lonely 🌐 planet

Paris

Montmartre &
Northern Paris
p117

Champs Élysées
& Grands Boulevards
p73

Louvre &
Les Halles
p88

Ménilmontant
& Belleville
p155

Eiffel Tower &
Western Paris
p56

Le Marais
p138

St-Germain
& Invalides
p225

The Islands
p187

Bastille
& Eastern
Paris
p168

Latin
Quarter
p204

Montparnasse &
Southern Paris
p246

**Alexis Averbuck, Fabienne Fong Yan,
Madeleine Rothery, Nicola Leigh Stewart,
Jean-Bernard Carillet, Rooksana Hossenally**

CONTENTS

Pont
Alexandre III (p74)

Paris street view with the Eiffel Tower (p60) in the background

MATHIEU FEVRY/SHUTTERSTOCK ©

The Seine (p189)

PARIS
THE JOURNEY BEGINS HERE

Since I was a small child, revelling in tiny, aromatic strawberries in a French springtime, Paris has been a lodestar, calling me back, inspiring me. A city that always changes, and remains fresh, fascinating and rich. I return every year, usually with no set plan, just to be here. To see what face it presents, who I meet, what I notice and how it feels.

Now, as the city gears up to host the Olympics, there's an additional frisson of preparation, but the hidden corners and untrod streets are always there. Waiting for you to step out and see what you find. In the words of Gertrude Stein, who hailed from Oakland, California, like me: 'America is my country and Paris is my hometown.' It has become an emblem to me of how nationality is a mirage, only given power if we believe in it.

Alexis Averbuck

alexisaverbuck.com

Alexis is a writer and painter who lives a nomadic life between California, France, Italy, Iceland and Greece. She paints her travels and writes about them for Lonely Planet.

My favourite experience is a walk along the Seine (p189). By day for fresh air, clouds and people-watching. By night for shimmering lights and ambience, the best in the world.

WHO GOES WHERE

Our writers and experts choose the places which, for them, define Paris.

The **13e arrondissement** (p257) is one of Paris' most underrated. It has a smattering of village-like neighbourhoods, parks, cafes, bistros, bars and restaurants. It's a fast-changing area - this is where the future of Paris lies!

Jean-Bernard Carillet

@jb.carillet_photography

Based in Paris, Jean-Bernard is a writer, photographer and videographer.

I love the diversity Paris offers: you can people-watch with a coffee, admire architecture at the **Louvre** (pictured, p92) and embark on a street-art tour in **Belleville** (p155) before ending your day with wine and cheese by the **Seine**.

Fabienne Fong Yan

@a.fab.journey, a-fab-journey.com

French-Chinese born and raised on Réunion Island, Fabienne has been based in Paris for 17 years.

The north of Paris is the most varied and ethnically diverse area of the city, with neighbourhoods like **Gare du Nord**, (p129) **Barbès** (p129) and **Pigalle** (pictured, p121) seeing a second lease of life thanks to young entrepreneurs opening exciting new businesses.

Rooksana Hossenally

@whatsup.paris

Rooksana is a travel and culture journalist based in Paris.

I will never tire of a *chocolat chaud* at **Café de Flore** (p235). I love to while away an afternoon on the *terrasse*, dreaming of when Ernest Hemingway and Simone de Beauvoir came here.

Madeleine Rothery

@mad.e.leiner

An Australian, Madeleine puts her love for storytelling into her experiences of France.

What I love in Paris, other than living in the most beautiful city in the world, is that even after nearly a decade there is always something new to discover: a restaurant, an exhibition or one of the city's many stories.

Nicola Leigh Stewart

@nicolaleighstewart

Nicola is a Paris-based writer for Condé Nast Traveller, Robb Report *and the* Telegraph.

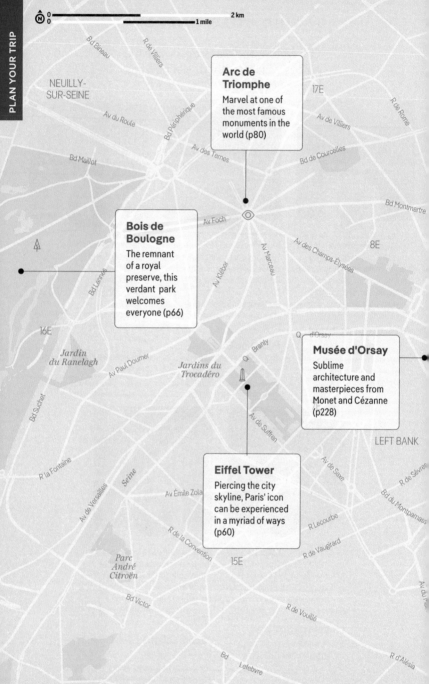

N 0 _____ 2 km
0 _____ 1 mile

NEUILLY-
SUR-SEINE

17E

8E

16E

LEFT BANK

15E

*Jardin
du Ranelagh*

*Jardins du
Trocadéro*

*Parc
André
Citroën*

**Arc de
Triomphe**

Marvel at one of
the most famous
monuments in the
world (p80)

**Bois de
Boulogne**

The remnant
of a royal
preserve, this
verdant park
welcomes
everyone (p66)

Musée d'Orsay

Sublime
architecture and
masterpieces from
Monet and Cézanne
(p228)

Eiffel Tower

Piercing the city
skyline, Paris' icon
can be experienced
in a myriad of ways
(p60)

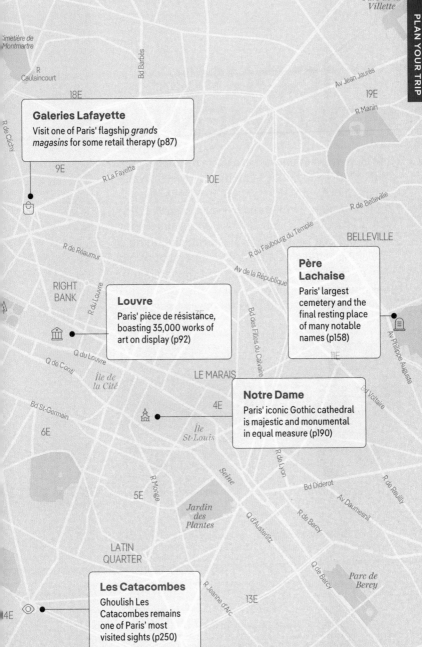

Parc de la Villette

Cimetière de Montmartre

R Caulaincourt

Bd Barbès

Av Jean Jaurès

18E

19E

R Manin

Galeries Lafayette

Visit one of Paris' flagship *grands magasins* for some retail therapy (p87)

9E

R La Fayette

10E

R de Belleville

R du Faubourg du Temple

Av de la République

BELLEVILLE

R de Réaumur

RIGHT BANK

R du Louvre

Louvre

Paris' pièce de résistance, boasting 35,000 works of art on display (p92)

Père Lachaise

Paris' largest cemetery and the final resting place of many notable names (p158)

Av Philippe Auguste

Q du Louvre

Q de Conti

Île de la Cité

Bd des Filles du Calvaire

LE MARAIS

4E

Île St-Louis

Bd St-Germain

6E

Notre Dame

Paris' iconic Gothic cathedral is majestic and monumental in equal measure (p190)

11E

Bd Voltaire

R de Lyon

R Monge

Seine

5E

Jardin des Plantes

Q d'Austerlitz

Bd Diderot

Av Daumesnil

R de Reuilly

R de Bercy

Q de Bercy

LATIN QUARTER

Les Catacombes

Ghoulish Les Catacombes remains one of Paris' most visited sights (p250)

R Jeanne d'Arc

13E

Parc de Bercy

14E

R d'Alésia

ICONIC MONUMENTS

Paris' famous monuments such as its triumphal arch, grand plazas and quintessential tower have become synonymous with the city itself. Its streetscapes – lamplit bridges, awning-shaded cafe terraces filled with wicker chairs and broad boulevards lined with cream-coloured Haussmannian apartment buildings – are emblematic, too. Always dynamic, more recent structures like the Louvre's glittering pyramid and the Fondation Louis Vuitton's glass sails have meshed into the architectural fabric of the city as well.

Eiffel Tower

No one could imagine Paris without its signature spire, though Gustave Eiffel only constructed it as a temporary exhibit for the 1889 Exposition Universelle (World Fair).

The Islands

The bridges, quays, parks, architecture and views on Paris' lovely Seine islands are the heart of the city. They change with the light and photo-ops beckon.

Basilique du Sacré-Cœur

Whether you're a first-timer or a frequent visitor, the Sacré-Coeur's elegant, gleaming white basilica is always worth a glimpse.

BEST MONUMENTAL EXPERIENCES

Arc de Triomphe ❶ Take in some of Paris' best vistas atop this magnificent, intricately sculpted triumphal arch on the Champs-Élysées. (p80)

Cathédrale Notre Dame de Paris ❷ Behold the city's geographic and spiritual heart, recovered from the 2019 fire that felled its spire. (p190)

Louvre ❸ Visit at night for the marvellous ambience of this immense palace-turned-museum and its Seine-side gardens, the Tuileries. (p92)

Hôtel des Invalides ❹ Impress yourself at Louis XIV's 1670s home for 4000 disabled war veterans. (p241)

Place de la Concorde ❺ Imagine how Louis XVI and Marie Antoinette were among thousands guillotined where the obelisk now stands amidst circling traffic. (p75)

LEFT: MIKHAIL GNATKOVSKIY/SHUTTERSTOCK ©, RIGHT: JUAN HUNG-YEN/SHUTTERSTOCK ©, FAR RIGHT: PYTY/SHUTTERSTOCK ©

Bois de Vincennes (p183)

GREEN ESCAPES

While Paris is Europe's most densely populated capital, it's easy to unwind in fresh air. The city is graced with beautiful parks, gardens, squares and sprawling lawns such as the Champ de Mars, and its *poumons* (lungs) are the rambling forests of the western Bois de Boulogne and eastern Bois de Vincennes.

Waterway Explorations

Flanked by quintessentially Parisian landmarks, Paris' most beautiful 'boulevard' of all, the Seine, flows through the city's heart and around its islands.

Jardin des Tuileries

Part of the *axe historique* (historic axis), adjacent to the Louvre, these symmetrical formal gardens were designed by André Le Nôtre in the 17th century.

BEST OUTDOOR EXPERIENCES

Bois de Boulogne ❶ Explore this former royal hunting grounds packed with tropical greenhouses, boat rentals and more. (p66)

Canal St-Martin ❷ Amble shaded towpaths and iron footbridges along the charming, 4.5km-long canal. (p121)

The Islands ❸ Tuck into market fare or quaff French wine in quiet parks and on riverside quays with hidden island vistas. (p187)

Bois de Vincennes ❹ Create a Paris summer, paddling lazily around the central isles of Lac Daumesnil. (p183)

Paris Plages ❺ Join Parisians at summertime riverside beaches. (p42)

ARCHITECTURAL WORSHIP

It took disease, clogged streets, an antiquated sewerage system and Baron Georges-Eugène Haussmann to drag architectural Paris out of the Middle Ages. Yet since Haussmann's radical 19th-century transformation, Paris has never looked back. Today the skyline shimmers with a gamut of architectural styles, from Roman arenas and Gothic cathedrals to postmodernist cubes and futuristic skyscrapers.

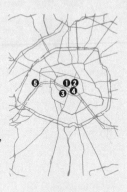

BEST ARCHITECTURE EXPERIENCES

Bourse de Commerce ❶ Appreciate the mesmerising glass-roofed circular building. (p102)

Centre Pompidou ❷ Soak up surprise at this controversial agglomeration of multicoloured pipes, which closes for renovation in 2025. (p99)

Église St-Germain-des-Prés ❸ Seek out the oldest church in Paris. (p232)

Hôtel de Ville ❹ Examine one of the city's most beautiful Renaissance façades. (p142)

Cité de l'Architecture et du Patrimoine ❺ Marvel at models of ancient monuments. (p65)

Shimmering Sainte-Chapelle

Classical concerts provide the perfect opportunity to appreciate the beauty of Paris' oldest stained glass at Sainte-Chapelle, consecrated in 1248.

Montmartre Magic

Channel pure Parisian charm in this former hilltop village with its huge villa homes surrounded by gardens and narrow streets lined with petite bars and cafes.

CULINARY WEALTH

France pioneered what is still the most influential style of cooking in the Western world and Paris is its showcase par excellence. Here, the food, wine and dining experiences are considered inseparable and whether you're in a charming neighbourhood bistro, an elegant brasserie or a once-in-a-lifetime *haute cuisine* restaurant, you'll find these places all pride themselves on the preparation and presentation of quality produce. Do as Parisians do and savour every moment.

Brilliant Bistros

Tucked in Paris' backstreets, you'll find exciting neobistros where creative young chefs forge reputations alongside timeless bistros honouring classic cookery techniques.

Brash Brasseries

Grand brasseries are a hallmark of Paris' dining scene. Seafood is typically a speciality. Montparnasse has a splendid line-up along bd du Montparnasse.

Gastronomic Extravaganzas

Paris has a galaxy of Michelin-starred restaurants helmed by legendary chefs – lunch reservations are easier to come by.

BEST DINING EXPERIENCES

Le Marché des Enfants Rouges ❶ Get your picnic from your market of the day (paris.fr), like this one with fresh produce stalls and counter-service eateries. (p152)

Le Gourmet ❷ Browse the temple of gourmet and artisanal foods at Galeries Lafayette. (p87)

Bouillon Chartier ❸ Embrace the bouillon meal trend – a vintage dining hall with cheap classic fare. (p132)

Grande Mosquée de Paris ❹ Honour France's North African heritage at this mosque's restaurant serving delicious tagines, couscous and grilled meats in a beautiful courtyard. (p210)

Le Procope ❺ Experience one of the oldest restaurants in Paris with a spectacular dining room in which traditional French fare is elegantly served. (p214)

LEFT: FRANCESCA SCIARRA/SHUTTERSTOCK ©, RIGHT: OLEG MEDVEDYTSKOV/SHUTTERSTOCK ©, FAR RIGHT: POLISH ©

La Brasserie de l'Isle Saint-Louis (p197)

CAFE LIFE

A visit to Paris doesn't seem complete without a leisurely session people-watching and sipping coffee or cocktails on a streetfront terrace. The art of being, noticing and relaxing comes alive. Every neighbourhood has its favourite hangs and best beating hearts, or there are the iconic magnets. You can always wander and pick one that suits.

Classic Neighbourhoods

Montmartre and St-Germain-des-Prés, legendary parts of Paris, have been cafe mainstays since before the time of Sartre, Cézanne and Stein.

Take Your Time

You buy your drink or coffee, and you buy the table for the duration. Waiters won't hurry you out. Sit back and enjoy.

BEST CAFÉ EXPERIENCES

La Brasserie de l'Isle Saint-Louis ❶ Bask under the buttresses of Notre Dame. (p190)

Café de Flore ❷ Sink back in time at the bd St-Germain watering holes of Sartre, de Beauvoir and Hemingway. (p235)

Le Petit Moulin ❸ Lounge on the cobblestone Montmartre street for prime people-watching. (p125)

Maison Maison ❹ Catch some rays on the Seine with views of Pont Neuf, Monnaie de Paris and Pont des Arts. (p113)

Stephane Bersia ❺ Let traditional pastries and speciality coffee take centre stage. (p180)

ARTISTIC TREASURES

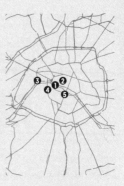

With an illustrious artistic pedigree – Renoir, Picasso, Monet, Manet, Dalí and Van Gogh are but a few of the masters who have lived and worked here over the years – Paris is one of the world's great art repositories. In addition to world-famous national museums, scores of smaller establishments feature every imaginable genre, diverse venues mount major exhibitions and offbeat installations, and the city is filled with vibrant street art.

BEST ART EXPERIENCES

Musée d'Orsay ❶ Thrill at preeminent impressionist and postimpressionist canvases within the grand former railway station Gare d'Orsay. (p228)

Jardin du Palais Royal ❷ Revel in this meeting of contemporary art and classical architecture. (p91)

Musée du Louvre

The *Mona Lisa*, *Venus de Milo* and *Winged Nike* are just three of countless priceless treasures inside this fortress turned royal palace turned France's first national museum.

Art Incubators

POUSH is one of Paris' largest art incubators, and hosts and supports more than 260 artists in a former industrial campus in Aubervilliers.

Palais de Tokyo ❸ Sample varied artistic styles in western Paris' smorgasbord of museums like this one, or Musée du Quai Branly – Jacques Chirac or the Musée Yves Saint Laurent. (p70)

Cluny Musée National du Moyen Âge ❹ Rise from the mosaic-adorned metro station to this brilliant museum in the 15th-century Hôtel de Cluny. (p218)

Street Art

All over town, denizens create inventive graffiti and magnificent murals, like those on our walking tour (p251).

Musée Rodin ❺ Be awed at Auguste Rodin's former workshop, showroom and garden filled with sculptural masterpieces such as *The Kiss*. (p245)

(FREE)

FOR FREE

Paris might be home to *haute couture, haute cuisine* and historic luxury hotels, but if you're still waiting for your lottery numbers to come up, don't despair. There are a wealth of ways to soak up the French capital without spending a centime (or scarcely any, at least). Simply walking and people-watching can fill countless days in this dynamic city, with beautiful parks and gardens, awe-inspiring architecture, and markets and shops (window-shopping never goes out of style). Try the Canal St-Martin, the gardens, the quays and bridges of the Seine, St-Germain or Montmartre's winding streets, for a start.

Magnificent Churches

Some of Paris' most magnificent buildings are free-to-enter places of worship. Not only exceptional architecturally and historically, they contain exquisite art and treasures.

Musical Life

Concerts and DJ sets happen for free (or for the cost of a drink) throughout the city. Buskers entertain crowds on Paris' streets and even aboard the metro.

Free Museums

Municipal museums (parismusees.paris.fr) are free! Many others have a free day per month, generally the first Sunday.

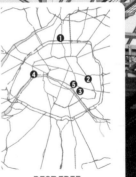

BEST FREE EXPERIENCES

Marché aux Puces de St-Ouen ❶ Enjoy many free hours of entertainment at this sprawling complex of 11 interconnected markets. (p126)

Cimetière du Père Lachaise ❷ Pay your respects to the likes of Oscar Wilde, Édith Piaf, Jim Morrison and Marcel Proust. (p158)

Promenade Plantée ❸ Amble the world's first elevated park, atop a 19th-century railway viaduct. (p171)

Musée d'Art Moderne de la Ville de Paris ❹ Be spoiled in relative peace in the outstanding permanent collection of 20th-century art and furniture. (p70)

Paris Greeters ❺ Take a free walking tour (donation encouraged) by booking in advance for a personalised excursion. (p41)

Find more information on free things to do in Paris on lonelyplanet.com

Rue des Lombards (p115)

LIVE IT UP

The reputation of the demure Parisian goes out the window when you click into nightlife mode. Neighbourhoods light up when cafes morph into bars, and concert halls and edgy alt-scene venues fill for live music and DJ sets. All you need is a spirit of adventure and a commitment to join in.

North Paris Music Scene

North Paris has a wealth of music venues: Boule Noire, Cigale, Elysée-Montmartre, Trabendo, Zénith Paris, Grande Halle de la Villette, Cabaret Sauvage, New Morning and Philharmonie.

Cocktail Renaissance

Paris' cocktail scene spans glitzy hotel bars and neobistros, backstreet speakeasies and former hostess bars in hip SoPi ('south Pigalle').

BEST NIGHTLIFE EXPERIENCES

Rue Oberkampf and rue St-Maur ❶ Hang out near happening Ménilmontant, where bars stay open late. (p179)

Coupe-Chou ❷ While away the evening at this old bar that used to serve night-shift workers. (p221)

Aux Folies ❸ Join a Belleville institution at one of the city's oldest cabaret-bars. (p162)

Le Bristol ❹ Dress to the nines for top hotel bars like this one or Hôtel Plaza Athénée and Hôtel de Crillon. (p84)

Café de la Danse ❺ Dance the night away at the beating heart of Bastille nightlife. (p178)

UNDER THE RADAR

Paris does not limit itself to iconic monuments and sights. For those in search of something quirkier or lesser-known, there are plenty of options. New developments are also always afoot in the French capital, from inspired culinary and fashion initiatives to major museum openings and reopenings, while neighbourhood establishments and markets are cornerstones of local life.

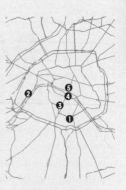

BEST OFF-THE-BEATEN-TRACK EXPERIENCES

La Butte aux Cailles ❶ Get lost in the village-like atmosphere of this tiny district near Place d'Italie (p255).

Maison de Balzac ❷ Immerse in old-school Paris at Honoré de Balzac's dreamy writing studio and garden with Eiffel Tower views. (p69)

Musée Atelier Zadkine ❸ Escape from the hustle-bustle in the peaceful sculpture garden at the home of Russian sculptor Ossip Zadkine. (p237)

Crypte Archéologique ❹ Hide in plain sight, under Notre Dame, where Roman ruins show the roots of the entire city. (p190)

Tour St-Jacques ❺ Climb to the top of this mysterious, solitary neogothic tower near Châtelet-Les Halles. (p113)

Alternative Arts & Music Hubs

Explore Paris' independent creative spirit at alt-art hubs like 59 Rivoli, La Bellevilloise, La Gare-Le Gore, Hasard Ludique, La Recyclerie, 104 or Flèche d'Or.

Bastille Industrial Passages

Secret courtyards, private alleys and picturesque passages, once occupied by workshops, now give an impression of a small village around Bastille.

Grand Paris

Beyond Paris' ring road, suburbs like Pantin and St-Ouen have awakened with canal bars and hybrid spaces like the Cité Fertile and Mains d'Œuvres.

PARIS WITH KIDS

Paris is an endlessly entertaining destination for kids. Crammed with cultural riches that can be explored with audioguides, smartphone apps and high-quality tours, the city is also rich in outdoor escapes, from its rambling gardens, urban playgrounds and river-based activities, to its climbable monuments and street-front cafe terraces.

Summiting Paris

Paris' tippy tops offer exhilarating climbs and thrilling views: from the Eiffel Tower to the Arc de Triomphe, Notre Dame's towers or the village of Montmartre.

Garden Play

Craft outdoor adventures in the iconic Jardin du Luxembourg with its merry-go-round and toy sailboats, the giant Bois de Boulogne or iconic Tuileries and Seine river parks.

Endless Museums

Museums, many of them free for kids, abound: machine museums (Musée des Arts et Métiers), Muséum National D'histoire Naturelle, Aquarium de Paris Cinéaqua, Musée Rodin...and on, and on, and on.

BEST FAMILY EXPERIENCES

Atelier des Lumières ❶ Discover, in sound and colour, animated works of the world's greatest painters like Klimt and Chagall. (p180)

Musée en Herbe ❷ Introduce your tots to art and culture at this museum designed for children three and up. (p111)

Privé de Dessert ❸ Dazzle the kids at this tricky restaurant where starters look like desserts and desserts look like savoury dishes. (p175)

Château de Versailles ❹ Get the energy out in vast gardens with enormous fountains and an equestrian show. (p268)

Cité des Sciences et de l'Industrie ❺ Immerse in science at the huge industrial-style children's exploratorium. (p135)

Find more information on things to do with kids in Paris on lonelyplanet.com

Perfect Days

Monument-lined boulevards, museums, bistros and boutiques are enhanced by newer multimedia galleries and design shops. Plenty to pack your days. But always leave time for wandering and noticing – this is a city for the flâneur.

Musée d'Orsay (p228)

PYTTY/SHUTTERSTOCK ©

DAY 1

Louvre & Les Halles

☼ Start with a stroll thro ugh the elegant **Jardin des Tuileries** (p98), stopping to view Monet's enormous *Water Lilies* at the **Musée de l'Orangerie** and/or photography exhibits at the **Jeu de Paume**.

Lunch Savour classic fare with art nouveau style at **Le Grand Colbert** (p106).

Louvre & Les Halles

☼ IM Pei's glass pyramid is your compass point to enter the labyrinthine **Louvre** (p92). Visiting this monumental museum could easily consume a full day, but once you've had your fill, browse the colonnaded arcades of the exquisite **Jardin du Palais Royal** (p91), and visit the beautiful church **Église St-Eustache** (p110). Tap into the soul of the former Les Halles wholesale markets along backstreet legacies like the old oyster market, **rue Montorgueil** (p110). Linger for a drink on rue Montmartre, then head to the late-opening **Centre Pompidou** (p99) for modern art and amazing views.

Dinner Pair tapas and wine at **Les Dessous de la Robe** (p108).

Le Marais, Ménilmontant & Belleville

☾ There's a wealth to see in Le Marais by day (**Musée National Picasso-Paris** (p149), **Musée Carnavalet** (p143), **Maison de Victor Hugo** (p149), **Musée des Arts et Métiers** (p145)...), but the neighbourhood really comes into its own at night.

DAY 2

Champs-Élysées & Grands Boulevards

☀ Climb the mighty **Arc de Triomphe** (p80) for a pinch-yourself Parisian panorama. Stroll Paris' most glamorous avenue, the **Champs-Élysées** (p81), and flex your credit card in the **Triangle d'Or** (p86), **Galeries Lafayette** (p87) or **place de la Madeleine** (76) before going behind the scenes of Paris' opulent opera house, the **Palais Garnier** (p83).

Lunch Café Jacques (p50): casual yet classy, with ringside tower views.

Eiffel Tower & Western Paris

☀ Check out global indigenous art at the **Musée du Quai Branly** (p63). This cultural neighbourhood is also home to the world's largest Monet collection at the **Musée Marmottan Monet** (p64), contemporary installations at the **Palais de Tokyo** (P71) and **Musée d'Art Moderne de la Ville de Paris** (p70), and Asian treasures at the **Musée Guimet** (p64). Sunset is the best time to ascend the **Eiffel Tower** (p60), to experience both dizzying views during daylight hours, and glittering la ville lumière (City of Light) by night.

Dinner Traditional French bistro fare with flare at **Le CasseNoix** (p259).

Montparnasse & Southern Paris

☾ Detour for a drink at a historic Montparnasse brasserie like **Le Select** (p235) or continue down the Seine to party at **Les Docks** (p258) or aboard floating nightclubs moored near the **Bibliothèque Nationale de France** (p257).

DAY 3

The Islands

☀ Start your day on the Île de la Cité, the site of **Notre Dame** (p190), open again and restored after the 2019 fire. For gobsmacking stained glass, don't miss the island's **Sainte-Chapelle** (p196). Cross the **Pont St-Louis** (p200) to buy a **Berthillon** (p199) ice cream before browsing the Île St-Louis' varied boutiques and art galleries.

Lunch Deliciously Parisian hangout **Café Saint Régis** (p197).

St-Germain & Les Invalides

☀ Swoon over impressionist masterpieces in the magnificent **Musée d'Orsay** (p228), scout out the backstreet boutiques and storied shops of St-Germain, sip coffee on the terrace of literary cafes like **Les Deux Magots** (p235) and laze in the lovely **Jardin du Luxembourg** (p216), the city's most popular park.

Dinner French classics in art nouveau jewel **Bouillon Chartier** (p132).

Latin Quarter

☾ Scour the shelves of late-night bookshops like the legendary **Shakespeare & Company** (p214), then join Parisian students and academics in the Latin Quarter's bars, cafes and pubs on **rue Mouffetard** (p208) or hit a jazz club like **Caveau de la Huchette** (p220).

WHEN TO GO

Paris is timeless. A city of life and light, you can ebb and flow like the Seine and adapt to the changing conditions.

A highlight of virtually all traveller's lifetime itineraries, Paris is a magnet for all. Spring (especially April and May) and autumn (particularly September and October) are ideal with gentle weather and less-crowded central streets. Summer (June to August) is the main tourist season, but many establishments close during August when Parisians generally leave. Sights are quieter and prices lower during winter (November to February).

When planning a visit it's also worth checking out Paris' extensive festival and events calendar. One of the world's best cultural cities, you can dictate a trip that includes anything from special operas and hip-hop dance premieres to French Open tennis.

Accommodation Lowdown

Paris' plentiful accommodation spans all budgets, but it is often fully booked well in advance, particularly during peak times (April to October, as well as public and school holidays). Reservations are essential at these times, but are also recommended year-round.

⊙ I LIVE HERE

SUMMER BLOOM

Janine Eberle is a local writer.
@janinemaree

Sometime in May, a run of warm days unofficially heralds the beginning of summer and the city transforms. Winter gloom lifts; we're suddenly a city of giddy optimists, determined to profit from every sunny moment, rushing en masse to find a *terrasse* and order a glass of rosé. Picnickers swarm the banks of the Seine and canals, armed with baguettes, *fromage*, and charcuterie, and COVID-era temporary outdoor seating (allowed during the warm months) reclaims parking places.

MAY HOLIDAYS

The temperate month of May, which is a top time to visit Paris, also has more public holidays than any other month in France. Watch out for widespread closures, particularly on May Day (1 May).

LEFT: KIRILL CHERNYSHEV/SHUTTERSTOCK ©
RIGHT: D.BOND/SHUTTERSTOCK ©

Jardin du Luxembourg (p216)

Weather Through the Year

JANUARY	FEBRUARY	MARCH	APRIL	MAY	JUNE
Avg daytime max: **8°C**	Avg daytime max: **9°C**	Avg daytime max: **13°C**	Avg daytime max: **17°C**	Avg daytime max: **20°C**	Avg daytime max: **24°C**
Days of rainfall: 9	Days of rainfall: 8	Days of rainfall: 9	Days of rainfall: 8	Days of rainfall: 9	Days of rainfall: 8

WINTER ICE SKATING

Come winter, ice-skating rinks pop up across the city, including in some truly picturesque spots, such as Galeries Lafayette's panoramic rooftop. Skating is usually free, with a charge for skate hire. Venues change from year to year; check parisinfo.com.

Rocking Out

Bastille Day The capital celebrates France's national day with a morning military parade along av des Champs-Élysées, accompanied by a fly-past of fighter aircraft and helicopters. *Feux d'artifice* (fireworks) light up the sky above the Champ de Mars by night. ☀ **July**

Fête de la Musique This national music festival (p179) welcomes in summer on the solstice with fabulous staged and impromptu live performances of jazz, reggae, classical and more. Held at venues all over the city. ☀ **June**

Rock en Seine Headlining acts perform at the Domaine National de St-Cloud, on the city's southwestern edge, at this popular three-day music festival. ☀ **August**

We Love Green This music festival (p184) lights up the Bois de Vincennes with international bands and top-tier DJ sets. ☀ **June**

Culture & Cycling

Chinese New Year During Chinese New Year (p252), get thrilled by parades thronging through the 13e *arronidissement* and firecrackers lighting up the night. ● **Date varies**

Tour de France The last of 21 stages of this prestigious, 3500km-long cycling event finishes with a race up the av des Champs-Élysées on the third or fourth Sunday of July. ☀ **July**

Quartier du Livre The Latin Quarter comes even more alive than usual during this festival (p213) when independent booksellers and writers set up stands or take over cafes throughout the neighbourhood. **Late May/ early June**

Nuit Blanche From sundown until sunrise on the first Saturday and Sunday of October, museums stay open, along with bars and clubs, for one 'White Night' (ie 'All Nighter'). ☁ **October**

AUTUMN ENCOUNTER

Rafael Sinclair Mahdavi is co-author of The Dishwasher Dialogues, a memoir of 1970s Paris. *rafaelmahdavi.com*

It was an autumn afternoon by the Louvre, I jumped off the bus and joined the queue at the glass pyramid. I struck up a conversation with an elderly woman. She hailed from Wichita, Kansas, and I told her my mother was from there. 'You see,' I said. 'That's Paris for you. You queue up to meet Caravaggio and you meet a lady from Wichita.'

Autumn , Musée du Louvre (p92)

SUMMER SUN

During the Parisian summer, when daylight can last around 16 hours, 'beaches' – complete with sunbeds, lounge chairs and palm trees – line the banks of the Seine, Paris Pride rocks the June streets and shoppers hit the summer *soldes* (sales).

JULY	**AUGUST**	**SEPTEMBER**	**OCTOBER**	**NOVEMBER**	**DECEMBER**
Avg daytime max: **26°C**	Avg daytime max: **25°C**	Avg daytime max: **22°C**	Avg daytime max: **17°C**	Avg daytime max: **11°C**	Avg daytime max: **8°C**
Days of rainfall: 7	Days of rainfall: 6	Days of rainfall: 7	Days of rainfall: 8	Days of rainfall: 9	Days of rainfall: 9

LEFT: ARDANME/SHUTTERSTOCK ©. RIGHT: MORE THAN PRODUCTION/SHUTTERSTOCK ©

Valentino fashion store, Paris

GET PREPARED FOR PARIS

Useful things to load in your bag, your ears and your brain.

Clothes

Stylish togs As the cradle of *haute couture*, Paris is chic: don your smarter threads and accessories. But keep in mind, Parisians have a finely tuned sense of aesthetics. They take meticulous care in their presentation and every component fits perfectly. They favour style and simplicity over bling, mixing basics from chains like H&M with designer pieces, vintage and flea-market finds, and statement-making accessories. You'll also stand out less and therefore be less of a target for pickpockets.
Cruising shoes Bring sturdy shoes whatever the season, whether trainers, which are ubiquitous, or walking shoes – cobbled streets aren't kind on high heels.

Manners

Always greet and say goodbye to anyone you interact with, using 'bonjour' ('bonsoir' at night) and 'au revoir'. It's not viewed as a formality but as basic respect.

Take your time at meals or in cafes – recreation is relaxation in Paris.

Talking about money (salaries or spending outlays) in public is taboo. Food and drink aside, conversations often revolve around philosophy, art and sports.

Scarf A scarf can double as a style accessory and covering for bare shoulders in cathedrals and other religious sites where you should dress respectfully.

📖 READ

A Moveable Feast
(Ernest Hemingway;
1964) Hemingway's
posthumously published
memoir about his life in
1920s Paris.

Notre Dame de Paris
(Victor Hugo; 1831)
The classic tale of the
hunchback of Notre
Dame who saved the
cathedral.

Life: A User's Manual
(Georges Perec; 1978)
Intricate novel about
an apartment block's
inhabitants between
1833 and 1975.

**The Most Secret
Memory of Men**
(Mohamed Mbougar
Sarr; 2023) Tour de force
about literature and
colonialism.

Words

'Bonjour' (bon-zhoor) is how you say 'hello' in Paris.
'Au revoir' (o-rer-vwa) translates to something close to 'til next time', and is used for 'goodbye'.
'Excusez-moi' (ek-skew-zay-mwa) is how you interrupt someone or get attention ('excuse me').
If you bump into someone, say **'pardon'** (par-don).
To say 'yes', use **'oui'** (wee), or make it more informal, almost like yeah, by drawing out the pronunciation (weah).
'No' is easy: **'non'** (noh).
'S'il vous plaît' (seel-voo-play) is the way to say 'please', and you can also use it to get the waiter's attention.
'Thank you' is a must. Just say **'merci'** (mair-see).
And if someone thanks you, reply with **'de rien'** (der ree-en) for 'you're welcome'.

If someone hits you with a stream of French, you can let them know 'I don't understand' by saying **'Je ne comprends pas'** (zher ner kom-pron pa).
Then you can ask them: 'Do you speak English?' with **'Parlez-vous anglais?'** (par-lay-voo ong-glay).
To enquire of a hotelier or a shopkeeper the price of something, say **'Quel est le prix?'** (kel ay ler pree).
To ask someone how they are doing, **'Comment allez-vous?'** (ko-moh ta-lay-voo) is the more formal way to go. Or more casually, ask **'Ça va?'** (sa va), which is similar to 'How's it going?'
If they ask how you are, and you're doing well, you can respond 'Fine, thank you, and you?' with **'Bien, merci. Et vous?'** (byun mair-see ay voo).

📺 WATCH

Call My Agent! (various directors; 2015–present) Lighthearted look at life in a Parisian talent agency, choc-a-bloc with celeb cameos.

Amélie (Jean-Pierre Jeunet; 2001, pictured) Story of a winsome young Parisian in a whimsical Montmartre.

Paris, Je T'Aime (various directors; 2006) Eighteen short films about love in different *arrondissements*.

Les Misérables (Ladj Ly; 2019) Another side of life in and near the City of Light by a Parisian director.

Revoir Paris (Alice Winocour; 2022) A Parisian woman works to remember and rebuild her life after a fateful event.

🎧 LISTEN

Navigating the French (Paris Underground Radio; 2021–present) American journalist Emily Monaco's podcast deep dives into French culture via one word per episode.

La Vie en Rose (Édith Piaf; 1946) One of many stirring classic *chansons* by Belleville-born La Môme Piaf (the Little Sparrow), covered by Grace Jones and others.

NI (Ninho; 2023) Latest hip-hop release in a string of number-one albums by rapper from the Parisian suburb, Yerres.

DNK (Aya Nakamura; 2023) Most recent album from Malian French hitmaker, preceded by platinum-selling albums *Aya* and *Nakamura*.

OKCAMERA/SHUTTERSTOCK ©

Outdoor restaurants, Paris

DINING OUT

Home to one of the world's greatest culinary traditions, Paris wows –
whether with multicourse meals, crusty baguettes or gooey Camembert.

The inhabitants of some cities rally around local sports teams, but in Paris they rally around *la table* – and everything on it. Pistachio macarons, shots of tomato consommé, decadent *bœuf bourguignon*, a gooey wedge of Camembert running onto the cheese plate...food isn't fuel here; it's the reason you get up in the morning.

Blessed with access to a rich and varied French landscape and farmers with a strong sense of regional identity, plus a culture that celebrates life's daily pleasures, it's no surprise that Parisian chefs have long been synonymous with gastronomic genius. In recent decades, a new generation of chefs has emerged, displaying a willingness to push the boundaries of traditional tastes. They are open to culinary traditions originating outside France

while at the same time downplaying the importance of Michelin stars and instead embracing street-front bistro and style-forward settings. Decadent work-of-art pastries aren't going anywhere. Instead, Parisian cuisine is continuing to innovate and shine. For more on Food, Drink & Nightlife, see p294.

Vegetarians & Vegans

Vegetarians and vegans make up a small minority in a country where *viande* (meat) once also meant 'food', but in recent years they have been increasingly well catered for with a slew of new vegetarian and vegan addresses, from casual vegan burger, pizza and hotdog joints to gourmet vegetarian and vegan restaurants. Many places also offer vegetarian choices on their set menus. Another good

Best Paris Dishes	BAGUETTES	PARISIAN BRIE	ONION SOUP	MACARONS
	Fresh from a *boulangerie*, topped with local butter, jam or ham.	Stand-out cows-milk *bries* include Provins, Melun, Montereau and Meaux.	Delicious beef broth and onions with crispy croutons and melted Gruyère.	Pillows of almond flour with fillings, from chocolate to rose or matcha.

bet is non-French cuisine, like Middle Eastern food. See happycow.net for vegan and vegetarian options in Paris.

Food Shopping Parisian Style

One of the excellent privileges of life in Paris is to buy food from small neighbourhood shops, each with its own speciality. Prepare for a cultural moment, standing in little queues to fill the fridge (or assemble a picnic), chatting with the purveyor at each stop.

Patisseries (cake shops) are similar to *boulangeries* (bakeries) but are generally a notch up on sophistication. *Fromageries* specialise in cheese: whether hard goat's cheese or creamy *Époisses*. The *boucherie* (butcher's shop) sells a huge array of animal products, but short-term visitors usually focus on *charcuterie* (prepared meats) such as *pâtés*, *saucissons* (salami) and *rillettes* (meat spreads). Similar to a deli, the traiteur specialises in prepared dishes. *Marchés alimentaires* (open-air and covered markets) are also a staple of Parisian life. And don't forget the *caviste* (wine shop), with wines usually much more affordable than overseas.

Paris Food Websites

Le Fooding *(lefooding.com)* The French movement that's giving Michelin a run for its money, with a mission to shake up the establishment. A balance of under-the-radar reviews and truly fine dining.

PIPPILONGSTOCKING/SHUTTERSTOCK ©

Macarons, Champs-Élysées

Paris by Mouth *(parisbymouth.com)* Capital dining and drinking with articles and recommendations searchable by *arrondissement*.

David Lebovitz *(davidlebovitz.com)* Expat US pastry chef and cookbook author with insights and recommendations.

La Fourchette *(thefork.com)* Offers user reviews and great deals of up to 50% off in Paris restaurants.

MAXEW/SHUTTERSTOCK ©

FOOD & WINE FESTIVALS

Paris Cocktail Week Participating bars citywide create signature cocktails. March.

Salon International de l'Agriculture Appetising nine-day agricultural fair with France-wide fare. February-March.

Paris Café Festival Coffee roasters from France and beyond celebrate the bean. May.

Paris Beer Festival Craft beer's popularity in Paris peaks over 10 days across the city. May.

Asian Street Food Festival Day-long extravaganza at La Grande Pagode de Vincennes. June.

Fête des Vendanges de Montmartre (pictured) Five days celebrating the grape harvest with costumes, concerts, food and parade. October.

Salon du Chocolat Chocaholics shouldn't miss this five-day festival of tastings, workshops, demonstrations and kids' activities. October–November.

PARISIAN MICROBREWS	CROISSANTS	STEAK TARTARE	PARIS-BREST
Excellent local beers include Paname, Outland and Charbonnière.	Perfect place to try these lovelies from a different *boulangerie* every day.	Raw ground beef paired with everything from capers to raw egg.	Hoop of choux pastry filled with hazelnut and/or almond praline cream.

ERIC GLENN/SHUTTERSTOCK ©

Bistro, Montmartre (p117)

Eat & Drink Like a Parisian

Eating well is of prime importance to most French people, who spend a sumptuous amount of time thinking about, discussing and enjoying food and wine. Yet dining out (learn more at p294) doesn't have to be a ceremonious occasion or one riddled with pitfalls for the uninitiated. Approach food with even half the enthusiasm *les Français* do, and you will be welcomed, encouraged and exceedingly well fed.

Enjoy the Prix-Fixe Menus

Daily *formules* or *menus* (prix-fixe menus) typically include two- to four-course meals. In some cases, particularly at market-driven neobistros, there is no *carte* (menu). Lunch menus are often a fantastic deal and allow you to enjoy h*aute cuisine* at very affordable prices.

Take a Seat

Bread Order a meal and within seconds a basket of fresh bread will be brought to the table. Butter is rarely an accompaniment. Except in the most upmarket of places, don't expect a side plate – simply put it on the table.

Water Asking for *une carafe d'eau* (jug of tap water) is perfectly acceptable, although some waiters will presume you don't know this and only offer mineral water, which you have to pay for. Should you prefer bubbles, ask for *de l'eau gazeuze* (fizzy mineral water). Ice (*glaçons*) can be hard to come by.

Embrace Wine

Wine is easily the most popular beverage in Paris and house wine can cost less than bottled water. Of France's dozens of wine-producing regions, the principal ones are Burgundy, Bordeaux, the Rhône and the Loire Valleys, Champagne, Languedoc, Provence and Alsace. The best wines are Appellation d'Origine Contrôlée (AOC; also labelled Appellation d'Origine Protégée, AOP).

Paying the Bill & Tipping

Trying to get *l'addition* (the bill) can be maddeningly slow. The French consider it rude to bring the bill immediately – you have to be persistent when it comes to getting your server's attention. A *pourboire* (tip) on top of the bill is not necessary as service is always included.

RESERVE AHEAD

It's not only a safe bet to reserve ahead so you are sure to get a table, but it makes the restaurant staff happy, which is a grand way to kick off your meal.

Nonetheless, midrange restaurants will usually have a free table for lunch (arrive by 12.30pm), but book a day or two in advance for dinner.

Reservations up to one or two months ahead are crucial for lunch and dinner at popular/high-end restaurants. You may need to reconfirm on the day, so do pick up if a strange French number calls your mobile.

ARDANNE/SHUTTERSTOCK ©

Cafe, Rue de Rivoli

LEFT: GALLOFILM/SHUTTERSTOCK ©, RIGHT: PETR KOVALENKOV/SHUTTERSTOCK ©

Bread for sale, Paris

HOW TO... Explore Paris' Bread & Cheese Purveyors

Few things in France are as tantalising as the smell of just-baked buttery croissants wafting out of an open bakery door, and few can resist the temptation of the hundreds of cheese varieties available in the capital. Here, we give you a quick primer on how to dive right in to two of Paris' signature foods.

Sample the Daily Bread

With roughly 1200 *boulangeries* in Paris – or 11.5 per sq km – you should absolutely find your way to one (or more!) at some point during your stay.

As you'll notice in the extravagant display windows, bakeries bake much more than *baguettes*: they also sell croissants, chocolate éclairs, quiches, pizzas and an astounding array of pastries and cakes. If you're eating lunch on the cheap, a trip to the closest bakery will do you right.

Specialist *patisseries* (pastry shops), often headed by big-name pastry chefs, create astonishing works of art. Their delicacies fall into several categories: *bavarois* (gelatin-set, cream-based desserts), *gateaux* (literally 'cakes', but spanning everything from a sponge-based chocolate-and-coffee opéra to layered-pastry *mille-feuille*), cookie-style treats like shell-shaped madeleine cakes and macarons, *choux* (puff pastry, such as éclairs

and profiteroles), *entremets* (eg flans) and *viennoiseries* (yeast-based baked goods including croissants and *pains au chocolat*). When buying bread from a *boulangerie*, try to familiarise yourself with the varieties on sale while you're standing in the queue – not all baguettes are created equal. Most Parisians today will ask for a baguette *tradition* (traditional-style baguette), distinguished by its pointy tips and coarse, handcrafted surface. Other breads you'll see include *boules* (round loaves), *pavés* (flattened rectangular loaves) and *ficelles* (skinny loaves that are half the weight of a baguette).

The shape of a *baguette* (literally 'stick' or 'wand') evolved when Napoléon Bonaparte ordered army bakers to create loaves for soldiers to stuff down their trouser legs on the march.

Every spring *boulangers* (bakers) battle it out in the official *Grand Prix de la Meilleure Baguette de Paris* (Best Baguette in Paris). The winner is not only awarded a cash prize but

TOP BOULANGERIES & PATISSERIES

Atelier du Geste à l'Émotion Île de la Cité mainstay for precious patisserie and *viennoiseries*.

Boulangerie MieMie Turns out distinctive croissants, some of the best in Paris.

La Briée Celebrate brioche at this neighbourhood bakery.

Sacha Finkelsztajn – La Boutique Jaune Traditional Jewish bakery in the Marais.

Monsieur Caramel Korea meets France in delectable baked goods.

Stohrer Rue Landmark in business since 1730.

Laurent Duchêne Croissants vie with macarons.

VG Pâtisserie Indulge in plant-based vegan treats.

Jacques Genin Assembled-to-order mille-feuilles.

Fou de Pâtisserie Treats by some of France's top pastry chefs.

also provides the French president with baguettes for a year.

Choose Cheese

Charles de Gaulle once famously asked how it was possible to govern a country with 246 types of cheese (now countless more). So how on earth to choose what to buy at the *fromagerie* (cheese shop)?

The variety on offer can be overwhelming, but vendors will always allow you to sample before you buy, and they are usually very generous with their guidance and pairing advice.

Seek the Five Basic Cheese Types

Fromage à pâte demi-dure
'Semi-hard cheese' means uncooked, pressed cheese. Try Tomme de Savoie, made from either raw or pasteurised cow's milk; Cantal, a cow's-milk cheese from Auvergne that tastes something like cheddar; St-Nectaire, a pressed cheese that has a strong, complex taste; and Ossau-Iraty, a ewe's-milk cheese made in the Basque Country.

Fromage à pâte dure
'Hard cheese' is always cooked and then pressed. Try Beaufort, a grainy cow's-milk cheese with a slightly fruity taste from Rhône-Alpes; Comté, a cheese made with raw cow's milk in Franche-Comté; and Mimolette, an Edam-like dark-orange cheese from Lille aged for up to 36 months.

Fromage à pâte molle
'Soft cheese' is moulded or rind-washed. Camembert, a classic moulded cheese from Normandy, and Brie de Meaux are both made from raw cow's milk. Munster from Alsace, mild Chaource and strong-smelling Langres from Champagne are rind-washed, fine-textured cheeses.

Stohrer (p110)

Fromage à pâte persillée
'Marbled' or 'blue cheese' is so called because the veins often resemble *persille* (parsley). Roquefort is an ewe's-milk veined cheese that is to many the king of French cheeses. Fourme d'Ambert is a mild cow's-milk cheese from Rhône-Alpes.

Fromage de chèvre
'Goat's-milk cheese' is usually creamy and both sweet and slightly salty when fresh, but it hardens and gets much saltier as it matures. Try Ste-Maure de Touraine, a mild cheese from the Loire region, or Crottin de Chavignol, a saltier variety from Burgundy.

Cheese, Marché d'Aligre (p173)

LILLY TROTT/SHUTTERSTOCK ©

Cafe, Le Marais (p138)

BAR OPEN

You'll find all types of thirst-quenching or caffeine-quaffing venues, from chic wine bars and neighbourhood dives to speciality taprooms.

For the French, drinking and eating go together like wine and cheese, and the boundary between a cafe, *salon de thé* (tearoom), bistro, brasserie, bar and even a wine bar is blurred.

The line between drinking and clubbing is often nonexistent – a cafe that's quiet mid-afternoon might have DJ sets in the evening and dancing later on.

For most Parisians living in tiny apartments, cafes and bars have traditionally served as the salon they don't have – a place where they can meet with friends over *un verre* (glass of wine), read for hours over a *café au lait*, debate politics while downing an espresso at a zinc counter, swill cocktails during *apéro* (*apéritif*; predinner drink) or get the party started aboard a floating club

on the Seine. Clubbing here tends to be underground and extremely mobile. The best DJs and their followings have short stints in a venue before moving on, and the scene's hippest *soirées clubbing* (clubbing events) float between venues – including the many dance-driven bars (check internet listings).

Rooftop Bars

Innovative drinking and dining spaces are carving out their place on the city's rooftops, with panoramic views over the skyline strung with Parisian landmarks.

One of the best rooftop bars is **Le Perchoir** (leperchoir.fr), atop a former industrial building in Ménilmontant.

The same team also runs the rooftop bar **Le Perchoir Marais** at department store

Lonely Planet's Top Bars	MOONSHINER Vintage vibe with cocktails and beaucoup ambience (p175).	BAR HEMINGWAY Legendary cocktails inside the Ritz (p108).	LES DEUX MAGOTS Watch St-Germain go by from this cafe's terrace (p235).	ST JAMES Just one of many high-end hotel bars (eg Le Bristol, Hôtel de Crillon) (p70).

BHV, and the bar and restaurant at **Pavilion 6** of Paris Expo Porte de Versailles, using produce grown at their 14,000-sq-metre urban rooftop farm (the world's largest).

Seasonal rooftop bar-restaurants crown department stores **Galeries Lafayette** and **Le Printemps** (printemps.com), the rooftop terrace of cultural centre **Point Éphémère** (pointephemere.org) on the banks of Canal St-Martin, and **Perchoir de l'Est**, above railway station Gare de l'Est. Or try **Café Oz Rooftop** on the Institut Français de la Mode.

Many Parisian hotels also have spectacular rooftop bars, such as **Hôtel des Grands Boulevards**, **Mama Shelter** and **Terrass" Hôtel**.

Beer & Breweries

Beer hasn't traditionally had a high profile in France and mass-produced varieties such as Kronenbourg 1664 (5.5%), brewed in Strasbourg, used to dominate.

Paris' growing bière artisanale (craft beer) scene, however, is booming, with city breweries, such as **Brasserie BapBap** and **Brasserie la Goutte d'Or**, microbreweries and cafes offering limited-production brews on tap and bottled. The city's artisan-beer fest, the **Paris Beer Festival**, takes place in brasseries, bars and specialist beer shops throughout the city. An excellent resource for hopheads is hoppyparis.com.

Coffee Decoded

Coffee has always been Parisians' drink of choice to kick-start the day. So it's surprising that Parisian coffee long lagged behind world standards, with poor-quality beans and unrefined preparation.

However, Paris' coffee revolution has seen local roasteries like **Belleville Brûlerie** and **Coutume** priming cafes citywide.

Un café Single shot of espresso.

Un café allongé Espresso lengthened with hot water (sometimes served separately).

Un café au lait Coffee with milk.

Un café crème Shot of espresso lengthened with steamed milk.

Un double Double shot of espresso.

Une noisette Shot of espresso with a spot of milk.

ROMAN PIP/SHUTTERSTOCK ©

NEED TO KNOW

Tiered Pricing

Drinking in Paris means paying for the space you take up. So it costs more to sit at a table than to stand at the counter, more for coveted terrace seats, more on a fancy square than a backstreet, more in the 8e than the 18e.

Average Costs

Glass of wine from €4. Cocktail €9 to €16. *Demi* (half-pint) of beer €4 to €7. In clubs and chic bars, prices can double. Club admission is free to €20, often cheaper before 1am.

Happy 'Hour'

Parisian 'happy hour' – called just that (no French translation) – ushers in reduced-price drinks for two or three hours, usually between 5pm and 8pm.

Closing Time

Cafes and bars close around 2am, though some have licences until dawn. Club hours vary depending on venue and event but start late.

Aperol Spritz cocktails, Paris

CANDELARIA	LE FREEDJ	LA DAME DE CANTON	AUX FOLIES
Famous speakeasy behind a door in a taqueria in the 3e (p152).	Le Marais staple gay bar, better for mingling and dancing than drinks.	Floating Chinese junk in the 13e with live music and DJs (p260).	BELLEVILLE Iconic 1870s cabaret turned bar with a large, lively terrace (p162).

Moulin Rouge (p127)

SHOWTIME

Catching a performance in Paris is a treat. French and international opera, ballet and theatre companies and cabaret dancers take to the stage in fabled venues, while elsewhere a flurry of young, passionate, highly creative musicians, thespians and other artists make the city's fascinating fringe art scene what it is.

Opera & Dance

France's **Opéra National de Paris** and **Ballet de l'Opéra National de Paris** perform at Paris' two opera houses: the **Palais Garnier** and **Opéra Bastille**. **Théâtre National de Chaillot** (dance) is in the Trocadéro area. The season runs between September and July – buy tickets well in advance.

Check out what modern dance and hip-hop spectacles are on while you're in town... they're a direct route to current French culture.

Live Music

Street music is a constant in this busker-filled city, with summer adding open-air concerts along the Seine and in city parks to the year-round serenade of accordions. The rue des Lombards (p115) near Châtelet is the best for jazz with three iconic clubs. Sainte-Chapelle holds classical concerts (p196).

Theatre

Theatre productions, including those originally written in other languages, are invariably performed in French. Non-French speakers should check out **Theatre in Paris**

(theatreinparis.com), whose bilingual hosts provide an English-language program and direct you to your seats. Typically there are upwards of 10 shows on offer, from French classics to contemporary comedies and Broadway-style productions with English surtitles.

Cabarets

Whirling lines of feather-boa-clad, high-kicking dancers at grand-scale cabarets like cancan creator **Moulin Rouge** are a bit retro to modern eyes, but remain a quintessential fixture on Paris' entertainment scene – for many but Parisians. A favourite drag queen venue is **Madame Arthur** for exuberant, light-hearted shows.

Cinema

Foreign films (including English-language films) screened in their original language with French subtitles are labelled 'VO' (*version originale*). Films labelled 'VF' (*version française*) are dubbed in French. Lost in Frenchlation (lostinfrenchlation.com) hosts English-subtitled screenings of French films accompanied by drinks.

Tickets

Purchase most concert, theatre and other cultural and sporting-event tickets from electronics and entertainment megashop Fnac (fnactickets.com), whether at the *billeteries* (ticket offices) throughout Paris or online, or directly from the venue.

Discount Tickets

On the day of performance, theatre, opera and ballet tickets are sold for half-price (plus €3.50 commission) at the Kiosque Théâtre Madeleine (kiosqueculture.com).

Street musician, Paris

LONELY PLANET'S TOP...

Listings for Entertainment & Clubbing

L'Officiel des Spectacles *(offi.fr)* Paris' top listings guide is in French but is easy to navigate online. The print booklet is available from newsstands on Wednesday, and is crammed with everything on in the capital, including concert, theatre and cinema listings.

LYLO *(lylo.fr)* Short for Les Yeux, Les Oreilles ('eyes and ears'); offers the low-down on concerts, festivals and more.

Le Figaro *(lefigaro.fr/culture)* Music, cinema and theatre listings.

Paris Nightlife *(parisnightlife.fr)* All-encompassing listings site.

Paris Bouge *(parisbouge.com)* Comprehensive listings site.

Sortir à Paris *(sortiraparis.com)* Click on 'Soirées & Bars', then 'Nuits Parisiennes'.

Tribu de Nuit *(tribudenuit.com)* Parties, club events and concerts galore.

ENTERTAINMENT BY NEIGHBOURHOOD

Eiffel Tower & Western Paris	Visit Palais de Chaillot's Théâtre National de Chaillot or the nearby Maison de la Radio, with their many dance and live music performances.
Champs-Élysées & Grands Boulevards	Famous revues and Paris' palatial 1875-built opera house take top billing here.
Louvre & Les Halles	Swinging jazz clubs, centuries-old theatres and cinemas mix it up with pumping nightclubs.
Montmartre & Northern Paris	Show-stopping cabarets, mythologised concert halls and cutting-edge cultural centres. Place du Tertre, Montmartre's original main square, is Paris' busiest busker stage.
Le Marais, Ménil-montant & Belleville	Rockin' live-music venues, old-style *chansons* and arts centres.
Bastille & Eastern Paris	Opera, old-time tea dancing and France's national cinema institute are big drawcards.
The Islands	Look for buskers on Pont St-Louis, the bridge linking Paris' two islands.
Latin Quarter	Swing bands, cinema retrospectives and jam sessions.
St-Germain & Les Invalides	Atmospheric cinemas, cultural centres and theatres inhabit this chic, sophisticated neighbourhood.
Montparnasse & Southern Paris	Some of this area's most happening venues are aboard boats moored on the Seine.

OLIVEROUGE 3 /SHUTTERSTOCK ©

Marché aux Puces de St-Ouen (p126)

TREASURE HUNT

Paris has it all: broad boulevards lined with international chains, luxury avenues studded with designer fashion houses and fabulous markets. But the real charm lies in strolling the city's backstreets, where tiny speciality shops and quirky boutiques selling everything from strawberry-scented Wellington boots to heavenly fragranced candles are wedged between cafes, galleries and churches.

Fashion is Paris' forte. Yet although its well-groomed residents sometimes make the city look and feel like a giant catwalk, fashion here is about style and quality first and foremost, rather than status or brand names. A good place to get an overview of Paris fashion is at the city's famous *grands magasins* (department stores).

Paris is also an exquisite treasure chest of gourmet food (including cheeses, macarons and foie gras), wine, tea, books, beautiful stationery, art, art supplies, antiques and collectables. Ask for *un paquet cadeau* – free (and very beautiful) gift wrapping, offered by most shops.

Paris' twice-yearly *soldes* (sales), lasting four weeks, start in mid-January and again in late June.

Fashion Deals & Shows

Parisian fashion doesn't have to break the bank: find fantastic bargains at secondhand and vintage boutiques, and outlet shops selling previous seasons' collections, surpluses and seconds by top-line designers. **Paris**

Good Fashion aims for sustainability by improving sourcing and making processes more eco-friendly.

Although tickets for Paris' high-profile fashion shows are like hens' teeth, you can still see some runway action: reserve ahead to attend shows (haussmann.galeries lafayette.com) at Galeries Lafayette.

Street Markets

Paris' street markets are social gatherings for the entire neighbourhood, and visiting one will give you a true appreciation of Parisian life. Nearly every little quarter has its own (never on Monday) where tarpaulin-topped tables bow beneath fresh, cooked and preserved delicacies. *Marchés biologiques* (organic markets) are sprouting up across the city. Many street markets also sell clothes, accessories, homewares and more.

The city's flea markets brim with bric-a-brac, antiques, retro clothing, cheap brand-name clothing, footwear, African carvings and electronic gear. But watch out for pickpockets! Every Parisian market is listed on paris.fr/pages/les-marches-parisiens-2428, including speciality markets for flowers or ephemeral *brocantes* (secondhand markets) and *vide-greniers* ('empty the attic' sales).

Souvenirs

For distinctive souvenirs, visit the **City of Paris' Paris Rendez-Vous** (paris.fr/equipements/paris-rendez-vous-17644) boutique at the Hôtel de Ville. Its online shop ships worldwide. At major museums, the **Boutiques de Musées** (boutiquesdemusees.fr) have high-quality replicas and a digital framing service: browse masterpieces, choose a frame and have it mailed home.

Art, Antiques & Homewares

From venerable antique dealers to edgy art galleries, browse and buy one-off conversation pieces and collectibles. A good starting point is the Carré Rive Gauche ('Left Bank Square'), bounded by quai Voltaire and rues de l'Université, des St-Pères and du Bac, in St-Germain, where you'll find scores of specialist merchants.

Parisian creativity comes to the fore during **Paris Design Week** (maison-objet.com/en/paris-design-week), featuring launches, workshops and more for 10 days in September. Other design shows accessible to the public include the 12-day **Foire de Paris** (foiredeparis.fr).

MAKEW/SHUTTERSTOCK ©

LONELY PLANET'S TOP...

Independent Shops

Marin Montagut Stock up on gifts for home at this housewares shop. (p233)

Opulence Vintage Ogle this tiny storefront on Île St-Louis selling vintage couture. (p201)

Empreintes Paris Choose between French-made wares from all over the country. (p150)

Stohrer (pictured) Sample patisserie and decadent takeaway at Paris' oldest bakery. (p110)

Lorette & Jasmin Find designer boutique deals or rent a handbag. (p71)

Le Studio des Parfums Take a workshop in making your signature scent in the Marais. (p151)

Librairie Gourmande Browse cookbooks and volumes related to cuisine and drink. (p111)

Merci Source anything from clothes to beauty products and homewares. (p181)

SHOPPING BY NEIGHBOURHOOD

Eiffel Tower & Western Paris	Top brands and couture mingle with independent boutiques.
Champs-Élysées & Grands Boulevards	*Haute couture* houses and famous department stores.
Louvre & Les Halles	Cookware shops, high-street chains and covered arcades.
Montmartre & Northern Paris	Gourmet food shops, art and quintessential souvenirs.
Le Marais, Ménilmontant & Belleville	Quirky homewares, art galleries and up-and-coming designers in Haut Marais.
Bastille & Eastern Paris	Great markets, Viaduc des Arts workshops.
The Islands	Enchanting gift shops and boutiques but tourist tat on Île de la Cité.
Latin Quarter	Late-opening bookshops and music shops.
St-Germain & Les Invalides	Art, antiques and chic designer boutiques.
Montparnasse & Southern Paris	Discount fashion outlets, Asian groceries.

MARC BRUXELLE/SHUTTERSTOCK ©

Paris Plages (p43)

SPORT &
THE OUTDOORS

In the run-up to Paris' 2024 Summer Olympics and Summer Paralympics, you'll find ample opportunities to watch spectator sports or take part yourself. Thwack a tennis ball, stroll in style, admire art or break out some wine and cheese. And ply the waters and banks of the Seine to combine fresh air with thrilling vistas.

The Seine

The lifeline of Paris, the Seine sluices through the city, spanned by 37 bridges. Its Unesco World Heritage–listed riverbanks offer picturesque promenades, parks, activities and events, including summertime beaches. After dark, watch the river dance with the limpid reflections of city lights and tourist-boat flood lamps.

The Seine's riverbanks are where Parisians come to cycle, jog, in-line skate and stroll. Staircases along the banks lead down to the water's edge.

Particularly picturesque spots for a riverside promenade include the areas around Paris' two elegant inner-city islands (p187), the Île de la Cité and Île St-Louis. Up at street level, the city's Right and Left Banks are lined with distinctive green-metal *bouquiniste* stalls selling antiquarian books, sheet music and old advertising posters.

A lesser-known island stroll is the ar-

Paris' Top Parks

JARDIN DU LUXEMBOURG
Tennis courts, puppet shows and coveted picnic benches by a palace-museum with ponds.

JARDIN DES TUILERIES
Stately royal gardens are now open to all along the banks of the Seine where you can view Monet's *Water Lilies* at the Musée de l'Orangerie.

PARC MONCEAU
Beautiful 18th-century English-style park with whimsical follies in the 8e.

FAMILY ADVENTURES

A Seine river cruise is a joy for all ages. Myriad companies run day- and night-time boat tours, lasting around an hour, with commentary in multiple languages. Many also offer lunch and dinner cruises like Bateaux-Mouches or Bateaux Parisiens. But there is something extra special about the one-hour 'Paris Mystery' tours designed especially for children by Vedettes de Paris.

Batobus is a handy hop-on, hop-off service that stops at quintessentially Parisian attractions: the Eiffel Tower, Invalides, Musée d'Orsay, St-Germain des Prés, Notre Dame, Jardin des Plantes, Hôtel de Ville, Musée du Louvre and place de la Concorde. The next-most popular activity after cycling has to be skating, whether on the

street or on ice. Rent a pair of in-line skates at **Nomadeshop** and join the Friday-evening skate, **Pari Roller**, that zooms through the Paris streets, or join the more laid-back Sunday-afternoon skate, **Rollers & Coquillages**. Paris Greeters (greeters.fr) guides walking tours are with local volunteers, invariably in their own 'backyard' and well away from the madding crowd.

tificial Île aux Cygnes (264) via its tree-shaded walkway, the Allée des Cygnes. Walking from west to east gives you a stunning view of the Eiffel Tower.

The river also acts as a giant backyard for apartment-dwelling Parisians. All along its banks you'll find locals reading, picnicking, canoodling or just basking in the sunshine. Among the best-loved spots is the tiny triangular park, square du Vert-Galant (p201), beneath the Pont Neuf.

In addition to riverside park activities, entertainment options include nightclubs aboard boats moored in the 13e (p257), such as Bateau El Alamein, with live-music gigs, and more bars and restaurants along the Parc Rives de Seine on both riverbanks.

Sports

Paris hosts a great variety of sporting events throughout the year, from tennis' French Open and Paris Masters to local football matches. There's a handful of stadiums in and around the city – for upcoming events, click on Sports & Games (under the Going Out menu) at parisinfo.com. If you can read French, sports daily *L'Équipe* (lequipe.fr) provides more depth.

Local teams include football's Paris Saint-Germain (psg.fr), and rugby's sky-blue-and-white-dressed Racing 92 (racing92.fr) and pink-clad Stade Français Paris (stade.fr). Catch France's national football team, Les Bleus (fff.fr), at the Stade de France.

The city's three **horse racing tracks** can make for a thrilling afternoon. The **Hippodrome d'Auteuil** and the

FANCY A SWIM?

See our picks of the best swimming spots on the Seine (p42).

Bateau, the Seine (p70)

JARDIN DES PLANTES	BOIS DE BOULOGNE	BOIS DE VINCENNES	PARC DE LA VILLETTE
The city's beautiful botanic gardens shelter rare plants and 18th-century glass-and-metal greenhouses.	A vast forest including gardens, horse-racing arenas, French Open tennis complex and more.	Eastern forest that offers easy escape from the concrete into nature.	Urban oasis of greenery, waterways, concert venues, bars and science museum.

Hippodrome de Longchamp are in the Bois de Boulogne. **Hippodrome de Paris-Vincennes** is in the Bois de Vincennes. Every October the **Prix de l'Arc de Triomphe** (prixarcdetriomphe.com), Europe's most prestigious horse race, is held at the Hippodrome de Longchamp.

The city of Paris website (paris.fr/sport) has info on everything from skating and badminton to stadiums and equipment rental. Also useful is quefaire.paris.fr/sports, which lists venues for football and **climbing**, and has info on **swimming pools** open at night and other activities.

Boules

You'll often see groups of earnest Parisians playing boules (aka *pétanque*, France's most popular traditional game, similar to lawn bowls) in the Jardin du Luxembourg and other parks and squares with suitably flat, shady patches of gravel. The Arènes de Lutèce boulodrome in a 2nd-century Roman amphitheatre in the Latin Quarter is a fabulous spot to absorb the scene. There are usually places to play at Paris Plages.

If you want to try out the sport indoors, head to **Chez Bouboule**, which has a packed-sand *boulodrome* and a bar.

Cycling

Everyone knows that the Tour de France races up the Champs-Élysées at the end of July every year, but you don't need Jonas Vingegaard's leg muscles to enjoy Paris on two wheels. Between the Paris bike-share scheme **Vélib'**, and the hundreds of kilometres of urban bike paths, cycling around the city has never been easier. Sign up for one of the great city bike tours or hire a bike yourself. Some streets are closed to vehicle traffic on Sundays – see paris.fr/pages/paris-respire-2122 – great news for cyclists! Bring your own helmet.

At the time of research, Parisians had banned rental scooters like Lime, which used to be hugely popular.

Olympics

The 2024 Summer Olympic Games and Summer Paralympic Games (2–18 August 2024; paris2024.org) brought renovations, redevelopments and a flurry of construction projects around the city. A cornerstone of the Games is that 95% of the venues will be pre-existing or temporary, in an effort to minimise not only costs but also the impact on the environment. Landmark buildings overhauled and redeployed for the Olympics include the Grand Palais, just off the av des Champs-Élysées in the 8e. Originally built for the 1900 Exposition Universelle (World's Fair) and topped by a 8.5-tonne art nouveau glass roof, it will host Olympic fencing and taekwondo, and Paralympic wheelchair fencing.

SWIMMING

- By the Bassin de la Villette there are three clean-water-zoned swimming pools of varying depths. There's also a floating swimming pool, Piscine Joséphine Baker, accommodating children and swimmers with disabilities, near Bercy. The pools are patrolled by life guards and are typically open 11am to 9pm during the Paris Plages season. Check the annual program at parisinfo.com.

- Although swimming has been banned in the waterways due to maritime traffic and water quality, efforts have been successful to ensure the Seine is clean enough to host open-water swimming events like the triathlon and marathon during the 2024 Summer Olympics. And, as a part of Mayor Hidalgo's initiative, three open-air swimming areas will open to the public in 2025: Bercy, Bras Marie and Bras de Grenelle.

- Paris' vintage swimming pools add a dash of style to your paddle. The art deco Piscine Pontoise in the Latin Quarter dates from the 1930s and has night openings – particularly moody – or try the minimalist, white Piscine de la Butte aux Cailles (p255) or the maximalist Piscine Molitor (p59). The historic Piscine Georges Vallerey, which was built as part of the 1924 Olympic Games, is getting a bit of a makeover for the 2024 Games, when it will be used as a training venue.

Find more places to swim on lonelyplanet.com

TOMMY LAREY/SHUTTERSTOCK ©

Bassin de la Villette

Paris' 80,000-seat Stade de France, in St-Denis, which was built for the 1998 FIFA World Cup, will be the Games' main stadium. The year prior to the Olympics, it was also the site of the 2023 Rugby World Cup being hosted by France.

Adjacent to the Eiffel Tower, the Parc du Champ de Mars will have a temporary arena where Olympic wrestling and judo competitions will take place. The Champ de Mars will also be the site of beach volleyball and Paralympic boccia (a precision ball sport similar to bowls and *pétanque*) competitions.

Only three Olympic venues were built from scratch: the Aquatics Centre, next to the Stade de France; the 51-hectare Olympic and Paralympic Village, 7km north of central Paris and less than 2km from the Stade de France; and the 9-hectare Media Village at Le Bourget, some 10km northeast of central Paris, which forms part of a larger 'garden city' being developed to link the Dugny and Le Bourget communes and the Georges-Valbon parkland. After the Games, all three newly built venues will be repurposed for public use.

Also constructed at the Olympic village is a transport hub with five metro lines and

SUMMERTIME BEACHES

Each summer, the Paris Plages (Paris Beaches) see *pétanque* (a variant on the game of bowls), pop-up bars and cafes, sun lounges, parasols, water fountains and sprays line the river from around mid-July to early September (exact dates vary year to year). Established in 2002 for Parisians who couldn't escape to the coast to cool off in the summer months, they now typically set up at the Parc Rives de Seine (between the Pont de Solferino and Pont Alexandre III on the Left Bank, and between the Pont de Sully to the Pont Neuf on the Right Bank), as well as along the quays by the Bassin de la Villette in the 19e.

two RER lines. It will form part of the mammoth Grand Paris (Greater Paris) redevelopment project that will ultimately connect the outer suburbs beyond the bd Périphérique ring road with the city proper. Grand Paris' principal goal is to connect the suburbs with one another, instead of relying on a central inner-city hub from which all lines radiate outwards, with a target completion date of 2030.

Playground, Paris

PARIS WITH KIDS

Parisians adore *les enfants* (children) and the city's residential density means you'll find playground equipment in parks and squares throughout the city. Families have an overwhelming choice of creative, educational, culinary and 'pure old-fashioned fun' things to see, do and experience. Plan ahead to get the best out of kid-friendly Paris.

Science Immersion

Cité des Sciences *(cite-sciences.fr)* If you have time for just one museum, make it this one. Book interactive Cité des Enfants sessions (for children aged two to 12) in advance to avoid disappointment.

Musée des Arts et Métiers *(arts-et-metiers. net)* Crammed with instruments and machines, Europe's oldest science and technology museum is fascinating. Activity- and experiment-driven workshops are top-notch.

Galerie des Enfants *(mnhn.fr)* Natural-history museum for six- to 12-year-olds within the Jardin des Plantes.

Art Exploration

Centre Pompidou *(centrepompidou.fr)* Modern-art hub with great exhibitions, workshops (for kids aged three to 12) and teen events in Studio 13/16.

Musée en Herbe *(museeenherbe.com)* Thoughtful art museum for children with an excellent bookshop and art workshops for kids aged two to 12.

Palais de Tokyo *(palaisdetokyo.com)* Palais de Tokyo offers interactive installations, art workshops (for kids five to 10 years old) and storytelling sessions (for three- to five-year-olds) as well as family activities for everyone.

Treasure Hunts with THATMuse *(thatmuse. com)* All ages will get a burst of art adrenaline with a THATMuse treasure hunt at the Louvre or Musée d'Orsay. Play alone or in teams.

Hands-On Activities

Crafty Happenings at the Musée du Quai Branly – Jacques Chirac *(quaibranly.fr)* Mask making, boomerang hurling and experimenting with traditional instruments...the ateliers enfants (for three-year-olds to teenagers) at this Seine-side museum, devoted to African, Asian and Oceanic art and culture, are diverse and creative.

Music at Philharmonie de Paris
(philharmoniedeparis.fr) Concerts, shows and instrument workshops are part of the world-music repertoire at the city's cutting-edge philharmonic hall in Parc de la Villette.

Bag Painting with Kasia Dietz
(kasiadietzworkshops.com) Design and paint a reversible, hand-printed canvas tote with Paris-based New Yorker Kasia Dietz during a half-day bag-painting workshop – ideal for fashion-conscious teens (and parents).

Musée National de la Marine *(musee-marine. fr)* Explore interactive exhibits at the newly remodelled marine museum with all things nautical.

Continued on p46

LONELY PLANET'S TOP...

Amusement Parks

Disneyland Resort Paris A magnet for families, this park 32km east of Paris incorporates both Disneyland itself and the cinema-themed Walt Disney Studios Park.

Parc Astérix Shuttle buses run from central Paris to this summer-opening theme park, 35km north of the city, which covers prehistory through to the 19th century with its six 'worlds', adrenaline-pumping attractions and shows for all ages (pictured).

Jardin d'Acclimatation The Bois de Boulogne's popular amusement park with rides, a small train, petting zoo, playgrounds, puppet shows and paddling pool.

Canal St-Martin (p121)

PARIS' BEST PARK ACTIVITIES

Sailing boats in Jardin du Luxembourg	Playgrounds, puppet shows and a carousel: this legendary park has pandered to children for generations. But it's vintage toy sailing boats that are the real heart-stealers.
Jardin des Tuileries	These elegant gardens stage kids' activities and a summertime amusement park.
Parc Floral de Paris	Easily the best playground for kids eight years and older: concerts, puppet shows, giant climbing webs, 30m-high slides and a zip line.
Locks on Canal St-Martin	Watching canal boats navigate the many locks is fun, fascinating and free.
Boat cruising on the Seine	The Seine is also a perfect venue for family adventures (p41).
Riverside play on Parc Rives de Seine	Giant board games, a climbing wall, a 20m-long blackboard, tepees and events galore line this expressway-turned-promenade.

(continued from p45)

Model Building at Cité de l'Architecture et du Patrimoine (citedelarchitecture.fr) Workshops at Paris' architecture museum see kids (aged four to 16 years) build art deco houses, châteaux and towers in miniature form. Text

Animals & Other Creatures

Equestrian Shows at Versailles
(chateauversailles.fr) World-class equestrian shows at Château de Versailles are mesmerising. Show tickets and training sessions include a stable visit.

Sharks at Aquarium de Paris Cinéaqua
(cineaqua.com) Centrally located, Cinéaqua has a shark tank and 500-plus fish species, and screens ocean-themed films.

Ménagerie du Jardin des Plantes (mnhn.fr) The collection of animals in Jardin des Plantes includes snow panthers and pandas; combine with the neighbouring natural-history museum, particularly its Grande Galerie de l'Évolution.

Parc Zoologique de Paris
(parczoologiquedeparis.fr) Observe lions, cougars, white rhinos and a whole gaggle of other beasties at this state-of-the-art zoo in Bois de Vincennes.

Dazzling Screentime

Digital Exhibitions at Gaîté Lyrique
(gaite-lyrique.net) La Gaîté Lyrique features digital-driven exhibitions, video games for older children and teens, laptops to use in the digitally connected cafe and a library with desks shaped like ducks for kids under five to sit at and draw while older siblings geek.

Special-Effect Movies at Cité des Sciences
(cite-sciences.fr) This museum boasts two special-effect cinemas: Géode with 3D movies, and Cinéma Louis-Lumière screening animation and short films. Top it off with a cinematic trip through the solar system in the planetarium.

Behind-the-Scenes Tour at Le Grand Rex
(legrandrex.com) Whizz-bang special effects stun during behind-the-scenes tours at this iconic 1930s cinema. Stand behind the big screen and muck around in a recording studio.

Art Illuminations at Atelier des Lumières
(atelier-lumieres.com) Artworks projected on this former foundry's bare walls dazzle kids and adults alike.

Practicalities

Babysitting Hotels can often organise sitters for guests.

DELPIXEL/SHUTTERSTOCK ©

RAINY-DAY IDEAS

Cirque d'Hiver Bouglione (cirquedhiver.com) Clowns, trapeze artists and acrobats have entertained children of all ages at the city's winter circus since 1852. The season runs October to March and performances last around 2½ hours.

Musée des Arts Forains (arts-forains.com/en) Check for seasonal events at this nostalgic fairground museum, such as its Christmas season during Le Festival du Merveilleux.

Musée des Égouts de Paris (musee-egouts.paris.fr) Romping through sewerage tunnels, learning what happens when you flush a loo in Paris and spotting rats is all part of the kid-cool experience at this quirky museum.

Les Catacombes (catacombes.paris.fr) Teens generally get a kick out of Paris' most macabre sight, but be warned: this skull-packed underground cemetery is not for the faint-hearted (pictured, p250).

An Afternoon at the Theatre Paris' diverse theatre scene stages bags of spectacles (shows), théâtre classique (classical theatre) and other performances for kids, some in English; weekly entertainment mag L'Officiel des Spectacles (offi.fr) lists what's on.

Musée de la Magie (museedelamagie.com) This museum is pure magic!

Creative Endeavours (seizeparis.com) Crafting workshops at Seize will fire up kids' creativity.

Equipment Rent strollers, scooters, car seats, travel beds and more while in Paris from companies such as Kidelio (kidelio.com).

Paris Mômes (parismomes.fr) Covers Parisian kid culture (up to 12 years); print off playful kids' guides for major art exhibitions before leaving home.

Parc Zoologique de Paris (p185)

The Louvre (p92)

MUSEUMS & GALLERIES

If there's one thing that rivals Parisians' obsession with food, it's their love of art. Hundreds of museums and galleries pepper the city, and whether you prefer classicism, impressionism or exhibits of French military history, you can always be sure to find something new just around the corner.

Paris Museum Passes

If you think you'll be visiting more than two or three museums or monuments while in Paris, the single most important investment you can make is the Paris Museum Pass (parismuseumpass.com; two/four/six days €55/70/85). The pass is valid for entry to over 50 venues in and around the city, including the Louvre, Centre Pompidou, Musée d'Orsay and Musée Rodin (but not the Eiffel Tower), the châteaux at Versailles and Fontainebleau, and the Basilique de St-Denis.

One of the best features of the pass is that you can bypass the long ticket queues at major attractions (though not the security queues). But be warned: the pass is valid for a certain number of days, not hours, so if you activate a two-day pass late Friday afternoon, for instance, you will only be able to use it for a full day on Saturday. Also keep in mind that most museums are closed on either Monday or Tuesday, so think twice before you activate a pass on a Sunday. The Paris Museum Pass is available online as well as at participating museums, tourist desks at the airports, branches of the Paris Convention & Visitors Bureau, and other locations listed on the website. EU citizens under 26 years and children under 18 years get free entry to national museums and monuments, so don't buy this pass if you belong to one of those categories.

If you have the Passion Monuments Pass (monuments-nationaux.fr), which covers over 90 national monuments around France, 11 are in the Paris area.

Art Incubators

In addition to the traditional high-toned and venerated galleries in the centre of Paris, alternative arts and music hubs (p19) are springing up all around the city. They blend art exhibitions and gallery spaces with musical performance venues, and often cafes and other attractions. Check local listings (p36) for what's on when you're in town.

Children's Workshops

If you have kids in tow, make sure you check out the day's *ateliers* (workshops; p44). Although these are usually in French, most activities involve hands-on creation, so children should enjoy themselves despite any language barrier. At major museums (eg the Centre Pompidou and the Louvre), it's best to sign up in advance.

PETR KOVALENKOV/SHUTTERSTOCK ©

FLORIN CNEJEVIC/SHUTTERSTOCK ©

Children painting

LONELY PLANET'S TOP...

Performances

Many museums and historic sights host excellent concerts and performances, with schedules that generally run from September to early June.

Musée du Louvre Hosts a series of lunchtime and evening classical concerts.

Musée d'Orsay Concerts at 12.30pm Tuesday mid-October to early June, plus various evening classical performances (pictured).

Musée du Quai Branly – Jacques Chirac Folk performances of theatre, dance and music from around the world.

Centre Pompidou Film screenings and avant-garde dance and music performances.

Sainte-Chapelle Evening concerts of classical music and song, a lit by summer-time stained-glass glory.

Musée d'Orsay (p228)

ART BY NEIGHBOURHOOD

Eiffel Tower & Western Paris	Paris' largest concentration of museums, from the Quai Branly to Musée Marmottan Monet.
Champs-Élysées & Grands Boulevards	Musée des Beaux-Arts de la Ville de Paris, Musée National Gustave Moreau and more.
Louvre & Les Halles	The Louvre, Centre Pompidou, Musée de l'Orangerie and others.
Montmartre & Northern Paris	Musée Jacquemart-André, Cité des Sciences, Le 104 and others.
Le Marais, Ménilmontant & Belleville	Musée National Picasso, Mémorial de la Shoah, Lafayette Anticipations and L'Atelier des Lumières.
Bastille & Eastern Paris	Cinémathèque Française and others.
Latin Quarter, St-Germain & Les Invalides	Musées National du Moyen Âge et d'Histoire Naturelle, Institut du Monde Arabe and Musée d'Orsay.

KIEVVICTOR/SHUTTERSTOCK ©

Musée d'Orsay (p228)

LONELY PLANET'S TOP...

Museum Dining

Café Jacquemart-André

Lunch or tea in the sumptuous dining room of the 19th-century mansion and museum of the same name.

Halle aux Grains at

Collection Pinault – Paris

A restaurant by renowned chef Michel Bras complements the exhibitions at the Bourse de Commerce.

Bambini, Forest and Monsieur Bleu

Multiple cafes and restaurants at the Palais du Tokyo, some with courtyard seating and Eiffel Tower views.

Le Restaurant and Café Campana

Within the Musée d'Orsay; the former was the art nouveau railway station's showpiece restaurant.

Les Ombres and Café Jacques

These two dining options at the Musée du Quai Branly have ringside seats for the Eiffel Tower.

Public Art

Museums and galleries are not the sole repositories of art in Paris. Indeed, art is all around you, including *murs végétaux* (vertical gardens adorning apartment buildings), and street art ranging from small murals to artworks covering entire high-rises to Invader tags (tiled *Space Invaders*–inspired creations) marking street corners. Enjoying art in Paris is simply a matter of keeping your eyes open.

Big-name installations have become destinations in their own right. Niki de Saint Phalle and Jean Tinguely's playful *Stravinsky Fountain* – a collection of 16 colourful animated sculptures based on the composer's oeuvre – is located next to the Centre Pompidou. Daniel Buren's zebra-striped columns of varying heights at the Palais Royal are another beloved Paris fixture. The installation was originally greeted with derision but has since become an integral part of the historic site. Both the Jardin des Tuileries and the Jardin du Luxembourg are dotted with dozens of sculptures that date from the 19th and early 20th centuries. The Jardin des

Tuileries also contains an area with more contemporary works from the likes of Roy Lichtenstein and Magdalena Abakanowicz. You can also check out our mural walking tour (p251) in the 13e.

One of the best areas to go hunting for contemporary public art – and architecture – is out in the business district of La Défense, where you'll find dozens of works by well-known artists such as Miró, Calder and Belmondo. Metro stations, too, often contain some iconic or unusual additions, from Hector Guimard's signature art nouveau entrances to the crown-shaped cupolas at the Palais Royal.

How to Avoid Museum Fatigue

• Visit early in the day or late in the evening to avoid the crush of crowds.
• Choose less-visited museums to feel space and leisure.
• Choose less-visited portions of the famous museums (at the Louvre, you'd be amazed how the rooms around the *Mona Lisa* are slammed but those with the Greek masterpieces or Vermeers can be empty).
• Wear comfortable shoes and make use of the cloakrooms.
• Drink plenty of water.
• Sit down as often as you can – standing still and walking slowly promote tiredness.
• Plan breaks at the cafes or outdoor terraces in some museums to martial your energy.

Viewing Tips

• Studies suggest that museum-goers spend no more than 10 seconds viewing an exhibit and another 10 seconds reading the label. To avoid this, choose a particular section to focus on, or join a guided tour of the highlights.
• Reflecting on the museum's exhibits and materials and forming associations with it causes information to move from your short- to long-term memory. Your experiences will thus amount to more than a series of visual 'bites'. Take your time and know that you can't see it all. Focus on the pieces that speak to you. Using an audioguide or smartphone app (many museums have their own) is also a good way to provide context.

Ticket Tips

Book online to avoid queues where possible (eg for the Louvre, Musée d'Orsay, Centre Pompidou).

Print tickets before you go if necessary. In some cases, you can download the tickets onto a smartphone, but check beforehand. Also, ensure you can download more than one ticket onto your phone if you're doing so for a group or family.

If you can't book online, look for automated machines at museum entrances, which generally have shorter queues. Note that credit cards without an embedded smart chip (and some non-European chip-enabled cards) won't work in these machines.

City museums (eg Petit Palais, Musée Cognacq-Jay) are free; many other museums have one free day per month.

Temporary exhibits almost always have a separate admission fee, even at free museums.

Check if you qualify for a reduced-price ticket (*tarif réduit*): students, seniors and children generally get discounts or free admission with valid ID.

PANDORA PICTURES/SHUTTERSTOCK ©

Musée du Louvre (p92)

PARIS

THE GUIDE

Chapters in this section are organised by hubs and their surrounding areas. We see the hub as your base in the destination, where you'll find unique experiences, local insights, insider tips and expert recommendations. It's also your gateway to the surrounding area, where you'll see what and how much you can do from there.

View from the Panthéon (p207)

ERICBERY/SHUTTERSTOCK ©

NEIGHBOURHOODS AT A GLANCE

Find the neighbourhoods that tick all your boxes.

Eiffel Tower & Western Paris

ELEGANT AND ICONIC,
BEJEWELLED BY TREASURES

p56

Montmartre & Northern Paris

HISTORIC HILLTOP VILLAGE,
NEW PARIS MUSINGS

p117

Champs-Élysées & Grands Boulevards

GRAND MONUMENTS AND LES
GRANDS MAGASINS

p73

Louvre & Les Halles

BLENDING HISTORY AND
PARISIAN LIFESTYLE

p88

Le Marais

HISTORY, BEAUTY
SHOPPING AND
CREATIVITY

p138

Ménilmontant & Belleville

ARTS, VIEWS AND
MULTICULTURAL WALKS

p155

The Islands

CHIC, HISTORIC
AND DELIGHTFUL

p187

St-Germain & Les Invalides

IN THE FOOTSTEPS OF
CREATIVE GIANTS

p225

Bastille & Eastern Paris

HISTORY, NIGHTLIFE AND
INDUSTRIAL HERITAGE

p168

Latin Quarter

MEDIEVAL MARVELS AND
LITERARY LUMINARIES

p204

Montparnasse & Southern Paris

UNDERRATED, ECLECTIC
AND FULL OF SURPRISES

p246

Eiffel Tower & Western Paris

ELEGANT AND ICONIC, BEJEWELLED BY TREASURES

With its hourly sparkles that illuminate the evening skyline, the Eiffel Tower dazzles any time of day.

Ascending to its viewing platforms will offer you a panorama over the whole of Paris, with the prestigious neighbourhood of Passy (the 16th *arrondissement*) stretching along the far banks of the Seine to the west. In the 18th and 19th centuries, Passy was home to luminaries such as Benjamin Franklin and Balzac. Defined by its harmonious, elegant buildings from the Haussmann era, it was only annexed to the city in 1860. Nowadays, chic restaurants and cool cafes vie for your attention, along with excellent shopping: from farmers' markets to couture boutiques.

Home to very well-heeled Parisians, this *grande dame* of a neighbourhood is where you can get up close and personal with the city's symbolic tower as well as art deco and art nouveau architecture. More contemporary towers are found in the high-rise business district of La Défense just outside the *Périphérique* (ring road) encircling central Paris. Fringing the area's western reaches, the glorious green Bois de Boulogne, a former royal hunting ground, is the city's escape for fresh air and is home to everything from a fine-arts museum (Fondation Louis Vuitton) to a kids' amusement park and famous Stade Roland-Garros, home of the French Open.

Fabulous museums in the 16th include the Musée Marmottan Monet, with the world's largest collection of Monet paintings; the hip Palais de Tokyo and venerable Musée d'Art Moderne, with modern art installations; the Musée Guimet des Arts Asiatiques, France's standout Asian art museum; the fascinating Cité de l'Architecture et du Patrimoine, with captivating sculptures and murals; and a host of smaller collections.

On the Left Bank the prominent Musée du Quai Branly – Jacques Chirac showcases indigenous art and culture from outside Europe.

ULYSSEPIXEL/SHUTTERSTOCK ©

DON'T MISS

EIFFEL TOWER
Ascend the icon at dusk to watch its sparkling lights blink across Paris. **p60**

TROCADERO & PALAIS DE CHAILLOT
Snap selfies with the Eiffel Tower in the background and take in top museums. **p59**

QUAI BRANLY MUSEUM
Find inspiration in exquisite art and craftsmanship from around the world. **p63**

TOP TIP

Though excellent top-end restaurants dot the 16e, it's substantially more affordable to picnic in one of the many green spaces (Bois du Boulogne, Palais Galliera, Champs de Mars). Build a feast with goodies from *boulangeries* (bakeries), *fromageries* (cheese shops, like La Fromagerie de Grenelle), markets and speciality shops (like cured meat at Boucherie Maison Le Bourdonnec).

MICHAEL VON AICHBERGER/SHUTTERSTOCK ©

Left: Parc de Bagatelle (p67); Above: Eiffel Tower (p60), as seen from Palais Chaillot

MARMOTTAN MONET MUSEUM
Revel in the world's largest collection of Monet canvases, alongside other impressionist and post-impressionists. **p64**

CITY OF ARCHITECTURE AND HERITAGE
Wander cathedral portals, gargoyles and scale models in this standout museum. **p65**

BOIS DE BOULOGNE
Explore Paris' green oasis: from bike rides to rowboats, an art foundation to an amusement park. **p66**

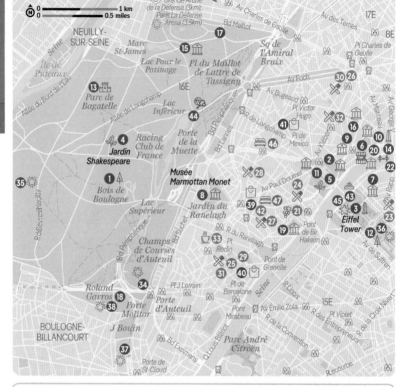

TOP SIGHTS

1 Bois de Boulogne
2 Cité de l'Architecture et du Patrimoine
3 Eiffel Tower
4 Jardin Shakespeare
5 Jardins du Trocadéro
6 Palais de Tokyo
7 Musée du Quai Branly – Jacques Chirac
8 Musée Marmottan Monet
9 Musée National des Arts Asiatiques Guimet
10 Musée Yves Saint Laurent Paris
11 Palais de Chaillot
12 Parc du Champ de Mars

SIGHTS

see 5 Aquarium de Paris Cinéaqua
13 Parc de Bagatelle

14 Flame of Liberty Memorial
15 Fondation Louis Vuitton
16 Hôtel d'Heidelbach
17 Jardin d'Acclimatation
18 Jardin des Serres d'Auteuil
19 Maison de Balzac
20 Musée d'Art Moderne de la Ville de Paris
see 11 Musée de la Marine
see 11 Musée de l'Homme
21 Musée du Vin
see 6 Palais de Tokyo
see 6 Palais Galliera
22 Pont de l'Alma
see 13 Pré Catelan

SPORTS & ACTIVITIES

43 Bateaux Parisiens
44 Lac Inférieur Boat Hire

45 Vedettes de Paris

SLEEPING

46 Hôtel Villa Glamour
47 Hôtel Villa Nicolo

EATING

23 Arnaud Nicolas
24 Aux Cocottes
see 6 Bambini
25 Boulangerie Basil
26 Bustronome
see 5 Ducasse sur Seine
see 6 Forêt
27 HSP La Table
28 L'Archeste
see 3 Le Jules Verne
29 Les Gros Gâteaux
see 3 Madame Brasserie
30 Prunier
31 Sables
32 Sogno Paris

DRINKING & NIGHTLIFE

33 Bô Zinc Café

ENTERTAINMENT

34 Hippodrome d'Auteuil
35 Hippodrome de Longchamp
36 Les Marionnettes du Champ de Mars
37 Parc des Princes
38 Stade Roland Garros
see 2 Théâtre National de Chaillot see 6 Yoyo

SHOPPING

see 6 Agnès B
39 La Grande Épicerie Rive Droite
40 Lorette & Jasmin
41 Mouty
42 Passy Covered Market

MASSIMO TODARO/SHUTTERSTOCK ©

Eiffel Tower (p60)

Parc du Champs de Mars
Grand Green Parade Ground

Running southeast from the Eiffel Tower, the grassy green jewel of the Champ de Mars – an ideal summer picnic spot – was originally used as a parade ground for the cadets of the 18th-century **École Militaire** (Military Academy). This school in the vast French-classical building commissioned by Louis XV at the southeastern end of the park counts Napoléon Bonaparte among its illustrious graduates.

Until 2024, the park is hosting a temporary Grand Palais while the original undergoes renovations.

Children flock to the puppet shows at **Les Marionnettes du Champ de Mars** (check online for schedules).

Trocadéro & Palais de Chaillot
Gracious Gardens, Stellar Views and World-Class Museums

Across the river from the Eiffel Tower, the Trocadéro is a beautiful complex of of fountain-bedecked gardens surrounding the Palais de Chaillot. The curved, colonnaded wings of this building and its central terrace afford an exceptional panorama of the **Jardins du Trocadéro**, the Seine and the Eiffel Tower. The eastern wing houses the **Cité de l'Architecture et du Patrimoine** (p65), devoted to French architecture, as well as the **Théâtre National de Chaillot**. The **Musée de la Marine** (p71) and the **Musée de l'Homme** are housed in the western wing. **Aquarium de Paris Cinéaqua** (p71) is also in the complex, a great hit for the kids. The place du Trocadéro et du 11 Novembre on the northwestern side of the palace is ringed by large cafes.

59

NOVIKOV ALEKSEY/SHUTTERSTOCK ©

PRACTICALITIES

Scan this QR code to
pre-book tickets (crucial)
and plan your visit:

TOP SIGHT

Eiffel Tower

Piercing the city skyline, Paris' icon beckons. Experience the **Eiffel Tower** in myriad ways, from a daytime trip or an evening ascent amid twinkling lights to a stroll in the gardens at its base. Even though some seven million people visit annually, few would dispute that each time is unique – it's something that simply has to be done at least once.

DON'T MISS

2nd-floor panorama

Top-floor vertigo enhanced by the Champagne bar

1st-floor Pavillon Ferrié

Tactile descent down the stairs near the base

Strolling the gardens under the tower

Catch the tower's nightly twinkle-show

Exploring an Icon

Named after its designer, Gustave Eiffel, the Tour Eiffel was built for the 1889 Exposition Universelle (World's Fair). It took 300 workers, 2.5 million rivets and two years of nonstop labour to assemble. Upon completion, the tower became the tallest human-made structure in the world (324m) – a record held until the 1930 completion of New York's Chrysler Building. A symbol of the modern age, it faced opposition from Paris' artistic and literary elite, and the 'metal asparagus', as some snidely called it, was originally slated to be torn down in 1909. It was spared only because it proved an ideal platform for the transmitting antennas needed for the newfangled science of radiotelegraphy. Now a local nickname for the tower is *La dame de fer* (Iron Lady).

1st Floor

Of the tower's three floors, the 1st (57m) has the most space, with a broad wooden deck for lounging, but the least impressive views. The glass-enclosed **Pavillon Ferrié** houses an immersion film along with a small cafe, pizza bar and souvenir shop. On the outer walkway follow a discovery circuit to learn more about the tower's ingenious design and history. Check out the sections of glass flooring that offer a dizzying view of the ant-like people walking on the ground far below. This level also hosts the restaurant **Madame Brasserie**. The 1st floor's commercial areas are powered by two sleek wind turbines within the tower.

2nd Floor

Views from the 2nd floor (115m) are grand – impressively high but still close enough to see the details of the city below. Pinpoint locations in Paris and beyond using telescopes and panoramic maps placed around this level. Story windows give an overview of the lifts' mechanics, and the vision well allows you to gaze through glass panels to the ground. Also up here are toilets, souvenir shops, a macaron bar, and Michelin-starred restaurant **Le Jules Verne** (accessible by a dedicated lift in the south pillar).

Top Floor (Summit!)

Views from the wind-buffeted top floor (276m) stretch up to 60km on a clear day. At this height the sweeping panoramas are more thrilling than detailed. You'll exit the lift onto a glass-enclosed level with directional panels orienting many of the world's cities. Then take one of the two small sets of metal stairs to the highest tier, which is open-air. Celebrate your ascent with a glass of bubbly from the **Champagne bar** at this topmost level – or opt for mineral water, lemonade and macarons. Afterwards, peep into Gustave Eiffel's restored top-level **office** where wax models of Eiffel and his daughter Claire greet Thomas Edison. Somewhat unbelievably, there are also toilets up here.

Guide

The Eiffel Tower's online visitor's guide (guide.toureiffel.paris) is packed with info and can be accessed by the tower's wifi network. There's also an information booth at the base, near the west pillar, which has brochures and information on guided tours and activities for kids.

Ticket Purchases & Queueing Strategies

Even on a good day the base of the Eiffel Tower can be a chaotic scrum of confused travellers. A bit of preparation can cut down on joining that fray, and save time waiting in often atrocious queues, especially in high season (May to September) and during holidays like Easter.

External Security

Nowadays, bullet-proof glass barriers surround the tower's base. Visitors must pass through external security at one of the two entrances to the glass enclosure on av Gustave Eiffel. The two exits are on quai Branly. The security lines are divided between walk-in visitors, people with pre-booked tickets, and people with reservations at the restaurants. You are allowed through this point without a ticket if you just want to stroll the gardens directly under the tower itself.

NIGHTLY SPARKLES

Every hour on the hour, the tower sparkles for five minutes with 20,000 6-watt lights. They were first installed for Paris' millennium celebration in 2000 – it took 25 mountain climbers five months to install the current bulbs and 40km of electrical cords. For the best view of the light show, head across the Seine to the Jardins du Trocadéro.

TOP TIPS

- Book tickets well in advance.
- Ascend as far as the 2nd floor (on foot or by lift), where a separate lift on the 2nd-floor mezzanine serves the top floor (closed during heavy winds).
- The top floor and stairs aren't accessible to people with limited mobility.
- At the time of writing, the stairs to the very top were closed to the public. You must book (or buy at the tower base) a lift ticket.
- Minimise queuing for lifts by descending via the stairs from the 1st or 2nd levels.
- Bring a jacket as it can be breezy at the top.

CHECK BOTH QUEUES

A great trick to make the most of your time is to double-check which queue is shortest. In the busy swirl many people are not aware that there are usually two queues for the lifts, both ascending and descending, once you are up in the tower (that is, two queues on each layer: 1st floor, 2nd floor, 2nd floor mezzanine, and top floor). Most folks unwittingly line up for whichever they come to first. If you're willing to take a quick reconnoiter, you may find the other of the pair of queues on your floor is much shorter. Or if you're on the 2nd floor, the mezzanine queues are shorter, etc.

Tickets

Once inside, there are ticket booths (with long queues) at the south pillar. It is well worth pre-booking online to reduce waiting. And, at certain times, only people with pre-booked lift tickets to the top will be allowed up there (ie sometimes there are no tickets available on the day). But most days you can buy a stairs ticket or a stairs-plus-ticket-to-the-top. If you can't reserve your tickets ahead of time, expect lengthy waits both for tickets and for lifts.

Pre-purchasing tickets online gives you an allocated timeslot – print your ticket or show it on your phone.

Taking the Stairs

The climb consists of 360 steps to the 1st floor and another 360 steps to the 2nd floor. As of the time of writing, the stairs to the top are no longer open to the public. You must buy a lift ticket at the base or online (there are no ticket sales for the top on the 2nd floor). Plan for about 10 minutes between floors.

Top-Floor Lift

Ascend as far as the 2nd floor, and from there a separate lift goes up to the top floor (closed during heavy winds). This lift to the top is only accessible by walking up a small flight of stairs to the 2nd-floor mezzanine where the lift is located. Note that the top floor and stairs aren't accessible to people with limited mobility. Pushchairs must be folded in lifts and bags or backpacks larger than aeroplane-cabin size aren't allowed. You will need your ticket to access the lift, after, once again, waiting in a queue.

Eating at Eiffel

The tower's eateries range from snack bars to sit-down 1st-floor Madame Brasserie or 2nd-floor Le Jules Verne. With restaurant reservations, you get post-security access to lifts, and Le Jules Verne has its own lift. On the 1st floor, there's a cafe (called, confusingly, Bistro) and a pizza bar (slice €5–6) and on the 2nd floor a snack bar (sandwiches €8–9). Nearby, don't get tourist-trapped: rue de l'Exposition has a good range, from Pertinence and Le P'tit Troquet to Ryukishin Eiffel.

Paintjob

Sporting six different colours throughout its lifetime, the tower has been painted red and bronze since 1968. Work is underway to strip the previous 19 coats and apply the yellow-brown shade originally conceived by Gustave Eiffel, giving it a new golden hue in time for the 2024 Olympics.

Steam Power

Originally, construction and the earliest lifts were all steam-powered. Coal-driven steam engines inside the south pillar powered the hydraulic pumps that move the passenger lifts. The smoke flushed through a flue venting through the red-brick chimney you can still see today near Sortie 1 (Exit 1).

Musée du Quai Branly

Craftsmanship from Around the World

No other museum in Paris provides such inspiration for travellers, budding anthropologists and those who simply appreciate the beauty of traditional craftwork. A tribute to the incredible diversity of human culture, the **Musée du Quai Branly – Jacques Chirac** presents art from around the world.

Divided into four main sections (Oceania, Asia, Africa and the Americas), the museum showcases an impressive array of artefacts, all displayed in a refreshingly unique interior without rooms or high walls. Highlights include remarkable carvings from Papua New Guinea (Oceania); clothing, jewellery and textiles from India to Vietnam (Asia); an excellent collection of masks (Africa); and artefacts from great American civilisations – the Mayas, Aztecs and Incas. Numerous aids on hand help you navigate the vast collection and delve deeper. Multimedia touch screens provide context, while tailored walks (available online and upon request at the entrance) focus on specific themes, from masks and funerary objects to jewellery and musical instruments.

Temporary exhibits and performances are also generally excellent. Café Branly is pleasantly set in the gardens.

Musée Yves Saint Laurent Paris

Musée Yves Saint Laurent Paris

Celebrate YSL's Fashion Brilliance

Housed in the studios of the legendary designer Yves Saint Laurent, this **museum** holds retrospectives of YSL's avant-garde designs, from early sketches to finished pieces. Temporary exhibitions give an insight into the creative process of designing a *haute couture* (high fashion) collection and the history of fashion throughout the 20th century. Details like his actual workshop, collections of hats, shoes and buttons and polaroids of models wearing his designs are fascinating glimpses into his universe. The building can only accommodate a small number of visitors at a time, so buy tickets online or expect to queue outside.

Musée du Quai Branly

Musée Marmottan Monet

World's Largest Monet Collection

Housed in the duc de Valmy's former hunting lodge (well, let's call it a mansion), the charming **Musée Marmottan Monet** houses the world's largest collection of Monet paintings and sketches. Take this unique chance to immerse in a real cross-section of his work, beginning with paintings such as the seminal *Impression, soleil levant* (1873) and *En promenade près d'Argenteuil* (1875), passing through numerous waterlily studies, before moving on to considerably more abstract pieces dating to the early 1900s. Masterpieces to look out for include *La barque* (1887), *Cathédrale de Rouen* (1892), *Londres, le Parlement* (1901) and the various *Nymphéas* – many of these were smaller studies for the works now on display in the Musée de l'Orangerie (p104).

Also on display are a handful of canvases by Renoir, Pissarro, Gauguin and Morisot, and a collection of 13th- to 16th-century illuminations, which are quite lovely if somewhat out of place. Temporary exhibitions, included in the admission price, are always superb. It sometimes offers joint tickets with Monet's gardens at Giverny (p279).

Musée National des Arts Asiatiques Guimet

Masterworks of Asian Art

France's foremost **Asian arts museum** entices with a superb collection of sculptures, paintings and religious articles from the vast stretch between Afghanistan and Japan. In fact, it's possible to observe the gradual transmission of both Buddhism and artistic styles along the Silk Road in some of the museum's pieces, from the 1st-century Gandhara Buddhas from Afghanistan and Pakistan to the later Central Asian, Chinese and Japanese Buddhist sculptures and art.

Keep an eye out for the world's largest collection of Khmer artefacts outside Cambodia and Nepalese and Tibetan bronzes and mandalas. The enormous China collection encompassing everything from ink paintings and calligraphy to funerary statuary is housed in nearby **Hôtel d'Heidelbach** with a wonderful Japanese garden.

ULYSSEPIXEL/SHUTTERSTOCK ©

Musée National des Arts Asiatiques Guimet

Marché Président Wilson

Food Markets

Sample Fresh Delicacies

Stroll the open-air **Marché Président Wilson** across from Palais de Tokyo where swathes of fresh-cut flowers crowd vendors of organic wines, heirloom vegetables, fish and crustaceans and artisanal charcuterie. The many temptations are available Wednesday and Saturday mornings, and it's one of the most convenient to reach in the 16e *arrondissement*.

Other days you can head southwest about 1.7km to the **Passy covered market** (open daily 8am to 1pm, and also 4pm to 7pm Monday to Saturday) or **La Grande Épicerie Rive Droite**. While there, bivalve lovers can swing over to the oyster bar at **HSP La Table**.

Cité de l'Architecture et du Patrimoine

Soaring Tribute to French Architecture

Celebrate French architecture and heritage to great effect in the eastern wing of the Palais de Chaillot (p59), with thrilling views from the **museum** directly across to the Eiffel Tower. This museum's skylit rooms showcase 350 gob-smacking plaster casts taken from the country's greatest monuments. This collection was started following the desecration of many buildings during the French Revolution, and indeed some of the original art pieces, such as sculptures from the Reims Cathedral, were destroyed in later wars.

Wandering through this magnificent collection of church portals, gargoyles, saints and sinners is an incomparable experience for anyone interested in the elemental stories and craftwork of the country. At the time of writing, there was also an excellent exhibit on the restoration of Notre Dame, complete with fascinating interviews with the working artists and craftspeople.

The upper floor showcases modern architecture, including a complete Le Corbusier apartment, as well as reproduced murals and stained-glass windows from France's most important monuments. Head to the basement for excellent rotating exhibitions.

ULYSSEPIXEL/GETTY IMAGES ©

PRACTICALITIES

Scan this QR code to learn more about the park on the city's website.

TOP SIGHT

Bois de Boulogne

On the western edge of Paris, vast **Bois de Boulogne**, the remnant of a royal hunting preserve, was once the province of kings. Now it welcomes one and all for verdant strolls and picnics, row-boat rides on ponds, an array of formal gardens and greenhouses, plus a famous art foundation, children's amusement park and the clay courts of Roland-Garros.

DON'T MISS

Parc de Bagatelle

Fondation Louis Vuitton

Jardin des Serres d'Auteuil

Jardin d'Acclimatation

French Open

Lac Inférieur rowboats

Jardin Shakespeare historical plantings

Playground for All

The 845-hectare Bois de Boulogne (Forest of Boulogne) was originally part of the forest of Vouvray and changed hands from kings, to monks and back again. It takes it name from Notre Dame de Boulogne la Petite, a 13th-century church. At times it was the home of castles and a convent, at other times a haunt of brigands and a site of robberies and battles. The British and Russian armies camped here after the defeat of Napoléon.

The park as you see it now owes its informal layout to Baron Haussmann, who, inspired by London's Hyde Park, planted 400,000 trees here in the 19th century. Along with its gardens and other sights, the park has 15km of cycle paths and 28km of bridle paths through 125 hectares of forested land.

Fondation Louis Vuitton

Designed by Frank Gehry, this striking **contemporary-art centre** in the northwestern corner of the park opened its doors in late 2014. It's next to the Jardin d'Acclimatation, and the soaring glass-panelled building hosts one or two temporary shows at a time, from Olafur Eliasson to Basquiat × Warhol. A shuttle runs between the Arc de Triomphe and the museum during opening hours.

Jardin d'Acclimatation

Families adore this green, flowery amusement park on the Bois de Boulogne's northern fringe, which was renovated in 2018. Enjoy swings, roundabouts, playgrounds, a paddling pool, a petting zoo and puppet shows several times per week.

Parc de Bagatelle

Few Parisian parks are as romantic as this one, created as the result of a wager in 1775 between Marie-Antoinette and her brother-in-law, the Count of Artois. Surrounding its **chateau**, an array of gardens bloom, part of Paris' Botanical Garden — irises open in May, the famous **10,000 roses** between June and October, and waterlilies in August and September. The small, 19th-century Chinese-style **pagoda**, **waterfalls** and **summer classical-music concerts** are also a hit.

Pré Catelan

Stroll this area within Parc de Bagatelle for its wonderful **Jardin Shakespeare** full of plants, flowers and trees mentioned in Shakespeare's plays. Watch for summer performances in the attached **open-air theatre**. The restaurant here, also called Pré Catelan, is a gastronomic temple, helmed by Frédéric Anton to the tune of three Michelin stars.

Lac Inférieur

On the eastern side of the park, rent an old-fashioned **rowing boat** to explore Lac Inférieur, the largest of Bois de Boulogne's lakes – romance guaranteed.

Jardin des Serres d'Auteuil

It's worth the pilgrimage to the southeastern end of the Bois de Boulogne, for this manicured **garden** with impressive conservatories, which opened in 1898. Peruse six contemporary **greenhouses** with a large collection of tropical plants. Plus, there's a small kids' **playground** alongside.

Horse Racing

Follow in the footsteps of Hemingway and head to the track. In the south, the **Hippodrome de Longchamp**, on the site that once had a convent, holds races, the highlight of the year coming on the first Sunday in October, when it hosts the Prix de l'Arc de Triomphe. The **Hippodrome d'Auteuil** hosts steeplechases.

FRENCH OPEN & LOCAL SPORTS

The park's Stade Roland Garros is the home of the red-clay-court French Open (late May to early June). At other times, the tennis museum traces the sport's 500-year history (closed for renovation-reinvention at time of writing). Parc des Princes hosts Paris St-Germain (PSG) football and Paris La Défense Arena hosts rugby.

TOP TIPS

- Dogs must be kept on a leash.
- Buy picnic supplies outside of the park and bring them with you. Amenities are thin on the ground inside.
- Vélib' bike-share stations are near most park entrances, but not within the park itself.
- Metro lines 1 (Porte Maillot, Les Sablons), 2 (Porte Dauphine), 9 (Michel-Ange-Auteuil) and 10 (Michel-Ange-Auteuil, Porte d'Auteuil), and the RER C (Avenue Foch, Avenue Henri Martin) serve the park.
- Be warned that the area can be distinctly adult, especially along allée de Longchamp and allée de la Reine Marguerite, where sex workers cruise for clients.

CELEBRATE ARCHITECTURE

The Passy and Auteuil areas of the 16e are a festival of gorgeous art nouveau, art deco and modernist masterpieces. Start a study of art nouveau designs by famed Hector Guimard (1867–1942) at **1 Porte Dauphine metro** with its fanning entrance. Tree-lined **2 Av Georges Mandel** was opera star Maria Callas' last home (No 36) and look for No 59 with its elaborate glass awning and balconies. Continue on to **3 39 rue Scheffer**, an art nouveau stunner.

Then, get your architecture orientation at **4 Cité de l'Architecture et du Patrimoine** (p65). Upstairs in the museum, find the maquette of **5 25bis rue Benjamin Franklin** (named for the fellow who lived at 66 rue Raynouard) – it's just down the street with an elaborate inlaid floral facade. Guimard's glory, **6 Castel-Béranger** at 16 rue Jean de la Fontaine, won the award for Par-

is' best facade in 1898 – spot wild seahorses and peek into the psychedelic gate. Guimard built his home and studio, an asymmetrical celebration, in 1909 at **7 122 ave Mozart**. His **8 Hôtel Jassedé** at 41 rue Chardon Lagache showcases elaborate brickwork.

Swing by **9 Gustave Eiffel's 1912 aerodynamic lab** at 67 rue Boileau, the first of its kind. Pop into the **10 Hôtel Molitor pool complex**, an art deco icon built in 1929. Now, the south-facing facade is the only original remnant. The pool had fallen into disrepair, becoming a skater and raver hangout, before being renovated into this hotel. If you time it correctly, visit Unesco-listed **11 Le Corbusier studio apartment**. Designed from 1931–1934, the world's first glass-fronted apartment building was the renowned architect's home and studio.

🔖 TAKE A SELFIE ON THE BRIDGE TO CYGNES

Passy and the bridge across the Seine via the islet called **Île aux Cygnes** (p264) provide some of the best shots of the Eiffel Tower. Stroll over the bridge or zip over on Metro line 6.

View of the Eiffel Tower (p60) from Île aux Cygnes

Immerse Yourself at Balzac's Home

Revel in the Life of a Literary Icon

Transport yourself back in time at the pretty, three-storey spa **house** where realist novelist Honoré de Balzac (1799–1850) lived and worked from 1840 to 1847. In a small pocket of old-school Passy streets (look over the wall at the intact lane rue Berton below), his office is well-preserved, including the desk where he edited the entire *Comédie Humaine*. Peruse rooms of memorabilia, correspondence, prints and portraits – perfect for fans of literature and letters. The Maison Balzac app (wi-fi onsite for downloading) is crammed with audio commentary, including fascinating details about how Balzac maintained his manically intense work habits. Settle in at the on-site **cafe**, with fresh-baked treats and quiche at tables dotted around the lush **garden** with the Eiffel Tower high in the distance, and contemplate your next great work.

FLAME OF LIBERTY MEMORIAL

The bronze Flame of Liberty Memorial above the northern end of the **Pont de l'Alma**, now called place Diana, is a replica of the one topping the Statue of Liberty. It was placed in 1987 as a symbol of friendship between France and the USA, but even more famous is its location above the place d'Alma tunnel where, on 31 August 1997, Diana, Princess of Wales, Dodi Fayed and their driver, Henri Paul, were killed in a car wreck. The statue is usually surrounded by tributes.

WHERE TO FINE DINE IN EIFFEL TOWER & WESTERN PARIS

L'Archeste
Haute française fuses with *haute japonaise* in creative, artful dishes amid soothingly minimalist surrounds. €€€

Arnaud Nicolas
Charcuterie maestro artfully stocks a boutique and runs this restaurant with a menu that changes every two weeks. €€€

Sogno Paris
Tuck into hearty Italian fare with terrace views of the Eiffel Tower – book ahead to ensure a spot outside. €€

ART & ARCHITECTURE IN LA DÉFENSE

More than just office space, the La Défense district is an engaging, open-air art gallery. Calder, Miró and Torricini are among the international artists behind colourful and surprising sculptures and murals peppering the central 1km promenade. Pick up a map and English info on art and surprising green spaces at **Défense Info** (parisladefense. com), at the heart of the promenade. La Défense's landmark edifice is the marble **Grande Arche**, a squared-off arch built in the 1980s to house offices. Danish architect Johan-Otto von Sprekelsen deliberately placed it fractionally out of alignment with the promenade. A lift whisks you up for spectacular views from the rooftop. Temporary photojournalism exhibits are held in the museum (included in the rooftop visit).

Marvelous Modern Art

Play at Palais de Tokyo and Paris' Modern-Art Museums

Palais de Tokyo was created for the 1937 Exposition Internationale des Arts et Techniques dans la Vie Moderne (International Exposition of Art and Technology in Modern Life). The western wing, also called **Palais de Tokyo**, has no permanent collection. Instead, its concrete-and-steel interior is a slick host to interactive contemporary-art exhibitions and installations. The art- and design-focused **bookshop** is fabulous and its eating, drinking and entertainment options – including **Bambini** and **Forêt**, with tables in the central courtyard over a reflecting pool with the Eiffel Tower in the distance, and basement nightclub **Yoyo** – are magic.

In the west wing of the palace, don't miss the **Musée d'Art Moderne de la Ville de Paris**, Paris' modern-art museum. It displays a vast collection of fine works representative of just about every major artistic movement of the 20th and 21st centuries, with works by Modigliani, Matisse, Braque, Chagall and Soutine. The real jewels, though, are two enormous installations, one hung with canvases by Dufy and the other murals by Matisse. These permanent exhibitions are all – somewhat unbelievably – completely free. And superbly peaceful compared to the slammed Orsay and Louvre. Look out for excellent temporary exhibitions (not free), like a recent retrospective of Norwegian painter Anna-Eva Bergman. Download the free multilingual app online.

If you time your visit right, you can grab lunch out front at the bodacious Marché Président Wilson (p65).

A Moveable Feast

Cruising Rivers and Boulevards with Ace Views

Seine cruises elevate any Parisian stay. **Vedettes de Paris** offers 30-minute trips on small boats, a more intimate experience, or one-hour family cruises. **Bateaux Parisiens** runs hour-long circuits with audioguides in 14 languages and themed lunch and dinner cruises. The hop-on-hop-off **Batobus** stops at the Eiffel Tower.

Or put on the ritz with **Ducasse sur Seine**. Launched by multi-Michelin-starred chef Alain Ducasse, this 'floating restaurant' sails past icons such as the Louvre. The eco-friendly electric boat's silent motors allow you to concentrate on the ultra-refined French cuisine and, of course, the views.

A true moveable feast, **Bustronome** is a voyage into French gastronomy aboard a glass-roofed bus, with Paris' famous monuments – the Arc de Triomphe and Eiffel Tower – gliding by as you dine on seasonal creations.

WHERE TO DRINK IN THE 16E

St James Paris
Winter drinks in a wood-panelled library; summer drinks on a romantic garden terrace with balloon-shaped gazebos.

Bô Zinc Café
Buzzing pavement terrace and long bar, perfect for hanging with locals over coffee or after-work cocktails.

Musée du Vin
Book ahead for a museum visit and tastings in 15th-century vaulted cellars on a charming Passy courtyard.

Riding the Waves
New Marine Museum and Popular Aquarium

Get both above and below sea level at the Trocadéro. Located in the western wing of Palais de Chaillot, the recently renovated **Musée de la Marine** (Maritime Museum) celebrates France's grand naval adventures from the 17th century until the present day, and has one of the world's finest collections of model ships, as well as ancient figureheads, compasses, sextants, telescopes and paintings.

Kids love Paris' aquarium, **Aquarium de Paris Cinéaqua**, on the eastern side of the Jardins du Trocadéro, where a shark tank and 500-odd fish species entertain families on rainy days. Three cinemas screen ocean-related and other films (dubbed in French, with subtitles). On Saturday nights, nocturnal visits include a glass of bubbly or a soft drink.

Fashion Forward
Browse Couture Then Shop for Your Own

Paris' Fashion Museum, **Palais Galliera**, showcases over 200,000 outfits, spanning royal costumes to contemporary **haute couture** by designers such as Jean Paul Gaultier, in rotating shows. Enjoy a picnic on the elegant grounds of the sumptuous Italianate palace dating from the mid-19th century (the gardens are free to enter).

It's perfect inspiration for shopping in the neighbourhood's many top boutiques: from **Agnès B** to **Mouty**, with its slick, cheerful streetwear, and vintage- and couture-consignment cool Lorette & Jasmin.

BEST PLACES TO EAT

Tour the 16th *arrondissement's* rich delicacies, from fresh fruit tarts to gastro-temples.

Sables
Delectable seafood with refined flair served in a cheeky, sun-warmed space, accompanied by cool grooves. €€
Aux Cocottes
Reserve ahead to escape the tourist traps at this intimate bistro tucked into a side street near Trocadéro. €€
Le Casse Noix
Cheerful, buzzy service and ambience near the Eiffel Tower, with creative seasonal menus. €€
Les Gros Gâteaux
Small neighbourhood artisanal bakery spinning out superb, seasonal cakes and tarts. €
Boulangerie Basil
Delish sandwiches and pastries. €

CELEBRATE CHRISTIAN DIOR

Paris' 16e teems with boutiques and fashion museums like Palais Galliera and Yves St Laurent. But you'll need to head to the neighbouring 8e for fabulous La Galerie Dior (p84).

 WHERE TO STAY IN EIFFEL TOWER & WESTERN PARIS

Hôtel Villa Glamour	**Rayz Eiffel**	**Hôtel Villa Nicolo**
Beautifully designed classic rooms in a leafy, luxe residential area of the 16e. €€	Contemporary-chic hotel near Eiffel, with tower views from top-floor rooms and roof. €€€	In a quiet courtyard in Passy's shopping streets, a tidy hotel with friendly staff. €€€

TOP TIP

As the metro exit brings you out to the right of the Arc de Triomphe, this is where you'll find most tourists snapping their pics and Instagramming – cross over to the other side of the street to get a quieter shot. And in case you need them, there are also public toilets on this side.

Above: Petit Palais (p81); Right: Hôtel de la Marine (p85)

DON'T MISS

PALAIS GARNIER
Architectural masterpiece among Paris' most storied addresses, famously home to the mythical phantom. p75

ARC DE TRIOMPHE
Napoléon's victorious arch comes with one of the city's best views. p80

CHAMPS-ÉLYSÉES
Take a stroll along the world's most famous street.
p81

Champs-Élysées & Grands Boulevards

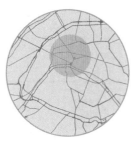

GRAND MONUMENTS AND LES GRANDS MAGASINS

On first impressions, the Champs-Élysées and Grands Boulevards areas might not seem to have all that much in common, other than being connected by Haussmann's wide boulevards, lined with rows of his now iconic buildings.

The world's most famous avenue, home to designer shops and surrounded by palace hotels, sits quite at home in the prestigious 8th *arrondissement* whilst next door in the 9th, the streets around Grands Boulevards offer a more down-to-earth slice of Parisian life, and one that's increasingly young and hip thanks to design-led boutique hotels and cool and creative restaurants.

However, as home to some of the city's most historic and majestic monuments – the Arc de Triomphe, the Petit Palais, La Madeleine, and place de la Concorde, to name just a few – these two neighbourhoods tell some of Paris' most fascinating stories; tales of various kings, both Napoléons, and one very big and bloody revolution. In the pres-

ent day, the *haute couture* boutiques in the prestigious Triangle d'Or (Golden Triangle) and the more accessible mix of high street, vintage and designer shops in and around the department stores of Printemps and Galeries Lafayette also make this area a top shopping destination. Once you've finished hitting the shops, you can also hit the bars (and your wallet) at one of the glitzy, *grande dame* hotels around the Champs-Élysées or take in the view from one of the rooftop terraces. And as home to some of Paris' most historic cinemas and live-music venues, and of course the magnificent Palais Garnier, you're also in the right place for capping off the evening with a film, a concert or a grandiose night at the opera.

PETIT PALAIS
This magnificent museum houses a wonderful collection of fine art set around a leafy courtyard. p82

LA GALERIE DIOR
Fashion fans will swoon over this stunning collection of Dior's loveliest creations. p84

HÔTEL DE LA MARINE
Step back in time as you wander through the Hôtel de la Marine's 18th-century gilded apartments. p85

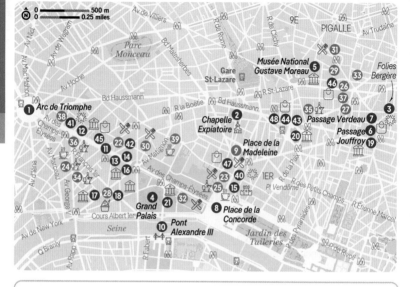

TOP SIGHTS
1 Arc de Triomphe
2 Chapelle Expiatoire
3 Folies Bergère
4 Grand Palais
5 Musée National
Gustave Moreau
6 Passage Jouffroy
7 Passage Verdeau
8 Place de la Concorde
9 Place de
la Madeleine
10 Pont Alexandre III

SIGHTS
11 Avenue des
Champs-Élysées
12 Home of Alberto
Santos-Dumont
13 Home of Colette
14 Home of the
Count of Monte Christo
15 Hôtel de la Marine
16 Hôtel de la Païva
17 Hôtel Plaza Athénée
18 La Galerie Dior
19 Musée Grévin
20 Palais Garnier
21 Petit Palais

SLEEPING
see 6 Hôtel Chopin
see 7 Hôtel Panache

EATING
see 3 Ardent
22 Brasserie Baroche
23 Butterfly Pâtisserie
24 Four Seasons
Hôtel George V

25 Hôtel de Crillon
26 Jeanne-Aimée
27 Juste
28 La Pâtisserie Dior
29 Le Bon Georges
see 24 Le George at
Four Seasons George V
30 Le Mermoz
see 6 Miznon
31 Norma the Bakery
32 Pavyllon
33 Pompette

DRINKING & NIGHTLIFE
34 Bulgari Bar
35 Créatures
36 Hôtel Barrière
Le Fouquet's
37 Ibrik

38 Le Balzac
see 24 Le Bar
39 Le Bristol
see 25 Les
Ambassadeurs

ENTERTAINMENT
40 Boutique Maille
41 UGC Normandie

SHOPPING
see 7 À la Mère de Famille
42 Cave Ponthieu
43 Galeries Lafayette
44 Galeries Lafayette –
Home & Gourmet
45 Guerlain
46 Le Drugstore
see 9 Mariage Frères
47 Patrick Roger
48 Printemps

Pont Alexandre III

Paris' Most Emblematic Bridge

Another monument built for the 1900 Universal Exhibition, along with the Petit Palais and Grand Palais, the gilded gold Pont Alexandre III is one of the city's art nouveau masterpieces. It was named after Tsar Alexander III, who finalised the Franco-Russian alliance in 1892, and it was Alexander's son Nicholas II who laid the bridge's foundation stone in 1896. Its opulent design features four imposing columns, two at each end, topped with golden bronze sculptures of winged horses that represent Arts, Sciences, Commerce and Industry, which are accompanied by a series of sculpted fantastical creatures such as nymphs, cherubs, water spirits and sea monsters. With such an opulent setting, and an Eiffel Tower view, it's obviously a popular spot for photos.

Grand Palais

A Grand Setting for Paris' Biggest Shows

Built at the same time as the Petit Palais, at the time of writing the Grand Palais was undergoing a refurbishment to restore it to its full glory and partially reopen as one of the venues for the 2024 Olympics. Before its temporary closure, it hosted a variety of exhibitions, from fashion by Louis Vuitton to art by Alphonse Mucha, and set the stage for the grandest of fashion shows by the likes of Chanel. Look out for more of the same after it fully reopens its doors in 2025.

Folies Bergère

TOP RIGHT: VERNERIE YANN/SHUTTERSTOCK.©
BOTTOM LEFT: JEANLUCICHARD/SHUTTERSTOCK.©

Place de la Concorde

Folies Bergère

One of Paris' First – and Most Enduring – Music Halls

You can't miss the gold art deco façade of the Folies Bergère, one of Paris' most iconic music halls. It's passed through various owners since its 1869 inauguration as the Folies Trévise, who each had their turn switching up the entertainment programme, but will forever be associated with Josephine Baker – it's here where she danced on stage in her iconic banana skirt. Charlie Chaplin, Dalida, Vanessa Paradis, and more recently Jean-Paul Gaultier's autobiographical Fashion Freak Show are some of the other big names to have graced its stage over the years.

Place de la Concorde

The Former Home of France's Grizzly Guillotine

Created in 1772, place de la Concorde sits on what was once a dry moat and fields surrounding the Jardin des Tuileries and the former royal palace, Le Louvre. It's famously where Louis XVI and Marie-Antoinette were guillotined in 1793 during the French Revolution, along with many others, gaining the square the name place de la Révolution. It was later renamed place de la Concorde in 1795 (although it briefly became place Louis XVI between 1826 and 1830) and redesigned between 1836 and 1846 by the architect Jacques-Ignace Hittorf, who added the two fountains, Fontaine des Mers and Fontaine des Fleuves, and the statues representing the French cities of Bordeaux, Brest, Lille, Lyon, Marseille, Nantes, Rouen and Strasbourg which sit around the edge of the square. But its most famous monument is the 3300-year-old Egyptian Luxor Obelisk, erected in 1836 after France received it as a gift from the King of Egypt and capped with a gilded gold pyramidion, gifted by the President of Egypt in 1998.

FOOD SHOPS NEAR PLACE DE LA MADELEINE

Patrick Roger
The minimalist boutique mirrors the pared-back collection of chocolates, which focuses on the purity of chocolate and praline.

La Maison de la Truffe
The luxurious truffle-infused range runs from affordable truffle crisps to the chance to splurge hundreds on whole white and black truffles.

Mariage Frères
With more than 800 tea references from 36 countries, Mariage Frères has the largest tea selection in the world. A canister is almost worth buying for the iconic packaging alone.

Boutique Maille
While you can buy jars of France's most famous brand of Dijon mustard in the supermarket, the mustard-obsessed will love the choice at the dedicated Maille boutique.

La Maison de la Truffe

Musée National Gustave Moreau

A Beautiful 'House Museum' Dedicated to the Artist

Gustave Moreau spent the last years of his life converting his home and studio at 14 rue de La Rochefoucauld into a **museum** before leaving all his belongings to the State upon his death in 1898. France honoured his dying wishes and the museum is now a unique time capsule of 19th-century design (there's an identical copy of the painter's apartment on the 1st floor) and a full immersion into Moreau's work, which was full of Greek mythology, Biblical stories and religious allegory. It's also home to one of the most Instagrammable staircases in Paris.

Place de la Madeleine

Place de la Madeleine

A Must Visit for Gourmands

The Greek-inspired L'église de la Madeleine dominates the centre of place de la Madeleine, the square named after it, with an imposing façade of Corinthian columns that makes it one of Paris' most unusual churches. It received its distinctive neoclassical look from Napoléon, who changed the design originally commissioned by Louis XV to create a pantheon that would honour his armies. After starting in 1764, construction wasn't finished until 1842, by which time the royal family had returned (albeit briefly) and Louis Philippe I was ruling from the reinstated throne. But like the Arc de Triomphe – another Napoléon-approved monument that was completed under the king's reign – the emperor's design plans held strong, even if his plans for world domination didn't. It's open every day for visitors and also holds classical music concerts; check the church website for more information. But a bigger draw than the church, for gastronomes at least, is the collection of France's most prestigious gourmet flagships that sit around the square, some of which, like Caviar Kaspia, have been here for nearly 100 years. There's also a flower market every day except Sunday.

PETR KOVALENKOV/SHUTTERSTOCK ©

Passage Jouffroy

Les Passages Couverts

Hunt for Secondhand Treasures in these 19th-Century Arcades

Paris' 19th-century *passages couverts* are among the most charming architectural features in the city, and three are located around Grands Boulevards. Built in 1800, **Passage des Panoramas** (p107) is the oldest and the liveliest, full of good restaurants and secondhand shops. **Passage Jouffroy** is just opposite on the bd Montmartre and opened in 1847. It's most famous for housing the **Musée Grévin**, a Parisian Madame Tussauds, but there's also a good selection of secondhand shops selling books and vintage posters. A three-minute walk away is **Passage Verdeau**, which dates to the same year as Jouffroy and shares some of the same architectural details – note the large glass roofs. It's definitely the quieter of the three for browsing vintage and antique shops away from the crowds. Book guided tours in English with the Association Passages and Galeries – best value is the group deal of €250 for 20 people.

Chapelle Expiatoire

A Royalist Monument in the Heart of a Hidden Square

This neoclassical building was commissioned by Louis XVIII when the monarchy made a brief, post-Revolution reappearance and so, perhaps unsurprisingly, it's dedicated to the memory of the royal family. It sits on the site of the former Madeleine cemetery, the burial place for those executed during the Revolution, including King Louis XVI (Louis XVIII's brother) and Marie Antoinette, before they were moved to the Basilica of St-Denis. For royalists, it's still one of France's major commemorative sites. For everyone else, its setting in place Louis XVI makes a tranquil haven away from the noise of the boulevards and the often-packed *grands magasins* (department stores).

Arc de Triomphe to Palais Garnier

You'll take in some of Paris' most famous sites and most beautiful architecture on this one-hour (4.8km) walk, which has plenty of coffee and shopping breaks along the way.

Start at the **1 Arc de Triomphe** (p80), and try to hit it early to avoid the crowds. From here, stroll down the 2km of the tree-lined **2 Champs-Élysées** (p81) with its many designer and luxury stores. The avenue might be the most famous in the world, but not for its food. If you need a pitstop, try Ladurée and L'Occitane x Pierre Hermé (for macarons), Le Deauville (for pastries by Carette) and Flora Danica (for coffee and a cinnamon roll). At the Champs-Élysées Marcel Dassault roundabout (look out for the beautiful Hôtel Marcel Dassault on your right at No 7, now home to auction house Artcurial), continue the walk through the leafy gardens to the **3 Stat-**

ue of General Charles de Gaulle. Turn right down av Winston Churchill to visit the art nouveau **4 Petit Palais** (p82), built as a fine-art museum for the 1900 Paris Exposition. Walk past the entrance to find a **5 Winston Churchill statue** on the corner of the museum towards the Pont Alexandre III, opposite the grand glass-roofed **6 Grand Palais** (p75). Once you've got your art fix, walk back to join the Champs-Élysées and cross over the road to find the path allée Marcel-Proust in the gardens, where you'll continue east to **7 place de la Concorde** (p75). See if you can spot which major French cities are represented by the sculptures on the edge of the square and in

HJBC/SHUTTERSTOCK ©

Printemps (p87)

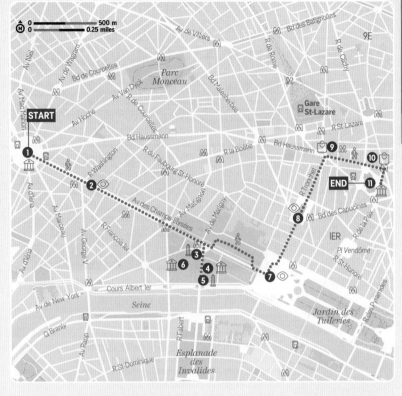

the middle, just by the gold-tipped Egyptian obelisk, look for the plaque that marks the execution site of King Louis XVI and Marie-Antoinette.

Cross the street and take rue Royale towards **8 place de la Madeleine**; it sits in between the twin buildings designed by Louis XV's chief architect, Ange-Jacques Gabriel, that now house the Hôtel de Crillon (p84) and Hôtel de la Marine (p85). The street's designer boutiques include some of France's most famous heritage brands, Cristofle, St Louis and Lalique, as well as another Ladurée (with a tea room) on your right and the fancy Le Village Royal shopping street on your left. Sitting in the centre of place de la Madeleine is the Greek-inspired church Église de la Madeleine, which gives the square its name. After visiting you can browse the surround-

ing gourmet shops (p82) and flower market. Continue north along rue Tronchet, another shopping street with French brands such as Le Creuset, Aubade and Petit Bateau. You'll know when you make it to bd Haussmann, you'll spot the golden and mosaic *coupoles* (cupolas) of **9 Printemps** (p87) and the large signs of **10 Galeries Lafayette Haussmann** (p87). If you want to skip the shopping then make a beeline for the department stores' grand terraces (p87) or wander around the delicious Galeries Lafayette Le Gourmet in search of the finest French foods. From here, head down rue Halévy to reach the magnificent **11 Palais Garnier** (p83). If you don't mind paying to sit where the likes of Victor Hugo, Ernest Hemingway and Emile Zola sat before you, you can finish with a coffee on the terrace of the historic Café de la Paix.

CHAMPS-ÉLYSÉES FILM FESTIVAL

Founded in 2012, the Champs-Élysées Film Festival builds on the avenue's rich cinema history to showcase both French and American independent films (great for English-speaking cinephiles) across all of the Champs-Élysées' movie theatres. The festival takes place every June and screens a mix of feature films, shorts, previews and more, supporting independent productions and emerging filmmakers, and showing off some more daring films. Whilst it's not quite Cannes, you can catch some high-profile films and actors here, the multi-Oscar winning *Everything Everywhere all at Once* was the closing film at the 2022 edition of the festival while recent past guests have included Jeff Goldblum, Christopher Walken, Kyle Maclachlan, and James Bond actor Ben Whishaw.

Arc de Triomphe

Marvel at the Arc de Triomphe

A Symbol of Both Military Power and Peace

Now one of the most famous monuments in the world, Napoléon commissioned the **Arc de Triomphe** after his victory at the Battle of Austerlitz in 1805, but by the time it was finished in 1836, the emperor had abdicated, died and the monarchy had made its brief return.

Although it was built as a symbol of military power, it now stands more as a symbol of peace and remembrance at the site of the Tomb of the Unknown Soldier, where the eternal flame has been burning continuously since 1923. A committee is in charge of making sure it is rekindled at 6.30pm each day; you can come and watch the event or catch it on the live video inside the museum.

The 200 original steps (although they have been restored over the years) will take you up to the museum and a further 40 lead up to the terrace, also original, although tourists snapping photos probably weren't what the designers had in mind at the time. It's easily one of the best views in Paris, partly because it also includes a clear view of the Eiffel Tower.

As one of Paris' most visited monuments, it's hard to visit at a quiet moment or predict when that might be, although first thing in the morning might be your best chance. The

WHERE TO SPLASH OUT ON FINE DINING ⸻

Pavyllon
Yannick Alléno's *haute cuisine*; the set lunch menu offers a more affordable taste of his Michelin-star cooking. €€€

Prunier
Another Yannick Alleno address, the French chef has breathed new life into this historic seafood restaurant. €€€

Le George at
Four Seasons George V
Mediterranean-inspired cuisine with vegetarian and vegan tasting menus. €€€

most beautiful time, however, is sunset, and although you're likely to be caught up in an even bigger crowd of tourists, it's worth it to catch the view at its prettiest. Two days a year, you can even see the sun fall right through the arc's centre, usually on or around 10 May and 1 August (the year's exact date isn't posted on the website but you can find it through a Google search). To get the ultimate shot, don't stand at the arch itself, you need to be on the Champs-Élysées, or even as far back as Jardin des Tuileries.

Meander the Avenue des Champs-Élysées

The World's Most Famous Avenue

Often called the most beautiful avenue in the world, the **Avenue des Champs-Élysées** is now largely avoided by Parisians, other than those who work in the area, but still, it's a sight to be seen and has a richer history than the high-street shops would lead you to believe.

Although it's hard to imagine now, the avenue sits on what was once fields just outside of the city limits, although close to the French palace of Le Louvre, before everything moved to Versailles. The king at the time, Louis XIV, wanted to develop the area and commissioned his principal gardener André Le Nôtre (who would go on to design the gardens at Versailles) to do something about it. The resulting avenue started out as a popular place for the aristocracy to stroll under Le Nôtre's pristine line of hedge-trimmed trees.

The avenue began to be developed in the 19th century; you'll recognise the distinctive Haussmann style, and later when aviation was taking off (literally), the wide-open avenue became a popular place for trying out the latest technology. Based on this, many car manufacturers opened showrooms in the early 19th century (it was also a great place to show off their expensive automobiles to the strolling high society) and you'll still spot brands such as Renault here today.

In the 1930s, it became better known for its movie theatres, giving it the nickname, 'Avenue de Cinéma'. Amazingly, 40 to 80 people still live on the avenue, surrounded by approximately 80 shops and 20 restaurants (and the five cinemas that are still on or just off the avenue). But of course, the most famous site sits at the finish line, the Arc de Triomphe.

BEST CONTEMPORARY CUISINE & NATURAL WINES

Le Mermoz
This elegant neobistro serves up a produce-driven menu that puts a modern riff on French classics. €€

Pompette
Delicious sharing plates (and desserts!) based around seasonal produce, served alongside artisan natural wines. There's a terrace to enjoy in summer. €€

STÉRÉO
Another cool and creative sharing-plates spot and bar à vin focused on natural wines. Also open on Sundays. €€

Ardent
Large sharing plates of meat cooked over fire are the focus here but there are great veggie options too. €€

Jeanne-Aimée
This hidden-away restaurant serves up a seasonal and creative menu (and a great-value lunch menu) under a lovely large glass verrerie. €€

 WHERE TO EAT CLASSIC FRENCH FOOD

Bouillon Chartier
Expect to queue for an hour (or more) but the classic dishes are great value at this Paris institution. €

Le Bon Georges
One of the more expensive bistros in Paris, but every dish is delicious and portions are generous. €€€

Brasserie Baroche
A perfect spot for people-watching with a slice of the signature paté en croute and a glass of wine. €€

BEST GOURMET SOUVENIRS

Le Drugstore
The fashionable concept store sells a selection of ultra luxe French products, including food and drink at its *épicerie fine* (delicatessen).

Cave Ponthieu
Owners (and wine producers) David and Paul champion French wines at their friendly wine shop.

Printemps
The department store's *épicerie fine*, Printemps du Goût, spans the whole of the 7th floor.

Galeries Lafayette
The Haussmann location has its own store dedicated to food, Le Gourmet, with three floors of fresh produce, cakes, chocolates, wines and spirits.

Palais Garnier

Magnificent Fine Arts at Petit Palais
The Museum of Paris

Commissioned by the city of Paris to showcase fine arts at the 1900 Paris Exposition (Exposition Universelle in French), the **Petit Palais** was one of the monuments built for the event which, for the first time, were designed to remain a permanent fixture after the world fair had ended.

Designed by architect Charles Girault, the idea was to create a crowd-pleasing, classical monument that everyone would like (think classic marble and moulding) but which also drew inspiration from Greek classical influences (note the grand columns) and the fashionable art nouveau style. Girault's previous life as an ironmonger also influenced the design, as seen in the gold ironwork entrance and the main curved staircase in the permanent collection, where floral motifs reference art nouveau.

Outside, the central garden was added to offer a moment of peace and tranquillity away from the city's crowds (especially during the exhibition) and can be enjoyed now from the terrace of the museum's cafe.

Notable works include *Les Halles* by Léon Lhermitte; *The Sleepers* by Gustave Courbet, a commission from a Turkish diplomat who then kept it hidden behind a curtain due to its

HISTORIC ADDRESSES ON THE CHAMPS-ELYSÉES

Guerlain
The luxury French beauty brand was one of the first stores to open, with perhaps the most beautiful façade at No 68.

Home of Alberto Santos-Dumont
No 114 is the former home of pilot Alberto Santos-Dumont, where he landed his airship in 1903.

Vuitton Building
Georges Vuitton, son of Louis, lived behind the 1914 art nouveau façade at No 70. It's now a Marriott Hotel.

racy subject matter (and who also commissioned Courbet's most famous work, *Origin of the World*, now in the Musée d'Orsay); and the recently restored *Portrait de l'Artiste en Costume Oriental* (*Self-Portrait in Oriental Attire*) by Rembrandt, who added the dog later to his only full-length self-portrait to hide his legs as he wasn't happy with the final result.

Downstairs you'll find an Arts and Crafts collection intended to shine a light on the works as an art form in their own right, a collection of art nouveau treasures, including Hector Guimard's (the man behind the now iconic Paris metro entrances) entire dining room, and a collection of Monets in the Impressionist Room. Unfortunately, information isn't given in English at the museum, but excellent guided tours are available with the museum's one English-speaking guide, or you can find more info about the works on the Petit Palais website.

Napoléon III's great Palais Garnier
Sumptuous Celebration of Music and Dance

In an emperor power move, Napoléon III commissioned a new Paris opera house to his liking after an assassination attempt at the former opera house on nearby rue Le Peletier. Charles Garnier was just 35 years old, and as yet unknown, when he won the commission to build it. He surprised everyone including Empress Eugénie, who was less than impressed when Garnier presented his designs. Napoléon III died before he ever got to see it. It's now visitors who get to use what would've been his private entrance to protect him from would-be attackers.

Once inside, the 'show' starts not in the auditorium but on another stage: the grand staircase. With its sweeping steps and numerous balconies to observe who was sashaying up them, Garnier purposefully designed it for posing. In the auditorium, he flattered high society again by choosing red velvet seating to complement the gilded gold, saying that the pink tinge reflected on women's faces helped them look 'more youthful and radiant'. Crowning the space is a fresco ceiling by Marc Chagall, a recent design addition, and the opera house's impressive chandelier, which inspired an event in Gaston Leroux's *The Phantom of the Opera* when it fell from the ceiling in 1896.

Aside from the auditorium, one of the Palais Garnier's most prestigious rooms is the Grand Foyer, inspired by the Hall of Mirrors at Versailles and recently restored to its full splendour. You can wander around just admiring all of this grandeur but it really is worth taking a tour of some kind: the audio tour is excellent and cheaper than taking a private group tour (bookable on the website), but with the latter you'll be able to actually sit in the auditorium, unless it's in use for practice.

BEST SWEET TREATS

Norma the Bakery
The French owners took inspiration from an English grandmother for treats such as scones, cinnamon rolls and brownies. €

Butterfly Pâtisserie
A taste of Matthieu Carlin's desserts in a relaxed setting. The ultra-creamy flan is the signature. €€

Fou de Pâtisserie
Pastries and desserts from the best names in Paris. Find a small counter at Le Drugstore. €

À la Mère de Famille
Beautifully packaged chocolates and traditional French *confiseries* (confectionery). €

La Pâtisserie Dior
Fashionistas can find Dior's patisserie inside its flagship boutique. €€

 HISTORIC ADDRESSES ON THE CHAMPS-ELYSÉES

Home of the Count of Monte Christo
Fans of Alexandre Dumas should pass by No 30, the site of the Count's Parisian home.

Home of Colette
No 31–33 is where the writer Colette lived briefly before moving to the Palais Royal.

Hôtel de la Païva
No 25 is the former *hôtel particulier* (private mansion) of courtesan Esther Lachman, aka La Païva.

NOVIKOV ALEKSEY/SHUTTERSTOCK ©

Avenue Montaigne (p86)

MOST BEAUTIFUL HOTEL BARS

Le Bar at Four Seasons Hotel George V
The whole team contributes to developing the menu at this elegant and cosy gentlemen's club-style bar. Service is impeccable.

Bulgari Bar at Hotel Bulgari
The sleek black bar hidden at the back of Hotel Bulgari makes a cool and sexy setting for after-dark cocktails.

Les Ambassadeurs at Hôtel de Crillon
One of Paris' most palatial hotels of course has an equally opulent bar: the gilded gold Les Ambassadeurs.

Sashay at La Galerie Dior

Dior's New Look ash a New Home

If you didn't manage to catch the stunning 'Christian Dior, Designer of Dreams' exhibition at the Musée des Arts Décoratifs (p104), or on its travels around the world, then you can now see Dior's most beautiful creations in this permanent space dedicated to the designer. Sitting next to Dior's huge flagship boutique, the museum takes you into the world of Dior and its complete history as you walk through 13 fabulously designed rooms.

The visit starts on the museum's immaculate white curved staircase, a popular photo spot, which highlights the colourful backdrop of 1874 miniature Dior creations, all 3D printed except for the 452 dresses, which have been hand sewn in the Dior workshops. From here you'll wander into an enchanted garden, past a Paris skyline and through a mini atelier where Dior's artisans can be found showcasing their savoir-faire before finishing the grand tour with the *pièce de résistance*, a room full of glittering Dior ball gowns.

There'll also be a chance to briefly visit the famed 30 av Montaigne where Monsieur Dior opened his couture house in 1946 and where you can see the original changing rooms

WHERE TO STAY AROUND GRANDS BOULEVARDS

Hôtel des Grands Boulevards
A hip hotel from the owners of the Experimental Cocktail Club, who also shake great drinks here. €€

Hôtel Chopin
A rare affordable hotel in Paris, and in the unique location of one of the city's historical *passage couverts*. €

Hôtel Panache
A retro-styled boutique address from the cool Parisian hotel group, Touriste. €€

used by the Dior models before they sashayed out in the latest *haute couture* collection. The exhibition changes twice a year so the delicate dresses can return to storage, and to tempt you back to see more of Dior's incredible archives. Book tickets in advance to avoid the long queues outside (and try to get the first slot to have more of the museum to yourself). As well as exiting through the gift shop you can also revive yourself at Café Dior before you leave, which comes with Dior prices, *bien sûr*, but it's a great spot for people-watching over a coffee.

Crowning glory at Hôtel de la Marine

An Architectural Masterpiece Reborn

Responsible for conserving the crown's collection of furniture, tapestries, arts, jewels, and weapons, as well as crafting new furnishings on demand, La Garde-Meuble de la Couronne ('Royal Furniture Depository' in English) was also France's first museum and welcomed the curious public to admire the most precious treasures in the royal collection. It's a similar case today, after the Hôtel de la Marine reopened its doors as a museum in 2021 after a large-scale restoration.

Make sure to get an audioguide when purchasing your ticket to understand what you're looking at as you move through the various gilded rooms, once the personal apartments of Marc Antoine Thierry de Ville d'Avray, La Garde-Meuble's last *intendant* (high official). Following the abolition of the monarchy (and de Ville d'Avray) it's where some of the most important events in French history took place, including the signing of Marie Antoinette's death warrant (she was executed just outside on place de la Concorde) and the signing of the bill to abolish slavery in France.

In a separate part of the building, two rooms are dedicated to the Al Thani Foundation, a non-profit organisation that brings together incredible works of art from antiquity to the modern day. The signs aren't in English, so, again, it really is worth paying for the audioguide which provides some fascinating information. The final room hosts a series of two temporary exhibitions each year in collaboration with world-class institutions such as London's Victoria and Albert Museum. You'll exit through the gift shop, of course, which sells an excellent collection of books on French history and various arts and crafts if the visit has piqued your interest.

WHERE TO TAKE AFTERNOON TEA

Hôtel Plaza Athénée
World Pastry Champion and *Meilleur Ouvrier de France* (Best Craftsperson of France) Angelo Musa puts a contemporary twist on classic French cakes.

Hôtel de Crillon
Housed in a monument commissioned by King Louis XV in 1758, the gorgeous Jardin d'Hiver is one of the most opulent and historic rooms in Paris for tea, cakes, and freshly baked scones.

Le Bristol
Palace hotel famed for its gastronomy (with five Michelin stars) serving tea in the 18th century-style Café Antonia or in the lush garden in summer.

Four Seasons Hotel George V
La Galerie makes an elegant setting for afternoon tea by the hotel's pastry chef Michael Bartocetti, surrounded by 19th-century works of art.

 WHERE TO GO TO THE CINEMA

Grand Rex
The iconic cinema has the largest cinema room in Paris.

UGC Normandie
Opened in 1937 and often used for premieres, this historic cinema has the second-largest room in Paris.

Le Balzac
This art-house cinema (screenings mainly in French) opened just off the Champs-Elysées in 1935.

OLIVEROUGE 3/SHUTTERSTOCK ©

Hôtel Plaza Athénée

WHERE TO STAY AROUND THE CHAMPS-ÉLYSÉES

Hôtel de la Boétie
A design-led address from the Tourist group amongst Paris' five-star and *grande dame* hotels. €€

CitizenM Paris Champs Elysées
This functional but fun hotel group offers a more affordable place to stay in the upmarket 8e. €€

Hotel Pley
A design-led lifestyle hotel; think restaurant, bar, fitness room and rooftop. Family- and pet-friendly. €€

Hotel Nuage
A tranquil boutique hotel (with its own private cinema room) based around the concept of slow living. €€

Splash out on Avenue Montaigne
Paris' Ultimate Shopping Street

The city's shopping Mecca is not the obvious Champs-Elysées but **Avenue Montaigne**, one of the three exclusive streets that make up the borders of Paris' prestigious Triangle d'Or (Golden Triangle) neighbourhood. While it's now best known for its ultra-luxe designer stores (think Dior, Chanel, Louis Vuitton), it's undergone various reinventions through the years: it was nicknamed 'allée des Veuves' back in the 18th century, a cheeky reference to the lonely widows who strolled the street looking for company, and in the 19th century, high society flocked to the open-air dance hall Le Bal Mabille, where the polka and world-famous cancan were reportedly created.

The **Théâtre des Champs-Elysées**, where Josephine Baker would later make her Paris debut in 1925, and **Hôtel Plaza Athénée**, where courtesan and spy Mata Hari was arrested outside in 1917, both opened their doors in 1913. Fashion couturiers arrived in the 1920s, and Paul Poiret, Maison Caillot and Madeleine Vionnet all opened their *maisons* on the avenue. But the most famous is Christian Dior, who opened his flagship at No 30 in 1946. Other addresses to look out for include No 12, where actress Marlene Dietrich lived and died, the Hô-

WHERE TO GRAB A COFFEE

Ibrik
This Balkans-inspired cafe makes a great pitstop for Turkish coffee and a doorstop slice of pistachio cake.€

Coffee Shades
Brothers Charles and Raphaël Corrot are sourcing and roasting some of the best coffee beans in Paris.€

Certified Panoramas
A sleek and stylish espresso bar hidden at the back of the Passage des Panoramas.€

tel Plaza Athénée's restaurant **Le Relais Plaza** at No 21, once a haunt of Yves Saint Laurent and the Dior models, and No 49, where Jackie Kennedy's fashionista sister Lee Radziwill lived on the 6th floor. At the end of the avenue is the **Hôtel Marcel Dassault**, now home to auction house Artcurial, whose grand balcony can be seen in the 1917 film, *Au Revoir Là-haut*.

Browse Les Grands Magasins

Paris's Monuments to Commerce

In true Paris style, the city's *grands magasins* (department stores) are more than simply a shopping destination, they're also historical monuments and architectural feats of their time. The 9th *arrondissement* is home to two of the grandest, the flagships of **Galeries Lafayette** and **Printemps**, which sit nearly side by side as neighbours (and competitors) on bd Haussmann. Both specialise in high-end luxury, whether you're looking for womenswear or kitchenware, but with nearly everything for sale under their stained-glass and gilded roofs, there's pretty much something for everyone.

If you're not here to shop, they're worth a visit for the architecture alone. The stained-glass art nouveau *coupole* (cupola) is the most famous sight of the 19th-century Galeries Lafayette Haussmann, and all of Paris during Christmas time when it crowns the store's annual festive installation.

Printemps has its own *coupoles* to match, four in fact, shimmering with gold and mosaics on the outside and housing cafes and a fantastic vintage section on the inside. If you're interested in the history then Printemps offers tours booked through Cultival website, with after-hours tours also available. Galeries Lafayette brings the store to life through guided visits, as well as fashion shows, cooking and pastry classes. As with most shopping expeditions, avoid going on weekends if you want to dodge the crowds. And if you can't decide on something to buy, a drink from one of the panoramic terraces or bars admittedly costs more than what you'd pay on the ground, but are worth the splurge for the view.

BEST ROOFTOP BARS

Hôtel Barrière
Le Fouquet's
Rooftop bars in the 8e tend to draw a certain moneyed crowd, but for a rooftop drink on the Champs-Élysées, this is the place to go.

Printemps
You'll need a reservation for Printemps Homme's Restaurant Perruche but you can pop by the leafy bar for an aperitif with panoramic views.

Créatures at Galeries Lafayette Haussmann
Anyone can access the terrace for a free view from Galeries Lafayette Haussmann, but if you want to soak it up with a drink in hand, stop by bar and restaurant Créatures.

The Shed at Hôtel des Grands Boulevards
This rooftop bar is tucked away from the buzz of the street and serves up drinks from the cocktail connoisseurs at the Experimental Group.

AFFORDABLE EATS

Miznon
A Middle Eastern restaurant with some of the best falafel in town. The mezze plates are great for sharing. €

Juste
Affordable and good oysters. The lunchtime prix fixe menu of *moules frites* also comes with a bonus glass of wine. €

Raviolis Nord Est
This down-to-earth restaurant is known for its tasty dumplings (*ravioli* in French) and noodles. €

Louvre & Les Halles

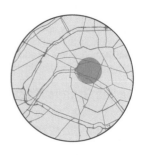

BLENDING HISTORY AND PARISIAN LIFESTYLE

Immerse yourself in the vibrant heart of Paris, where the Louvre and Les Halles commercial hub take centre stage.

This quarter serves as a focal point for historical landmarks, architectural marvels, dynamic cultural venues and a thriving food scene. Additionally, the Palais Royal gardens and the Centre Pompidou, a museum of modern art, stand prominently within the area.

Follow the right bank of the Seine to discover internationally renowned architectural wonders. As you stroll through the expansive avenues of the Jardin des Tuileries, adorned with captivating sculptural masterpieces, you'll be transported back in time. Take a moment to marvel at the iconic Louvre glass pyramid, juxtaposing the classical architecture of the former royal palace. Don't miss the opportunity to visit two architectural gems: the Bourse de Commerce and La Samaritaine, both reopened in 2021. Picture yourself as an 'Élégante', exploring the exquisite high-jewellery boutiques and palaces of place Vendôme.

Once the residence of kings, this district has undergone continuous transformation throughout its history. While Baron Haussmann's urban planning largely shapes the present-day layout, the district's essence can also be found in the bustling small businesses around Les Halles, rue Montorgueil and Sentier. Narrow cobblestone streets and preserved 19th-century shopfronts, as well as glass-roofed galleries, offer glimpses into the past.

Described as 'the womb of Paris' by French writer Émile Zola, Les Halles and its surroundings remain vibrant places of passage, commerce and encounters. During your explorations, take a break at one of the numerous cafes to observe the diverse crowd, whether nestled under the elegant arches of rue de Rivoli or tucked away in the more underground atmosphere of rue Quincampoix. These moments provide a true sense of Paris' cosmopolitan and timeless charm, showcasing the captivating blend of past and present that defines the city centre.

ARDANME/SHUTTERSTOCK ©

DON'T MISS

MUSÉE DU LOUVRE
Explore the countless masterpieces housed within one of the world's largest museums. **p92**

JARDIN DU PALAIS ROYAL
Wander in the galleries of this former royal palace, now an open-air museum. **p91**

CENTRE POMPIDOU
Visit this extraordinary museum of modern art before it temporarily closes for renovation in 2025. **p99**

BOURSE DE COMMERCE
Immerse yourself in the exhibitions in this circular architectural gem. **p102**

TOP TIP

The area offers a multitude of cultural visits, activities and food experiences. If you have limited time and wish to make the most of it, it's advisable to plan your days in advance. Prioritise booking tickets to the main museums as they tend to attract the largest crowds, and arrange your itineraries accordingly..

D.BOND/SHUTTERSTOCK ©

Left: La Samaritaine (p112); Above: Musée du Louvre (p92)

RICHELIEU SITE (FRENCH NATIONAL LIBRARY)
Go through centuries of archives and books, preserved for the sole purpose of advancing human knowledge. **p105**

RUE MONTORGUEIL
Discover the vibrant market scene, where cafes and restaurants create a lively atmosphere. **p108**

LA SAMARITAINE
Shop at this iconic 19th-century mall, or simply admire its breathtaking art nouveau and art deco architecture. **p112**

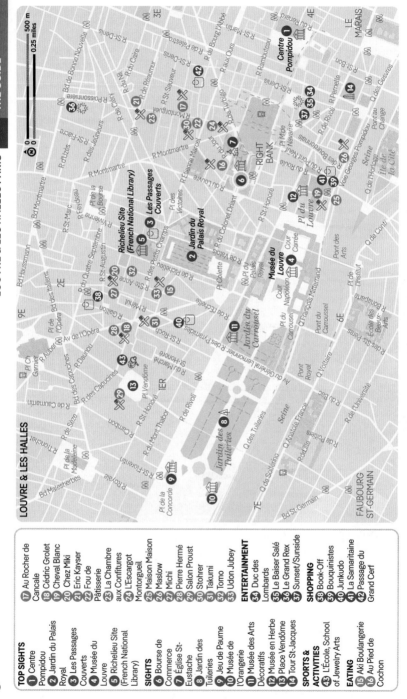

LOUVRE & LES HALLES

TOP SIGHTS
1. Centre Pompidou
2. Jardin du Palais Royal
3. Les Passages Couverts
4. Musée du Louvre
5. Richelieu Site (French National Library)

SIGHTS
6. Bourse de Commerce
7. Église St-Eustache
8. Jardin des Tuileries
9. Jeu de Paume
10. Musée de l'Orangerie
11. Musée des Arts Décoratifs
12. Musée en Herbe
13. Place Vendôme
14. Tour St-Jacques

SPORTS & ACTIVITIES
43. L'Ecole, School of Jewelry Arts

EATING
15. Aki Boulangerie
16. Au Pied de Cochon
17. Au Rocher de Cancale
18. Cédric Grolet
19. Cheval Blanc
20. Chez Miki
21. Éric Kayser
22. Fou de Pâtisserie
23. La Chambre aux Confitures
24. L'Escargot Montorgueil
25. Maison Maison
26. Maslow
27. Michi
28. Pierre Hermé
29. Salon Proust
30. Stohrer
31. Takumi
32. Tomo
33. Udon Jubey

ENTERTAINMENT
34. Duc des Lombards
35. Le Baiser Salé
36. Le Grand Rex
37. Sunset/Sunside

SHOPPING
38. Book-Off
39. Bouquinistes
40. Junkudo
41. La Samaritaine
42. Passage du Grand Cerf

Jardin du Palais Royal
Historical Cradle of the Arts

Tucked between the Louvre and the bustling av de l'Opéra, the Jardin du Palais Royal provides a serene haven loved by locals. It is bordered by impressive arcaded galleries – Galerie de Valois, Galerie de Montpensier and Galerie Beaujolais – dating back to the late 18th century. They used to house stores, cabarets and residences when Philippe d'Orléans (later known as Philippe Egalité) transformed the former palace into a popular square.

The place has long attracted prominent figures and artists. Among the original establishments is Le Grand Véfour, where Napoléon Bonaparte met Joséphine, and where Victor Hugo often had lunch. Parisians now simply enjoy daily coffee breaks in the shaded pathways of the garden. Take a closer look at the metal chairs scattered around the central fountain and read the poetic messages: known as 'Les Confidents', they celebrate moments of daydreaming in Paris' public gardens.

The southern section is a playground for modern art, where you can engage with Daniel Buren's zebra-striped columns, or capture your reflection in Pol Bury's silver *Fontaine des Spheres* (Fountain of Spheres). A bit further on at place Colette, named after the writer who once resided here, you can descend into the metro beneath Jean-Michel Othoniel's *Kiosque des Noctambules* (Kiosk of the Night Owls), made up of hundreds of colourful glass balls. On the same square, people often dance and play classical music. Take a break at the terrace of Le Nemours to enjoy this scene, reminiscent of a picturesque Parisian postcard.

WATCH A PLAY À LA FRANÇAISE

Housed in the front building of the Palais Royal, the **Comédie Française** showcases plays by classical French playwrights like Molière and Racine. French-speaking theatre enthusiasts will love catching a performance in the Salle Richelieu. The main theatre follows the Italian style, featuring a horseshoe-shaped auditorium, balconies and a richly decorated ceiling. Awaiting the start of the show in one of the red velvet seats feels like travelling back in time!

The institution also offers guided tours. Before booking, check if they're available in your preferred language.

OLRAT/SHUTTERSTOCK ©

Jardin du Palais Royal

CAVAN-IMAGES/SHUTTERSTOCK ©

Scan this QR code to check for special rates and room closures.

TOP SIGHT

Destination Louvre

The Musée du Louvre is undeniably Paris' pièce de résistance, boasting 35,000 works of art on display, including iconic masterpieces, spread across four floors. Glancing at each piece for one minute would take 24 days without sleeping. Careful planning is therefore essential to fully experience the world's largest art museum.

DON'T MISS

Mona Lisa

Winged Victory of Samothrace

Venus de Milo

Ballroom's Cariatides

Salon Carré

Sphinx' Crypt

Cour Khorsabad

Cour Marly and Cour Puget

Great Pyramid

First Time at the Louvre?

Entering the museum for the first time can be intimidating. The key to approaching the vast collections of the Louvre is to consider them from two significant perspectives: Western art spanning from the Middle Ages to the mid-19th century, and the art and crafts of five ancient civilisations that preceded and influenced it. Simultaneously, immerse yourself in the museum's captivating architecture shaped by multiple sovereigns. To navigate the museum, just remember that there are three wings: Sully (East) and the parallel Richelieu (North) and Denon (South). The Louvre can be both awe-inspiring and overwhelming. Maybe the best way to visit it is to allow yourself to choose, explore and be pleasantly surprised. Don't worry about seeing every masterpiece – enjoy the journey itself.

Guided by Ancient Civilisations

The antiquities department showcases pieces dating from the Neolithic period to the decline of the Roman Empire. Exploring chronologically the treasures of ancient civilisations will primarily lead you through the ground floor, with additional areas dedicated to Egyptian antiquities on Level 1. Begin your journey in the Richelieu Wing, exploring Mesopotamian art (from what is considered the earliest human civilisation). Continue to the Sully Wing to descend into the Sphinx' Crypt and uncover Egyptian art. Proceed to the Denon Wing to see Greek, Etruscan and Roman art.

Gardens of Sculptures

Sculpture enthusiasts should not miss the **Cour Marly** and **Cour Puget**, on Level -1 of the Richelieu Wing. These indoor courtyards bathed in natural light house French masterpieces created under Louis XIV. The Cour Marly provides an atmospheric setting reminiscent of its original location in one of the king's residences. Interestingly, in an arrangement that may seem counterintuitive, ascending to the upper level will transport you back in time to medieval French sculpture. Moving through the Richelieu Wing on the ground floor, you'll then encounter more sculptures from the 17th to the 19th centuries.

A European Tour of Masterpieces

The top floors showcase European paintings and decorative arts from the Middle Ages to the mid-19th century. Many visitors explore these floors towards the end of their visit, following the sequential order of the rooms. If you're a painting enthusiast, it's advisable to prioritise these floors during your visit! They are must-visit areas for iconic artworks like the *Mona Lisa*, as well as monumental paintings such as *The Wedding Feast at Cana* and *The Raft of the Medusa*. In addition, don't miss the impressive **Great Gallery**, the historic **Salon Carré** (the precursor to exhibition salons) and the opulent **Galerie d'Apollon**, adorned with stunning murals and golden embellishments.

Around the Louvre, Around the World

Like no ordinary museum, the Louvre takes you on a journey to different eras and continents. Don't miss the **Napoleon III Apartments**, almost untouched for nearly 150 years, at the end of the Richelieu Wing on Level 1. For a broader cultural experience, explore the small section dedicated to American, African, Asian and Oceanic arts, situated in a remote part of the Denon Wing (access through Level 1).

From Fortress to Museum

The Louvre wasn't always the seemingly unchanging, spectacular palace we recognise today. Built as a stronghold by King Philippe-Auguste from 1190 to 1202 in order to protect Paris from potential invasions, it remained mostly untouched through the Middle Ages. But during the Renaissance, from 1546 onwards, there were no less than 20 phases of destruction, reconstruction and enhancements. Its modern appearance only emerged after the French Revolution, with the Cour Carrée's addition and its connection to the Jardin des Tuileries. IM Pei's Great Pyramid is the latest addition to this enduring castle.

TOP TIPS

- Make sure you book your ticket online in advance, as you won't need to line up at the museum desk and there may be special pricing available.
- The website (louvre .fr/en) is a valuable resource for finding inspiration and planning your visit, with thematic itinerary ideas.
- Arriving early will give you the opportunity to explore the galleries with fewer crowds.
- Remember to wear comfortable shoes, as you will be walking through 403 halls and nearly 15 km of corridors!
- If you're visiting with children, you can take a break at the Studio (Richelieu Wing, Level -1), which provides creative materials for them to enjoy.

Louvre Itineraries

There are different ways to experience the museum, whether you have particular artworks in mind or prefer to discover freely. Here are some landmark suggestions and itinerary ideas to make the most of your time.

A Couple of Hours for the Essentials

If you're short on time, you can approach the Louvre by focusing on some iconic pieces, still seeking variety in both artworks and architecture. Start with a face-to-face with the **Great Sphinx of Tanis**, and explore the **Egyptian Antiquities** in the Sully Wing. On Level 1, view the **Seated Scribe** (Room 635), then proceed to the lavishly decorated **Rooms 600–622**, showcasing the 18th-century royal court lifestyle.

Head to the ground level using the central staircase and head directly to Room 345 to admire the **Venus de Milo**. From here, make your way up again via the magnificent staircase, where the **Winged Victory of Samothrace** awaits you.

Once on Level 1 again, continue your journey through the Denon Wing. Take a glance at the golden **Galerie d'Apollon** (Room 705) before immersing yourself in the painting galleries. Start with the **Salon Carré** (Room 708), which leads to the impressive **Great Gallery**, featuring masterpieces by renowned Italian artists, including Leonardo da Vinci's **Mona Lisa** (Room 711).

If you have extra time, visit the **Cour Marly** and **Cour Puget** in the Richelieu Wing to bask in the light and marvel at their imposing sculptures, including the Marly horses.

Half a Day at the Louvre

With additional time, you can further explore the remarkable surroundings of the former palace and appreciate the architectural additions made by successive residents over the centuries. In the magnificent Renaissance sections of the southern wings (Sully and Denon), attributed to Henri II and Henri IV, you can explore **Greek and Roman Antiquities** displayed across the Ballroom and the Salle du Manège. These rooms showcase the imported style from Italy, with notable features like the gate supported by the Cariatides, originally designed for hosting musicians. It's fascinating to imagine that Molière himself performed in front of King Louis XIV in this very space a century later.

Ascend the grand Mollien staircase to Level 1, where you'll find the Red Galleries housing masterpieces by French artists, including Delacroix' Liberty Leading the People (Room 700). For a refreshing break, head to Café Mollien, offering a splendid view of the Carrousel du Louvre from its terrace.

To end your visit with a spectacular experience, head to Cour Khorsabad (Room 229 in the Richelieu Wing), where the monumental vestiges of the Assyrian city and palace of King Sargon II at Dur-Sharrukin (now Khorsabad) are presented.

Jardin des Tuileries (p98)

The Full Louvre

If you're up for a more extensive exploration, you can delve deeper into the historical layers of the Louvre.

As you enter from the Carrousel's entrance, you may have already seen some of the medieval remains, dating back from 1190 when King Philippe-Auguste decided to build a fortress around Paris. Descending beneath the Cour Carrée and witnessing the surviving elements of the **original moats and drawbridge** makes you realise how complex the former palace's architecture is.

Make a jump in time, exploring the well-preserved **Napoleon III Apartments** in the Richelieu Wing (Rooms 535–49) for a taste of lavish Second Empire style. Visit **Café Richelieu**, run by the Angelina team, to enjoy a meal or sample their famous hot chocolate.

Art enthusiasts shouldn't miss the top floor of the Sully Wing, showcasing two centuries of **European and French masterpieces**. But if you're more into **decorative arts**, you will prefer to spend time wandering the Richelieu Wing galleries on Level 1.

Alternatively, discover a small collection of **artworks from Asia, Africa, Oceania and the Americas** in a more intimate section (Rooms 424–33). Note that these regions are better represented in other dedicated museums in Paris, like the Musée du Quai Branly.

ANTIQUE MYSTERY

The Louvre's oldest displayed piece is the statue of Ain Ghazal (Room 303, Sully Wing), unearthed in the 1980s in Jordan. Its subject is still a mystery: was it a man, a child or a god? To compare its age, note that more than 8000 years separates this enigmatic statue from the Winged Victory of Samothrace and the Venus de Milo, which date back to the 3rd and 1st centuries BCE.

The Louvre

A Half-Day tour

Successfully visiting the Louvre is a fine art. Its complex labyrinth of galleries and staircases spiralling across three wings and four floors renders discovery a snakes-and-ladders experience. Initiate yourself with this three-hour itinerary – a playful mix of Mona Lisa–obvious and up-to-the-minute unexpected.

Arriving in the **1 Cour Napoléon** beneath IM Pei's glass pyramid, pick up colour-coded floor plans at an information stand, then ride the escalator up to the Sully Wing and swap passport or credit card for a multimedia guide (there are limited descriptions in the galleries) at the wing entrance.

The Louvre is as much about spectacular architecture as masterful art. To appreciate this, zip up and down Sully's Escalier Henri II to admire **2 Venus de Milo**, then up parallel Escalier Henri IV to the palatial displays in **3 Cour Khorsabad**. Follow signs for the escalator up to the 1st floor and the opulent **4 Napoléon III apartments**. Next traverse 25 consecutive galleries (thank you, floor plan!) to flip conventional contemplation on its head with Cy Twombly's **5 The Ceiling**, and the hypnotic **6 Winged Victory of Samothrace**, which brazenly insists on being admired from all angles. End with the impossibly famous **7 Raft of the Medusa**, **8 Mona Lisa** and **9 Virgin & Child**.

BRIAN KINNEY/SHUTTERSTOCK ©

Napoléon III Apartments
Rooms 544 & 547, 1st Floor, Richelieu
Napoléon III's gorgeous gilt apartments were built from 1854 to 1861, featuring an over-the-top decor of gold leaf, stucco and crystal chandeliers that reaches a dizzying climax in the Grand Salon and State Dining Room.

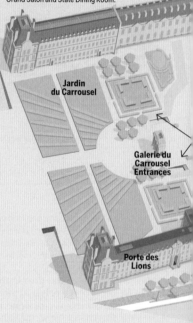

Jardin du Carrousel

Galerie du Carrousel Entrances

Porte des Lions

LOUVRE AUDITORIUM

Classical-music concerts are staged several times a week at the Louvre Auditorium (off the main entrance hall). Don't miss the Thursday lunchtime concerts featuring emerging composers and musicians. The season runs from September to April or May, depending on the concert series.

TOP TIPS

- Floor plans for navigating the Louvre's maze of galleries are free from the information desks in the Hall Napoléon.
- The Denon Wing is always packed; visit on late nights (Wednesday or Friday) or trade Denon in for the notably quieter Richelieu Wing.

Mona Lisa
Room 711, 1st Floor, D
No smile is as enigmat or bewitching as hers. Da Vinci's diminutive *L Joconde* hangs oppos the largest painting in the Louvre – sumptuou fellow Italian Renaissa artwork *The Wedding a Cana*.

The Raft of the Medusa
[Roo]m 700, 1st Floor, [De]non
[Dec]ipher the politics [beh]ind French [rom]anticism in [The]odore Géricault's [Raf]t of the Medusa.

Cour Khorsabad
Ground Floor, Richelieu
Time travel with a pair of winged human-headed bulls to view some of the world's oldest Mesopotamian art. **Detour»** Night-lit statues in Cour Puget.

PRYZMAT / SHUTTERSTOCK ©

The Ceiling
Room 663, Sully
Admire the blue shock of Cy Twombly's 400-sq-metre contemporary ceiling fresco – the Louvre's latest, daring commission. **Detour»** The Braque Ceiling, Room 662.

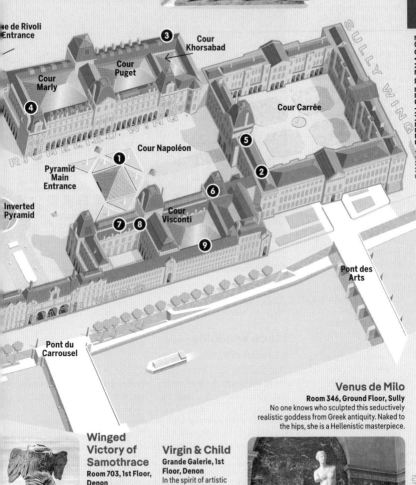

[Ru]e de Rivoli [E]ntrance

❸ Cour Khorsabad

Cour Puget

Cour Marly

Cour Carrée

❹

❺

Cour Napoléon ❶

Pyramid Main Entrance

❷

❻

Inverted Pyramid

❼ ❽ Cour Visconti

❾

RICHELIEU WING

SULLY WING

Pont des Arts

Pont du Carrousel

Venus de Milo
Room 346, Ground Floor, Sully
No one knows who sculpted this seductively realistic goddess from Greek antiquity. Naked to the hips, she is a Hellenistic masterpiece.

Winged Victory of Samothrace
Room 703, 1st Floor, Denon
Draw breath at the aggressive dynamism of this headless, handless Hellenistic goddess. **Detour»** The razzle-dazzle of the Apollo Gallery's crown jewels.

Virgin & Child
Grande Galerie, 1st Floor, Denon
In the spirit of artistic devotion save the Louvre's most famous gallery for last: a feast of Virgin-and-child paintings by Da Vinci, Raphael, Domenico Ghirlandaio, Giovanni Bellini and Francesco Botticini.

TUTTI FRUTTI / SHUTTERSTOCK ©

Jardin des Tuileries

The Splendour of a French Garden

This part of Paris has been home to a garden since 1564. The Jardin des Tuileries derived its name from the nearby tile (*tuiles*) manufacturers. However, we owe its current design to the royal gardener André Le Nôtre, renowned for creating the magnificent gardens of Versailles under King Louis XIV.

The garden was included in Baron Haussmann's west–east axis when he redesigned Paris in the early 19th century. Its central alley aligns perfectly with the city's main monuments, offering a sense of symmetry and infinite perspective as you stroll from the Louvre, with the Champs-Élysées unfolding beyond place de la Concorde.

As one of the rare expansive green spaces in the capital, this park is cherished by locals who enjoy early morning jogs amidst the many sculptures arranged among meticulously trimmed groves and flowerbeds. It is also a favourite among tourists, who appreciate taking a break from the cultural activities and museums in the vicinity. Two museums, the Musée de l'Orangerie and the Jeu de Paume gallery, can be found within the park itself.

PANDORA PICTURES/SHUTTERSTOCK ©

Place Vendôme

Place Vendôme

A Symbol of Parisian Luxury

Dominating the centre of this square is the 44m-high Colonne Vendôme, resembling a gem in a jewel case with richly decorated facades. Place Vendôme is famous for its opulent architecture, exquisite jewellery stores and the prestigious Ritz Hotel. The windows of high-jewellery houses like Cartier, Van Cleef & Arpels, Boucheron and Chaumet display creations like artworks exhibited in an open-air gallery. Place Vendôme has long been associated with luxury brands and *haute couture*. The stopper of the Chanel N°5 perfume bottle, for instance, is inspired by the square's distinctive octagonal shape. It pays tribute to Coco Chanel, who resided here for decades and loved the place.

Centre Pompidou

A Disruptive Museum of Modern Art

It is impossible to visit the centre of Paris without being awestruck by the audacious architecture of the Musée National d'Art Moderne, housed in the Centre Pompidou, which boasts one of the world's largest collections of contemporary art. With its exposed metallic structure and vertical pipes in vibrant green, blue, red and yellow, it gives the impression of being constructed inside out.

The architects, Renzo Piano, Richard Rogers and Gianfranco Franchini, initially aimed to avoid an intimidating cultural building and create a space where art and people could coexist freely, allowing the city to permeate through. The ground floor 'forum' is meant to be traversed by anyone, blurring the boundaries between inside and outside. As visitors ascend to the top floor on the transparent caterpillar-like elevators, they are visible from the outside. From the terrace they can enjoy one of the most spectacular views of Paris.

Inside, the Centre Pompidou offers a complete cultural ecosystem, with photography, films, paintings and drawings dating from 1905 to the present. Two floors house modern and contemporary masterpieces, featuring the works of renowned artists such as Andy Warhol, Niki de Saint Phalle, Marcel Duchamp and Jasper Jones, among others. The various galleries host timely exhibitions, and there is a vast public library cherished by students. Exploring the Centre Pompidou can captivate you for an entire day.

Note that significant renovation works are scheduled for 2025, resulting in the temporary closure of the museum.

IT DOESN'T ONLY TAKE PLACE INSIDE!

In line with the architectural philosophy of the Centre Pompidou, the idea of confining art within the building was inconceivable: artworks were intended to inhabit public spaces. Without even entering the main structure, you can witness Niki de Saint Phalle's colourful sculptures on the surface of **Fontaine Stravinsky**, located at the museum's base. **Brancusi's Studio**, a separate annex free of charge, faithfully recreates the sculptor's final studio and showcases his complete works. The plaza often hosts music performances and urban-art events.

ZDIG/SHUTTERSTOCK ©

Fontaine Stravinsky

The Louvre Inside Out

The experience of the Louvre isn't complete without an outdoor exploration. Landmark after landmark, history unfolds as you walk from the mesmerising Cour Carrée to the Jardin des Tuileries. Beyond the iconic Great Pyramid, a magnificent perspective of Paris unfolds, beginning with the smaller Arc de Triomphe. It continues with the Grand Obélisque, the Champs-Élysées and the bigger Arc de Triomphe. These guide the eye towards the impressive Grande Arche de La Défense.

1 Cour Carrée

You're standing on the hidden medieval remains of the original Louvre, which once occupied only the current courtyard's southwest corner. Over 250 years, this square courtyard underwent multiple construction phases. If you observe closely, you'll notice the monograms of the various commissioners engraved on the building, serving as evidence of their involvement.

2 Pavillon de l'Horloge

As you move to the Clock Pavilion, which separates the Cour Carrée from the grand Cour Napoléon, you'll be amazed by the exceptional acoustics under the arches, often attracting talented street musicians, especially cellists. Notable characteristics here

include a prominent clock, the imposing Cariatides supporting its frontispiece, and a domed roof that served as a model for all other domes in the Louvre. Inside, this section of the museum's exhibition focuses on the history of the building.

3 Great Pyramid

The main entrance to the museum was commissioned by President François Mitterrand and designed by Chinese American architect IM Pei. Despite initial controversy over its contrasting appearance, it has become an integral part of Paris' landscape and the museum's third-most visited artwork after the *Mona Lisa* and *Venus de Milo*. Standing at 21m high, it's constructed with 675 glass lozenges and

MAARTEN STEUNENBERG/SHUTTERSTOCK ©

Arc de Triomphe du Carrousel

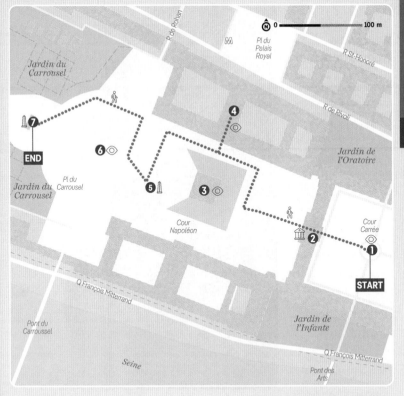

118 triangles. Esoteric rumours have suggested the presence of 666 triangles since Dan Brown's bestselling novel *The Da Vinci Code*.

4 Passage Richelieu

The Richelieu Wing houses three stunning courtyards covered by glass roofs: Cour Marly, Puget and Khorsabad. These are impressive sources of natural light. As you cross towards the Palais Royal through the central passage, you can catch a glimpse of these indoor sculpture gardens.

5 Louis XIV Statue

Peculiarly positioned in a non-central location within the Cour Napoléon, this statue was intentionally placed here by architect IM Pei. This was to accommodate the non-alignment of the Great Pyramid with the rest of the 'Great Axis of Paris' envisioned by Baron Haussman.

6 Inverted Pyramid of the Carrousel

An architectural tour de force, the inverted pyramid is visible from underground as you pass through the Carrousel du Louvre shopping mall. From the surface, its base is concealed by the vegetation of the central roundabout.

7 Arc de Triomphe du Carrousel

The Arc de Triomphe du Carrousel, a smaller version of the famous Arc de Triomphe, represents Napoléon's victories. Look down and you'll discover that it's also the central point of a giant sundial, formed by lines of paving stones on the ground. Walk beyond here into the Jardin des Tuileries to catch a glimpse of the Great Axis. Once in the garden, check out André Maillol's bronze statues, which seem to play hide-and-seek amidst the meticulously trimmed bushes.

Bourse de Commerce

Mesmerising Rotunda of Contemporary Art

Entering the Bourse de Commerce, which underwent a complete renovation and reopened to the public in 2021, is a unique experience. The circular walls and immense glass roof create a vast well of light, leaving the visitor with a sense of awe. It's hard to imagine that this place was once a bustling hub for commercial trades or even a wheat warehouse.

Today, the Bourse de Commerce stands as a modern architectural masterpiece. One remarkable feature is the glass cupola with its metallic structure, a tour de force of its time. The circular mural in its lower section, depicting international trade during an era of extensive colonial expansion, is compelling and deserves both an admiring and a critical eye.

The gallery now welcomes well-established and emerging contemporary artists alike. They are invited to create exhibitions tailored to the circular shape of the galleries surrounding the central space, achieving a perfect harmony between the building and the art it houses. Daily guided tours in English are available, providing insightful commentary on the site's rich heritage.

PASCALE GUÉRET/SHUTTERSTOCK ©

Bourse de Commerce

Passage du Grand Cerf

Pretty Shops for Crafts

Bridging the districts of rue St-Denis and rue Montorgueil, this covered passage is among the best preserved in Paris and is a pretty shortcut for locals. Its remarkable glass roof and vintage shop signs add to its appeal.

Unlike its more upscale counterparts near Palais Royal, Passage du Grand Cerf possesses two levels of fully glazed facades, which suggests that it was originally designed for production and craftwork (with shop below and workshop above). The current array of stores remains faithful to this heritage. A haberdasher, a soap maker, a jewel maker and an antique seller, among others, contribute to the essence of this not-so-hidden treasure.

ULYSSEPIXEL/SHUTTERSTOCK ©

épatant

Passage du Grand Cerf

HUNT FOR SMALL TREASURES

The area offers an array of unconventional shops, from antique stores to sophisticated haberdasheries. Here's a selection of offbeat finds:

Les Drapeaux de France
Located on place Colette, this unique workshop has been specialising in the art of miniature soldiers and figurines since 1949.

Rickshaw
In Passage du Grand Cerf, this charming store offers various objects (from lamps to doorknobs) and antiques from India.

Mokuba
This discreet Japanese haberdashery provides refined elegant ribbons to some of the greatest fashion designers.

A l'oriental
What if you were tempted to buy a pipe even if you don't smoke? At this eccentric specialised shop, situated in the Palais Royal, you'll find a vast collection.

CHRIS REDAN/SHUTTERSTOCK ©

Musée de l'Orangerie

A Visual-Art Museum Trip

Beyond the Louvre

Modern- and contemporary-art enthusiasts should not miss the **Musée de l'Orangerie** and **Jeu de Paume** gallery at place de la Concorde, as well as the **Musée des Arts Décoratifs (MAD)** in the Louvre's northern wing. They offer a slightly less overwhelming environment to explore, while remaining prominent cultural landmarks.

For those interested in impressionism, the Musée de l'Orangerie provides an absolutely unique experience with its display of Monet's *Nymphéas* (Water Lilies), the culmination of his life's work. Housed in specially designed oval rooms that create an immersive experience that's ahead of its time, the ensemble of immense canvases offers an almost meditative experience. Arriving early allows for a more tranquil viewing.

The Tuileries' other museum, the Jeu de Paume, stands in contrast with its programming: dedicated to contemporary art, it primarily focuses on modern photography and the exploration of new media. Embracing this innovative approach, it also features an online platform to showcase art projects specifically designed for the web.

 WHERE TO EAT NEAR PALAIS ROYAL

Eats Thyme
A Lebanese restaurant with vegan, vegetarian and meat options. Don't miss the manoush flatbread. €€

Ilang
Spicy-Asian-food enthusiasts will enjoy a bibimbap or tasty bulgogi at this Korean restaurant. €

Comme un Bouillon
A small establishment serving French popular classics, hidden in a street near the Palais Garnier. €

Last but not least, the MAD provides a rich testament to the French *art de vivre* and history of decorative arts. Its extensive collection pays tribute to artists and craftspeople who have brought beauty and functionality into our daily lives. It offers valuable insights into the history of various domains, including furniture making, glassware, ceramics, jewellery, fashion, graphic design and even advertising.

Explore Centuries of Archives

More Than a Mere Library

The **Richelieu Site**, the birthplace of the French National Library, is more than just a reading room. Its renowned Oval Room, along with the beautiful Salle Labrouste, houses 20,000 books and features breathtaking architecture that has earned it the nickname 'Oval Paradise'. You can indulge in reading one of the 9000 comic strips or marvel at the glass roof and the names of cities adorning the ceiling, each representing legendary libraries from around the world.

What truly sets the site apart and leaves a lasting impression is its role as the storage location for the 'Dépôt Légal', where every book, magazine, newspaper and even video game ever published in France is stored. This vast collection comprises over 40 million documents, a staggering number to comprehend.

To showcase its extensive archives, the National Library has ingeniously transformed part of its space into a rotating museum. In the Galerie Mazarin, a remarkable corridor boasting a 280-sq-metre Italian-style painted ceiling, the exhibited pieces are changed every four months. It's worth noting that, beyond their aesthetic value, each piece kept and catalogued at the National Library serves a purpose in advancing human knowledge.

Book a guided tour in advance to go deeper into both the architecture and the archives.

Teatime at the Palace

Ritz Hotel Indulgence

Under the watchful gaze of French writer Marcel Proust, indulge in the luxurious ambience of the **Salon Proust**. Sink into elegant, plush red chairs, bathed in a soft, warm glow that highlights the opulent surroundings. With rich wood panelling and delicate seasonal flowers on each table – a magnificent centrepiece bouquet overlooking a tantalising array of pastries – this part of the Ritz Hotel seems suspended in time. Treat yourself to a classic French teatime,

BEST SPECIALTY COFFEE SHOPS NEAR THE NATIONAL LIBRARY

Matamata
A small coffee shop on a quiet street, serving its own locally roasted coffee from Paris.

Café Nuances
This architect-designed coffee shop near place Vendôme offers ethically sourced coffee in an art deco setting.

Café Joyeux Opéra
This coffee-shop chain employs individuals with disabilities, offering them meaningful employment and a chance to connect with others. Try their blend in passage Choiseul.

Substance
A minimalist cafe where coffee is exclusively served at the bar and reservations are required to ensure an optimal coffee-tasting experience.

WHERE TO EAT NEAR PALAIS ROYAL

Astara Opéra	Daroco	Nodaiwa
A restaurant specialising in quality seafood, with an affordable lunch menu and a gourmet grocery store. €€	In a romantic covered passage, this Italian restaurant offers delightful pizzas and a wide selection of wines. €€	An elegant Japanese restaurant specialising in traditional grilled eel *(unagi)* served in various refined preparations. €€

A Sheltered Walk Back in Time

The area's covered galleries were inspired by the success of those at the Palais Royal, where shops cabarets, and other businesses thrived in the late 18th century. Landlords soon started constructing their own covered passages. They quickly gained popularity, as they offered the revolutionary experience of shopping indoors, sheltered and in a comfortable environment.

THE GUIDE

LOUVRE & LES HALLES PARIS

1 Galerie Beaujolais & Passage du Perron

The northern gallery of the Palais Royal, housing a few luxury shops, is connected to Passage du Perron, which used to be a meeting place for speculators due to its proximity to the stock exchange.
The Walk: Exit north and look for stairs on your right.

2 Passage des Deux Pavillons

Check out Olympia Le Tan's shop, famous for her original 'book clutch' concept. Exiting the passage, you'll be right across from Galerie Vivienne. Its owner bought and rebuilt Passage des Deux Pavillons, directing people from Palais Royal into his gallery, much to the annoyance of his rival, the owner of Galerie Colbert next door.
The Walk: Don't be tricked by this rivalry. Walk a few steps left and enter Galerie Colbert.

3 Galerie Colbert

At the heart of Galerie Colbert's rotunda stands a statue depicting the nymph Eurydice being bitten by a snake. You can stop and have lunch at Le Grand Colbert and admire its art nouveau decorum.
The Walk: Head left onto Rue des Petits Champs, then right towards the entrance of passage Choiseul.

CAVAN IMAGES/SHUTTERSTOCK ©

Galerie Vivienne

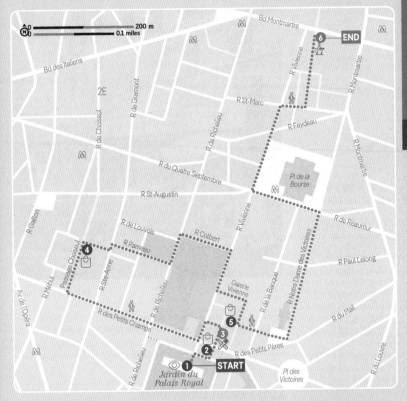

4 Passage Choiseul

Restored in 2007, this passage is one of the longest in Paris and used to have strong associations with literature and theatre. This heritage is still evident at Lavrut, a magnificent stationery store. Old upscale shops coexist with newer cafes and concept stores, blending the past and present.

The Walk: Exit at the north end of passage Choiseul. Enjoy square Louvois and its ornamental fountain as you head to 6 rue Vivienne.

5 Galerie Vivienne

One of the most stunning covered galleries in the area, Galerie Vivienne transports you to another world. It's bathed in light and adorned with a mosaic floor, beautifully decorated shopfronts and illuminated windows. Treat yourself to coffee and cake at Le Valentin Vivienne, appreciate the fine fabrics at Wolff and Descourtis, dis-

cover vintage postcards at Librairie Jousseaume and find a gift at the pretty Si tu Veux toy store.

The Walk: Leave through the rue de la Banque exit and walk up north towards Palais Brongniart. Make a detour to the charming place des Petits-Pères before continuing to rue St-Marc.

6 Passage des Panoramas

Opposite 7 rue St-Marc, this passage is interconnected with other galleries. Despite being a bit darker, it has its own charm, with vintage shop signs hanging overhead, and provides a picturesque view. If you're in a hurry, visit Culottées cafe near the entrance for a quick takeaway. With more time, sit down at Caffè Stern, housed in the former workshop of renowned engraver Stern.

You can finish here or continue the tour further north through Passage Jouffroy and Passage Verdeau (p77).

JUST ANOTHER PHOTOGRAPHER/SHUTTERSTOCK ©

Au Pied de Cochon

BEST HOTEL BARS NEAR THE LOUVRE

Bar Hemingway
American writer Ernest Hemingway frequented this bar during his time in Paris. Within the Ritz Hotel, it's renowned for its vintage decor reflecting the style of the 1920s and 1930s

Bar 228
In the prestigious Le Meurice hotel, this Philippe Starck-designed bar is primarily known for its extensive selection of premium spirits, wines and skillfully prepared cocktails.

Bar 8
Offering a sophisticated and contemporary atmosphere at the Mandarin Oriental, where guests can enjoy original cocktails crafted at the central oval marble bar.

curated by renowned pastry chef François Perret, which features a selection of nostalgic pastries. They are meant to evoke cherished childhood memories, much like the famous madeleine de Proust the writer depicted in the first volume of *In Search of Lost Time*.

Learn about Gemstones

Discover the Art of High Jewellery

Founded by the prestigious Maison Van Cleef & Arpels, **L'École, School of Jewelry Arts** hosts annual exhibitions that showcase the delicate world of jewellery and gemstones, inviting everyone to appreciate their beauty. Guided tours led by knowledgeable docents provide an opportunity to discover the intricate craftwork and discover the art of high jewellery. These can give more insight into the rich jewels displayed in the windows of place Vendôme. In addition, L'École offers a diverse range of courses and workshops dedicated to the art, history and craftwork of high jewellery. Due to their popularity, the courses are often fully booked, so it is advisable to check availability on the website beforehand.

 WHERE TO EAT NEAR LES HALLES

Boutique Yam'Tcha
The spin-off of the gourmet restaurant Yam'Tcha. This tearoom serves creative Hong Kong–style buns. €€

Les Dessous de la Robe
By day, have an affordable three-course meal; by night, a tapas-style dinner. Excels in wine pairing. €

Postiche
A beloved bistro among locals, offering occasionally audacious French classics, with a well-curated wine selection. €

Visit Little Tokyo
Take a Trip to Japan

Just a stone's throw from the Palais Royal, Paris' Japanese quarter has thrived on rue Ste-Anne and the surrounding streets since the 1980s. After the departure of the gay community, who had occupied the area until the 1960s, Japanese entrepreneurs began to settle here. Today, Little Tokyo, is a vibrant neighbourhood beloved by Parisians who appreciate Japanese culture. You can browse through books and Japanese stationery at **Junkudo**, which offers an extensive selection in both Japanese and French, or stop by **Book-Off**, known for its offerings of secondhand manga.

Above all, rue Ste-Anne is a favoured destination for Japanese-cuisine enthusiasts. With its fish-market decorum, **Kodawari Ramen Tsukiji** is among the most popular, although there are long lines as reservations are not available. More intimate, **Michi** serves delicate sushi at its very small counter, much in the style of tiny Tokyoite venues. **Chez Miki** offers bento boxes for lunch and transforms into an *izakaya* for dinner. **Udon Jubey** serves udon noodles in creamy broths. And don't skip dessert: try a delicate yuzu cheesecake from **Takumi**!

And what is a journey to Japan without a tea and pastry experience? Head to **Tomo**, a charming tearoom where you'll find *dorayakis* (Japanese pancakes) as delicate as the matcha green tea they serve. For a quick takeaway option, **Aki Boulangerie** offers a variety of choices, ranging from curry pork buns to matcha cakes.

Historical Overnight Brasserie
All-Night Roasted Pig's Trotter

Older Parisians treasure memories of dining at Au Pied de Cochon. Open 24/7, it embodies the spirit of a bygone era when Les Halles was the central market. Started in 1946 as a small postwar bistro by Clément Blanc, a visionary pork butcher, the establishment catered to market sellers, who used to work at night, and introduced the underrated pig's menu to its menu.

Over the years, it has expanded into a multiroom establishment, attracting both notable figures and everyday visitors. In 1981 even French President François Mitterrand celebrated his election here. Since 1990 the walls have been adorned with stunning murals and mirrors created by beaux-arts students, adding to its charm. What should you order late at night? Anything from the traditional French brasserie menu, to the famous roasted pig's trotter of course!

BRUNCH AT PLACE DU MARCHÉ ST-HONORÉ

This square nestled between rue St-Honoré and av de l'Opéra often goes unnoticed. However, it is favourite spot for locals to enjoy lunch during the work week or brunch on weekends. Its charm comes from the vibrant range of restaurants and boutiques surrounding the remarkable glass hall built by architect Ricardo Bofill in place of an ugly parking lot, now a covered shopping street, paying homage to the area's covered passages.

Reserve at **Nomad's** for a Sunday brunch on the terrace, especially on sunny days. Alternatively, try **Maison Popeille** to savour Mediterranean flavours.

If you visit on a market day (Wednesday and Saturday) or during an occasonal flea market, you'll be treated to an even livelier atmosphere.

WHERE TO EAT NEAR LES HALLES

Jtepadi	Maslow	La Tour Montlhéry – Chez Denise
A bistronomic restaurant tucked away from rue Montorgueil, serving impeccably presented dishes. €€	A 'slow food' eatery offering hearty meat-free and fish-free dishes from breakfast to late dinner. €€	A favourite among locals, this traditional restaurant serves classic and regional dishes. €€

Bouillon Julien

SHOP UNDER THE CANOPY

Once described as 'the womb of Paris', Les Halles underwent significant redevelopment after the relocation of the fresh-food market to Rungis in the 1970s. Today it remains a gathering place as the central transport hub, complemented by a vast green space welcoming people from all walks of life. The remarkable **Canopée des Halles**, an architectural gem, houses a vast underground mall featuring cultural venues such as the **Forum des Images**, a multimedia centre dedicated to the art of cinema. Among the notable shops, the flagship **Lego** store attracts both children and adults with its displays of monumental brick constructions. The official **Paris Olympic Store** is also located on the ground floor under the Canopée.

Organic Concerts
Music by Stained-Glass Light

Known for its impressive Gothic architecture, **Église St-Eustache** attracts visitors for its breathtaking stained-glass windows. However, the true masterpiece of the church is its renowned organ, considered one of the most beautiful instruments in France. It has 8000 pipes and its unique design allows the organist to play in the nave, close to the audience.

With a musical tradition dating back centuries, St-Eustache hosts many concerts and events. Listen to the glorious sound of the organ during the church service every Sunday. Additionally, on Sunday afternoons, organists present public auditions, and the church regularly hosts larger concerts and events. For detailed information about these truly immersive musical experiences, visit saint-eustache.org.

Montorgueil's Food Delights
Market-Street Shopping and Eating

Evoking the area's history as Paris' central market, rue Montorgueil continues to thrive, with an array of food shops, cafes and restaurants. Indulge in pastries at the oldest bakery in Paris, **Stohrer**, renowned for its *baba au rhum;* try *finan-*

 SWEET TREATS IN MONTORGUEIL

Cloud Cakes
A vegan coffee shop with delicious cakes to enjoy at small tables, enhanced by a sunbeam! €

Cookie Love
Chilli, chocolate and black-sesame cookies and other flavourful treats baked with love by Jean Hwang Carrant. €

Odette
Different flavours of cream puffs? This shop has it all! Try the raspberry and salted caramel choux. €

ciers at **Eric Kayser**; and shop for fruit jams at **La Chambre aux Confitures**, a great souvenir! Find iconic French dishes on your way: savour oysters at **Au Rocher de Cancale** and buttered snails at **L'Escargot Montorgueil**.

Every Thursday and Sunday the area comes alive with vibrant market stalls lining the paved streets around Église St-Eustache and rue Montmartre. It's an ideal time to purchase fresh fruit, meats, seafood, cheeses, bread and pastries. Be sure to visit before the bustling crowds of locals and tourists fill the neighbourhood.

A Sweet Tooth in Paris
Hunt for the Finest Pastries

Fraisier, Ispahan, Chocolate Entremêt, Éclair au chocolat, Flan marbré – all these sweet delights create a symphony for pastry lovers! **Fou de Pâtisserie** offers limited-time selections of renowned chefs' pastries, making them more accessible. Follow their Instagram for updates and indulge in their sweet treasure trove on rue Montorgueil.

Celebrated chefs from palace hotels such as the Ritz Hotel, Cheval Blanc and Le Meurice have established their own brands. For a taste of luxury and design, experience Maxime Frédéric's creations at **Cheval Blanc** in La Samaritaine. Visit the **Pierre Hermé** macaron shop and don't miss the flagship store of **Cédric Grolet** on av de l'Opéra, which is always bursting with visitors.

See the World Through a Child's Eyes
An Art Museum for Children

Musée en Herbe, located just behind the Louvre, is the only museum where children as young as three years old can come and not get bored, so it's a must-do if you're travelling with kids! It is dedicated to introducing children to the world of art and culture through interactive and educational exhibitions. Adults can also appreciate the original and interactive installations within the museum.

The museum is filled with vibrant colours, and offers regular workshops where children are encouraged to freely express their creativity. Adult storytellers accompany the visits, creating a dynamic and engaging experience. Children are encouraged to touch and interact with the artworks, as they are specifically tailored to their height and designed to pique their curiosity with a variety of shapes, sizes, textures and mediums. The museum takes a unique approach by working directly with artists to create exhibitions that are meaningful

BEST SHOPS TO WHET YOUR APPETITE

Librairie Gourmande
A bookstore specialising in culinary literature and cookbooks, with classic cookbooks, new releases and rare editions on two floors.

E Dehillerin
Step back into classic French culinary tradition at this kitchen-equipment store dating to the 1880s. The walls are decorated with copper pots and pans, creating a rustic, nostalgic atmosphere.

La Fermette
Cheese lovers might lose it at this small, well-stocked cheese shop on rue Montorgueil. Whether you're seeking creamy or hard cheese varieties, or even charcuterie to complement your platter, you'll find it all here.

 SWEET TREATS IN MONTORGUEIL

Tartelettes	Bo&Mie	Baltis
An intimate tearoom creating indulgent fruit tarts and other cakes – perfect for enjoying with a chai latte! €	A self-named 'creative bakery' offering a range of pastries and elevated *viennoiseries*. Try the flan praline! €	A Lebanese ice-cream parlour where you can taste traditional halwa with crushed pistachios, and more. €

A DREAM-LIKE CASTLE FOR ARTISTS

Known as an 'aftersquat', **59 rue de Rivoli** is a former squat that has been fully embraced and integrated into the cultural life of the city. It has transformed into an established contemporary-art venue and a collective of artists' studios. Despite its evolution, the space has managed to preserve its original essence: the facade is filled with hanging art pieces, and stepping inside feels like entering an artistic fortress. The spiral staircase is adorned with artworks and paintings, creating a mesmerising visual effect. The open studios offer visitors a chance to engage with the artists themselves and embark on an artistic voyage. Additionally, concerts and events are hosted every weekend and it's open to all.

HJBC/SHUTTERSTOCK ©

Booksellers along the Seine

and accessible to children. The featured artworks can range from pieces of historical significance to contemporary works that are making history. Musée en Herbe is not just a kindergarten-like environment; it is a museum that brings adults and children together around an immersive creative experience.

Shop at a Parisian Icon

A Timeless Feast for the Eyes

La Samaritaine holds a special place in Parisian hearts. Opened in 1869, it revolutionised shopping with its innovative concept of offering a wide range of goods under one roof. Like Le Bon Marché, it embraced modern merchandising and was known for its quality products and exceptional service. After years of uncertainty, **La Samaritaine** reopened in 2021. Inside and out, it showcases the beauty of art nouveau and art deco styles. Climb to the top floor to admire the meticulously restored murals, the grand geometrical staircase and the expansive glass roof. The 'Grand Magasin' offers a visual spectacle before even stepping into its shopping experience.

 WHERE TO EAT IN SENTIER

Mûre
A canteen with a seasonal menu sourcing most products from its own local farm. €

Frenchie
A rendezvous for gourmets seeking a delicate French gastronomic experience paired with excellent wines. €€€

Brasserie Dubillot
A lively art douveau setting where traditional French dishes with a modern twist are served. €

Take 300 Steps to Heaven

A Panoramic Embrace of Paris

Who would suspect that the most incredible panoramic view in Paris is also the starting point of the St-Jacques de Compostelle pilgrimage? Just steps away from Châtelet and the Centre Pompidou, in a small patch of green, the **Tour St-Jacque**s towers above the city. However, few people, including locals, are aware that during the spring and summer months, it is open to the public, giving visitors the unique opportunity to discover the history of what was once part of the Church of St-Jacques-de-la-Boucherie, dating back to the 16th century. Following your knowledgeable guide, you will ascend 300 steps on a narrow spiral staircase to marvel at breathtaking 360-degree views of Paris. Advanced booking on the City of Paris' website is strongly recommended, and it is advised to wear comfortable shoes for the climb.

A Riverside Stroll for Book Lovers

Read an Ancient Book Along the Seine

The *bouquinistes* (secondhand booksellers) lining up on quai du Louvre represent just a fraction of the 3km of ancient books, engravings and vintage posters along the riverside of the Seine. They contribute to the picturesque Parisian landscape and have become as iconic as the metro entrances and Wallace fountains since they adopted the same 'wagon green' colouring. Today, the *bouquinistes* are even part of Unesco's Intangible Cultural Heritage.

How about taking a leisurely stroll along the quayside and indulging in an ancient edition of a French classic that might evoke the nostalgia of your school days? Carefully choose from the countless books on offer, along with the charming souvenirs. To enhance your reading experience, find a spot at **Maison Maison**, a summer establishment located on the pedestrian riverbanks. Enjoy your book accompanied by a refreshing drink, while admiring the river and the Eiffel Tower in the background. In winter or on rainy days, find shelter at **Maslow**, a cosy cafe-restaurant promoting slow living.

CENTRAL RIVERBANK RECOMMEN-DATIONS

Julia Chican Vernin, co-founder of Maslow, a low-impact restaurant. *@maslow_restaurants*

Rue Montorgueil is a must-visit. The thought of it once being a hub for fresh food products, with oysters delivered by horse carriage to Rocher de Cancale, fascinates me. With kids, take a stroll along the quayside: they will enjoy the football cages and climbing walls. On sunny days, it's perfect for a picnic! As for historical landmarks, I have two favourites: La Samaritaine, and La Conciergerie, dedicated to the French Revolution. It's one of my personal highlights! For a unique souvenir, head to Vilmorin, the oldest seed shop in France. Buy some seeds and grow them when you return home!

 WHERE TO HAVE A DRINK IN SENTIER

Edgar	Player One	Hoxton
A spacious terrace opening on a quiet, almost hidden square to enjoy a sophisticated tapas-style apéritif.	A bar for fans of vintage video games and more, featuring a playful and geeky atmosphere.	A charming and inviting hotel with a secluded courtyard housing various wine and cocktail bars.

Discover a multifaceted neighbourhood often overlooked by tourists, yet possessing its own charm for travellers seeking an authentic, lived-in side of Paris.

Begin at **1 Tour Jean-sans-Peur**, a rare medieval vestige dating back to the 13th century. Then head east and turn left onto Rue de Palestro, into the narrow **2 Passage du Bourg l'Abbé**. Exiting it, you'll find yourself in the contrasting **3 Passage du Grand Cerf**, bathed in light. If you're taking the tour around lunchtime, indulge in delicious Afghan cuisine at **4 Kabul Kitchen**. Continue around the cobblestoned streets and make your way to **5 Passage du Caire**. Leaving the Montorgueil area, you'll enter Sentier, whose character was shaped by its history as a hub for merchants and craftsmen. Today it's undergoing a transformation, with the presence of start-ups and digital companies earning it

the nickname 'Silicon Sentier'. If the passage is closed, walk through rue du Caire towards **6 2 place du Caire**, where the building features heads of the Egyptian goddess Hathor. The location was once the heart of the 'cour des miracles', where beggars feigned disabilities and seemed to miraculously recover at night (its connection to Egypt commemorates Napoléon's victories). Head west to bookshop **7 Librairie Petite Égypte,** before walking north toward **8 L'Oasis d'Aboukir**, a vertical wall of plants bringing a refreshing touch to a village-like square with restaurants and terraces. A recommended place to end your walk is **9 Maison Constantine**, a unique hybrid establishment with Algerian inspiration, offering a multicultural experience that captures the essence of the area, with a beauty salon, coffee shop, delicatessen and designer concept store.

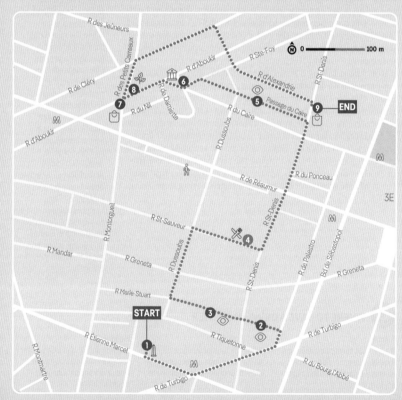

Jazz Your Night Out

One Street, Many Jazz Bars

Whether you're an ardent jazz enthusiast or simply seeking an evening of soul-stirring melodies, the jazz bars along **rue des Lombards** are your gateway to an unforgettable night out. Step into **Le Baiser Salé** to listen to contemporary or fusion jazz, with Afro-Caribbean influences. For a contrasting ambience, head to the spacious and sophisticated atmosphere of **Duc des Lombards**, where you can savour the sounds of classical jazz, swing or even Latin jazz. At **Sunset/Sunside**, get a taste of two clubs in one. Sunset highlights acoustic and traditional jazz styles, while Sunside showcases more contemporary jazz and improvisation. There's definitely something to satisfy every jazz lover along this street.

Singing at the Movies

Karaoke at Le Grand Rex

Known for its art deco aesthetics, **Le Grand Rex** offers an amazing experience for moviegoers with one of the most well-equipped auditoriums in Europe. However, it goes beyond cinema, offering diverse cultural activities to cater to changing interests, which in turn can reignite passion for the silver screen, especially among younger Parisians. From a cinema-themed escape game on the premises to karaoke nights featuring iconic musicals like *Mamma Mia!, We Will Rock You* and *Dirty Dancing,* Le Grand Rex offers an opportunity to unleash your inner performer. Say goodbye to singing in the shower and get ready to shine alongside 2,799 other people... fancy dress allowed! These immersive nights are organised by L'Ecran Pop, so be sure to book your tickets online in advance as they are incredibly popular. If you're looking for other activities, visit Le Grand Rex' website. And don't worry, you can still enjoy a regular movie screening!

FAVOURITE SPOTS IN SENTIER

Kenza Otmani, the founder of Maison Constantine, a hybrid beauty cafe.
@maison.constantine

Start at Boulangerie du Sentier for delicious bread. Don't miss the Egyptian facades on place du Caire. For lunch or brunch, try Café Madame or Baretto di Edgar for the best pizza in Paris. Take a stroll through the enchanting Passage du Grand Cerf and make sure to visit Rickshaw for one-of-a-kind treasures from India and East Asia. Don't forget to stop by 2plumes, a charming jewellery store with exquisite pieces. Wrap up your day with a delicious couscous dinner at Le Petit Zerda. Located at 17 rue René Boulanger near Porte St-Martin, this secret spot is definitely worth a visit.

 ## WHERE TO HAVE A DRINK NEAR LES HALLES

ROOF
Treat yourself to a cocktail on this rooftop with a panoramic view over the centre of Paris.

Café Compagnon
A modern-style cafe with a large open terrace and an excellent cheese and wine selection.

Experimental Cocktail Club
A bar with a speakeasy vibe and skilled mixologists, offering a sophisticated experience for cocktail enthusiasts.

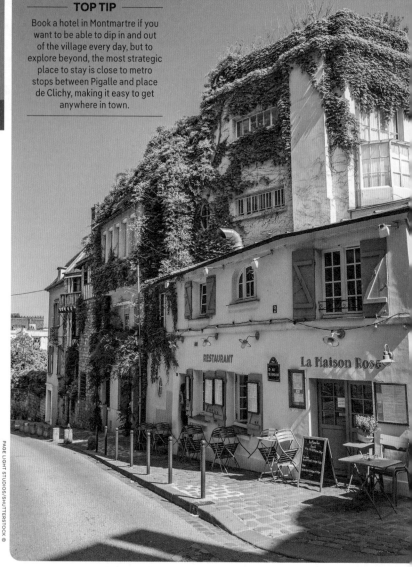

TOP TIP

Book a hotel in Montmartre if you want to be able to dip in and out of the village every day, but to explore beyond, the most strategic place to stay is close to metro stops between Pigalle and place de Clichy, making it easy to get anywhere in town.

PAGE LIGHT STUDIOS/SHUTTERSTOCK ©

Above: Rue de l'Abreuvoir (p122); Right: Marché aux Puces de St-Ouen (p137)

DON'T MISS

STROLLING MONTMARTRE
Get to know the area by walking its winding streets and taking in the surroundings. **p120**

DRINKS ON THE CANAL ST-MARTIN
Rub shoulders with the locals and join them for drinks by the water. **p121**

RUE DE L'ABREUVOIR
Discover one of Paris' prettiest streets, winding all the way up to the Sacré-Cœur from place Dalida. **p122**

Montmartre & Northern Paris

HISTORIC HILLTOP VILLAGE, NEW PARIS MUSINGS

While Montmartre, with its fabled artistic heritage, brings to mind clichés bolstered by the blockbuster film *Amélie* (2001), it remains one of the city's most enchanting areas that never stops giving.

Brimming with ivy-clad houses, restaurants, bars, artist ateliers and even a vineyard, and no matter how many times you've visited, you're bound to discover a street, monument or quirky house you've never seen before. And while Montmartre is one of Paris' more touristed areas, it's definitely worth the steep climb up the hill, elbowing your way through the swarms of visitors on place du Tertre, to get a look at the curved dome of the Basilique du Sacré-Cœur and the panoramic views across the city. Far from the madding crowds though, a local spirit lives on in spots where you're sure to soak up some of that Parisian soul that visitors travel far and wide to bask in. Despite Montmartre's many draws, there's plenty to explore beyond.

Northern Paris is packed with smaller, multicultural, creative neighbourhoods

that mesh together to form a more local picture of contemporary Paris. In the warmer months you'll find Parisians scattered along the banks of the Canal St-Martin and La Villette sipping cold rosé, or cocktail-hunting in the former red light district of Pigalle. You'll also spot them hauling back their market finds in Jules Joffrin, or eating in offbeat places around Gare du Nord, Barbès, Château Rouge or La Chapelle's Little India. There are also tons of things to see and do beyond the *Périphérique* (the ring road that delineates the city of Paris), in neighbourhoods like St-Ouen, Pantin and Aubervilliers, folded into the city proper thanks to an extended metro network. Here, cheaper rent and a slower pace of life have lured young families, artists and entrepreneurs, who are giving these areas an exciting new lease of life.

MUSÉE DE MONTMARTRE
Explore this offbeat museum to get under Montmartre's veneer of quaint houses and restaurants. **p123**

GUSTAVE MOREAU'S ATELIER
Snoop around the painter's former home and see his captivating works. **p126**

MARCHÉ AUX PUCES DE ST-OUEN
Set aside your weekend mornings to sift through the 11 markets for treasures. **p137**

MONTMARTE & NORTHERN PARIS

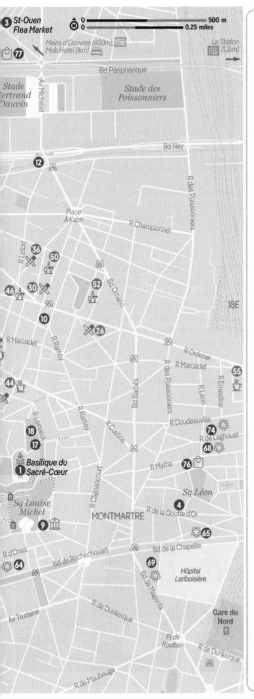

TOP SIGHTS
1 Basilique du Sacré-Cœur
2 Musée de Montmartre
3 St-Ouen Flea Market

SIGHTS
4 Brasserie de la Goutte d'Or
5 Cimetière de Montmartre
6 Cité des Fleurs
7 Clos Montmartre
8 Espace Dalí
9 Halle St-Pierre
10 Jules Joffrin Metro Station
11 La Petite Ceinture
12 La Recyclerie
13 Le Bateau-Lavoir
14 Place du Tertre
15 Promotrain
16 Rue Caulaincourt
17 Rue du Chevalier de la Barre
18 Square de la Turlure
19 Villa Léandre

EATING
20 Aléa
21 Chez Lucette
22 Chez Pradel
23 Gare au Gorille
24 Hôtel Eldorado
25 La Maison Rose
26 La Trincante
27 Le 975
28 Le Maquis
29 Le Moulin de la Galette
30 Le Nord Sud
31 Le Ruisseau
32 L'Envie du Jour
33 L'Esquisse
34 Lopin
35 Montcalm
36 Patakrep
37 STÉRÉO
38 Sunset
39 Superflu

DRINKING & NIGHTLIFE
40 Aux Vins Vivants
41 Beans on Fire
42 BlackBird Coffee
43 Café de la Butte
44 Café Francoeur
45 Dirty Dick
46 Dose
47 Hôtel Rochechouart
48 La Bossue
49 La Cavé
50 La Timbale
51 Le Hasard Ludique
52 Le Petit Joseph Dijon
53 Le Petit Moulin
54 L'Etoile de Montmartre
55 Lomi
56 Lulu White
57 Octopussy
58 Pimpin
59 Two Doors
60 Villa Frochot

ENTERTAINMENT
61 Au Lapin Agile
62 Chez Michou
63 Divan du Monde & Madame Arthur
64 Elysée-Montmartre
65 FGO Barbara
66 La Boule Noire
67 La Cigale
68 Le 360 Paris Music Factory
69 Le Louxor
70 Le Mansart
71 L'Européen
72 Manufacture des Abbesses
73 Moulin Rouge
74 Olympic Café

SHOPPING
75 Dizonord
76 Maison Château Rouge
77 Marché aux Puces de St-Ouen

Montmartre Through the Ages

MAP P118

From a Mining Site to Bohemian Nights

Montmartre's museum-like quality could be mistaken for being its only feature, but delve into its colourful backstory and it emerges as a multifaceted holder of many secrets. References to the hilltop village date to Gallo-Roman times. Perched on a windy 130m hill, the highest point in the city, it was populated with grain mills, like the **Moulin de la Galette**, where a replica stands today on rue Lepic. Montmartre was a gypsum mining site, leaving it riddled with underground tunnels; great hiding places for revolutionaries, artillery during various conflicts and for Russian soldiers during the Franco-Prussian War.

In 1860 Montmartre officially became part of the city's 18th *arrondissement* and later, the **Basilique du Sacré-Cœur** was built to expiate the city's sins. Its gleaming white dome towers above the city like a celestial mirage, floating up to the skies as close as possible to the gods. By the 19th century, Montmartre had become a place of debauchery, with cabarets like the **Au Lapin Agile**, still standing today. Montmartre drew artists like Pablo Picasso, Pierre-Auguste Renoir and Amedeo Modigliani, who came for the cheap rent and nightlife. Today, main artery rue des Abbesses and the narrow street-art-splattered lanes that tumble down steep hillsides are lined with bars, restaurants and boutiques, packed with visitors coming to get a taste of Montmartre's unique allure. However, get underneath the veneer and discover a parallel universe of local life that's miles from the seething hilltop **place du Tertre**.

Le Moulin de la Galette

VVOE/SHUTTERSTOCK ©

Canal St-Martin

MAP P130

Come Rain or Shine

The shabby chic neighbourhood of Canal St-Martin, behind Gare de l'Est (one of Paris' main train stations), is laid out along a picturesque, tree-lined canal. It comes alive during the warmer months when locals flock to the water's edge to enjoy drinks and picnics to the sound of people playing music. However, the plethora of trendy restaurants and bars, such as **Ake**, **Early June**, **Les Enfants Perdus** and **Le Comptoir Général** (p132), as well as boutiques scattered around the streets on the western bank, make it a year-round destination.

Pigalle

Canal St-Martin

Pigalle

MAP P130

From Red-Light District to Cocktail Strip

South of Montmartre, Pigalle is a patchwork of places that tells the story of its many lives. The remaining handful of sex shops, strip bars and adult cinemas are testimony to its past as a red-light district, while pocket-sized cocktail bars like **Dirty Dick** and **Lulu White**, as well as the magnificent **Villa Frochot**, with its art deco stained-glass window, point to its old absinthe and opium den days. A hotbed for raucous go-ings-on, especially during the Belle Époque (1871–1914), which brought a wave of cabarets, such as the world-famous Moulin Rouge, the area saw a second wind during the Années Folles (1920s). Today, Pigalle comes alive at night and on weekends when locals pack into its trendy bars and restaurants to let their hair down.

Jules Joffrin

MAP P118

Markets and Bohemian Bars

Jules Joffrin is a tangle of streets at the bottom of Montmartre's north side with bustling fruit and vegetable markets, especially on weekend mornings. Parisians shuffle along the cobblestone streets, stopping for a coffee or midday aperitif before heading for lunch. The area has some of the best-value drinking and dining, where you can rub shoulders with an arty local crowd. It's a diverse area of hole-in-wall bars such as **Le Petit Joseph Dijon** and **La Timbale**, go-tos like **Sunset**, old-world cafes such as **Le Nord Sud** and hidden culinary gems like **Le Maquis**, and is one of the last bohemian bastions that hasn't been steamrolled by gentrification.

121

Start in **1 Pigalle** and walk up rue Houdon, passing vintage perfume boutique **2 Abstraction**. Reach **3 rue des Abbesses**, with its shops and cafes. Avoid having to use the steep stairs by taking paved rue de la Vieuville, which turns into rue des Trois Frères and curves up behind the metro station. You'll pass the **4 Mur des Je t'aime (Wall of 'I Love Yous')**, always busy with visitors, the boutique **5 Spree** and the **6 Fotoautomat**, which usually has a queue but takes great snaps. At rue Androuet you'll pass **7 Au Marché de la Butte**, featured in the film *Amélie*, and then head to tree-lined place Emile Goudeau, where you'll see the storied studios **8 Le Bateau-Lavoir**, where major artists like Picasso once lived. Take rue d'Orchampt, passing by singer Dalida's former home, **9 Maison de Dalida**, then walk along rue Girardon and **10 rue de l'Abreuvoir**, one of the most scenic streets in the city. Pass by **11 La Maison Rose**, continue past ivy-clad houses and the vineyard, then go along rue des Saules and right onto rue St-Vincent to **12 square de la Turlure**, where you'll have a magnificent view of the back of the Sacré-Cœur. To reach the front of the basilica take **13 rue du Cardinal Guibert** and admire the dome and panoramic rooftop views. Make a detour west to the **14 place du Tertre** to see the crowded square of artists and restaurants. Back at Sacré-Cœur, walk left down the stairs through the **15 square Louise Michel** to the **16 Halle St-Pierre** in the area's textile neighbourhood, where you can see the basilica from the bottom of its pedestal.

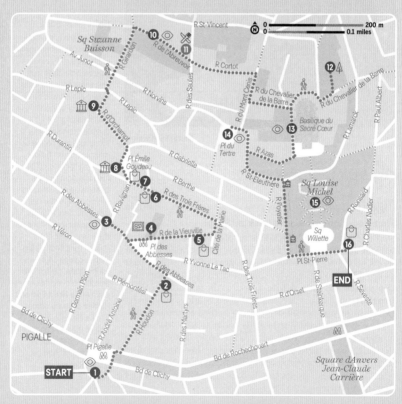

REPORT/SHUTTERSTOCK ©

Place du Tertre

Get Your Bearings in Montmartre
MAP P118

Old-World Charms Die Hard

Montmartre is a big village that brims with history at every turn. It begins in Pigalle with reams of souvenir shops that disappear as you ascend and reach the rue des Abbesses, the area's main artery. Bars, restaurants and high-street shops line the street and are often packed with visitors. Smaller streets like rue Lepic, rue Tholozé, rue Ravignan and rue des Trois Frères take you up to **place du Tertre**, planted with restaurants and their terraces in warmer months and artists with their easels, with Sacré-Cœur beyond. Montmartre was known for its vineyards for centuries but today, only the **Clos Montmartre** remains on rue des Saules, in place of an old *guinguette* (outdoor bar with dancing). Painter Pierre-Auguste Renoir lived next door in what is now the charming small **Musée de Montmartre**. Every October, during the **Fête des Vendanges** (the grape harvest celebration) the whole area comes alive with parties and a parade. Close by is the restaurant **La Maison Rose**, likely the most Instagrammed building in Paris, and probably built in the mid-1800s. Its pink walls came later and were inspired by a trip the then owner Laure Germaine Pichot took to Barcelona. She was also Picasso's lover

BEST PLACES FOR FRENCH FOOD IN MONTMARTRE

La Part des Anges
A bistro where real locals go to feast on heart-warming *magret de canard*. €€

Le Progrès
A favourite local cafe with wooden interiors, serving French staples from snails to steak tartare. €

La Vache et le Cuisinier
A lively upmarket evening spot for dining on hearty *côte de boeuf (rib steak)*. €€

Ma Biche
A laid-back spot where produce comes from nearby farms. There's a hearty brunch on Sundays. €€

Les Tantes Jeanne
Beautiful French cuisine that's perfect for a special occasion. €€€

 JULES JOFFRIN TASTEMAKERS: GOODIES TO TAKE HOME

Monsieur Caramel
This Korean pastry chef has mastered French delights, which he serves in his vintage patisserie. €€

Le Roi du Saucisson
Take a bite of France back with you with some *saucisson* (sausage) from this local go-to. €€

La Laiterie de Paris
A cheese shop where *affinage* (refining) actually takes place on-site. It also sells great natural wines. €€

BEST BARS IN MONTMARTRE

Chez Camille
Portraits of Elvis and Little Richard hang in gold frames and there's often live rock-and-roll music.

Le Tagada
This family-run bar is named after a red 1970s candy.

Soleil de la Butte
A tiny bar with a dance floor in the basement that's open till late.

Le Café des Deux Moulins
Featured in the film *Amélie*. Soak up the retro atmosphere.

Le Très Particulier
Known for its cocktails, this bar is hidden in the garden of a small, fancy hotel.

BORIS-B/SHUTTERSTOCK ©

Le Petit Moulin

and muse, who was often seen here having a *café crème* before returning to his quarters at **Le Bateau-Lavoir**, a cluster of artist studios on rue Ravignan that still exists to this day. Another famous resident of the area was the French-Italian singer Dalida, whose tomb is in the **Cimetière de Montmartre** as are those of writer Émile Zola and artist Gustave Moreau.

Montmartre's Present-Day Pleasures   MAP P118
Sacre-Cœur, Art and Cafes

Catch lesser-seen glimpses of the Basilique du Sacré-Cœur by veering to the back of the basilica, to **square de la Turlure** and the scenic **rue du Chevalier de la Barre**; you might catch Benedictine sisters strolling between their living quarters across the street to a secret entrance of the basilica. It took six architects to complete the Romano-Byzantine style basilica (1875–1919). It's built from calcite, ensuring it remains white. Inside, you'll find the glittering apse mosaic *Christ in Majesty*, one of the largest in the world. Above the high altar is the *Blessed Sacrament*. The prayer 'cycle' that began in 1885 before the basilica's completion still continues around the clock, with perpetual adoration of this sacrament – including at night. On Sunday you can hear the organ being played during mass and vespers.

 BEST PLACES TO STAY IN THE HEART OF MONTMARTRE

Hôtel Basss
Basic but clean; the location right on rue des Abbesses is the high point. €€

Le Village Montmartre
A well-priced hostel with dorm beds and an outdoor patio, on a quiet street in Montmartre. €

Le Relais Montmartre
A well-maintained classic abode that has lots of chintzy flower fabrics and a certain charm. €

Montmartre also has museums and theatres that should not be missed. As well as the Musée de Montmartre, visit the **Espace Dalí**, with 300 original works. The roster of performances at the **Manufacture des Abbesses** is also worth checking out, and make sure you pop into the **Halle St-Pierre**, an 'outsider' art gallery in a glass-and-iron structure that once served as a market in Montmartre's textile district of St-Pierre. The area's street art also makes it an open-air museum, with artists from all over the world coming to make their mark on the city.

When here, coffee fans should also take time to sit and watch the world go by at one of the many cafes, such as **Le Petit Moulin**, **La Bossue**, **Beans on Fire** or **BlackBird Coffee**. If pushed for time or if you have young children, take the **Promotrain**, which does a round trip up and down the hill in about 30 minutes to all the main sites.

Eating & People Watching in Jules Joffrin

MAP P118

Bohemian Bars and Restaurants

In Montmartre, start at **Le Moulin de la Galette** and head north on av Junot, taking in some of the most beautiful houses in the area and a peek at the townhouses on **Villa Léandre**, before winding your way down and crossing the beautiful **rue Caulaincourt**, with its cafes, then taking rue du Mont-Cenis all the way to **Jules Joffrin metro station**. Rue Ramey is also a local go-to for restaurants and cafes. Mornings in the low-key area between Clignancourt and Jules Joffrin can be spent soaking up the goings-on and people watching while hopping from one cafe terrace to the next. Over the road is the art deco–style cafe **Le Nord Sud**, and to the left, rue du Poteau comes alive at weekends with a lively produce market and locals enjoying a coffee or early aperitif in the sun at spots such as **Dose**. It's fun finding local gems in the streets in the surrounding area, like record shop **Dizonord** and, close to Clignancourt station. A disused railway circles Paris, with many of its stations now hybrid venues, like **La REcyclerie**. The area is also full of exciting yet relaxed restaurants to try, such as **La Trincante** for oysters, **Le Maquis**, **Montcalm** and **Aléa** for laid-back creative modern French cuisine, **Le Ruisseau** for burgers, **Patakrep** for crêpes and **Chez Pradel** for a typical French bistro experience.

ABANDONED TRAIN STATIONS TURNED ARTY HUBS

The 18-mile **Petite Ceinture**, or 'PC', railway built around Paris some 150 years ago, is the home of social recluses, homeless people and *cataphiles* that emerge from clandestine bars hidden below ground in the city's catacombs, a network of tunnels that runs underneath the city. A number of its abandoned train stations have also been turned into bars, such as **La REcyclerie**, and, in the area, **Le Hasard Ludique** and **La Station**. Elsewhere, check out La Gare jazz club, with a nightclub in the basement, La Muette restaurant and Poinçon cafe. The railway itself is slowly being reclaimed by city hall as a bucolic promenade.

BEST PLACES TO STAY IN THE HEART OF MONTMARTRE

Monsieur Aristide
A small, atmospheric and smart vintage-style hotel with a leafy courtyard cafe for sunny days. €€

Hôtel Littéraire Marcel Aymé
A clean and pleasant base to explore from, located in the heart of the neighbourhood. €

L'Hôtel Particulier
Push the black gate and follow the quiet path to this elegantly renovated mansion. €€€

ARTIST ATELIERS & VILLA MUSEUMS

Musée de Montmartre
Inside a 17th-century house, one of the oldest in the area, where artist Renoir lived. Displays tell the story of Montmartre's colourful past.

Musée de la Vie Romantique
A little piece of French countryside in the 9th *arrondissement*, it was Dutch painter Ary Scheffer's home; visitors included Dickens and Chopin.

Musée Gustave Moreau
The symbolist painter's former home. High points are his bewitching paintings and a gorgeous, creaky wooden spiral staircase leading to his studio.

Other small museums to have on your list in northern Paris include the atmospheric Musée Jacquemart-André, Musée Nissim de Camondo, Musée Cernuschi and Musée Jean-Jacques Henner.

PETR KOVALENKOV/SHUTTERSTOCK ©

Café Francoeur

Laid-Back Wanderings from Rue Lamarck to Marcadet

MAP P118

A Low-Key Foodie Paradise

A lot of places in Paris are about hitting the 'pause' button and lounging on a cafe terrace with friends, having coffee or wine, while having heated debates about politics or philosophy. It's a cliché but you might find it's not far from the truth. Around the tangle of streets north of Montmartre, just south of Jules Joffrin, are rue Lamarck, rue Marcadet (two of the longest streets in the 18th *arrondissement*) and rue Francoeur, where there are tons of laid-back bistros, coffee shops and bars to settle in at after a day's sightseeing. Favourites include cafes with postcard-perfect awnings at the top of the stairs near the Lamarck metro station on rue Caulaincourt, such as **Café de la Butte** and **Café Francoeur**. For craft coffee there is the old-timer **Lomi** (further along rue Marcadet) and trendy **Two Doors**, with a loyal, creative expat crowd. Bars to lounge at include **L'Etoile de Montmartre** and **La Cavé**, with a laid-back local atmosphere and sunny terraces, and **Aux Vins Vivants** for natural wines. For dinner, book to

VINTAGE HOMEWARE SHOPPING NORTH OF MONTMARTRE

Modernariato
A small vintage trove of treasures, including Rodney Kinsman lighting and Fritz Hansen consoles.

Jour de Broc
A photogenic boutique of countryside bric-a-brac, from old typewriters to porcelain figurines and cafe memorabilia.

Marché aux Puces de St-Ouen
Spend a day delving into this flea market, brimming with antique furniture and vintage jewellery.

eat at the excellent **L'Esquisse**, **Le 975**, **Lopin** or **Superflu**, which hosts DJs Fridays and Saturdays for after-dinner partying. Wherever you choose in the area, you're unlikely to go wrong as it's packed with restaurants helmed by creative chefs.

Discovering Pigalle & Beyond MAP P118
Red-Light District to Cocktail Bars

South of Montmartre between place de Clichy and Barbès is a part of Paris that meshes together various areas and histories. From cabarets to sex shops, Pigalle has always been known for its raucous nightlife, as immortalised in the works of painter Henri de Toulouse-Lautrec in the 1800s. Today, the goings-on might be tamer, but the area brims with places to dance, eat, drink, and incidentally, sleep. Book tickets for a night of drag cabaret at **Madame Arthur** or **Chez Michou**, or at the **Moulin Rouge** for traditional burlesque. The area is also packed with top music venues like **La Boule Noire**, **La Cigale**, **Elysée-Montmartre**, **Divan du Monde** and club **La Machine** (in the basement of the Moulin Rouge). There's a smattering of great places to eat and drink, such as the **Bar à Bulles**, at the top of the Moulin Rouge, the rooftop bar at **Hôtel Rochechouart**, with a jaw-dropping view of the Sacré-Cœur, local institution **Le Mansart** or cocktail kings **Dirty Dick** and **Lulu White**. Don't miss architectural gems like the magnificent **Villa Frochot**, said to have been a China-themed parlour, now a restaurant. Wrapped around Pigalle is the rest of the upscale 9th *arrondissement*. Here'll you find the produce boutiques of rue des Martyrs, the small restaurants of rue Condorcet and the elegant façades of the St-Georges area, with a sprinkling of quieter, chicer spots to eat and stay. These include Paris' very own **Soho House** and newly opened hotel **La Fantaisie**, with a restaurant led by three-star chef Dominique Crenn.

WHERE TO EAT IN PIGALLE

Bouillon Pigalle
Terrific value, this bouillon is one of several in the city not to miss for escargot and *steak-frites* at teeny prices.

Le Rochechouart
This vintage-style dining space with overhangs from its days as a 1920s dancing hall serves traditional French food.

Le Bon Georges
A local favourite for upscale French food and handpicked wines in classic bistro surroundings.

MESA (HOY Hotel)
A fantastic option for lesser-known flavours rooted in Latin American savoir-faire, rustled up with top-notch vegetarian produce. Meat lovers, you won't regret it.

 WHERE TO STAY IN PIGALLE

HOY
One of the most restful places to stay in town, it's focused on yoga and natural materials. €€

Le Pigalle
There's a retro-vintage vibe here, punctuated with record players, urban photography and squishy leather sofas. €€

Hotel Ballu
An intimate hotel with sleek rooms, a leafy outdoor courtyard and a little pool in the basement. €€

Once you've had a glimpse of the 1 **Moulin Rouge**, turn into the tangle of streets known as SoPi (South Pigalle), as the area became known in its latest heyday, pre-COVID-19. Walk along bd Rochechouart and make a stop at the 2 **Phono Museum**, with its collection of more than 100 fully working phonographs and thousands of records, which hint at the smattering of modern musical-instrument shops in the area. Walk to the south end of the 3 **square d'Anvers Jean-Claude Carrière** for an incredible view of the Sacré-Cœur towering above the city. Head southwards and stop at 9 rue de Douai, which was 4 **Henri de Toulouse-Lautrec's last abode**, before going to beautiful 5 **Buvette Paris** for a drink and nibbles. Continue to

6 **Hôtel Amour**, where you'll be lured by its hot-pink neon; the service and food are very average, but it draws creative types from major film stars to artists, giving the place an insider vibe. Then head to the atmospheric artist-atelier museum 7 **Musée Gustave Moreau**. Stroll the streets lined with restaurants and bars to 8 **St-Georges** area and to the 9 **Musée de la Vie Romantique**, with its bucolic setting. Then head a couple of minutes west to rue Ballu and the 10 **Villa Ballu**, where impressionist painter Edgar Degas is said to have lived, among other spots in Pigalle. Across the road, make sure you drop in at the intimate 11 **Hotel Le Ballu** and its tucked-away courtyard.

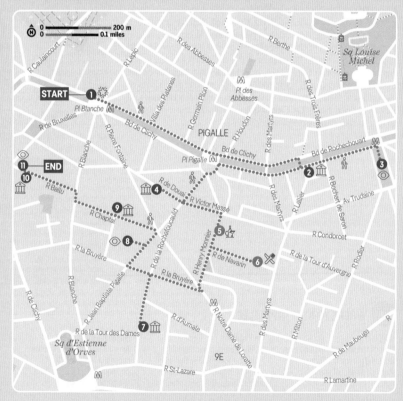

Le Louxor

The Beating Heart of Multiethnic Paris MAP P118

An Egyptian Cinema, a Hindu Festival...

Paris isn't all gilded bridges and grand buildings. It's also a patchwork of cultures from France's old colonies and beyond. East of Pigalle are the neighbourhoods of Barbès, sandwiched between Château Rouge and Gare du Nord (the Eurostar terminal) and La Chapelle. Usually heaving with people selling black-market cigarettes and other wares, the area is often cast aside due to its frenetic atmosphere. Look beyond the bustle though and dive into the area. Visit the art deco cinema **Le Louxor**, with its impressive neo-Egyptian façade, built in 1921. It also has a small rooftop bar. Along bd Rochechouart you'll also find **FGO Barbara**, a venue promoting French rap music that features a huge painting of a warrior by Franco-Congolese artist Kouka.

Close to La Chapelle metro station you'll find the impressive, all-wooden **Théâtre des Bouffes du Nord**, which hosts prominent plays. Beyond here is Little India, crammed with eating spots south of bd de la Chapelle around rue Cail. The area comes alive for Ganesh Chaturthi every September with a colourful procession. The area is also a hotbed for music events at places such as the **Olympic Café** and exceptional

WHERE TO EAT IN THE AREA

Saravana Bhavan
A big canteen packed with locals from the Hindu community who come for South Indian vegetarian specials like dosas and *idlis*.

Café des Deux Gares
Across the road from the hotel in the same group; excellent updated French fare is served in a laid-back atmosphere.

Pointe du Groin
A relaxed wine bar (little sister of Chez Casimir next door), offering hot and cold bites from rillettes to *accras*, with tables outside.

Terminus Nord
An age-old brasserie with Art Deco undertones that serves upscale French staples like *sole meunière*.

Lomi
A craft-coffee roasters and cafe institution, it could be credited with being the 'OG' before the wave took over the city.

WHERE TO STAY IN NORTHERN PARIS

Hôtel Bienvenue
A small, comfortable retro hotel with bold colours and a pretty courtyard restaurant. €€

Hôtel Providence
A cosy spot with a restaurant, terrace and homely rooms kitted out in flower-print velvet wallpaper. €€

Hôtel Grand Amour
Hôtel Amour's trendy little sister, with arty rooms, a fun atmosphere and a restaurant featuring small plates. €€

CANAL ST-MARTIN & AROUND

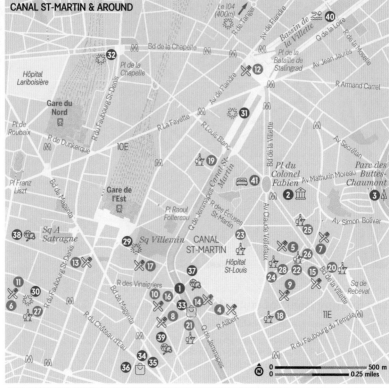

SIGHTS
1 Canal St-Martin
2 Communist Party Headquarters
3 Parc des Buttes-Chaumont

SPORTS & ACTIVITIES
37 Énergie Détente
38 Maison Alaena
39 Montgolfière Club
40 Paris Plages

SLEEPING
41 Generator Hostel

EATING
4 Ake
5 Au P'tit Curieux
6 Bonhomie
7 Candide
8 Debongout
9 Dixième Degré
10 Early June
11 Jah Jah
12 La Rotonde
13 L'Avant-Poste
14 Le Comptoir Général
15 Le Galopin
16 Le Verre Volé
17 Les Enfants Perdus

DRINKING & NIGHTLIFE
18 Abricot
19 Bizz'Art
20 Café Chérie
21 Chez Prune
22 La Cave à Michel
23 La Fontaine
24 La Palicave
25 Le Canon d'Achille
26 Le Renard
27 Le Syndicat
28 L'Iconique

ENTERTAINMENT
29 Café A
30 New Morning
31 Point Éphémère
32 Théâtre des Bouffes du Nord

SHOPPING
33 Artazart
34 Jamini
35 La Trésorerie
36 Thanx God I'm a V.I.P.

independent concert venue **Le 360 Paris Music Factory** in Château Rouge, which puts on gigs by artists from all over the world. Pick up some wax-style apparel at **Maison Château Rouge**, where the clothing is an ode to African cultures, and discover other colourful gems at local stores in the area. End at the **Brasserie de la Goutte d'Or** to taste some of its locally brewed beer.

The North's Final Frontier   MAP P130

Eating in the 9th Arrondissement

Cadet, Poissonnière and Chateau d'Eau are where the north filters out into the grand boulevards and eastern side of the city. Starting west, at the Notre-Dame de Lorette end, you'll find the casual **Lolo Cave à Manger**, serving up creative small plates to the owner's hand-picked tunes. Don't miss the upmarket **Caillebotte**, for its fresh seasonal cuisine. Taste French *haute cuisine* and natural wines at **La Condesa**, eat at ramen bar **Abri Soba**, one of the best in town, or try trendy Chinese dim-sum bar **Bleu Bao** (of the Bao family group), if you want to switch it up a bit from French food. Moving towards Gare de l'Est, **Jah Jah** and its laid-back vibe and vegan soul food make for a good pit stop, as does local-produce-focused **L'Avant-Poste** (little sister of Les Résistants on the Canal St-Martin). **Richer** and **Bonhomie** are fail-safe options for creative French cuisine.

In between eating your way across the area, stop for drinks in the courtyard of **Café A**, a part-converted chapel, or **Le Syndicat**. Hit the pause button and book a massage at the Biarritz-based skincare brand's **Maison Alaena**, hidden inside an office block with jaw-dropping views of Paris. See what's on at the **Folies Bergère**, a historical art deco theatre known in its heyday for cabaret, or check out the concert venue **New Morning**, with its fine line-up of live music by artists from all over the globe. You're also around the corner from the **World of Banksy**, a small immersive museum showcasing 70 of the famous artist's works.

Canal Cool in St-Martin   MAP P130

An Arty Pocket with Great Eats

The St-Martin Canal runs between Bastille in the south and Jaurès in the north and La Villette beyond. It's a favourite area with locals because its cluster of street-art-covered thoroughfares are packed with creative boutiques, trendy bars and restaurants. Make sure you leave time to browse the beautiful Indian homeware at **Jamini**, the carefully curated

WHERE TO EAT IN CANAL ST-MARTIN

Ake
An upscale, creative and contemporary experience of small plates.

Early June
Revolving chefs' residency with great wines.

Les Résistants
A must for its focus on farm-to-fork values and independent farmers and producers.

Hôtel du Nord
Refined classics, served in the location of a former hotel that's one of the area's oldest buildings (and from the eponymous 1930s film).

Les Enfants Perdus
Fantastic home-style French food offered in bistro surroundings.

Miznon
Easy and flavourful bites of grilled cauliflower and chicken.

 WHERE TO STAY IN THE CANAL ST-MARTIN AREA

Generator Hostel
Great-value, trendy individual or dorm rooms, plus a rooftop bar. €

Le Citizen
Right on the canal, with a relaxed atmosphere and simple but cosy rooms . €€

La Planque
A fun hotel with stylish rooms, located on a pretty little square on the canal's east bank. €€

THE LOWDOWN ON THE BOUILLONS OF PARIS

Originally restaurants for the working class, bouillons are wildly popular for their comforting classics and unbeatable prices.

Bouillon Chartier
Step back to 1896 at this art nouveau landmark with a lively atmosphere.

Bouillon Julien
An ornate art nouveau setting with a mint-green palette serving great *steak-frites*.

Bouillon Pigalle
A newer bouillon with a buzzy atmosphere. Visit outside of mealtimes to avoid queuing.

Petit Bouillon Pharamond
With original 1832 interiors, a laid-back atmosphere and food that probably tops that of the other bouillons.

Bouillon Chartier Montparnasse
Spectacular surroundings of brass railings and back-lit flower-painted ceilings accompany your dinner here.

PETR KOVALENKOV/SHUTTERSTOCK ©

Bouillon Chartier

homeware at **La Trésorerie**, vintage finds at **Debongout** and the treasures at thrift store **Thanx God I'm a V.I.P.**, where you might be able to dig out a Dior sports jacket or designer dress at a bargain price. If you're here to work and you want to work out, then the glass-roof **Montgolfière Club**, inside an old hot-air-balloon workshop, should be your go-to. For a different kind of relaxation, book a good-value massage at eastside **Energie Détente**. Pop into bookshop Artazart to leaf through the fantastic children's books and design magazines from all over the globe.

On warm evenings, sit by the canal with a beer or a glass of rosé like most of the locals, before going to see a live band at laid-back **Bizz'Art** further along the canal. Other bars to check out include **Le Comptoir Général**, with its fantastic curiosity-cabinet-meets-*Alice in Wonderland* interiors. Wine lovers will want to book a table at **Le Verre Volé**, one of the first wine bars to promote natural wines before they became mainstream. Alternatively, **Chez Prune** is a cafe that's always been popular for its simple salads and cheese and ham boards with wine. **Abricot**, on the east bank of the canal, is a successful newcomer to the scene due to its fun cocktails.

The Foodie & Historical Gems of Colonel Fabien
MAP P130

Communist Party and Hip-Hop Stronghold

Flanking the neighbourhoods of Canal St-Martin and Belleville, Colonel Fabien stems from the main square by the metro station and is named after a militant communist. In

WHERE TO STAY AROUND GARE DU NORD

25hours
Across from Gare du Nord, this colourful and comfortable hotel is a handy base. €

Hotel des Deux Gares
Part of the local Touriste group, this Luke Edward Hall-designed abode is quirky and fun. €€

Okko Hotels
Paris Gare de l'Est
This clean and functional pied-à-terre with clean lines is a good all-rounder. €

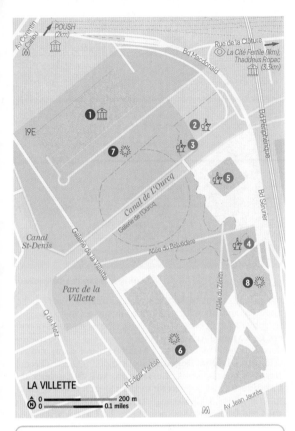

POUSH
(2km)

Av Corentin
Cariou

Rue de la Clôture
La Cité Fertile (1km);
Thaddeus Ropac
(3.3km)

Bd Macdonald

19E

**BEST INDY SPOTS
FOR PARTYING
ALL NIGHT LONG**

Kilomètre 25
An open-air house and
techno club under a
flyover, with events
held into the early
hours.

Glazart
Hosts club and DJ
nights of various
genres, from techno
and electro to rap and
metal. It has a beach
in summer.

La Station
An outdoor music
venue on the site
of an abandoned
coal factory that's a
platform for emerging
artists.

Le Gore
A basement
club under the
atmospheric La Gare
jazz club, located
inside a former train
station on a disused
railway.

Canal
St-Denis

Canal de L'Ourcq
Galerie de l'Ourcq

Galerie de la Villette

Allée du Belvédère

Bd Sérurier

Bd Périphérique

Allée du Zénith

Parc de la
Villette

Q de Metz

R Edgar Varèse

LA VILLETTE

0   200 m
0   0.1 miles

Av Jean Jaurès

THE GUIDE

MONTMARTRE & NORTHERN PARIS   PARIS

SIGHTS
1 Cité des Sciences
et de l'Industrie

**DRINKING
& NIGHTLIFE**
2 Cabaret Sauvage
3 La Péniche Cinéma
4 Le Trabendo
5 Le Zénith

ENTERTAINMENT
6 Grande Halle de
la Villette
7 La Géode
8 Philharmonie
de Paris

fact, the large rectangular building fronted by a dark glass
wave, designed by star architect Oscar Niemeyer, is the **Communist Party headquarters**. The interior feels like being
inside a giant space station, with its impressive curved main
hall. The building opens its doors to visitors on the Journées
du Patrimoine (Heritage Days) every September. The rest of
the area, lined up along bd de la Villette, might not look like

 WHERE TO EAT AND DRINK AROUND LA VILLETTE

Le Pavillon des Canaux
This relaxed cafe and bar,
close to the water, is modelled
to look like the inside of a
house. €€

**Paname Brewery Company
(PBC)**
A summer go-to for craft beer
that's brewed onsite, with a
deck overhanging the water. €€

Les Bancs Publics
A casual bistro with tables
and chairs set up on the canal
banks in warmer months. €

GRANGE AUX BELLES: THE BIRTHPLACE OF PARIS' HIP-HOP

In the early 1980s artists congregated at the Grange aux Belles club, off square du Colonel Fabien, for Sunday afternoon parties with DJ Chabin that mixed reggae, jazz-rock, zouk, funk and hip-hop. Music and graffiti came together here with breakdancing, and artists from Afrika Bambaataa to NTM passed through. The creative energy of the early days was documented by photographer, TV presenter and journalist Sophie Bramly, who recently published *Yo!*, a fanzine that includes some of her best photography from that time. The venue has long since closed but the memories are still very much alive.

KIEVVICTOR/SHUTTERSTOCK ©

Park near square des Batignolles

much at first, but tucked in its back streets are arty, bohemian restaurants with well-priced menus as well as bars to try for a different type of local Paris vibe. Some spots of note are **Le Canon d'Achille**, a natural-wine bar that offers produce-led small plates with a Mediterranean slant, and the colourful **Dixième Degrè**, an institution that serves French classics. Chicer spots like **Le Galopin**, **Au P'tit Curieux** and **Candide** are also popular for modern French food. For atmospheric drinks, walk to the place Ste-Marthe, a quiet square with laid-back bars, and nearby, try **La Cave à Michel** for the wines and **Le Renard**, a fun, casual bar with floor seating. Also around here are **L'Iconique**, **Café Chéri** and **La Palicave**. For rooftop musings, head to the **Generator Hostel**, across the square from the metro station. Take rue de la Grange aux Belles, the birthplace of hip-hop in Paris, to the Canal St-Martin area and you'll stumble upon the cafe **La Fontaine**, wildly popular for its coffee and simple French staples in an attractive bistro setting.

 ## THREE OF TODAY'S FRENCH RAP ARTISTS

Jul
Born and bred in Marseille, he's France's most prolific and biggest-selling artist.

Doria
Loved for her fast-paced, upbeat gangsta-style rap, she's one of the more established women artists on the scene.

Ninho
Rapping since he was 12, Ninho has a sound infused by Congolese music.

Along the Water from Jaurès to La Villette

MAP P130, P135

Canalside Culture and Clubbing

This last pocket of Paris before you officially reach the suburbs on the other side of the ring road (the *Périphérique*) is an eldorado for music fans and night owls. Packed with clubs, arty hubs and concert venues, there's something for everyone here. Starting on the canal between Stalingrad and Jaurès, **La Rotonde**, inside a circular 1700s building, is always heaving with people, as is **Point Ephémère** (or FMR), an alternative music and arts spot. Walk along the canal towards Riquet, where you'll find **Le 104**, a hybrid venue and arts incubator, with exhibitions and a restaurant, that's also a meeting place for local teens to come and practise their dance acts.

An expanse of greenery marks out Parc de la Villette, the location of the **Cité des Sciences et de l'Industrie**, which has some of the city's best immersive exhibits for kids. Also here is the 3D cinema **La Géode**, constructed as a monumental silver ball whose mirror surface reflects the sky. Some of the city's best clubs are nearby, such as **Le Zénith**, **Le Trabendo** and **Cabaret Sauvage**. Docked here is **La Péniche Cinéma**, a barge with a club on board. Also check out the **Grande Halle de la Villette**, a former meat market now hosting concerts and events. The must-see Philharmonie de Paris, a silvery, angular structure from architect Jean Nouvel, hosts a range of exhibitions and events, including classical and contemporary music concerts in its impressive main hall. Leave time to walk along the canal banks and stop at its many cafes, bars and restaurants, or have a snooze on a deck chair in summer, when the area is transformed into the 'urban beaches' of the **Paris Plages**.

Family-Friendly Batignolles & Les Epinettes

MAP P118

Restaurants and Parks for All

Northwest of Montmartre are a clutch of residential neighbourhoods to explore. One of the last areas to join the city of Paris, Batignolles still has a village atmosphere despite its rising popularity. Scattered with workshops and independent shops, since the arrival of French high-street stores it's become a more polished place. Streets fan out from place du Dr Félix Lobligeois, which has a church and a pretty garden in square des Batignolles. The area is a relaxed neighbourhood built around a covered market, good for families and

GETTING ON THE INSIDE TRACK

We've peppered our coverage with the best places to go, but find your own as well by staying behind when the sunlight filters out of the sky and the streets empty of visitors. Follow the sound of French, which once again becomes the dominant language, acting as a yellow-brick road to local bars and restaurants. While it's worth climbing to the basilica to see it up close and take in the rooftop views, explore the smaller streets that wrap around the village's hillsides too.

 WHERE TO EAT AND DRINK AROUND LA VILLETTE

Le Pavillon des Canaux
This relaxed cafe and bar, close to the water, is modelled to look like the inside of a house. €€

Paname Brewery Company (PBC)
A summer go-to for craft beer that's brewed onsite, with a deck overhanging the water. €€

Les Bancs Publics
A casual bistro with tables and chairs set up on the canal banks in warmer months. €

LEFT: POUSH ©. RIGHT: STANISLAVSKYI/SHUTTERSTOCK ©

WHY I LOVE NORTHERN PARIS

Rooksana Hossenally, writer

I've lived in the north of Paris for more than 10 years and have seen its many small neighbourhoods become exciting pockets of the city with their own distinctive identities. Before, visitors would zoom through up to Montmartre to see Sacré-Cœur, but thanks to a creative generation of young entrepreneurs reshaping northern Paris, areas like Pigalle, Barbès, Château Rouge and La Villette have become destinations in their own right. Ultimately, though, as well as exploring its architectural gems and blockbuster museums, Paris is about taking time to stroll its streets, and settling in at a cafe to watch life unfold, feeling the pulse of each neighbourhood, as you tuck into *steak-frites* or enjoy a coffee or glass of wine.

POUSH

shopping without the crowds. Further north, in Les Epinettes, an area of independent businesses with a community spirit, get a craft beer at hole-in-the-wall bar **Octopussy** or a coffee at **Pimpim**, or eat at **Chez Lucette**, where owner Rose, who's been here for decades, cooks everything herself out the back. Work off lunch with a walk through the whimsical passage **Cité des Fleurs**, where the magnificent houses were once the homes of the likes of actress Catherine Deneuve and painter Simon Hantaï. Explore a little further and head to **Le Hasard Ludique**, a bar and restaurant inside an abandoned train station where concerts are held every night.

There are some culinary gems in Batignolles to try, including Réunionese chef Kelly Rangama's Michelin-starred **Le Faham**, or **Gare au Gorille**, for contemporary French cuisine. **L'Envie du Jour** is also popular, for its traditional French food with a twist. Head towards busy place de Clichy and to street-art-adorned rue Biot, where you'll find more places to eat, plus the theatre **L'Européen**, which often puts on standup shows. Close by, push the door to the recently refurbished **Hôtel Eldorado** and take a seat at the chic restaurant in a leafy courtyard.

 ## THREE DON'T-MISS ANNUAL EVENTS IN NORTHERN PARIS

La Fête des Vendanges
For five days in October locals celebrate Montmartre's grape harvest with parties and a parade.

Paris Plages
From July to September, hit the urban beaches along the Seine or La Villette's canals.

Banlieue Bleues
Explore Pantin through its jazz scene from March to April, when top artists perform at various venues.

The 'Grand Paris' Expansion

Markets and an Art Incubator

Paris is expanding beyond the confines of the ring road, through an extension of its metro lines, which has accelerated due to the Olympic Games in 2024. 'Grand Paris' includes areas of the 93 department, which has suffered a bad rap due to reports of gangs and ghettos, like St-Ouen, St-Denis, Aubervilliers and Pantin, originally small industrial towns on the tram line. Young Parisian families wanting more space for their money have flocked to these areas, driving up prices and bringing trendy restaurants, bars and boutiques.

The star attraction remains the **Basilique de St-Denis**. Dating to the 1100s, it is France's largest royal necropolis (42 kings and 32 queens are buried here). The tombs in the crypt, adorned with lifelike gisants (recumbent figures) carved from death masks, are Europe's largest collection of funerary art and the main reason to make the trip out here.

The other high point is the **Marché aux Puces de St-Ouen**, open on weekends. Actually a labyrinth of 11 markets, it's a treasure trove for antiques and vintage finds. Several small bars within the market make great pit stops, while newer venues such the **Mob Hotel** offer good-value rooms. Arts and culture institution **Mains d'Oeuvres** is seeing a second lease of life, with a fresh program of events for the whole family.

In Aubervilliers, check out events at **POUSH**, the city's biggest contemporary art incubator, located inside a repurposed factory. Also in the area you'll find **La Station**, a platform for emerging musical artists.

While quieter, Pantin has also seen a revival around its canal, starting with an offshoot of prestigious gallery **Thaddeus Ropac**, along with iconic French fashion brand Hermès transferring its ateliers to the area. Subsequently, cultural hub **La Cité Fertile** opened its doors here too.

Marché aux Puces
de St-Ouen (p126)

EXPLORING NORTHERN PARIS ON A CANAL CRUISE

As well as a cruise along the River Seine, it's also possible to explore northern Paris on a canal cruise. Make a booking to explore the Canal St-Martin and Parc de la Villette and watch the locals sitting canalside enjoying drinks, and pass through swing bridges and banks covered in street art. Several companies offer cruises, such as **Canauxrama** in Jaurès, **Paris Canal Croisières** from Porte de Pantin, and **Marin d'Eau Douce**, from whom you can hire a self-drive boat with a group of people and putter along the Canal de l'Ourcq, bookended by Jaurès and La Villette.

WHERE TO EAT IN PANTIN AND ST-OUEN

Les Pantins
A relaxed restaurant serving modern French food rustled up with well-sourced produce and great natural wines. €€

Le Coq d'Or
Close to the St-Ouen flea market, with delicious couscous served by a friendly bunch. €

Bonne Aventure
Fresh French fare with a light Mediterranean touch that's perfect for summer; close to the flea market. €€

Le Marais

HISTORY, BEAUTY SHOPPING AND CREATIVITY

Le Marais is steeped in history, with an atmosphere that feels both timeless and cosmopolitan through its variety of architectural styles.

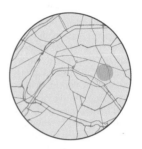

MAZIARZ/SHUTTERSTOCK ©

It's the only district in Paris that has preserved its narrow streets and occasionally crooked buildings from the pre-Revolutionary era, escaping Baron Haussmann's great transformations in 1853.

Le Marais holds many secrets about Paris' past. Prior to its transformation into a playground for the French aristocracy in the 17th and 18th centuries, it had played a significant role as a Jewish district since the Middle Ages. Although it's less prevalent today, traces of Jewish cultural heritage still remain. The opulent *hôtels particuliers* (private mansions) stand as elegant reminders of the area's period as the residence of French nobility, adding layer after layer of history.

However, Le Marais has undergone a transformation over the years, becoming synonymous with trendy boutiques, designer stores and art galleries. While retaining its historical charm, it is seen now as a fashion-forward haven, attracting the style-conscious and discerning shoppers alike. From renowned fashion houses to independent designers, Le Marais offers a unique and diverse shopping experience. Its northern part, Le Haut Marais (around Arts et Métiers), presents a more laid-back side, with a chill vibe, cosy cafes and restaurants.

The district is also renowned for its inclusivity and acceptance tradition. Its visible LGBTIQ+friendly policy has made it a safe place for the community, fostering an atmosphere of warmth, diversity and celebration. Its wealth of bars, clubs and establishments cater to all orientations, and in its lively streets it feels like everyone can truly be themselves and be at home.

All in all, Le Marais invites exploration of its winding lanes and never fails to surprise, whether you're looking for a historical discovery, an expansive museum, a fashion experience or a sense of belonging.

DON'T MISS

PLACE DES VOSGES
Discover this historic royal square's stunning architecture and serene gardens. p141

RUE DES ROSIERS
Explore Le Marais' Jewish heritage while soaking in this historic street's lively ambience. p141

HÔTEL DE VILLE
Marvel at the lively square and intricate façade of this historic neoclassical building. p142

TOP TIP

Don't underestimate the time and walking needed to fully appreciate Le Marais. It may not cover much ground in Paris, but this district is particularly dense, with its narrow, winding streets, and it isn't well connected by the metro. Note that the area can be particularly busy on weekends.

Left: Jewish quarter (p141); Above: Place des Vosges (p141)

RUE DES ARCHIVES
Stroll along this bustling street, where diverse architectural styles showcase various historical layers. **p143**

MUSÉE CARNAVALET
Visit the Museum of Paris, where rich exhibits chronicle the city's history through art and artefacts. **p143**

MUSÉE DES ARTS ET MÉTIERS
Examiner past and present inventions, delving into centuries of human ingenuity. **p145**

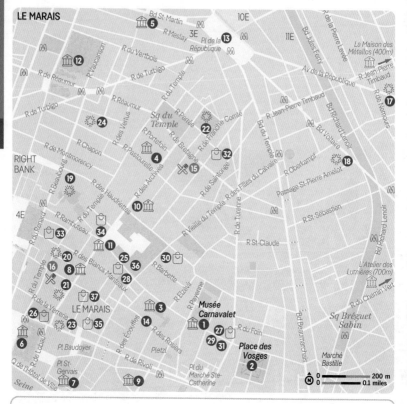

TOP SIGHTS
1. Musée Carnavalet
2. Place des Vosges

SIGHTS
3. 3537
4. Fondation Henri Cartier-Bresson
5. Galerie Sakura
6. Hôtel de Ville
7. La Galerie Rouge
8. Lafayette Anticipations
9. Maison Européenne de la Photographie
10. Musée de la Chasse et de la Nature
11. Musée des Archives Nationales
12. Musée des Arts et Métiers
13. Place de la République
14. Rue des Rosiers

EATING
15. Le Marché des Enfants Rouges
16. Tata Burger

ENTERTAINMENT
17. BAM Karaoke
18. Bataclan
19. Duplex Bar
20. Elles Bar
21. freedj
22. Le Carreau du Temple
23. Les Souffleurs
24. Tango

SHOPPING
25. Bâton Rouge
26. BHV
27. Diptyque
28. Fragonard
29. Frederic Malle
30. Korres
31. Le Studio des Parfums
32. Liquides Bar à Parfums
33. Little Biceps
34. Nicolaï
35. Officine Universelle Buly
36. Oh My Cream!
37. Trudon

LEMBI/SHUTTERSTOCK ©

Place des Vosges

An Enduring Royal Square

Place des Vosges has truly stood the test of time. The vision of King Henry IV, who wanted a grand square in Paris, this iconic landmark was constructed in 1605 and has remained a social hub throughout the centuries. During its early years as place Royale, it served as a gathering place for the aristocracy, a centre of both elegance and intrigue, as immortalised in Corneille's eponymous play.

Today, while the aristocratic ambience has disappeared, the essence of social connection persists, as visitors and locals alike converge upon the spacious lawns, refreshed by beautiful fountains, and beneath the shade of trees. It's an ideal place for picnicking and taking leisure strolls to admire the *hôtels particuliers* and art galleries, or for dining at one of the traditional French restaurants nestled under the arcades. This emblematic square captivates with its impeccable symmetry and is renowned for hosting illustrious inhabitants, notably the esteemed French writer Victor Hugo, whose former residence at number 6 has been transformed into a museum.

Rue des Rosiers

Rue des Rosiers

Explore the Centre of Jewish Heritage

Once a major street for the Jewish community, rue des Rosiers now continues to pay homage to Jewish culture. Since the street is particularly known for its culinary heritage, make sure to stop by Sacha Finkelsztajn's little yellow bakery, where his children continue to bring this heritage to life. Indulge in mouth-watering apple strudels, Polish cheesecakes and braided bagels! If you're looking for a savoury option, head to one of the tempting felafel shops that are plentiful on this historical street. As you explore, you'll also notice more discreet traces of Jewish heritage: commemorative plaques and the still-persisting Café des Psaumes.

Musée des Archives Nationales

Musée des Archives Nationales

Guardian of the Republic

Most locals frequently appreciate the **Musée des Archives Nationales** for its gardens, which can be visited free of charge, hidden behind the walls of the Hôtel de Soubise. However, it is also the custodian of precious documents forming the foundation of the French republic. The mission of the National Archives is to preserve and safeguard not only legislative acts but also significant objects that represent the establishment of the republic, such as seals and the Constitutional Act. The museum showcases its collections through temporary exhibitions.

Place de la République

Where History and Politics Intersect

Dominated by a statue of Marianne, the embodiment of the French republic, place de la République has become one of Paris' most renowned squares, largely due to the years of unrest that have marked recent decades in France. Symbolising democracy and the spirit of the people, the square serves as a gathering point for demonstrations, alongside place de la Bastille and place de la Nation. Situated at the intersection of vibrant districts, it offers an open space frequented by skateboarders, street performers and locals.

ARCHIVED TREASURES OF ALL SORTS

The Musée des Archives Nationales safeguards primarily legal documents, while the **Bibliothèque Nationale de France** (p257) has been entrusted with preserving manuscripts related to arts and sciences. Temporary exhibitions are also held at the **Richelieu Site** (p105).

Hôtel de Ville

Explore the Old Institutional Heart

The intricate neoclassical façade of Paris' town hall can evoke a sense of awe. The Hôtel de Ville features numerous statues representing notable figures from Paris' history, including politicians, scientists, artists and industry pioneers, as well as allegories of the arts.

The façade is often illuminated or displays symbolic messages through adornments.

The esplanade, now known as place de la Libération, was called place de Grève until President Charles de Gaulle delivered his 'liberation of Paris' speech at the Hôtel de Ville in

1944. It now regularly welcomes cultural events and street performers, creating an inviting and convivial atmosphere. These kinds of shows replaced another – for five centuries it had been the site where criminals were executed.

LOTSOSTOCK/SHUTTERSTOCK ©

Musée Carnavalet

Musée Carnavalet

Journey Back Through Paris' History

At the Musée Carnavalet, you're first welcomed by a grand hall adorned with old shop signs, reminders of Paris' vibrant commercial life throughout the centuries. As you wander through the museum's spacious rooms, you'll encounter artworks, artefacts and historical finds that recount the layered history of Paris. The city is showcased in all its forms and across all eras through numerous scale models, paintings, architectural remnants and modern masterpieces.

The exhibits provide a tangible glimpse into Parisian life over time. Murals, entire shops and even a hotel ballroom were all moved to the Hôtel Carnavalet to testify to their enduring magnificence. All this offers insights into the hands and spirits that shaped the city. Particularly captivating is the floor dedicated to the French Revolution. Spend half a day at Carnavalet and you will emerge knowing Paris inside and out.

After this journey through time, take a break in the impressive gardens, which hosts an outdoor restaurant in summer. Since admission to the museum is free, except for temporary exhibitions, arriving early is a good idea.

Musée Carnavalet

Rue des Archives

Stroll a Historical Street

From the Carreau du Temple, where the Templars established the first district by draining the marshes in the 12th century, to the magnificent *hôtels particuliers*, rue des Archives encapsulates the entire architectural history of Le Marais. While many mansions remain hidden behind closed gates, a few have been transformed into museums, such as the Hôtels de Guénégaud and de Montgelas (now the fabulous Musée de la Chasse et de la Nature), or the Hôtel de Soubise (now the Musée des Archives Nationales). Conclude your walk at the expansive **BHV** (Bazar de l'Hôtel de Ville), one of the first Parisian *grands magasins* (department stores) still operating today.

Le Marais has been home to Jewish communities since the Middle Ages. This walking tour guides you through significant sites where their heritage in Le Marais is still visible, as well as places of Holocaust remembrance, inseparable from the area's history.

Begin your journey on the cobblestone street of **1 rue des Rosiers**, renowned for its culinary delights and cultural importance. Take a moment to visit **2 Librairie du Temple**, a bookshop dedicated to Jewish books and culture. The most curious will take a peek at **3 Joseph Migneret Garden**. Named after a professor who played a vital role in rescuing Jewish children during WWII, this hidden garden now offers a peaceful sanctuary. Continue to rue Pavée, where you'll find a striking **4 synagogue** designed by Hector Guimard, famous for his art nouveau metro station entrances. Guimard created this synagogue as

a tribute to his Jewish wife. You're now at the former location of the Pletzel ('small square' in Yiddish). After experiencing the intersection of art and faith, proceed to the **5 Musée d'Art et d'Histoire du Judaïsme**, housed in the historic Hôtel de St-Aignan, one of the most impressive *hôtels particuliers* in Le Marais. Established in 1948 by Holocaust survivors, this institution showcases a diverse collection of artworks depicting Jewish history and culture, encompassing European and Maghreb communities. Conclude your tour at the **6 Mémorial de la Shoah**, accessible via the Allée des Justes de France. This narrow street often hosts open-air exhibitions that shed light on different aspects of Jewish history. The memorial itself comprises a museum and document centre dedicated to the Shoah, providing a solemn and contemplative setting, including the Tomb of the Unknown Jewish Martyr in the crypt.

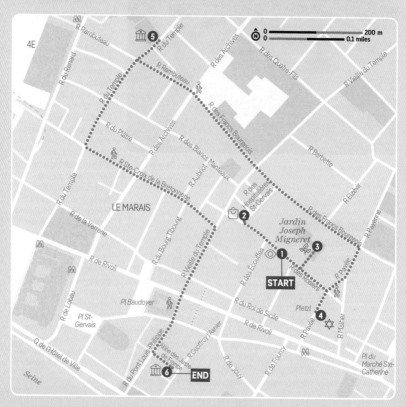

Musée des Arts et Métiers

Be Inspired by Human Ingenuity

Your journey begins at the Arts et Métiers metro station, where you are greeted by a steampunk ambience created by copper plaques that cover the entire station in celebration of the conservatory's bicentenary. Step out of this underground machine and enter the remarkable Musée des Arts et Métiers, located on the edge of Le Marais, in a former royal priory. It is a unique place where the past and future converge through countless displays of inventions, serving as a testimony to the human pursuit of knowledge and progress. From ancient scientific instruments to groundbreaking technological advancements, the museum explores the profound impact of science and technology on society.

The immersive collection includes scientific instruments, mechanical devices, vehicles, communication equipment and much more. It features iconic inventions such as Blaise Pascal's Pascaline, an early mechanical calculator, the original model of the *Statue of Liberty* designed by Bartholdi, Ader's plane number 3 (one of the earliest studies of military aviation), and even a reconstruction of the laboratory of chemist Antoine Lavoisier. Additionally, it offers educational opportunities for children through regular workshops that familiarise them with the spirit of invention and pioneering innovation.

This vertiginous exploration of past inventions and the history of transport, photography, energy and textiles provides visitors with a glimpse into how our human minds design and invent objects, while also prompting contemplation about the future of innovation. Let yourself be inspired and gain insight into contemporary technological advancements.

FOUCAULT'S PENDULUM

French physicist Léon Foucault invited scientists to see the Earth rotate when he built his first pendulum in 1851. While exploring the Musée des Arts et Métiers, one of the most awe-inspiring exhibits you'll see is Foucault's Pendulum. Located within the Church of St-Martin des Champs, this iconic invention visually demonstrated the rotation of the Earth at a time when it had not yet been scientifically proven. Its installation beneath the nave adds grandeur to this impressive perpetually moving experiment.

ELLA HANOCH/SHUTTERSTOCK ©

ETERNAL PENDULUM

You can also witness Foucault's spectacular invention at the **Panthéon** (p207). Attached to a 67m-long cable, the ball (weighing nearly 30kg) perpetually oscillates, following the Earth's rotation, under the magnificent dome that houses illustrious figures of the French nation.

Foucault's Pendulum

Le Marais' Secret Passages & Untold Stories

Take a tour back to the pre–French Revolution period and unravel the area's historical layers. As you navigate through bustling narrow streets, immerse yourself in the vibrant energy of the present, while discovering the tranquillity of 17th–century-mansions and hidden courtyards. Everywhere you turn in Le Marais, history lurks in its corners. This walking tour only scratches the surface of the district's untold stories.

1 Hôtel de Sens

Begin your journey at this remarkable medieval mansion dating to the 15th century, once a residence for Sens' archbishops. History remembers the execution of one of Queen Margot's suitors, which she supposedly witnessed from a window of the mansion.

The Walk: Take rue de l'Ave Maria and reach the entrance to Village St-Paul's courtyards.

2 Village St-Paul

Stroll this picturesque neighbourhood that preserves an old Parisian atmosphere. Initially known for its concentration of antique shops, it has now transformed into a network of charming courtyards with craft shops and hidden restaurants.

The Walk: Exit through rue des Jardins St-Paul.

3 Philippe Auguste's Wall

You'll find yourself across from the remnants of King Philippe Auguste's wall, a defensive fortification built at the end of the 12th century to protect Paris from potential attacks from the northwest. It was constructed before the king embarked on the Third Crusade.

The Walk: Turn right onto rue Charlemagne and then left onto rue St-Paul. Keep an eye out for the easily missed passage St-Paul and head left.

4 St-Paul St-Louis Church

Enter through the lateral door if the passage is open. This church showcases an impressive Gothic structure combined with Italian architectural elements of its time. As you

PACK-SHOT/SHUTTERSTOCK ©

Hôtel de Sens

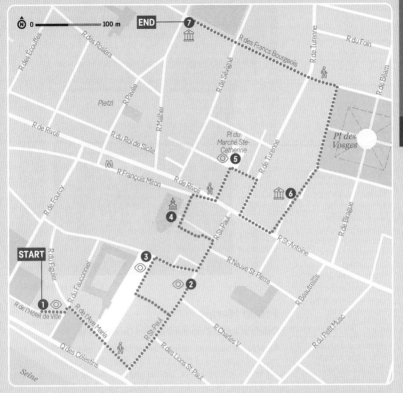

leave through the main door, note the holy-water stoups donated by Victor Hugo for his daughter Léopoldine's wedding.
The Walk: Turn right onto rue St-Antoine, and then immediately left onto rue Caron.

5 Place du Marché Ste-Catherine

Pause at this charming square surrounded by lively restaurants and bars. This tranquil place exudes an atmosphere reminiscent of the south of France, and it contrasts with the grandeur of nearby place des Vosges.
The Walk: Return to rue St-Antoine and enter the courtyard of Hôtel de Sully.

6 Hôtel de Sully

Built in 1624, this magnificent *hôtel particulier* represents the characteristic mansions of Le Marais during its fashionable era. Its façade is adorned with golden ornaments,

which you can admire from the gardens. The Sully family resided in this mansion until the 18th century. An interesting detail is that the estate features a secret passage leading to place des Vosges, providing a convenient shortcut.
The Walk: If you haven't discovered the secret passage, continue on rue de Turenne, then turn left onto rue des Francs-Bourgeois, one of the busiest shopping streets in the area.

7 Hôtel de Lamoignon

In 1759 the last resident of this mansion bequeathed 14,000 books to the city of Paris upon his death. Four years later, this *hôtel particulier* became the first public library in Paris, open to all. Today it houses the Historical Library of Paris (open from Tuesday to Saturday).

Passage Molière

PASSAGE MOLIÈRE

On the outskirts of Le Marais, under the shade of the Centre Pompidou, lies passage Molière, a haven of poetry and culture. This historic *passage* has been revitalised by local shopkeepers, dedicating it to literature and all things related to reading and writing. Find a spot at Café de la Poésie, with a book from ECX bookshop in hand: immerse yourself in a world of words or even jot down a few verses of your own. Poetry enthusiasts will be delighted by the program offered at the Maison de la Poésie, a venue dedicated to the art of poetry. While you're here, browse L'Ecritoire for unique cards and discover Japanese stationery at Misaki Iinuma's.

Proud Marais

Celebrating All Communities and Orientations

Le Marais has maintained its reputation as an inclusive area and a stronghold of the LGBTIQ+ community, welcoming people of all orientations. Unfortunately, rising property prices in the past decade have led to the displacement or closure of many emblematic establishments. Nonetheless, the inclusive identity of the area remains, and it continues to be a traditional district that celebrates Pride in summer as much as it does all year long. LGBTIQ+ establishments are often marked by rainbow flags, indicating their connection to the community and their friendly nature. Rainbow street art can be found throughout the neighbourhood, adding to the welcoming atmosphere.

While seamlessly blending into the fashionable ambience of Le Marais, the gay-friendly vibe is concentrated mainly around rue Ste-Croix de la Bretonnerie, the southern part of rue du Temple, and hidden place des Émeutes de Stonewall, tucked away behind the impressive BHV Marais Men's section.

Day or night, everyone is welcome at the surrounding restaurants, with **Tata Burger** being number one for a suggestive burger. But the real excitement begins when night falls, at the

WHERE TO HAVE A DRINK IN LE MARAIS

Piment Café
A small bar across from St-Paul's church, with a good vibe and affordable beer.

Le Chéper
Hidden on a former bank's top floor; an elegant venue for enjoying cocktails under a dome.

Sherry Butt
A quaint cocktail bar with excellent mixologists, ideal for intimate evenings in a dimmed atmosphere.

vibrant bars attracting a diverse crowd, such as **freedj**, **Duplex Bar** and **Les Souffleurs**. Just around the corner, **Elles Bar** provides a discreet venue for lesbians. And don't forget the recently reopened **Tango**, an iconic nightclub.

Learn About Animals in the City
A Museum about Hunting and Nature

The **Musée de la Chasse et de la Nature** is a surprising place to stumble upon in the heart of Le Marais. It is housed in one of the most beautifully restored private mansions in the area, which adds to the sense of wonder conveyed by this unexpected, almost uncanny place.

Exploring the historical, cultural and artistic aspects of hunting, as well as the relationship between humans and the natural world, the museum has an impressive collection of animal specimens. They are displayed in thought-provoking arrangements, aiming to evoke a sense of wonder and reflection about the relationship between humans and animals.

In a seemingly paradoxical approach, a wide range of exhibits also showcase various aspects of hunting, including firearms, taxidermy displays of animals, hunting equipment and art pieces related to hunting and nature. Sensitive hearts might think twice before visiting those rooms. Yet, the prompted contemplation upon our impact on nature is compelling.

Occasionally, visitors may encounter the melodies of hunting horn musicians rehearsing or performing concerts. This transports you to another realm, offering a unique opportunity to discover an activity far removed from Le Marais' narrow city streets.

Photographic Paris
Explore Contemporary Photography

Is there a city more photogenic than Paris, with its layers of architecture and hidden historical corners? Photo enthusiasts in search of the answer will find an abundance of resources on the art of photography in Le Marais.

Beyond Robert Doisneau's famous *The Kiss by the Hôtel de Ville* captured in front of Paris' town hall, it's worth noting that the Musée Carnavalet boasts many photographs showing the evolution of the city and the daily lives of its inhabitants over the years.

The **Maison Européenne de la Photographie** (MEP) is dedicated to contemporary photography and through temporary exhibitions features works by photographers from around the world. In a different vein, the

SOME PARTICULAR LE MARAIS MUSEUMS

Visiting the area's museums offers a double advantage, to learn about the exhibited topics while also exploring the magnificent *hôtels particuliers* that were built between the 16th and 18th centuries.

Musée Cognacq-Jay
Housed in the Hôtel Donon, the collections of Ernest Cognacq and Marie-Louise Jay, founders of La Samaritaine, include paintings and furniture characteristic of the 18th century.

Musée Picasso
Dating back to the 17th century, the Hôtel Salé's architecture contrasts with the unconventional works of Picasso; 5000 artworks are displayed in the grand building.

Maison de Victor Hugo
Located on place des Vosges, the residence (from 1832 to 1848) of this icon of French literature showcases his personal belongings, manuscripts and memorabilia.

WHERE TO EAT IN LE MARAIS

Benedict
Specialising in eggs Benedict, this is a perfect brunch place to pair egg toasts with cocktails. €€

Le Reflet
A convivial French *bistronomy* restaurant that employs people living with Down syndrome. €€

Le Colimaçon
A *bistronomy* restaurant serving traditional French recipes, often with an elegant and creative twist. €€

BEST CONCEPT STORES IN LE MARAIS

Empreintes Paris
The only concept store dedicated to French craftwork, showcasing ceramics, leather goods, jewellery, stationery and beauty products.

Fleux
Several shops on rue des Francs-Bourgeois, with a range of decoration and fashion objects.

L'Eclaireur Sévigné
A discreet but spacious store with contemporary, high-tech-inspired decor, where renowned *haute couture* houses present their creations.

BHV
A Le Marais institution, which remains faithful to its heritage as a Parisian *grand magasin*, offering a comprehensive range of products from fashion to DIY tools.

ERICBERY/SHUTTERSTOCK ©

Fleux

Fondation Henri Cartier-Bresson preserves and promotes the work of the renowned French photographer, considered a pioneer of modern photojournalism. The foundation exhibits Cartier-Bresson's iconic photographs as well as those of others who have significantly contributed to the field of photography.

Finally, **La Galerie Rouge** exhibits and sells fine art photography, both by established contemporary artists and emerging photographers.

Avant-Garde Galleries
A Hybrid Hub for Modern Design

The artistic exploration of Le Marais would not be complete without its numerous art galleries and alternative venues, which playfully contrast with the historical heritage of the buildings. The area actively supports experimental art practices, with venues like **3537** utilising the space of the ancient Hôtel de Coulanges to create a shared space of offices, concept stores and exhibition halls. **Lafayette Anticipations** offers a hybrid experience, with cultural events, temporary exhibitions of contemporary designers, a trendy bookshop and a cafe. For modern-design enthusiasts, is a cutting-edge pop-up store that showcases innovative brands and creators mainly focused on fashion, with a new exhibition each week. Addi-

WHERE TO EAT IN LE MARAIS

GrandCoeur
An elegant Mediterranean restaurant tucked away in a historical cobblestoned courtyard. €€€

Kitchen
A cosy and convivial vegetarian restaurant offering breakfast and lunch options, including healthy bowls and toasts. €€

Kaali Temple
An Indian street-food counter specialising in delicious takeaways, with both meat and vegetarian options available. €

tionally, numerous galleries in the area actively play with the boundaries of traditional art forms, such as **Galerie Sakura**, which is dedicated to pop culture and allows art lovers to discover emerging artists and designers.

From Fashion to Beauty

A Rendezvous with Yourself

Le Marais has long been known as a fashion shopping destination, but has also evolved into a hub for niche perfumery, natural beauty and luxury skincare brands in recent years. This shift has brought about a more personalised experience for beauty enthusiasts looking for a moment to themselves. If you're seeking a skincare boutique, head to **Oh My Cream!** or **Korres**, specialising in clean, natural or vegan products. Makeup aficionados should not miss **Bâton Rouge**, a French brand that creates tailored lipsticks, from colour to scent. For a holistic pampering session, make an appointment with Emmanuelle at **Little Biceps**. Her team of beauty experts will warmly welcome you into their serene salon, hidden in the heart of Le Marais, where they offer rejuvenating face massages and lymphatic draining sessions. From cosmetics to a full beauty session, who can resist a moment of self-care in one of Paris' most exclusive and exquisite neighbourhoods?

In Search of the Best Scent

Find Your Perfect Perfume

Did you know that Jean-Baptiste Grenouille, the infamous character from the novel *Perfume,* yet the greatest nose in literature, resided on the outskirts of Le Marais? In the real world, this neighbourhood also celebrates the art of perfumery. Perfume lovers will find a world of fragrances that perfectly align with their tastes and personality. Alongside renowned brands like **Fragonard** and **Nicolaï**, you'll also find niche and independent houses such as **Frederic Malle**, **Officine Universelle Buly** and perfume concept store **Liquides Bar à Parfums**. Each perfume shops unveils its own scents and aesthetics. If you're looking to bring home a fragrant memory, scented candles are popular at **Trudon** and **Diptyque**. Finally, for an immersive and personalised experience, join a workshop at **Le Studio des Parfums**. Here, you can learn about the art of perfumery and create your perfect scent under the guidance of experts in their fragrance laboratory, nestled in a medieval basement in Le Marais.

FOOD & BEAUTY TIPS

Emmanuelle Rodeghiero, founder of Little Biceps beauty salon in Le Marais.

Start with breakfast from SAIN bakery. For shopping, check out Open Dressing. Enjoy lunch at Oken or Le Bistrot de l'Alouette or if you're in a hurry, try Pulpa. Don't miss the chocolate cake at Kitchen! Treat yourself at Golden Nails. Rejuvenate with yoga and barre classes at Poses. Quench your thirst with a juice from Mandarine or end your day with a ginger margarita at La Perla and a pasta dinner at Assaggio Bistro.

A FOCUS ON LENS-BASED ARTS

With its commitment to exploring the artistic, cultural and social significance of photography, the **Jeu de Paume gallery** (p104) in the Jardin des Tuileries is a must-visit if you want to dig more into both contemporary photography and other visual media.

WHERE TO HAVE SWEET TREATS IN LE MARAIS

La Glacerie	Yann Couvreur	Pastelli Mary Gelateria
Upscale ice creams with bold flavours crafted by David Wesmaël, 'France's Best Craftsman'. €	The renowned French pastry chef's store, featuring his best creations, such as vanilla millfeuilles. €	Tiny shop with select quality flavours, offering an authentic Italian gelato experience. €

Brunch from the Stalls

The Oldest Parisian Covered Market

Le Marché des Enfants Rouges, dating back to the 17th century, still exudes plenty of charm after undergoing renovations in the 1990s. It has become a soulful gathering place for both locals and visitors. The market is home to a diverse array of food stalls and small eateries. Whether you're passing by or looking to sit down, take a moment to immerse yourself in the lively atmosphere and explore the generous, typically French market stalls offering fresh food, fruit, flowers, cheese and charcuterie products. Since the market is open on Sundays as well, one of the best experiences is to indulge in brunch at one of the numerous local or international food stalls surrounding the market. You can enjoy vegetarian delights at Au Coin Bio, order a Japanese bento at Chez Taeko or savour Italian antipasti at Mangiamo-Italiano. You can do a culinary world tour!

In the Footsteps of the Templars

Le Carreau du Temple Events

Street names like rue du Temple, rue Vieille-du-Temple and rue du Trésor in Le Marais hint at the Templars' presence here. While the treasure remains a mystery, the Templars' historical influence is undeniable. In the 12th century they were granted lands by the king, transforming the marshy area into what it is today. The Templar enclosure and dungeon are long gone, leaving only a blue trace on the ground near the town hall of the 3rd *arrondissement*. **Le Carreau du Temple**, once a market for various household and fashion goods, now hosts a range of cultural and sporting events, including the Food Temple Culinary Festival, the much-appreciated Paris Café Festival and Salon du Vintage.

A VISIONARY CULTURAL HUB

Cultural centre **La Gaîté Lyrique** exemplifies the successful transformation of historical establishments into hybrid spaces driven by a progressive cultural vision. A 17th-century former theatre, it has been reimagined as a multidisciplinary venue. From 2023 to 2028, the centre's programming aims to foster collective initiatives with an entrepreneurial spirit, providing a nurturing environment where ideas can flourish rather than succumbing to the anxieties of fast-paced and uncontrollable current events. Embracing this bold challenge, it organises family workshops and collaborative events, presents multifaceted exhibitions and promotes the dynamic use of its space. Visit their website to check the agenda and book your slot for some creativity.

WHERE TO HAVE A DRINK IN HAUT MARAIS

Maison Proust
Hotel bar with elegant library decor and plush armchairs, ideal for a late-night cocktail.

Little Red Door
Speakeasy with talented mixologists, accessible through a small, discreet entrance. Expect queues.

Candelaria
Hidden cocktail bar behind a taco restaurant, one of Paris' original speakeasies and still highly regarded.

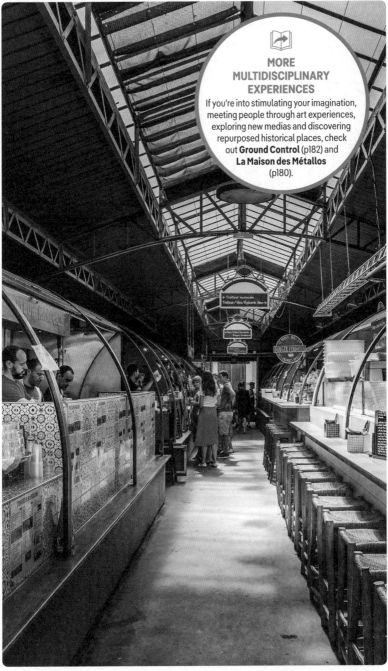

MORE MULTIDISCIPLINARY EXPERIENCES

If you're into stimulating your imagination, meeting people through art experiences, exploring new medias and discovering repurposed historical places, check out **Ground Control** (p182) and **La Maison des Métallos** (p180).

Le Marché des Enfants Rouges

TOP TIP

Wear comfortable shoes to navigate Belleville's hilly streets and occasionally steep areas – some parts can be quite a hike. Take your time to be pleasantly surprised by this lesser-known area, and don't hesitate to engage with its inhabitants for the opportunity to better understand the spirit of these neighbourhoods.

Above: Parc des Buttes-Chaumont (p157); Right: Cimetière du Père Lachaise (p158)

DON'T MISS

PARC DES BUTTES-CHAUMONT
Picnic on this park's grassy slopes, admiring the romantic hill in the middle of its central lake. p157

PARC DE BELLEVILLE
Don't miss the panoramic view from the Belvédère, one of the highest hills in Paris. p157

CIMETIÈRE DU PÈRE LACHAISE
Visit the famous resting place for iconic figures such as Oscar Wilde, Jim Morrison and Édith Piaf. p158

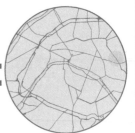

Ménilmontant & Belleville

ARTS, VIEWS AND MULTICULTURAL WALKS

The northeastern neighbourhoods of Belleville and Ménilmontant have a distinct character.

Originally separate villages outside Paris, they were incorporated into the city in 1860. But they have maintained a strong identity, with their vibrant artistic spirit, multicultural quarters and, to some extent, rebellious nature, inherited from the historical popular movements born on their streets.

Today, the Chinese side of Belleville is one of the most prominent, but with a rich history of immigration, the area has always embraced diversity in its narrow, hilly streets. Settled just beyond the famous Père Lachaise cemetery, these neighbourhoods still exude a village-like vibe and the legacy of working people. In Belleville, locals, while being from diverse communities, tend to feel a closer connection to one another. This cultural melting pot allows visitors to embark on a global journey without leaving Paris. Many locals proudly claim that Belleville is not Paris, it is Belleville!

As you wander through the narrow streets, you will sense the lively pulse where traditions and youth converge. From the breathtaking views atop Parc de Belleville or Parc des Buttes-Chaumont, two iconic landmarks of the area providing a refreshing escape from central Paris' busy boulevards, your journey will lead you through streets adorned with murals and urban art. These streets serve as canvases for creative expressions unlike anywhere else in Paris.

Day or night, Belleville and Ménilmontant offer a dynamic nightlife scene. Immerse yourself in live music performances in intimate venues and follow in the footsteps of Édith Piaf and other artists who have found inspiration in those city hills. Whether you seek cultural diversity, colourful street art, stunning views or an immersive nightlife experience, venture into the hidden corners of Belleville and Ménilmontant and let their rebellious spirit guide your adventure.

AUX FOLIES	RUE DÉNOYEZ	CHINESE BELLEVILLE
Grab a drink at this legendary Belleville bar, where Édith Piaf is said to have performed. **p162**	Stroll this ever-changing street, a sanctuary for street art in the heart of Belleville. **p162**	Dine in one of the many Chinese restaurants that are the soul of this new Chinatown. **p163**

MÉNILMONTANT & BELLEVILLE

20E

TOP SIGHTS	EATING	DRINKING	ENTERTAINMENT
1 Cimetière du Père Lachaise	**5** Best Tofu	**& NIGHTLIFE**	**12** La Maison des Métallos
2 Rue Dénoyez	**6** Chez Alex	**10** Aux Folies	**13** L'Atelier des Lumières
SIGHTS	**7** Pavillon aux Pivoines	**11** Belvédère de Belleville	**14** Les Plateaux Sauvages
3 Musée Édith Piaf	**8** Raviolis Nord-Est		
4 Parc de Belleville	**9** You Wei		

DELPIXEL/SHUTTERSTOCK ©

Parc de Belleville

Panoramic Paris

Starting at the foot of Parc de Belleville, you'll encounter a long mural depicting scenes from the historic Paris Commune, a pivotal moment in the city's history that unfolded on the streets of Belleville. The mural is a symbol of the neighbourhood's revolutionary spirit and the ongoing struggles for social change that remain relevant today. As you wander along the park's terraced slopes towards the summit, you'll cross the central waterfall that trickles between the meandering trails. The vines planted on some garden terraces serve as a reminder of Belleville's history as a winemaking village since the Middle Ages.

Upon reaching the **Belvédère** at the top of the hill, you'll be rewarded with a breathtaking vantage point. Welcome to the second-highest summit in Paris! This elevated platform not only offers panoramic views of Paris, stretching from Montparnasse to the Eiffel Tower, but is also a meeting point for street artists. Take a moment to admire the multitude of murals, which create a colourful frame for your panoramic view.

Parc de Belleville

Parc des Buttes-Chaumont

Picnic over the Hills

Discovering Parc des Buttes-Chaumont is a small adventure. With its undulating terrain, it requires a bit of stamina to fully explore and appreciate its beauty. However, the park's steep slopes offer excellent picnic areas that are highly appreciated by locals, especially during the summer. At the heart of the garden you'll discover an impressive artificial hill with characteristic elements of English gardens, including bridges, grottoes and Sybille's Temple, a reconstituted Greek ruin. When you need a break, have a drink at Le Pavillon Puebla or Rosa Bonheur, two cafes located within the park.

LEFT: PASCALE GUERET/SHUTTERSTOCK ©, RIGHT: LILA LOUISA/SHUTTERSTOCK ©

Scan this QR code to check the cemetery's opening hours.

TOP SIGHT

Monumental Garden of Eternity

The prestigious Cimetière du Père Lachaise serves as Paris' necropolis, aligned with the Panthéon, where figures who shaped the French nation are honoured. However, this cemetery is not only a resting place for the renowned. Today it stands as an otherworldly space where extraordinary funerary monuments coexist with the graves of both famous and lesser-known individuals, each still cherished by someone.

DON'T MISS

The Monument to the Dead

Lovers Héloïse and Abélard

Irish writer Oscar Wilde

Rock star Jim Morrison

French singer Édith Piaf

French writer Marcel Proust

The Columbarium

An Eternal English Garden

When commissioned to design the new Parisian cemetery in the early 19th century, architect Alexandre-Théodore Brongniart envisioned a space that embodied nobility without grandiosity, simplicity without neglect, and invoked religious sentiments without fear. He aimed to create a place of peaceful remembrance, with a melancholic charm based on a combination of nature and monuments. Inspired by English gardens, the cemetery was meticulously planned, with winding paths and a significant portion dedicated to nature. Today, as you enter, the cacophony of the city fades away and the graves seamlessly blend into the undulating landscape, creating a feeling of beautiful strangeness, as if you're suspended between two worlds.

The Construction of a Legendary Place

Overlooked at the time of its inauguration, the cemetery faced challenges in gaining popularity due to its location far from the city. However, efforts were made to enhance its appeal:

the relocation of famous figures like Molière and La Fontaine, as well as the creation of the impressive sepulchre for the mythical medieval lovers Héloïse and Abélard. Over time, politicians, scientists, artists and writers followed suit, solidifying Père Lachaise's reputation as the eternal resting place of the renowned.

Funerary Art for Posterity

The entire site of Père Lachaise is recognised for its historical heritage, with all funerary steles dating to before 1900 listed as Historical Monuments. Additionally, 14 monuments are classified. The classification is reserved for works that hold public interest from a historical or an artistic perspective. Works that are listed may not immediately qualify as Historical Monuments but present sufficient historical or artistic interest for preservation. Among the classified monuments are the Wall of the Federates; Godde's chapel on the former Jesuit house site; bd Ménilmontant's monumental gate; the Monument to the Dead and 10 sepulchres. These sepulchres include Héloïse and Abélard (Division 7), Molière and La Fontaine (Division 25), Oscar Wilde (Division 89), Frédéric Chopin (Division 11), Antoine de Guillaume-Lagrange (Division 29), Montanier-Delille (Division 11), Cartellier-Heim (Division 53), Georges Guët (Division 19) and Yakovleff (Division 82).

Rituals & Superstitions of Père Lachaise

Like all cemeteries, where the boundaries between worlds blur, Père Lachaise has its own superstitions and esoteric rituals associated with its iconic sepulchres. Couples renew their vows in front of Héloïse and Abélard's tomb, seeking eternal love. Oscar Wilde's tomb has long been the object of passionate kisses believed to bring luck in love. Victor Noir's effigy (Division 92) is central to erotic morbid fertility rituals. Laying hands at the dolmen of medium Allan Kardec (Division 44) is believed to grant wishes. Lastly, the ritual offerings left on Jim Morrison's grave (Division 6) perpetuate a cult mainly based on alcohol.

Famous tomb of lovers Héloïse and Abélard

A RURAL GARDEN IN THE CITY

Below Père Lachaise, Pierre-Emmanuel's **Natural Garden** hosts native plant species from Parisian regions and offers a glimpse into Paris'. With minimal mowing to honour natural cycles, the meadows allow vegetation to thrive.

TOP TIPS

- Download a map: this will help you navigate the grounds and locate specific graves or landmarks.
- Choose the right entrance: Père Lachaise has five distinct entrances. Pick the closest one to the area you wish to visit.
- Wear comfortable shoes and bring water: the cemetery is large, with uneven terrain. Be prepared for walking and stay hydrated.
- Show respect: remember that this is a graveyard where people come to pay their respects to their loved ones. Don't climb on tombs and keep noise levels low.
- Plan ahead: if you have limited time or specific graves you want to visit, plan your itinerary in advance.

Cimetière du Père Lachaise

A Half-Day Tour

There is a certain romance to getting lost in this jungle of graves spun from centuries of tales. But to search for one grave amid the million in this 44-hectare land of the dead requires guidance.

Approaching the main entrance on bd de Ménilmontant, pay your respects at the **1 Monument aux Morts Parisiens de la Première Guerre Mondiale**. Inside the cemetery, head up av Principle and turn right onto av du Puits to grab a map at the **2 Bureaux de la Conservation**.

Backtrack along av du Puits, turn right onto av Latérale du Sud, scale the stairs and bear right along chemin Denon to New Realist artist **3 Arman**, film director **4 Claude Chabrol** and **5 Chopin**.

Follow chemin Méhul downhill, cross av Casimir Périer and bear right onto chemin Serré. Take the second left (chemin Lebrun – unsigned), head uphill and near the top leave the footpath to weave through graves on your right to rock star **6 Jim Morrison**. Back on chemin Lauriston, continue uphill to roundabout **7 Rond-Point Casimir Périer**.

Admire the funerary art of contemporary photographer **8 André Chabot**, av de la Chapelle. Continue uphill for energising city views from the **9 chapel steps**, then zigzag to **10 Molière & La Fontaine**, on chemin Molière.

Cut between graves onto av Tranversale No 1 – spot potatoes atop **11 Parmentier's** headstone. Continue straight onto av Greffülhe and left onto av Tranversale No 2 to rub **12 Monsieur Noir's** shiny crotch.

Navigation to **13 Édith Piaf** and the **14 Mur des Fédérés** is straightforward. End with angel-topped **15 Oscar Wilde** near the Porte Gambetta entrance.

TOP TIPS

- Père Lachaise is a photographer's paradise any time of the day or year, but best are sunny autumn mornings after the rain.
- Cemetery lovers will appreciate themed guided tours (two hours) led by entertaining cemetery historian Thierry Le Roi (www.necro-romantiques.com).

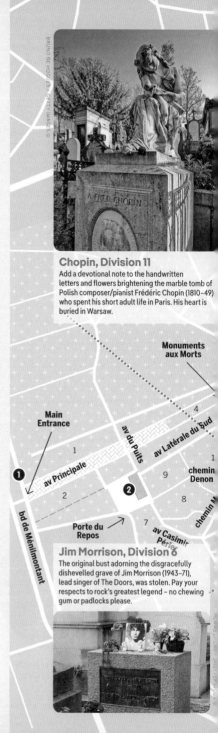

BRUNO DE HOGUES / GETTY IMAGES ©

Chopin, Division 11
Add a devotional note to the handwritten letters and flowers brightening the marble tomb of Polish composer/pianist Frédéric Chopin (1810–49) who spent his short adult life in Paris. His heart is buried in Warsaw.

Monuments aux Morts

Main Entrance

av du Puits

av Latérale du Sud

chemin Denon

chemin M

bd de Ménilmontant

av Principale

Porte du Repos

av Casimir Périer

Jim Morrison, Division 6
The original bust adorning the disgracefully dishevelled grave of Jim Morrison (1943–71), lead singer of The Doors, was stolen. Pay your respects to rock's greatest legend – no chewing gum or padlocks please.

André Chabot, Division 20

Contemporary photographer André Chabot (1941) shoots funerary art, hence the bijou 19th-century chapel he's equipped with monumental granite camera – and a QR code in preparation for the day he departs.

Molière & La Fontaine, Division 25

Parisians refused to leave their local quartier for Père Lachaise so in 1817 the authorities moved in popular playwright Molière (1622–73) and poet Jean de la Fontaine (1621–95). The marketing strategy worked.

Oscar Wilde, Division 89

Irish writer Oscar Wilde (1854–1900) was forever scandalous: check the enormous packet of the sphinx on his tomb, sculpted by British-American sculptor Jacob Epstein 11 years after Wilde died.

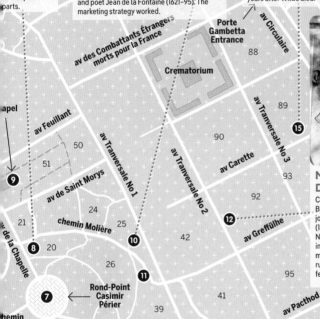

av des Combattants Étrangers morts pour la France

Porte Gambetta Entrance

Crematorium

88

av Circulaire

Chapel

av Feuillant

av Transversale No 1

av Transversale No 2

av Carette

av Greffülhe

av Transversale No 3

89 **15**

90

93

92 **12**

95

41

39

av Pacthod

Rond-Point Casimir Périer

chemin Lesseps

chemin Molière

av de Saint Morys

de la Chapelle

chemin Euriston

chemin Lebrun

chemin Serré

50

51

9

24

25 **10**

42

26 **11**

21

8 20

14

6

6

5

7

97

13 **14**

96

76

av Circulaire

35

Monsieur Noir, Division 92

Cemetery sex stud Mr Black, alias 21-year-old journalist Victor Noir (1848–70), was shot by Napoléon III's nephew in a botched duel. Urban myth means women rub his crotch to boost fertility.

Édith Piaf, Division 97

The archbishop of Paris might have refused Parisian diva Édith Piaf (1915–63) the Catholic rite of burial, but that didn't stop more than 100,000 mourners attending her interment at Père Lachaise.

Mur des Fédérés, Division 76

This plain brick wall was where 147 Communard insurgents were lined up and shot in 1871. Equally emotive is the sculpted walkway of commemorative war memorials surrounding the mass grave.

Porte de la Réunion

BRUNO DE HOGUES / GETTY IMAGES ©

BRUNO DE HOGUES / GETTY IMAGES ©

ALIZADA STUDIOS / SHUTTERSTOCK ©

IRINA KLYU CHNIKOVA / SHUTTERSTOCK ©

Aux Folies

Belleville's Iconic Bar

Who isn't familiar with this iconic establishment at the heart of Belleville? Aux Folies, a former cabaret turned cinema and now a beloved bar, has been open since 1872 and has always been a popular rendezvous place for entertainment. Adding a mythical aura, legend has it that Édith Piaf sang on stage here during her teenage years. With its large terrace opening onto the street-art haven of rue Dénoyez and the lively bd de Belleville, day or night, it maintains its affordability, diversity and welcoming atmosphere for all.

Aux Folies

La Bellevilloise

A Festive Cultural Celebration

Another iconic place in Belleville, with a focus on performing arts, dance and live music, is La Bellevilloise. This former cooperative hall, created by workers, has transformed into one of the favourite music and dancing venues for Parisians. Being the first-ever worker's cooperative in France, La Bellevilloise has always held the mission of promoting political education and culture for the wider community. Remaining faithful to its founding principles, the venue has evolved into a spacious and modern multidisciplinary stage, as well as a vibrant gathering place. Its weekend jazz brunch has gained particular popularity among visitors and locals alike.

Belleville

Rue Dénoyez

Street-Art Sanctuary

In no other neighbourhood in Paris will you find such a high concentration of street art as in Belleville and Ménilmontant. Graffiti and murals flourish, creating a visible dialogue among artists. While these artworks are constantly evolving, certain 'territories' have been established. Rue Dénoyez is a designated space where street artists can showcase their art. If you look at the walls closely, you'll notice layers of paintings on top of each other, leading some to nickname it 'the shrinking street'. You can visit one day and see a particular artwork, only to return the next and discover an entirely new mural.

Chinese Belleville

Flavours of China

Considered the newest Chinatown in Paris, Belleville has rich culinary offerings, which see locals flock here for the authentic Chinese cuisine. With a dynamic and close-knit community, mainly from the Wenzhou region of southeastern China, the neighbourhood boasts plenty of small businesses and restaurants, ranging from cosy family-owned establishments to larger dining venues. For an unusual experience, **Pavillon aux Pivoines** presents a setting with a reconstructed traditional living room and a calligraphy desk. As you enter the hall, you'll be greeted by a scale model of the Imperial City, crafted by the former chef himself. The restaurant is now run by his daughter. For those seeking a street-food experience, **Raviolis Nord-Est** and the bustling **Chez Alex** are among the local favourites. You can also indulge in pastries from **You Wei** pastry shop or join the queue at **Best Tofu**, where the staff predominantly speak Mandarin. Don't let the lines or language barrier discourage you though.

Belleville's Stories & Secrets

Explore with a Local Friend

Throughout the 20th century, waves of immigration brought diverse communities to Belleville: Armenians, Italians, Russian and Polish Jews in the 1920s; German Jews in the 1930s; Moroccan Jews in the 1960s; Africans, Chinese and people from the West Indies in the 1980s; and Yugoslavians and Pakistanis in the 1990s. They all coexist today, creating a unique atmosphere and a tapestry of languages. Exploring Belleville with an occasional 'translator' to unlock its nuances is a plus. Discover hidden treasures like a Mandarin-language Chinese pastry shop with delicious sesame biscuits or a Tunisian Jewish canteen where a rabbi imparts blessings every Sunday. Join expert guides **Donatien Schramm** (French only; book through exploreparis.com) or **Chloé Vasselin** (French or English; book via Instagram @bouiboui.leblog) to discover their beloved multicultural neighbourhood.

The Cradle of Street Art

Where Art Transforms the Public Space

Often associated with territorial boundaries, a competitive spirit or insider knowledge, street art has shaped the identity of Belleville and Ménilmontant. Don't miss the famous **Belvédère de Belleville** or Art Azoï's creations at

ART TO HEART

Belleville has always been a captivating neighbourhood to artists, effortlessly blending its industrial past with a picturesque landscape, capturing the essence of both a working-class town and a tranquil village. With a long tradition of welcoming writers, painters and film directors alike, it's no wonder the area continues to draw contemporary artists as well. In the heart of Belleville, the **Ateliers d'Artistes de Belleville** serves as a pulsating artistic hub, housing over 250 artists' studios. Throughout the year, the gallery showcases regular exhibitions, but the true highlight is the annual open-studio days (typically in June), when the entire neighbourhood comes alive with creative energy. Check their website for specific dates.

WHERE TO EAT IN BELLEVILLE

Paloma
A French lunchtime canteen offering a daily *menu* with a single option for starter, main course and dessert. €

Le Barbouquin
A cosy bookshop-cafe in street-art sanctuary rue Dénoyez that serves light food. €

Benoît Castel
A bakery-pastry shop known for its all-you-can-eat brunch, popular with locals. Online booking recommended. €€

With its rolling hills and winding streets, Belleville has a history as both a festive and idyllic area. Its slopes were covered in vineyards, and waterfalls ran down its hills. Notably, it provided water to Paris before the city's water tank was relocated to the south. Step back in time to discover Belleville's rustic legacy. Begin your tour in one of the most enchanting preserved neighbourhoods in Paris, reminiscent of a French countryside village with its colourful houses and gardens: **1 la Mouzaïa**. As there are just a few streets, you'll quickly leave this haven as you make your way towards the **2 Parc des Buttes-Chaumont**. Climb the artificial hill to Sybille's Temple within the park or proceed directly to metro Pyrénées, circling around it. Continue along rue Piat, leading you along the upper edge of Parc de Belleville, where you can admire the panoramic view over the city. Upon reaching the small cobblestoned square of **3 place Henri Krasucki**, take a break at one of the cafes or head to rue des Cascades. In this street, you'll encounter **4 Regard St-Martin**, a small surviving stone building that once served as a water-observation station, dating back to the time when Belleville was a water supplier. Just across from it, rue de Savies bears the name of the original farm that gave birth to the entire city of Belleville during the Middle Ages. Take the stairs to reach rue de l'Ermitage, running parallel to rue des Cascades, and continue to the narrow yet charming alleyway of **5 Villa de l'Ermitage**. Conclude your walking tour with a cultural pause at the **6 Pavillon Carré de Baudoin**. This 18th-century building, formerly a venue for parties, has been repurposed as a contemporary arts centre.

MÉNILMONTANT & BELLEVILLE PARIS

THE GUIDE

CATHERINE.LPROD/SHUTTERSTOCK ©

> **THE OTHER CHINATOWN**
> Parisians associate the 13th *arrondissement* with **Chinatown** (p252), although it is home to a diverse community of residents with Chinese, Vietnamese and Cambodian origins. It developed in the 1970s, and has since thrived into a centre of Southeast Asian culture.

Chinese New Year, Paris

Les Plateaux Sauvages cultural centre. As you wander around from place Henri Krasucki to rue des Couronnes, you'll encounter unmissable artworks by Nemo, known for his iconic black figure often chasing a red balloon – a nod to the film *Le Ballon Rouge* by French director Jacques Tati, which takes place in Ménilmontant. Also keep an eye out for Jérôme Mesnager's white figures representing the neighbourhood's people. Both are revered as the godfathers of French street art.

To delve deeper into this intriguing world that sometimes needs deciphering, seek the expertise of guides like Laurent from **Fresh Street Art Paris** (freshstreetartparis.fr). Their guided tours reveal the hidden layers and meanings behind what has become a true form of expression for the local community. With them, you'll not only gain insights into the soul and history of these historically rebellious neighbourhoods, but also get an opportunity to appreciate the transformative power of street art.

BEST MUSIC BARS & CONCERT HALLS AROUND BELLEVILLE

Le Zorba
A beloved bar that has become a Belleville institution. Renowned for its lively late-night parties.

Culture Rapide
This popular cabaret offers an eclectic program matching the diversity of its patrons, who gather for drinks on its open-air terrace.

Le Vieux Belleville
Known as the 'Singing Cafe', this French bistro embraces traditional French *musette* music with accordion melodies.

La Flèche d'Or
Occupying a former train station, this versatile perform-ing-arts venue offers a diverse program throughout the year.

WHERE TO DRINK IN BELLEVILLE

La Sardine
A bar with a charming terrace located on a square tucked away from the bustling avenues.

Floréal Belleville
A cafe with a bohemian vintage ambience, offering a complementary cultural space.

Le Perchoir Ménilmontant
One of the first rooftop bars in Paris, providing a perfect open-air setting to party.

Rediscover Édith Piaf
Follow La Môme's Voice

Walk in the footsteps of France's beloved national singer Édith Piaf. Born in Ménilmontant, she led a remarkably romantic, eventful and successful life, ultimately becoming an icon of early-20th-century French music. Parisians continue to pay tribute to her across the hills of Belleville, from the steps of 72 rue de Belleville to her grave in Cimetière du Père Lachaise. While legend suggests she was born on those steps, she actually entered the world a few blocks away at Tenon Hospital. At the nearby place Édith Piaf, her statue with arms raised towards the sky perfectly captures the essence of her songs of love and sorrow. In her former two-room apartment, now the **Musée Édith Piaf**, her life is told through carefully curated personal objects. Across these emblematic places, three music boxes playing her songs are hidden – see if you can uncover them.

Paris Village
A Patch of Countryside

Until 1860, the village of **Charonne** was nestled on the hills near Porte de Bagnolet. Though the village was incorporated into Paris' 20th *arrondissement*, there remain a few picturesque streets to be discovered, with cobblestone paths, townhouses and neatly lined gardens. Just before bd Périphérique, this preserved area is known as **La Campagne à Paris** (the Countryside in Paris). As you explore this tranquil enclave, soak in the charm of a bygone era – a time when the housing here was dedicated to working-class families, and was very affordable (it is obviously not the case today!).

 WHERE TO STAY NEAR BELLEVILLE

Babel Belleville	**The People–Paris Belleville**	**Mama Shelter Paris East**
Nestled in a serene street, this charming hotel offers a delightful brunch experience on weekends. €€	A youth hostel featuring a bar and local activities in tune with the neighbourhood's liveliness. €€	A contemporary hotel boasting comfortable rooms and a fantastic open-air rooftop bar and restaurant. €€€

La Campagne à Paris

Bastille & Eastern Paris

HISTORY, NIGHTLIFE AND INDUSTRIAL HERITAGE

Explore eastern Paris, extending from the historic place de la Bastille to the charming Bois de Vincennes along the Right Bank of the Seine.

Often overlooked by tourists, this area offers a captivating blend of history, nature and remnants of its industrial past.

While the place de la Bastille holds historic significance, it is the industrial heritage of the surrounding district, particularly the Faubourg St-Antoine and Popincourt districts, that have left the most visible mark today. Once a bustling centre of craftwork during the 19th and early 20th centuries, it was filled with workshops, mostly specialising in furniture making. As the industrial era has passed, the workshops have transformed into trendy cafes, small shops, vibrant concert venues and creative restaurants, infusing the area with a lively and contemporary ambience.

Going eastward, the landscape gradually transforms. The neighbourhood of Nation features broad residential avenues, while just beyond bd Périphérique, which marks the city limits, lies the tranquil town of Vincennes. One of its highlights is the expansive Bois de Vincennes, a forest serving as one of Paris' green lungs. The bois draws Parisians outside of the city, offering an easy opportunity to take a break from its frenzy.

Once connected by a now-vanished railway, these distinct areas have each evolved in their own unique way over the decades, but they retain their village-like charm, inherited from their history as *faubourgs* (small boroughs). It is this intimate atmosphere that often leads locals to say that Paris doesn't feel as vast as it may seem.

A journey around Bastille and towards the east of Paris offers the opportunity to discover lesser-known corners and facets of the city, , unveiling a different, more lived-in side of the capital, away from the most popular tourist spots.

JOAO PAULO V TINOCO/SHUTTERSTOCK ©

DON'T MISS

PLACE DE LA BASTILLE
Discover how the historic heart of the French Revolution has given way to a well-designed urban area. p172

COULÉE VERTE RENÉ-DUMONT
Stroll above the streets of Paris on this green pedestrian promenade along former train tracks. p171

MARCHÉ D'ALIGRE
Try typically French products at the indoor and outdoor venues of this vibrant, popular market. p173

TOP TIP

Utilise public transport effectively. While walking is a great way to explore the immediate surroundings, the distance between Bastille and Vincennes is significant. The transport system is quite efficient in the area so make extensive use of it to save time and energy.

PETR KOVALENKOV/SHUTTERSTOCK ©

Left: Coulée Verte René-Dumont (p171); Above: Bois de Vincennes (p183)

PALAIS DE LA PORTE DORÉE
Explore this art deco masterpiece housing the Musée de l'Histoire de l'Immigration and a tropical aquarium. p174

ARTISANS' COURTS
Wander the hidden alleys and courtyards that were home to skilled craftspeople for centuries. p176

BOIS DE VINCENNES
Rent a rowing boat for a romantic moment on Lac Daumesnil among its artificial isles. p183

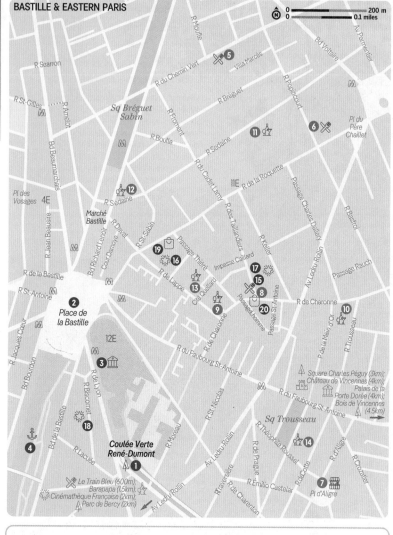

BASTILLE & EASTERN PARIS

TOP SIGHTS
1 Coulée Verte René-Dumont
2 Place de la Bastille

SIGHTS
3 Opéra Bastille
4 Port de l'Arsenal

EATING
5 Aujourd'hui Demain
6 Friendly Kitchen
7 Marché d'Aligre
8 Mori Café

DRINKING & NIGHTLIFE
9 L'Atelier Saisonnier
10 Les Cuves de Fauve
11 Les Mauvais Joueurs
12 Moonshiner
13 Street Art
14 Troll Café

ENTERTAINMENT
15 Badaboum
16 Café de La Danse
17 Les Disquaires
18 Supersonic

SHOPPING
19 Totale Eclipse
20 Verreglass

Coulée Verte René-Dumont

Walk the Green Line

One of Paris' most distinctive green pathways is the Coulée Verte René-Dumont (or 'Promenade Plantée'), which provides a surprisingly serene escape from the city streets. Stretching across 4.5km, it follows the former train tracks once linking Vincennes to a train station in Bastille – now the site of the opera house. Meticulously maintained flowerbeds and bushes pave the way, diligently tended to by three dedicated city gardeners.

From Bastille to Gare de Lyon, the pathway ascends above the city on a historic 19th-century viaduct. It's particularly popular in springtime when the roses are in bloom. Walking at the level of the surrounding red-brick buildings' windows, with vibrant flowers and lush trees in the foreground, is a unique experience.

Locals frequently gather at the Jardin de Reuilly for picnics, but you can venture even further east towards the Palais de la Porte Dorée. Along this stretch, you may encounter staircases that appear to lead nowhere. These purposefully designed structures offer observation points for spotting the small animals that reside among the bushes, although they can be scarce at peak hours.

Opéra Bastille

Opéra Bastille

A House to Democratise the Arts

With its striking glass and steel façade, the Opéra Bastille can be surprising at first glance. Inaugurated on 13 July 1989 to commemorate the bicentenary of the storming of the Bastille, it is part of a broader initiative to promote contemporary culture and contrast with its older counterpart, the Palais Garnier. The main stage for the Paris Opera and boasting Europe's largest performance stage, it hosts numerous ravishing music and dance performances, from contemporary to classical creations. Special viewings for young adults (up to 28 years old) continue democratising the arts. Check the website for enticing offers and discounts for a memorable experience.

LAYERS OF HISTORY

Nothing remains today of the ancient fortress, originally constructed in the 14th century. Only a small sign on a building near bd Henri IV indicates the boundaries of the former prison. Over the centuries, various urban designs were suggested for the place de la Bastille, including the peculiar concept of placing a monumental fountain in the shape of an elephant at its centre, though it was never realised. The square is now a spacious pedestrian area, dominated by the modern Opéra Bastille, symbolising the area's cultural revitalisation.

Place de la Bastille
Symbol of Liberty Throughout the Centuries

On 14 July 1789, the inhabitants of the Faubourg St-Antoine rose up to seize the Bastille prison, seeking additional weapons at a time of siege in Paris. But when the guards refused to surrender, the situation escalated rapidly. The people had been in rebellion against the authorities for several months due to prolonged periods of starvation and hardship, and this event is usually considered the first episode of the French Revolution.

The place de la Bastille not only stands as a powerful symbol of the events of 1789, but it also represents more broadly the freedom of the people. Its central column commemorates the Trois Glorieuses, the three-day July Revolution of 1830, crowned by the statue of the *Génie de la Liberté* (Genius of Liberty). Interestingly, the base of the column is composed of two funerary stones: one honouring the fallen during the 1830 revolution, with the remains of 500 individuals resting beneath the column, and the second commemorating the fighters who lost their lives in the 1848 revolution, which brought an end to the monarchy.

Today, the place de la Bastille shares a symbolic connection with its counterpart, the place de la République, and continues to be a site of frequent demonstrations and political events. Under the watchful gaze of the statue, the square remains a welcoming blend of tourists, artists, office workers, partygoers, waitstaff, teenagers and skaters, coming together day and night in a vibrant atmosphere.

WHAT HAPPENED DURING THE FRENCH REVOLUTION?
An extensive educational exhibition, featuring historical objects, is dedicated to the French Revolution at the **Conciergerie** (p189), notably the place of imprisonment for Queen Marie Antoinette.

Place de la Bastille

RCHAT/SHUTTERSTOCK ©

Fish for sale, Marché d'Aligre

Marché d'Aligre

The District's Living Soul

Locals and tourists alike adore the Marché d'Aligre for its extensive selection of produce, ranging from fresh fruits and vegetables to cheese, fish, meat, spices, sweets and prepared dishes. What sets the Aligre market apart and makes it one of the most comprehensive in Paris is its three distinct sections.

Halle Beauvau is a covered market housing permanent vendors where you can spend a morning indulging in cheese, wine, Italian olives, Malagasy specialities, or you can simply grab a speciality coffee before venturing to the open-air market for fresh produce.

The outdoor section is particularly popular for its affordable prices, attracting early-morning grocery shoppers seeking the freshest goods. Aligre has a tradition of catering to those with limited means. Closed only on Mondays, the market offers a perfect opportunity to experience the typical French way of purchasing fresh food.

The flea market section, located in the northern part of Aligre, is a true gem. It traces its roots back to a time when royal edicts allowed anyone to sell whatever they wanted on place d'Aligre. Antique enthusiasts, African mask collectors, book lovers and treasure hunters will find themselves falling in love with this area.

Beyond the market, Aligre forms a community, with many shop owners here established for decades, and the area seems to have managed to resist gentrification better than others. It even hosts its own independent radio station, Aligre FM, which has been broadcasting since 1981.

NOT-TO-BE-MISSED SHOPS OF ALIGRE

The shops surrounding the market contribute to its lively atmosphere and enhance the experience.

La Graineterie du Marché
This unique shop specialises in seeds and infusion leaves, and is possibly one of the few remaining stores of its kind in Paris.

Sweet Romance
Located inside Halle Beauvau, this pastry shop will tempt your taste buds with its cakes and tarts, perfectly paired with a coffee.

Aux Merveilleux de Fred
While Fred may be famous for his meringue pastries, don't miss out on his underrated yet delicious mellow brioche.

Palais de la Porte Dorée

Colonial Propaganda to Educational Institution

The 'Palais des Colonies' was originally built for the 1931 Colonial Exhibition. An art deco jewel boasting a grand design that leaves a lasting impression, in 2012 it was officially renamed Palais de la Porte Dorée after its golden gates.

Today, it houses a tropical aquarium and the **Musée de l'Histoire de l'Immigration**, highlighting the history of immigration and promoting cultural understanding. However, back in 1931, it showcased the history of the French Empire and the reciprocal contributions between the colonies and France. Inside, Ducos de la Haille's mural represents the contribution made by France to overseas territories. Although it is spectacular and holds historical value, it serves as a reminder of the building's initial propagandist nature.

Reopened in June 2023, the permanent collection sheds light on immigrants' experiences and contributions to French history, in an effort to provide insight into often controversial topics. The exhibition employs a pedagogical approach to engage younger visitors. For those interested in the architectural aspects of the building, guided tours are available (contact the Palais de la Porte Dorée directly).

A JOURNEY BACK TO THE MIDDLE AGES

Visitors with an interest in medieval lifestyle shouldn't miss the renovated **Cluny Museum** (p218), which showcases restored artefacts within a building that combines medieval vestiges with contemporary architecture, creating a harmonious blend of the old and the new.

TUPUNGATO/SHUTTERSTOCK ©

Château de Vincennes

Château de Vincennes

An Underrated Medieval Fortress

What began as a small hunting lodge has transformed over the centuries into a defensive fortress, a royal residence and prison. Located on the outskirts of Paris, Château de Vincennes attracts fewer visitors compared to more-central landmarks. Its massive dungeon, one of the tallest in Europe, is particularly remarkable amidst the fully urbanised town of Vincennes. Immerse yourself in the building's rich history, exploring the embattlements and ascending to the top of the tower for a panoramic view of the surroundings. Don't miss Sainte-Chapelle, a smaller version of its Parisian counterpart in the 1st arrondissement, and its delicate stained-glass windows.

A Drink at the Port
A Surprising City Harbour

It's so tranquil at the Bassin de l'Arsenal that you might question whether the boats docked here ever venture out onto the River Seine or beyond. The **Port de l'Arsenal** (built on the ancient ammunition store belonging to the Bastille fortress) is a small harbour tucked between two bustling avenues. It feels like a mini getaway from the city, where you can enjoy a refreshing drink at a bar with a terrace overlooking the harbour or in one of the small gardens. Despite occasional lively gatherings at night (perhaps a bit too lively for some), the space provides a calm setting for a stroll past the boats on sunny days. Photographers will appreciate the view of the Colonne de Juillet from the Bassin.

Pick Your Night Out
A Bar for Every Taste

Place de la Bastille and its surroundings come alive at night. Rue de Lappe holds a special place in the hearts of many Parisians who spent their younger years in the area. While the street has become less rough over time, it still maintains its emblematic status, with an abundance of bars and restaurants. The festive atmosphere extends to the surrounding streets. Beer enthusiasts will enjoy a pint or two at the **Troll Café** or **Les Cuves de Fauve**, a large brewpub concept also serving bistro food. Visit the bar **Street Art** for painted walls and an underground atmosphere. If you're more into wine, enjoy a glass or two, along with an apéritif at **L'Atelier Saisonnier**. Board-game enthusiasts can have a great time at **Les Mauvais Joueurs**. And if you're looking for a more discreet, yet original experience, don't miss the famous **Moonshiner** speakeasy...look for its hidden entrance.

Out All Night for Good Fun
Bastille Music Beats

How can you have a great night out without a vibrant live music scene? If you're looking for a good evening out, take your chance at **Les Disquaires**, a cafe concert venue with an eclectic program, where you can enjoy a drink and catch a live show. When it ends, DJs take over the dance floor, until 5am on weekends. Alternatively, you can check out the nearby **Badaboum** – renowned for its funk parties – or the club **Supersonic**. Another option is the

A VOYAGE THROUGH LIGHT & SOUND

Located within an underground section of Opéra Bastille known as the 'modular stage' (salle modulable), one of the opera house's most remarkable technical features, the **Grand Palais Immersif** presents two digital exhibitions per year. Curated by the renowned team of Grand Palais, famous for their monumental installations, these exhibitions aim to fully immerse visitors in a selected artist's work or a specific artistic theme, via wall projections, olfactory experiences, musical installations and interactive devices. Some projections are so realistic that the characters presented seem to come to life. This innovative museum transports visitors into a living universe of art. Note that the entrance is separate from the Opéra's.

 WHERE TO EAT NEAR ALIGRE

Mokonuts	Table	Privé de Dessert
Cosmopolitan cafe offering hearty breakfast and lunch, prepared with love. Reservations recommended. €€	A Michelin-starred gourmet restaurant from chef Bruno Verjus, who excels at creating sublime dishes. €€€	A creative trompe-l'oeil concept where starters resemble desserts (but taste like starters) and vice versa. €€

EXPLORE THE ARTISANS' COURTS

Since the 15th century there has been a tradition of artisanship among Faubourg St-Antoine's inhabitants. These include woodworkers, furniture makers, boilermakers and earthenware artisans, who honed their skills in narrow courtyards, which, on weekends, are now mostly hidden behind closed doors. While some workshops remain, they are gradually being taken over by modern businesses. Nonetheless, the picturesque *passages* on this walking tour will immerse you in the atmosphere of these occupations.

Start at **1 cour Damoye**, a site founded by an ironmonger, once home to ragpickers and scrap dealers. The contrast with today's charming townhouses in this cobblestoned *passage* is striking. Exit onto rue Daval and head towards rue de Lappe, renowned for its bars and nightlife. Continue to **2 passage Lhomme**, which retains a nostalgic atmo-

sphere. Don't miss the game shop's window. As you walk towards the end, you'll notice remnants of warehouses and old workshops mixed with newly established offices.

Go back on rue de Charonne and make you way along **3 passage Josset**, past Les Fleurs, a pretty jewellery and beauty store. Head back to rue du Faubourg St-Antoine and to **4 passage de La Main d'Or**. Look for the engravings and sculptures throughout the passage before turning into rue de la Main d'Or, having a coffee at Passager, or just continuing your tour past metro Ledru-Rollin. Take a final detour through **5 passage du Chantier**, where you'll find yourself among Bastille's legacy of furniture makers. The *passage* still has its old shop signs hanging overhead, adding to the charm. If it's open, take the chance to glance at **6 cour du Bel-Air**, almost entirely adorned with lush vines.

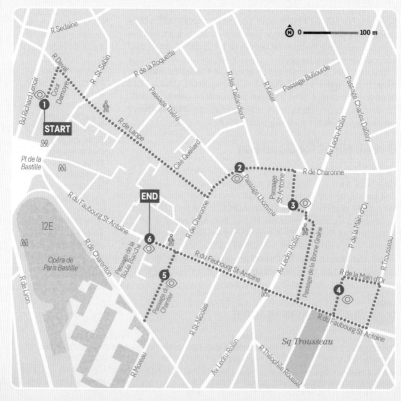

TOM PLEVNIK/SHUTTERSTOCK ©

CUIR AU CARRE

POLÈN

J4S

HEAVEN FOR COFFEE ENTHUSIASTS

Every year, the Paris Café Festival is held at the cultural space **Le Carreau du Temple** (p152) in Le Marais. The event attracts coffee roasters, makers and fans from around the globe.

Cour Damoye

BASTILLE & VOLTAIRE FOOD TIPS

Martin Herbelin, co-founder of food guide *Le Food Trip*, shares his personal recommendations. *@le_food_trip*

First, I must mention the family-friendly square Gardette, where you can try some of the best crepes in Paris at Krugen. For lunch, visit Café Content, a typical neighbourhood cafe, or grab a sandwich at Chez Aline, a former horse-butcher shop. Don't miss the renowned cheese selection, especially the Roquefort, at La Fromagerie Gilbert, and grab fresh bread from MieMie bakery. I could give many more food addresses... Dersou for unique food and cocktail pairings, the great Isola bar for the best spritz in Paris, and for beer, Brasserie BapBap – one of the first Parisian breweries.

Le Bataclan

Café de La Danse, a lively place that offers seated concerts. During the day, the area continues to cater to music enthusiasts, particularly vinyl lovers, as there are numerous record shops in the area to explore.

Shop Until You Drop
A Mix of Independent Finds

Paris offers a plethora of shopping options, and while rue du Faubourg St-Antoine is dominated by chain brands, you'll discover plenty of independent shops around rue de Charonne that will satisfy your desire for unique finds. The area has a special charm when it comes to shopping for clothing, with a mix of trendy French brands with a bohemian touch on rue de Charonne, complemented by independent shops towards rue de la Roquette or further east around metro Ledru-Rollin.

Besides fashion, you can find small treasures like jewellery at **Totale Eclipse**, or antiques in the few remaining shops that reflect the area's artisan heritage, such as **Verreglass**, though absolutely don't enter if you're carrying a backpack and could risk breaking a crystal flask or Murano glass bowl – just marvel at the vintage finds from the window.

 WHERE TO EAT NEAR BASTILLE

Café de l'Industrie
A timeless establishment serving robust French favourites and satisfying desserts in a convivial and warm setting. €

Mokoloco
A kitchen welcoming talented chefs in residence, curated by the Mokonuts team, with a beautiful wine selection. €€€

Do&Co
An intimate restaurant specialising in Vietnamese cuisine, featuring delicately crafted dishes. €

A Creative Food Scene

Delicious Vegan Diversity

The streets from Bastille to Charonne offer a vibrant and diverse food scene with a wide range of options. Alongside the variety of food origins, you'll find a great selection of dietary choices. Vegan restaurants are not uncommon in the area, and offer more than just healthy options. They are known for their creative and delicious dishes, challenging preconceived notions about vegan cuisine. Among the appealing and cosy places to visit, **Mori Café** stands out, providing a taste of Japan within its charming wooden walls. **Aujourd'hui Demain** is a larger cafe-restaurant where you can indulge in hearty quesadillas or burgers. For an upscale experience, the **Friendly Kitchen** is a must-visit. Make sure you try one of their gluten-free cakes: your taste buds will be grateful!

Top Streets for Celebrating Music

Nightlife and Live Performances

If you're looking for a place in Paris to celebrate World Music Day (Fête de la Musique), which takes place on 21 June every year and marks the arrival of summer, look no further. The district around rue d'Oberkampf and rue St-Maur stands out as one of the few areas in central Paris that has successfully preserved its active nightlife, offering a variety of bars, cocktail clubs and music venues. On World Music Day this area becomes even more vibrant as it embraces the spirit of the celebration.

The area remains lively throughout the year. Many bars regularly host live music performances and DJ sets, ensuring there is always something happening. Check out the lineup at nearby concert hall **Le Bataclan**, which has shown resilience following the tragic terrorist attacks of 2015 and continues to host performances. If you prefer a more intimate gathering, **BAM Karaoke** provides private booths where you can enjoy karaoke and drinks. Simply head to the Oberkampf, Parmentier or rue St-Maur metro stations and you're in for an evening of fun!

Living Art Meets Industrial Past

From Industrial Buildings to Cultural Centres

From République to Charonne, the Popincourt district serves as a perfect example of repurposed industrial heritage. This part of Paris developed around metallurgy and mechanics. The architectural style of the streets, characterised by

CREATE YOUR OWN FOOD TRIP

If you find yourself overwhelmed by the abundance of food in Paris and the limited time or stomach space to try them all, fear not! *Le Food Trip* allows you to navigate the city and discover the best food artisans through carefully curated recommendations in a 'food passport' entitled *The Paris Food Trip*. Parisians Martin and Adrien have gathered 30 exceptional places, mostly in eastern Paris, which introduce you to the richness of French gastronomy, and the art of creating happiness through good products. How it works: each stamp in your 'passport' grants you a tasting. You can buy *The Paris Food Trip* at local bookshops or even better, order it in advance before your visit to Paris.

WHERE TO EAT NEAR BASTILLE

Les Bariolés de Maud
Homemade colourful stuffed triangles with meat or vegetarian fillings – a perfect brunch option. €€

Brasserie Rosie
A friendly brasserie offering traditional French dishes such as sausages and mashed potatoes, as well as tartare. €

Amendula Cafe
A cosy Italian cafe tucked away in a quiet alley offering generous plates and delicious cakes. €

Summer on the Seine

BEST PLACES FOR A COFFEE FIX IN THE 11TH ARR

Beans on Fire
A pioneering Parisian coffee roaster offering delicious blends in a serene setting across from square Gardette.

Back in Black
A trendy coffee shop run by friendly staff, where you can enjoy freshly roasted beans and all-day breakfasts.

COMETS
Experience the best of both worlds at this unique space that combines a coffee shop with a record shop.

Stéphane Bersia
Discover the combination of speciality coffee and fine French pastries at this one-of-a-kind coffee shop, with a new pairing every month.

geometric shapes and brick structures, reflects this history, in contrast to the city centre's prevalent Haussmannian architecture. Instead, buildings here were constructed to house workers and can be considered the ancestors of social housing.

As part of an initiative to repurpose Paris' 19th-century industrial buildings, two emblematic projects have thrived in the area. **L'Atelier des Lumières** is a digital art centre that showcases immersive exhibitions that project artworks by renowned artists such as Klimt, Chagall and Van Gogh onto the walls, floors and ceilings of a former foundry. It's very interactive and is particularly loved by children. Adults may find more enjoyment in the cultural programming at **La Maison des Métallos** and appreciate its cast-iron gate adorned with a lyre, a reminder of the building's initial purpose as a musical-instrument manufacturer (before serving as an administrative building for the Union of Metallurgists). Originally established as a performing-arts centre, it has evolved into a multidisciplinary space where every month new artists are invited to explore the transformative power of art in shaping our present and future.

 WHERE TO EAT NEAR OBERKAMPF

La Petite Peña
A tapas bar with a laid-back atmosphere, perfect for enjoying drinks and tasty foods late into the night. €

Chanceux
Charming, family-style restaurant with a refreshing countryside ambience and a daily changing menu. €

Basique
Modern restaurant serving beautifully crafted shared plates, hidden away from the bustling tourist streets. €€

Summer Seine

Open-Air Riverside Bars

Among the best places to grab a drink when summer arrives is along the banks of the Seine, where a variety of riverboats transform their docking spaces into vibrant bars. While these riverside terraces used to be rare and reserved for concert boats or VIP dining experiences, they have flourished in recent years, reviving the 19th-century tradition of the *guinguette* (open-air dance hall) and bringing life to the once neglected riverbanks. Situated across from the architecturally stunning Cité de la Mode et du Design, one of the most popular options on this side of the Seine is the **Barapapa**, which returns every summer with a festive atmosphere, diverse musical offerings and a great, chill vibe along the Port de la Rapée quayside.

Staying on Track

An Urban Trail to the Past

Gradually replaced by the more convenient and less polluting underground railway system in the early 20th century, steam and coal trains had completely disappeared from the Parisian transport network by the 1970s. However, traces of their existence remain, and the heritage of that time, a symbol of the city's industrialisation, still holds a strong presence in the imagination of eastern Paris.

Embarking on an urban trail starting from **square Charles Péguy**, located on a section of the Petite Ceinture (the former train belt encircling Paris), allows you to rediscover this history. Follow the former Vincennes line towards the city centre. This route was once very popular, as it used to transport workers between Faubourg St-Antoine and the charming town of Vincennes, taking them to the *guinguettes* along the Seine for Sunday parties. As you continue along towards the ancient Gare de Reuilly (now converted into a cultural centre), you will pass by a former water-refill station and go through a train tunnel now housing urban-art installations. For the more persistent walkers, you can continue all the way to the Viaduc des Arts and conclude the experience at **Le Train Bleu**. This unique establishment, over 100 years old, is located within the walls of Gare de Lyon. It has exceptional neobaroque decorations, reminiscent of the vibrant Belle Époque era – dining here is like stepping back to a period in history when the train was just beginning to make its mark.

BEST INDEPENDENT STORES AROUND POPINCOURT-CHARONNE

Merci
An iconic store in a 19th-century building curating high-quality sustainable items with a philanthropic approach.

Maison Béguin
A welcoming decoration shop with carefully curated vintage and contemporary designs.

La Maison – Nad Yut
A charming homewares store with a Scandinavian touch, tucked away in a hidden courtyard.

Les Fleurs
One shop for jewels and accessories, another for vintage homeware and designer decoration – both beautifully arranged in a bohemian setting.

We Are Paris
A tiny shop offering a selection of home and beauty products, including handmade and locally sourced items.

 WHERE TO EAT NEAR OBERKAMPF

Le Grand Bréguet
A canteen co-working space with a welcoming atmosphere. Homemade food is served daily. €

La Mi-Fa
A *bistronomique* restaurant with French dishes and a personal touch, hidden away from the busy streets. €€

Brasserie Martin
A spacious brasserie known for its specialisation in roasted meat. Don't miss the succulent roast pork. €

A POPULAR TRAIN TREND

Other train stations that have been repurposed into multidisciplinary spaces, providing vast, alternative cultural options for Parisians, include **La Recyclerie** (p125), a cafe and bike-repair shop, and **La Cité Fertile** (p137), an immensely popular urban project.

THOMAS STOIBER/SHUTTERSTOCK ©

FROM MAIL HALL TO VIBRANT CULTURE COURT

Located in a former mail-sorting hall owned by SNCF (the French national railway company), **Ground Control** is a sprawling multidisciplinary space, a hub where people can gather, explore innovative ideas through cultural events, or simply relax, grab a drink and indulge in finger food from a wide array of food stalls. It also offers areas with lounge chairs, and can get quite crowded, especially during the summer months, as there are few places like this in Paris. In keeping with its multicultural and open-minded approach, it is home to the Refugee Food Festival. Beyond its physical presence, Ground Control also hosts its own podcast series (in French).

La Recyclerie

The Richness of the Earth
From Vineyards to Parisian Gardens

As spring and summer arrive, the **Parc de Bercy** blossoms into a tapestry of colourful flowerbeds. Often overlooked by tourists, the park holds an interesting connection to Paris' winemaking legacy. Located on the grounds of former wine warehouses, it serves as a reminder of the city's prestigious past as the world's largest hub for the wine and spirits trade during the 19th century. This tradition, dating as far back as the Middle Ages, persisted until the 1950s. The vinicultural history endures through the park's 400 grapevines, which are still harvested annually, and the **Chai de Bercy**, a converted wine warehouse now serving as an exhibition space.

The park offers even more than its winemaking heritage: it has become a haven for gardening enthusiasts. Beyond the meticulously flowerbeds and pathways, the park celebrates the art of gardening and the integration of nature within the urban environment. **The House of Gardening**, an educational space in a charming little house in the heart of the park, offers guidance for all who want to develop their green thumbs, through the advice of gardening experts and various other resources.

WHERE TO BUY SWEET TREATS IN EASTERN PARIS

La Briée	Tapissier	Scoop Me a Cookie
A bakery specialising in brioche (sweet airy bread) with a variety of forms and fillings. €	A tiny pastry shop where you can have a delicious brownie or pecan pie with speciality coffee. €	Very indulgent cookies with soft dough, from banana and peanut butter to three-chocolate-chip and fudge. €

Behind the Screens

Uncover the Magic of Cinema

The French have a profound affinity for the art of film, with many directors having left an indelible mark on the history of cinema – Jean-Luc Godard, Jacques Audiard, Agnès Varda, Jean-Pierre Jeunet and François Truffaut, to name just a few. Moreover, going to the cinema ranks among the top experiences in Paris. The city boasts over 350 cinema theatres, each cherished by Parisians.

It's no surprise, then, that there's an entire museum dedicated to this seventh art form. Nestled within the Parc de Bercy, **Cinémathèque Française** offers a comprehensive journey not only through the history of French cinema but also into the secrets of this artistic medium. And of course, there's a cinema at the museum! With a diverse program that allows you to watch classic French films every day, some introduced by experts and followed by conferences, it presents a unique opportunity to delve deeper into the nuances of French cinema. Young cinephiles can also enjoy a tailored program and occasional workshops designed to help them grasp this intricate yet profoundly contemporary art form.

Most importantly, don't miss the permanent exhibition, constructed from an extensive archive collection housed in a new museum spanning over 800 sq metres. A special focus is given to director Georges Méliès and his surrealistic imagery, offering a captivating journey through decades of cinema, exploring various techniques and showcasing vintage equipment. To wrap up your visit and bring your cinematic knowledge into the modern era, head to the large cinema complex in Bercy Village, featuring 18 cinema theatres amidst a bustling shopping and entertainment area.

Around the Lake

Take a Romantic Boat Ride

On sunny days, the grassy banks near **Lac Daumesnil** in Bois de Vincennes evoke a scene reminiscent of Edouard Manet's painting *Le Déjeuner sur l'Herbe*, albeit without the undressed ladies. Highly popular among Parisians residing in the eastern part of the city, **Bois de Vincennes** is a tranquil haven and a escape from the week's frenzy. The lake and its central isles in this section of the park were artificially created in 1860.

One of the highlights here is renting a rowing boat to enjoy the serene surroundings, an activity in the immediate vicinity of Paris that's only available here. For a 30- to 60-minute ride, it costs €15 for up to four people in one boat. Enhance

BEST CULTURE & ENTERTAINMENT SPOTS IN BERCY

Musée des Arts Forains
This unusual museum offers a glimpse into the enchanting world of amusement rides, carousels and other carnival artefacts. Online booking is mandatory.

Bercy Village
Formerly a wine depot, this area next to the Parc de Bercy has been transformed into a pedestrian village, with food venues, entertainment and shops (convenient if you have children).

Accor Arena
The stage here has a seating capacity of 20,000 and hosts major concerts and sports events. The arena is a 2024 Olympics venue.

 WHERE TO BUY SWEET TREATS IN EASTERN PARIS

Diamande	**VG Pâtisserie**	**Manufacture Ducasse**
An exceptional pastry shop renowned for its delectable almond creations with Algerian and French influences. €	A pastry shop specialising in delicate plant-based cake recipes, as well as vegan pastries. €	The flagship workshop of master chocolatier Alain Ducasse, also offering delicious ice creams. €

your countryside outing with a picnic on the banks or with a short walk around the lake to the central isles. Don't miss the **Romantic Temple**, a small reproduction of a Greek-inspired temple at the top of the central hill, visible from the banks. Check out the grotto and sculpted waterfalls below the temple, designed in the manner of an English garden where ruins and waterfalls are meant to blend naturally into the landscape.

Conclude your leisurely afternoon at **Le Chalet des Îles**, an open-air bar with live music, perfect for engaging in endless conversations over cocktails that continue on after sunset.

THE LARGEST BUDDHA STATUE IN FRANCE

One of the most intriguing attractions in Bois de Vincennes is undoubtedly the **Great Pagoda**, which houses the largest Buddha statue in France. Just a stone's throw from Lac Daumesnil, and rather ironically located in repurposed pavilions from the 1931 Colonial Exhibition, it serves as a vibrant gathering place for Asian communities on the outskirts of Paris. Regular spiritual festivals are organised, maintaining the tradition of communal food sharing. They are generally open to the public. Since 2021 an Asian Street Food Festival has also been held at the pagoda, which often attracts large crowds. The Tibetan temple also on the premises is not open to the public.

Paris' Greenest Festival

Music, Talks and Chilling In Nature

If raising awareness about ecological issues through music and art is nothing new, the **We Love Green** festival in the heart of Bois de Vincennes stands as the pioneering event of its kind in Paris. If you're a festivalgoer visiting Paris in June, hop on the metro or bus (as coming by car is discouraged), leave your cash behind and dive headfirst into an exciting music lineup. With five stages, including the dedicated Think Tank stage for environmental talks and discussions, the festival takes over the forest for three full days. It showcases performances by established and emerging French and international artists, while also featuring art installations and workshops, fostering connections and exchanges beyond the musical stages.

**Buddha,
Great Pagoda**

 WHERE TO HAVE A DRINK NEAR BERCY

3bis
This board-game/karaoke bar is famous for its immersive decor and themed room inspired by the TV show *Friends*.

Le Triangle
A friendly bouldering club with a bar. It's accessible, and more exciting when combined with a climbing session!

La Javelle
A spacious open-air bar located towards the outskirts of Paris that creates a lively *guinguette*-style atmosphere.

THE BEST OF BOIS DE VINCENNES FOR KIDS

Parc Zoologique de Paris
Paris' zoo has a variety of exciting activities; eg having breakfast with giraffes.

Aquarium Tropical
This aquarium houses small crocodiles and other aquatic creatures.

Parc Floral de Paris
This vast park has tree activities and zip lines. Keep an eye out for the roaming peacock in the garden.

La Cartoucherie
A cultural complex in the forest, showcasing theatre, dance and circus arts.

Jardin d'Agronomie Tropicale
Lush vegetation, with remnants of the 1931 Colonial Exhibition, including a Chinese gate and Cambodian stupa.

Parc Floral de Paris

WHERE TO SLEEP & DRINK IN EASTERN PARIS

**The People –
Les Piaules Nation**
A youth hostel known for its rooftop terrace overlooking place de la Nation. €

Mk2 Hotel Paradiso
A unique cinema-themed hotel featuring a large screen in each room, and an open-air rooftop cinema. €€

The People – Paris Marais
Conveniently located near Bastille, this youth hostel boasts a popular glass-wall restaurant, Titi Palacio. €

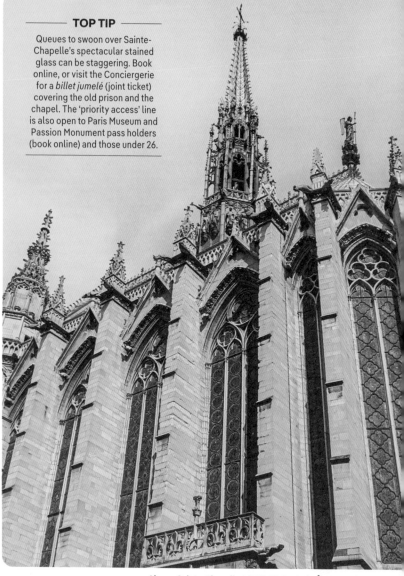

TOP TIP

Queues to swoon over Sainte-Chapelle's spectacular stained glass can be staggering. Book online, or visit the Conciergerie for a *billet jumelé* (joint ticket) covering the old prison and the chapel. The 'priority access' line is also open to Paris Museum and Passion Monument pass holders (book online) and those under 26.

NADIA_FOTO/SHUTTERSTOCK ©

Above: Sainte-Chapelle (p196); Right: Cafe, Île St-Louis (p189)

DON'T MISS

PICNIC ON THE SEINE
Crunch crusty baguettes and savour the sweetness of famous Parisian Berthillon ice cream on the islands' sunny riverbanks. **p189**

CONCIERGERIE
Learn how Marie Antoinette and thousands of others spent their final days at this 14th-century palace turned prison. **p189**

CATHÉDRALE NOTRE DAME DE PARIS
Thank the heavens that the crowning glory of Gothic architecture survived the 2019 fire. **p190**

The Islands

CHIC, HISTORIC AND DELIGHTFUL

Paris' geographic, historic and spiritual heart lies here, in the Seine. This is where Romans set up shop and slowly the entire city radiated outwards.

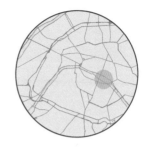

The larger of these two inner-city islands, Île de la Cité, is home to majestic Notre Dame, being restored after its devastating 2019 fire, and Sainte-Chapelle, with its exquisite stained glass. Its serene neighbour, little Île St-Louis, is graced with charming boutiques and sun-bathed quays beckoning to picnickers. Where better to start your explorations than Notre Dame? After an amazingly detailed and mightily rapid €850 million restoration, the cathedral is slated to open in time for the 2024 Olympics. And its massive towers and dramatic flying buttresses always radiate magnificence. Much less well-known but equally thrilling, Sainte-Chapelle, the chapel of kings and queens, is a symphony of kaleidoscopic 13th-century stained glass in slender stonework – fantastic during evening concerts in summer, when the light is still high. It sits a mere few footsteps from today's

SIMONA SIRIO/SHUTTERSTOCK ©

functioning Palais de Justice and the dungeons in the French Revolution prison, the Conciergerie.

Cross Pont St-Louis to enchanting Île St-Louis to have brunch or lunch at the deliciously Parisian hangout Café Saint Régis, then browse the island's boutiques and art galleries. Restore yourself with iconic Berthillon ice cream, perfect to enjoy while strolling the river's edge or gawking at the island's many historic *hôtels particuliers* (grand mansions).

Come late afternoon, cruise back over to Pont St-Louis – where you're likely to catch buskers – for a predinner apéritif and allow ample time to lap up the quaint, old-world vibe of pretty, car-free place Dauphine on Île de la Cité. Then watch the lights come up on Pont Neuf, with its dramatic busts of ogres and kings and the lights sparkling on the length of the Seine. Revel in it – you're in Paris.

SAINTE-CHAPELLE
Bathe in richly coloured biblical tales, told through stained-glass imagery with a grace and beauty impossible to find elsewhere. **p196**

CAFÉ LIFE ON ÎLE ST-LOUIS
Settle in with a coffee or cocktail for people-watching with the soaring backdrop of Notre Dame. **p197**

PLAY ON THE PONT NEUF & ISLAND BRIDGES
Stroll and snap selfies or dance to buskers on some of Paris' most romantic bridges. **p199**

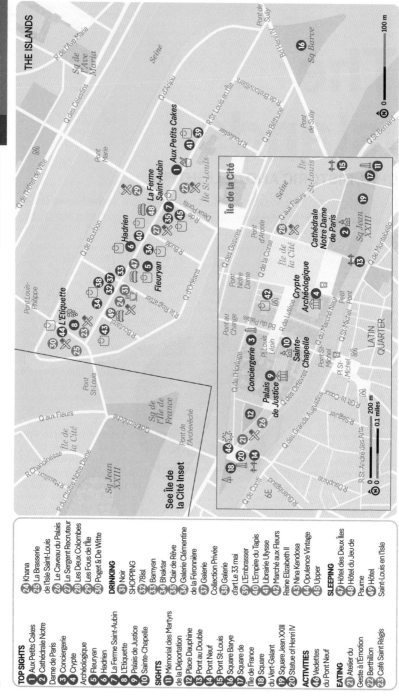

THE ISLANDS

Seine

Sq de l'Ave Maria

R de l'Ave Maria

Pont de Sully

16 Sq Barye

Bd Henri IV

Q des Célestins

Q d'Anjou

R Poulletier

R St-Louis en l'Île

Pont de Sully

Q de Béthune

Q de l'Hôtel de Ville

Pont Marie

1 Aux Petits Cakes

La Ferme Saint-Aubin

R St-Louis

Île St-Louis

Q St-Bernard

41 **39**

22

29

Hadrien **6**

48 **35** **7**
R de Deux Ponts

27 **45**

40

36

Fleuryan

5

R Budé

Île de la Cité

Q aux Fleurs

Île St-Louis

15

17 **11**

Seine

Pont Louis-Philippe

L'Étiquette

8

30 **25**

44

23

38 **37**

32 **31**

34

49 **24**

43

R Regrattier

Q de Bourbon

Q d'Orléans

33 **47**

Cathédrale Notre Dame de Paris

2

19 Sq Jean XXIII

28

13

Q de Montebello

Q des Grands Augustins

Pont St-Louis

Q aux Fleurs

Île de la Cité

Q aux Fleurs

R Chanoinesse

R du Cloître Notre Dame

R Massillon

Sq Jean XXIII

Q de l'Archevêché

Sq de l'Île de France

Pont de l'Archevêché

See Île de la Cité Inset

Pont de la Tournelle

100 m

THE ISLANDS

Q des Gesvres

Pont d'Arcole

Île de la Cité

Pont Notre Dame

Crypte Archéologique

4

Pont au Change

Bd du Palais

R de Lutèce

R d'Arcole

Pont au Double

Conciergerie **3**

Pl Louis Lépin

10

Sainte-Chapelle

R de la Corse

Pont St-Michel

Petit Pont

42

Palais de Justice **9**

12

26

Q de l'Horloge

Q des Orfèvres

Q du Marché Neuf

Pl St-Michel

LATIN QUARTER

Q St-Michel

18 **4** **6**

20 **21**

14

R de Harlay

Pl St-André des Arts

R Séguier

R Dauphine

Q de Conti

R St-André des Arts

R Git-le-Cœur

9E

200 m
0.1 miles

N

Conciergerie

Conciergerie

Prisons Through the Ages

A royal palace in the 14th century, the Conciergerie later became a prison. During the Reign of Terror (1793–94), alleged enemies of the Revolution were incarcerated here before being brought before the Revolutionary Tribunal next door in the 13th-century **Palais de Justice** (still a working courthouse, which you can enter for free; p202).

Of the almost 2800 prisoners held in the Conciergerie's dungeons at that time (in various 'classes' of cells, no less) before being sent to the guillotine, the star prisoner was Queen Marie Antoinette. You can see a display of some of her delicate personal items. As the Revolution began to turn on its own, radicals Danton and Robespierre made an appearance at the Conciergerie and, finally, the judges of the tribunal themselves.

Rotating exhibitions fill the beautiful Rayonnant Gothic **Salle des Gens d'Armes**, Europe's largest surviving medieval hall.

Rent a HistoPad (tablet-device guide; €5) to explore in augmented reality and take part in an interactive, 3D treasure hunt.

Picnic on the Banks of the Seine

The Sweet Island Life

You can't miss the happy Parisians dotting the quays and parks of the islands, relaxing, reading, romancing and, of course, picnicking. Join them! Outfit yourself at the islands' lovely purveyors – from luxe sandwiches and tarts at **Atelier du Geste à l'Émotion** (p199), excellent breads at **Aux Petits Cakes**, *fromage* (cheese) from **La Ferme Saint-Aubin** or a little of everything at the small grocery store on rue St-Louis en l'Île or lovely **Fleuryan**. Pick up a bottle of wine, too, at **L'Etiquette**. Dessert? Chocolate from **Hadrien** or ice cream from **Berthillon** (p199), *bien sur!*

ARDANME/SHUTTERSTOCK ©

PRACTICALITIES

Scan this QR code for opening hours and tours of Notre Dame.

TOP SIGHT

Notre Dame

Majestic and monumental in equal measure, Paris' iconic French Gothic cathedral is now reopened after the 2019 fire, its resplendent art and architecture, from bell towers to stained glass, shining like new. The capital's most visited unticketed site – more than 12 million cross its threshold annually – remains, as always, a Parisian beacon.

DON'T MISS

Rose windows

Bell towers

Flying buttresses

Treasury

The *Mays* paintings

Underground ruins

Cathedral concerts

Reigning Masterpiece

Notre Dame represents a generous history of building and re-building, long before the fire of 15 April 2019. It's constructed on the site occupied by a Gallo-Roman temple and was preceded by several earlier churches. The masterpiece we see today was begun in 1163 and largely completed by the early 14th century. It was badly damaged during the Revolution, prompting architect Eugène-Emmanuel Viollet-le-Duc to oversee extensive renovations between 1845 and 1864. That's when many of the magnificent forest of ornate flying buttresses that encircle the cathedral chancel and support its walls and roof were added.

With the devastating 2019 fire, this French Gothic landmark, long considered the city's geographic and spiritual heart, went through a massive restoration and, amazingly, has reopened its doors in 2024. Highlights include its three spectacular rose windows, treasury and bell towers, calling to be climbed. In the North Tower, about 400 steps spiral to the top of the western façade, where you'll find yourself face-to-face with frightening gargoyles and a spectacular view of Paris.

Fire of April 2019

On the evening of 15 April 2019, a blaze broke out under the cathedral's roof. Firefighters were able to control the fire and ultimately save the church, including its iconic bell towers, rose windows and western façade. But the damage remained catastrophic: both the roof and slender spire – actually a 19th-century addition – were completely destroyed and the interior was severely damaged. Several statues and artefacts had already been removed from the cathedral as part of a restoration program underway prior to the fire. While flames engulfed the cathedral, Paris firefighters and the fire brigade's chaplain formed a human chain to save many of the remaining cathedral treasures.

Rebuilding Notre Dame

After the fire, French President Emmanuel Macron said he'd like the cathedral to be rebuilt by 2024, in time for the Olympic Games. It took more than two years to clean and stabilise the structure, and while construction is ongoing at the time of writing, the doors are, indeed, slated to reopen in 2024.

Overall, the restoration, involving over 1000 artists and journeymen, at a cost of approximately €850 million (raised via donations), will not only repair fire-damaged elements, but clean and restore everything – pipe organ, 3000 sq metres of stained glass, paintings, copper sculptures, inside and out – to the untarnished condition of the era of Viollet-le-Duc, a requirement of the charters the government must follow. Even the oak beams (cut from over 2000 oak trees) have been hand-hewn using traditional axes. The pipe organ alone will take six months to reassemble and tune – only at night because it requires complete silence.

Grand Plan

Notre Dame is known for its sublime balance, though if you look closely you'll see all sorts of minor asymmetrical elements introduced to avoid monotony, in accordance with standard Gothic practice. These include the slightly different shapes of each of the three main **portals**, whose statues were once brightly coloured to make them more effective as a *Biblia pauperum* – a 'Bible of the poor' to help the illiterate faithful understand Old Testament stories, the Passion of the Christ and the lives of the saints.

Landmark Occasions

Historic events at Notre Dame abound. Henry VI of England was crowned here in 1431 as King of France. In 1558 Mary, Queen of Scots married the Dauphin Francis (later Francis II of France). At the unusual 1600 marriage of Marie de Médici to Henri of Navarre, he, as a Protestant who couldn't enter the church, stood outside. In 1804 Napoléon I was crowned by Pope Pius VII. And Joan of Arc was beatified in 1909 and canonised in 1920.

CENTRE OF FRANCE

Notre Dame has always been the heart of Paris – distances from Paris to every part of France are measured from a bronze star embedded in the cobbles of the cathedral's front square (called Parvis Notre Dame or place Jean-Paul II). It's also the centre of the city. A statue of Charlemagne (742–814 CE) is nearby.

TOP TIPS

● Huge queues just get longer throughout the day – arrive early.

● Shorten bell-tower queues by reserving a same-day visit with the free JeFile smartphone app.

● Some of the best views of the cathedral's flying buttresses are from square Jean XXIII (the little park behind it) or bridges St-Louis and de l'Archevêché.

● Collect an audioguide from Notre Dame's information desk, inside the entrance.

● Metro stops Cité (line 4) and St-Michel (line 4 and RER B and C) are each a five-minute walk away.

● Remember that Notre Dame is an active place of worship.

Notre Dame

Towers

A constant queue marks the entrance to the **Tours de Notre Dame** (tours-notre-dame-de-paris.fr), the cathedral's bell towers. Climb the 400-odd spiralling steps to the top of the western façade of the **North Tower**, where gargoyles grimace and grin on the rooftop (Galerie des Chimères). These grotesque statues divert rainwater from the roof to prevent masonry damage, with the water exiting through their elongated, open mouths. They also, purportedly, ward off evil spirits. Although they appear medieval, they were installed by Viollet-le-Duc in the 19th century. From the top there's a **spectacular view** over Paris. In the **South Tower** hangs Emmanuel, the cathedral's original 13-tonne bourdon **bell** (all of the cathedral's bells are named, as is the tradition).

During the night of 24 August 1944, when the Île de la Cité was retaken by French, Allied and Resistance troops, the tolling of the Emmanuel announced Paris' approaching liberation.

Emmanuel's peal purity apparently proceeds from the precious metals Parisian women threw into the pot when it was recast from copper and bronze in 1631. As part of 2013's celebrations for the 850th anniversary of the start of Notre Dame's construction, nine new bells were installed, replicating the original medieval chimes.

Galerie des Chimères

OLRAT/SHUTTERSTOCK ©

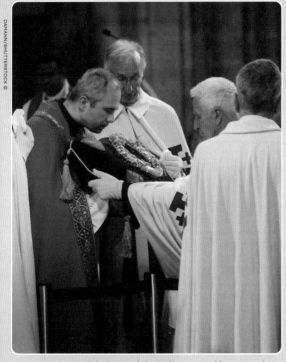

DAMANN/SHUTTERSTOCK ©

Holy Crown of Thorns is presented for veneration

Treasury

It is absolutely worth the small fee to enter the *trésor* (treasury), which houses Notre Dame's dazzling sacred jewels and relics in the cathedral's southeastern transept.

The **Ste-Couronne** (Holy Crown), the wreath of thorns believed to have been placed on Jesus' head before he was crucified, was given to Notre Dame in 1239 by St Louis. It is only exhibited between 3pm and 4pm on the first Friday of the month and Fridays during Lent, plus 10am to 5pm on Good Friday.

Easier to see is the wonderful collection, **Les Camées des Papes** (Papal cameos). Sculpted with incredible finesse in shell and framed in silver, the 268 pieces depict every pope in miniature from St Pierre to Benoît XVI.

ROSE WINDOWS & ORGAN

Behold the three rose windows colouring the cathedral's vast 127m-long, 48m-wide interior. The 13m-wide southern window is the largest and depicts the theme of the Last Judgement. The window on the northern side of the transept remains virtually unchanged since the 13th century. Admire the 10m-wide window over the western façade, with the Virgin Mary in the centre, above the organ. The organ is one of the largest in the world, with 8000 pipes (900 of which have historical classification), 115 stops, five 56-key manuals and a 32-key pedalboard.

Notre Dame

Timeline

1160 Maurice de Sully becomes bishop of Paris. Mission: to grace growing Paris with a lofty new cathedral.

1182–90 The choir with double ambulatory is finished and work starts on the nave and side chapels.

1200–50 The **1 west façade**, with rose window, three portals and two soaring towers, goes up. Everyone is stunned.

1345 Some 180 years after the foundation stone was laid, the Cathédrale de Notre Dame is complete. It is dedicated to notre dame (our lady), the Virgin Mary.

1789 Revolutionaries smash the original Gallery of Kings, pillage the cathedral and melt all its bells except the great bell **2 Emmanuel**. The cathedral becomes a Temple of Reason and then a warehouse.

1831 Victor Hugo's novel *The Hunchback of Notre Dame* inspires new interest in the half-ruined Gothic cathedral.

1845–64 Architect Viollet-le-Duc undertakes its restoration. Twenty-eight new kings are sculpted for the west façade. The heavily decorated **3 portals and spire** are reconstructed. The neogothic treasury is built.

1860 The area in front of Notre Dame is cleared to create the **4 parvis**, an alfresco classroom where Parisians can learn a catechism illustrated on sculpted portals.

1935 A rooster bearing part of the relics of the Crown of Thorns, St Denis and Ste Geneviève is put on top of the cathedral spire to protect those who pray inside.

1991 The architectural masterpiece of Notre Dame and its Seine-side riverbanks become a Unesco World Heritage Site.

2013 Notre Dame celebrates 850 years since construction began with a bevy of new bells and restoration works.

2019 A fire causes devastating damage to the cathedral interior, destroys most of the roof and topples the spire.

2024 The cathedral is due to reopen to visitors and resume church services in December 2024.

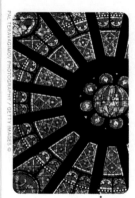

North Rose Window

See prophets, judges, kings and priests venerate Mary in vivid blue and violet glass, one of three beautiful rose blooms (1225–70), each almost 10m in diameter.

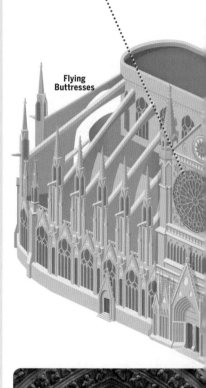

Flying Buttresses

...asury

...ash reserve of French kings – who ordered
...ces, crucifixes, baptism fonts and other
...ed gems to be melted down in the Mint
...g times of financial strife (war, famine and
...) – was stored in the Notre Dame treasury.
...e April 2019 fire, priceless relics, such as the
...d Ste-Couronne (Holy Crown), purportedly
...reath of thorns placed on Jesus' head before
...as cruclfied, were saved by a human chain of
...e workers.

...re & Roof

...thirds of the roof, and the 19th-century spire,
...destroyed in the 2019 fire.

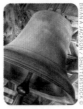

Great Bell
The peal of Emmanuel,
the cathedral's great
bell, is so pure thanks
to precious gems and
jewels Parisian women
threw into the pot when
it was recast from
copper and bronze in
1631. Admire its original
siblings in square Jean
XXII.

Chimera Gallery
The north tower is graced with grimacing gargoyles
and grotesque chimera, including celebrity
chimera Stryga, who has wings, horns, a human
body and sticking-out tongue. This bestial lot
wards off demons.

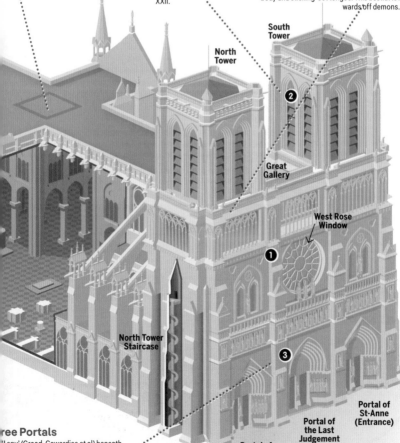

South
Tower

North
Tower

2

Great
Gallery

West Rose
Window

1

North Tower
Staircase

3

Portal of
St-Anne
(Entrance)

Portal of
the Last
Judgement

Portal of
the Virgin
(Exit)

4   Parvis
Notre Dame

...ree Portals

..."I spy" (Greed, Cowardice et al) beneath
...e sculpted doorways, which illustrate
...easons, life and the 12 vices and virtues
...side the Bible.

STAINED GLASS

Statues of the Apostles, foliage-adorned capitals and beatific angels decorate this sumptuous, bijou chapel. But it is the 1113 biblical scenes, from Genesis through to the Crown of Thorns reaching Paris, depicted in its 15 soaring stained-glass windows – 15m high in the nave, 13m in the apse – and monumental, 9m-wide rose window that stun visitors. They were crafted by the artists who worked on Chartres and are generally best read from left to right and top to bottom to follow the stories.

Sainte-Chapelle

Shimmering Stained-Glass Bedazzlement

No sight in Paris is as dazzling as this radiant **Holy Chapel**, hidden away like a precious gem within the city's original, 13th-century Palais de Justice (Law Courts) and Palais de la Cité, the former royal residence. Paris' oldest, finest stained glass laces its sublime Gothic interior – best viewed on sunny days when light floods in, creating an entrancing rainbow of bold colours.

Sainte-Chapelle was built in just six years and consecrated in 1248. It was conceived by French king Louis IX to house his collection of holy relics, including the famous Ste-Couronne (Holy Crown, Jesus' wreath of thorns), which he acquired in 1239 from the Emperor of Constantinople for a sum easily exceeding the amount it cost to build the chapel. In reality, it was safeguarded in the treasury at Notre Dame (and saved from the 2019 fire).

Enter through the lower chamber of the chapel, used by palace staff, and mount a spiral stair signposted 'Chapelle Haute' to reach the glorious upper chapel where royals, such as Catherine de Médici, and their close friends worshipped. The relatively squat lower chamber supports the delicate masonry above, allowing for such a seemingly impossible array of windows.

Stir your soul at a classical music **evening concert** (check schedules and buy tickets at fnac.com).

You can also join a free one-hour guided tour in English (daily at 11am and 3pm); rent an audioguide (€3); or download the Sainte-Chapelle Windows smartphone app to study the windows in intricate detail.

FROM HIGH TO LOW

Explore the neighbouring **Palais de Justice** (p202) and **Conciergerie** (p189) to see the darker side of life, in the courts and prisons where prisoners were tried and held before the guillotine.

MIKHAIL VARENTSOV/SHUTTERSTOCK ©

View of Sainte-Chapelle

RAFFAELLA GALVANI/SHUTTERSTOCK ©

Croque monsieur

Cafe Life

Lounge the Day Away in Style

When Parisians relax, they relax. A morning coffee, lingering lunch or predinner drink can stretch on, and Paris' islands offer top chances to while the day away. For excellent people watching, head to the point where **Pont St-Louis** meets the island of the same name. There, you'll find one of the islands' best dining experiences: Café Saint Régis. Waiters in long white aprons, a ceramic-tiled interior and retro vintage decor make this buzzy spot a deliciously Parisian hangout any time of the day, from breakfast pastries, organic omelettes and mid-morning croques monsieurs (cheese and ham toasties) to Parisian classics – garlicky snails, onion soup, tartare – and late-night cocktails.

Or pop across the street to **La Brasserie de l'Isle Saint-Louis** for its broad patio with ace views. From coffees to crisp glasses of Chablis you can graduate up to hearty *choucroute* (a decadent pile of sauerkraut topped with sausage and ham), peachy to set you up for a night out.

ISLANDS THROUGH TIME

Île de la Cité was the site of the first settlement in Paris (c 3rd century BCE) and later the centre of Roman Lutetia. The island remained the hub of royal and ecclesiastical power, even after the city spread to both banks of the Seine in the Middle Ages. Smaller Île St-Louis was actually two uninhabited islets called Île Notre Dame (Our Lady Isle) and Île aux Vaches (Cows Island) in the early 17th century – until a building contractor and two financiers worked out a deal with Louis XIII to create one island and build two stone bridges to the mainland. The agreed future redevelopment of part of historic hospital Hôtel Dieu into commercial offices, shops and restaurants heralds a new era for the island.

THE GUIDE

THE ISLANDS PARIS

WHERE TO EAT ON THE ISLANDS

Poget & De Witte
Oysters! Paired with a crisp Chablis or a frothy Champagne. €€

Le Sergent Recruteur
The islands' Michelin-starred treat, where plates look like art and service is impeccable. €€€

Khana
Excite your palate with Afghan fare on the main street of Île St-Louis. €€

Start strolling through island life Paris-style as the **1 Pont Neuf** hits the tip of Île de la Cité. The emerald **2 square du Vert-Galant**, just down the stairs at the original level of the island offers a bracing breath of fresh air, with stellar views, on the point where Hemingway and his pals used to fish. Stroll to hidden **3 place Dauphine**, built on a former marsh. If you're lucky there'll be a heated game of *pétanque* underway beneath the shade trees. You can dive into Notre Dame (p190), Sainte-Chapelle (p196) or the Conciergerie (p189), or make a beeline to lovely **4 rue des Ursins**, which was Paris' first dock. Keep an eye out for the Roman ramparts (at the junction with rue de Colombe), before ambling to the pocket park complete with lion's-head fountain.

Meander across **5 Pont St-Louis** (p200) to the peaceful island named after the only sainted French king, Louis IX. Find your own quiet stretch of shade-dappled quay to picnic (p189) or embrace history and architecture on **6 quai de Bourbon**. Read the plaques as you go, naming venerable residents: for example, at No 19 artist Camille Claudel had her studio. Continuing on, **7 29 quai d'Anjou** was where Ford Madox Ford founded the influential *Transatlantic Review* in 1924 with John Quinn, James Joyce and Ezra Pound.

Finish your tour of the island's *hôtels particuliers* with crowning-glory **8 Hôtel Lambert** (1 quai d'Anjou), built by King Louis XIV's architect Louis Le Vau – also responsible for the Versailles we know today. French telecom magnate Xavier Niel bought it in 2022 and is rumoured to be making it the home of his cultural foundation.

Seek a cool and contemplative retreat in French-baroque **9 Église St-Louis en l'Île**, built between 1664 and 1726.

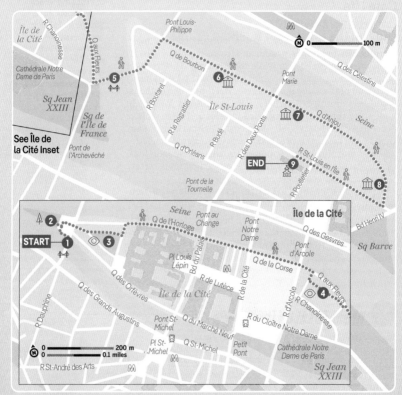

Pont Neuf

BEST BOAT CRUISES FROM THE ISLANDS

Vedettes du Pont Neuf
One-hour cruises depart year-round from Vedettes' centrally located dock at the western tip of Île de la Cité. Commentary is in French and English. Tickets are cheaper if you buy in advance online. They also offer 90-minute lunch cruises, evening Champagne cruises and two-hour dinner cruises.

Batobus
Batobus runs glassed-in trimarans that dock every 20 to 25 minutes at nine small piers along the Seine, including at Notre Dame.

Play on the Pont Neuf & Island Bridges
Gorgeous History, Modern Musicians

Paris' oldest bridge, confusingly named Pont Neuf, or 'New Bridge', has linked the western end of Île de la Cité with both riverbanks since 1607, when the king, Henri IV, inaugurated it by crossing the bridge on a white stallion. The bridge's epic arches (seven on the northern stretch and five on the southern span) are decorated with 381 *mascarons* (grotesque figures) depicting barbers, dentists, pickpockets, loiterers etc.

The inaugural crossing is commemorated by an equestrian **statue of Henri IV**, known to his subjects as the Vert Galant ('jolly rogue' or 'dirty old man', perspective depending).

The Pont Neuf and nearby peaceful and tree-adorned **place Dauphine** were used for public exhibitions in the 18th century. In the last century, the bridge became an objet d'art in 1963, when School of Paris artist Nonda built, exhibited and lived in a huge Trojan horse of steel and wood on the bridge; in 1985, when Bulgarian-born 'environmental sculptor' Christo famously wrapped the bridge in beige fabric; and in 1994 when Japanese designer Kenzo covered it with flowers.

 WHERE TO EAT ON THE ISLANDS

Berthillon
Founded here in 1954, the flagship of the esteemed *glacier* (ice-cream maker) is still run by the same family. €

Atelier du Geste à l'Émotion
The best bakery on Île de la Cité with superb croissants and exquisite pastries. €

Pierre Hermé
Island outpost of the famed macaron-maker, perfect for a pick-me-up. €

WHY I LOVE PARIS' ISLANDS

Alexis Averbuck, writer

Every time I come to Paris I make a pilgrimage to the islands. By day, by night, the views offer the soaring romance and twinkling lights we all dream about when we think of the City of Light. There's great people-watching too, as locals and tourists alike cut through on their way elsewhere or seek a picnic spot on the quay. I also love thinking about how these islands are the very root of the original city, built layer-upon-layer of history, from pre-Roman to Notre Dame and Sainte-Chappelle (with its heart-thrilling stained glass) and the bustling brasseries of today. I almost feel like you haven't fully experienced Paris until you've come to its islands.

Île de la Cité

The islands' bridges are top spots for buskers. Take in the street entertainment at **Pont au Double** (linking Notre Dame with the Left Bank) and **Pont St-Louis** (linking both islands), which buzz with street performers in summer.

In fact, the current postcard-perfect bridge Pont St-Louis connecting Île de la Cité and Île St-Louis dates from 1969. It is the seventh bridge built on this spot to link the two islands. The first – made from wood – went up in the 1630s.

Chic Shopping

Browse Île St-Louis Galleries and Boutiques

Île St-Louis is a shopper's delight for craft-filled boutiques and tiny, enticing specialist stores and galleries. A saunter down the main street, rue St-Louis en l'Île, will take you by your picnic purveyors (p189) as well as myriad locally owned emporia.

Browse antiques at **Bhaktar**, handmade carpets at **L'Empire du Tapis** and Asian-influenced fashion at **Bamyan**. Or hit the concept store **Upper**, which is part boutique, art gallery and cafe (serving coffee, tea, beer, wine and cocktails). It carries everything from men's and women's fashion, hats, handbags, jewellery and sunglasses to stationery and homewares, displayed alongside works by Parisian, French and

WHERE TO DRINK ON THE ISLANDS

L'Etiquette
Coolcat *caviste* (wine merchant) and wine bar with a couple of tables on the pavement.

Noir
High-end coffee shop with delectable small baked goods on rue St-Louis en l'Île.

Cafes at Quai de Bourbon & Pont St-Louis
Cafes here have the best busker- and people-watching, with a Notre Dame backdrop.

international artists. **Galerie Collection Privée** and **Galerie d'art Le 33 mai** are combined in one storefront, displaying compelling contemporary art, while **Galerie Clémentine de la Féronnière** exhibits fine photography and excellent painters.

Or slide back in time at **Clair de Rêve**, a toy store where stringed marionettes made of papier-mâché, leather and porcelain bob from the ceiling. It also sells wind-up toys and music boxes.

Towards the eastern end of the street at **L'Embrasser**, a glass-and-steel façade opens onto the minimalist interior of this stylish gallery dedicated to Japanese art: think prints, paintings and pottery.

Nearby **Librairie Ulysse** is stuffed to the rafters with antiquarian and new travel guides, *National Geographic* back editions and maps. It was the world's first travel bookshop when it was opened in 1971 by the intrepid Catherine Domaine. Hours vary, but ring the bell and Catherine will open up if she's around.

If, on the other hand, you're after souvenirs and tourist kitsch, head to Île de la Cité.

Quiet Parks & River Vistas

Slip into Verdant Views

In all the beauty of central Paris it's easy to forget that the Seine is a living river with a rich ecology. The islands' small parks offer glimpses of both wildlife and manicured gardens.

At the westernmost tip of the Île de la Cité, migratory birds and chestnut, yew, black walnut and weeping willow trees grace the picturesque park **square du Vert-Galant**. Sitting at the islands' original level, 7m below their current height, the waterside park is reached by stairs leading down from the Pont Neuf. Especially romantic for drinks or a picnic at sunset, it can get crowded in the evenings at the beginning of summer or *la rentrée* (back to school).

Tucked behind Notre Dame, **square Jean XXIII** is a welcome respite from the cathedral's crowds with an ornate fountain and quiet(er) benches.

Immediately across the quai de l'Archevêché, the fenced **square de l'Île de France** gives superb river views and is less packed as well. It's also home to the **Mémorial des Martyrs de la Déportation** (Memorial to the Victims of the Deportation), erected in 1962. This monument commemorates the 200,000 French (including 76,000 Jews, of whom 11,000 were children) who were deported to and murdered in Nazi concentration camps during WWII. A single barred 'window'

FLOWER MARKET

As you stroll the Île de la Cité, look out for the sweet **Marché aux Fleurs Reine Elizabeth II**. Bang in the middle of the island, blooms have been sold at this quaint covered flower market since 1808, making it the oldest market of any kind in Paris. Browse blooming orchids, garden statuary and lavender sachets.

WHERE TO SHOP FOR FASHION ON ÎLE ST-LOUIS

Opulence Vintage
Vintage couture in a tiny storefront featuring everything from Chanel to Valentino and Versace.

Nina Kendosa
On rue St-Louis en l'Île with soft, casual styles often made from natural fibres.

78isl
Sporty, contemporary, bright and cheerful clothing and accessories.

separates the bleak, rough-concrete courtyard from the waters of the Seine. Inside lies the Tomb of the Unknown Deportee.

Continuing along to the eastern tip of Île St-Louis, the park at **square Barye**, just across bd Henri IV, sports a jaunty kids' playground plus views along the river towards the Jardin des Plantes, and access to the quays below.

Feeling the Seat of Power
From Palace to Courthouse

The **Palais de Justice**, which you enter by its own security line (don't get sucked into the queue at Sainte-Chapelle, which lies in its central courtyard), stands on ground once occupied by the Romans' administrative buildings. Over time, they were replaced by other seats of power (the Merovingian and Capetian kings ruled here). That all ended when Charles V (1338–80) moved out (over to the Louvre and other palaces) after he was forced to watch his trusted counsellors killed here.

During the Revolution, the old ways were overthrown and new courts were installed here, in what has ever since been known as the Palais de Justice. Its current façade dates from the latter half of the 19th and turn of the 20th century. The experience of walking its near-empty halls (as most tourists only stop to take photos on its stairs in the central **Cour du Mai**) instils a sense of monumental power. Court proceedings are private, but much of the large building is open to the public and it's interesting to look out its large windows at Sainte-Chapelle.

TOP BISTROS ON THE ISLANDS

Les Deux Colombes
Charmingly tucked into a quiet corner of Île de la Cité with friendly service and hearty classics. €€

Le Caveau du Palais
Half-timbered dining room and alfresco terrace invariably packed with diners tucking into bountiful fresh fare. €€

Les Fous de l'Île
Recently renovated local favourite featuring the French national symbol (cockerel) and a new chef, Jonathan Lafon. €€

ISLAND INCOGNITO
A lesser-known island stroll is the artificial Île aux Cygnes (p264) via its tree-shaded walkway, the Allée des Cygnes. Walking from west to east gives you a stunning view of the Eiffel Tower.

WHERE TO STAY ON ÎLE ST-LOUIS

Hôtel du Jeu de Paume
Contemporary hotel in a former royal tennis court on Île St-Louis' main street, with rooms inspired by modern artists. €€€

Hôtel des Deux Îles
Elegantly floral decor with top-floor rooms peeping out over Parisian rooftops and chimney pots. €€€

Hôtel Saint-Louis en l'Isle
Swank and subtle, this stellar abode includes a 17th-century stone-cellar breakfast room. €€€

PARISIAN MARKETS

For market lovers, check out more on Paris' wonderful street markets and old-fashioned covered markets (p106), a study in joyful abundance.

Replica of the Statue of Liberty with Eiffel Tower (p60) in the background

Latin Quarter

MEDIEVAL MARVELS AND LITERARY LUMINARIES

The Latin Quarter is one of the oldest neighbourhoods in Paris. Explore its spectacular medieval architecture and soak up the unique atmosphere, stemming from its heyday as the heart of literary Paris, when it drew writers like Ernest Hemingway and James Joyce.

The star attraction is the neoclassical Panthéon, inspired by the Roman edifice of the same name, where some of France's most brilliant figures are laid to rest. The Latin Quarter spans parts of the 5th and 6th *arrondissements* and runs between the Jardin du Luxembourg and the Jardin des Plantes, culminating at 'Mount' Ste-Geneviève (more of a hill), where you'll find the Panthéon and the prestigious Université Panthéon-Sorbonne. The Latin Quarter was the centre for higher education, with many of the top schools established here from the Middle Ages. It gets its name from Latin being the language of choice at these schools; it was spoken throughout the area until the French Revolution.

In this neighbourhood you can rub shoulders with ghosts of the past, such as Roman royalty, which sat in the 2nd-century Arènes de Lutèce amphitheatre; philosophers Simone de Beauvoir and Jean-Paul Sartre, who sat at a cafe on place de la Contrescarpe and went dancing nearby; or Ernest Hemingway, who frequented the area's many bars. Visit arthouse cinemas and museums such as the Muséum National d'Histoire Naturelle, with its brilliant Grande Galerie de l'Évolution and Galerie de Paléontologie et d'Anatomie Comparée. Grab a bite to eat at a top restaurant, stroll medieval rue Mouffetard, or check out the new arty hub Césure, inside a repurposed Sorbonne building. Delve into Paris' diverse cultural heritage too, with a look around the Institut du Monde Arabe, lunch in the courtyard of the Grande Mosquée de Paris, or an evening of live jazz at a local hangout.

SYMEONIDIS DIMITRIOS/SHUTTERSTOCK ©

DON'T MISS

THE PANTHÉON
Delve into the stories of the bright minds buried here. **p207**

ÉGLISE ST-ÉTIENNE DU MONT
See the intricate carvings adorning the façade of the most beautiful building in the area. **p210**

DINE AT A STORIED RESTAURANT
Book dinner at a historic eatery, such as Polidor, La Tour d'Argent or Le Procope. **p214**

TOP TIP

If you can, it's best to avoid visiting the Latin Quarter in the height of summer (July and August) as overtourism here is real. Queues for sites are long and you'll be hard pushed finding a free table at restaurants and bars, so book ahead if you are here then.

ZVONIMIR ATLETIC/SHUTTERSTOCK ©

Left: Panthéon (p207); Above: Église St-Étienne du Mont (p217)

JARDIN DES PLANTES	CATCH AN OLD CINEMA	THE LATIN QUARTER'S ARCHITECTURE
Come rain or shine, the gardens and history museums here are must-dos. **p210**	Watch a film at an atmospheric art deco cinema like Le Champo. **p215**	Get lost in the tangle of age-old stone streets to really soak up the singular atmosphere. **p219**

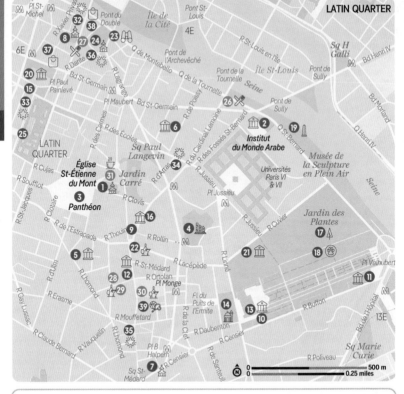

LATIN QUARTER

TOP SIGHTS
1 Église St-Étienne du Mont
2 Institut du Monde Arabe
3 Panthéon

SIGHTS
4 Arènes de Lutèce
5 Centre Culturel Irlandais
6 Collège des Bernardins
7 Église St-Médard
8 Église St-Séverin
9 Ernest Hemingway's Apartment
10 Galerie de Minéralogie et de Géologie
11 Galerie de Paléontologie et d'Anatomie Comparée
12 George Orwell's Boarding House
13 Grande Galerie de l'Évolution
14 Grande Mosquée de Paris
15 Institut Finlandais
16 James Joyce's Flat
17 Jardin des Plantes
18 La Ménagerie
19 Musée de la Sculpture en Plein Air
20 Musée National du Moyen Âge
21 Muséum National d'Histoire Naturelle
22 Place de la Contrescarpe
23 Quai de Montebello
24 St-Julien-le-Pauvre
25 Université Panthéon-Sorbonne

SPORTS & ACTIVITIES
39 Bowling Mouffetard

EATING
26 La Tour d'Argent
27 Odette

DRINKING & NIGHTLIFE
see 28 Brewberry
28 Le Bar'ouff
29 Le Chouff'Bar
30 Margen's
31 TRAM

ENTERTAINMENT
32 Caveau de la Huchette
33 Le Champo
34 Le Grand Action
35 L'Epée de Bois
36 Studio Galande

SHOPPING
37 Abbey Bookshop
38 Shakespeare & Company

Inside the Panthéon, the Star of the Latin Quarter
Where France's Greatest Thinkers Rest

Until the Eiffel Tower was finished in 1889, the Panthéon was the highest building in Paris. The imposing neoclassical building is still a fixture on the Paris skyline and boasts some of the best views of the city. Its huge dome is accessible via 203 steps (open to visitors between April and October), and its pediment portrays the central figures of the Nation and Liberty (statespeople and scholars to the left, soldiers to the right).

An architectural masterpiece, the Panthéon was commissioned by King Louis XV around 1750 as an abbey dedicated to Ste Geneviève, Paris' patron saint, in gratitude for his recovery from illness. It wasn't until 1790, a year after the French Revolution, that it opened, when it played a secular role as the temple of the nation and mausoleum for the remains of key figures. It did, however, revert back to religious purposes several times.

It is the final resting place for some of France's greatest intellectuals, including two-time Nobel Prize–winner Marie Curie, who was the first woman to be interred based on achievement – she was exhumed and reburied here. The interior is decorated with mosaics, intricate frescoes and grand paintings depicting scenes in French history. In 2018 Auschwitz survivor, feminist icon and human-rights activist Simone Veil became the fifth woman to be interred at the Panthéon. Note that since July 2023 all visitors must have a valid ticket to enter. Demand is high, so book online as far in advance as possible.

FOUCAULT'S PENDULUM

Taking pride of place at the very heart of the Panthéon is Foucault's pendulum, named after French physicist Léon Foucault. In 1851 he demonstrated the rotation of the Earth using laboratory apparatus rather than astronomical observations for the first time, by suspending the revolutionary device from the Panthéon's ceiling. The original pendulum is now housed at the Musée des Arts et Métiers (p145), while a working copy has been displayed at the Panthéon since 1995.

CELLO7/SHUTTERSTOCK ©

Foucault's Pendulum's

Odéon cinema

Odéon
Where French Film and History Converge

Odéon flanks St-Germain-des-Prés and the Jardin du Luxembourg, and is named after the Greco-Roman Théâtre de l'Odéon located near the metro station on picturesque **place Henri Mondor**, which has a statue of Danton, a French lawyer credited with being the leader of the French Revolution. Although you will find an Odéon cinema at the metro station, the area is actually known more for its arthouse cinemas, such as the art deco Le Champo and small, offbeat Christine21, owned by Golden Globe–winning actress Isabelle Huppert and her son.

Rue Mouffetard

St-Michel
Seine-side Landmarks

St-Michel is a bustling neighbourhood with medieval charms, such as rue de la Huchette, with the storied jazz club Caveau de la Huchette; rue la Bûcherie, where you'll find the popular bookshop Shakespeare & Company; and rue Galande, with atmospheric cafe Odette. Notable landmarks include the huge **Fontaine St-Michel**, with its red Languedoc marble colonnades that were finished in 1860. The fountain marks the start of the busy bd St-Michel, which ends at the Jardin du Luxembourg.

Rue Mouffetard
Literary Past and a Medieval Setting

Another remnant from the Middle Ages is the narrow rue Mouffetard, which measures only 7m wide in some places and slopes down from the Panthéon. Lined with fruit and vegetable stalls near metro Censier Daubenton, it abounds with touristy restaurants and studenty bars, but nevertheless retains a certain charm. The street culminates at **place de la Contrescarpe**. Called a 'cesspool' by Hemingway, it was once a hub for wild nights of drinking and dancing, popular with literary figures such as Simone de Beauvoir, François Rabelais and René Descartes, as well as Ernest Hemingway himself and James Joyce, who both lived nearby. Today, it's full of visitors who come to people-watch on cafe terraces while tucking into a croque monsieur.

France's Academic Centre

Prestigious Universities and Student Culture

The Latin Quarter has been the beating heart of the French academic system since the Middle Ages. The grand honeycomb-hued university buildings of the **Université Panthéon-Sorbonne**, including the jaw-droppingly beautiful Faculty of Medicine, glow gold in the summer sun and take you way back in time. Meanwhile, the poky bars and pubs lined up along rue Mouffetard and its tributaries recall hazy nights of debauchery incarnated by the likes of Hemingway, who lived in the area and had a penchant for partying into the early hours.

The crème de la crème of academia have flocked to the distinguished Sorbonne for centuries, making it one of the world's most famous institutions. Today La Sorbonne comprises 10 autonomous universities and some 55,000 students in total. It was created when the University of Paris was reorganised after the student protests of May 1968. The university buildings are open to the public only during the Journées Européennes du Patrimoine (European Heritage Days) every September, when it is possible to book to enter a selection of buildings across the city. However, the Sorbonne Chapel is open to visitors all year.

BRIAN KENNEY/SHUTTERSTOCK ©

Pain au chocolat, Pâtisserie Viennoise

PÂTISSERIE VIENNOISE

Make time for pastry at the age-old institution Pâtisserie Viennoise (open weekdays only). Next door to the Faculty of Medicine, it first opened in 1928 and is one of the rare places that have remained unchanged over time, with art nouveau lettering on the windows, bevelled mirrors, mosaic floors and a mahogany bar counter. It offers all the usual French staples, which are all handmade, as well as actual Viennese pastries like strudel and *Sachertorte*. There are also savoury options like croque monsieur and vegetable soups.

GRANDE MOSQUÉE DE PARIS

One of the biggest mosques in France and Paris' central mosque, the Grande Mosquée de Paris has a striking Moorish-style minaret, which peeps out from behind smooth white walls as you approach along the street. Visit the interior to see the intricate tile work and calligraphy. There is also a North African hammam (steam bathhouse), a pretty courtyard restaurant that serves delicious couscous, tagines and meat skewers, as well as a tearoom where staff serve sweet, fragrant mint tea and traditional cakes. There is also the possibility of smoking shisha in the front garden.

A Garden Oasis & its Museums

Dinosaurs and Botanical Gardens

A gorgeous botanical garden of 24 hectares with a double alley of plane trees, the **Jardin des Plantes** was originally created as a medicinal herb garden in 1626. Far from the hustle and bustle of the rest of the Latin Quarter, the garden is perfect for a picnic or a refreshing stroll. There's plenty to see here too, like the wealth of exotic plants, from cacti to a small rainforest, inside four elegant greenhouses (the Grandes Serres), each growing like mini-worlds of their own.

Set aside some time to delve into the exceptional **Muséum National d'Histoire Naturelle** located at the north end of the garden. A must-visit is the Galerie de Paléontologie et d'Anatomie Comparée on the eastern edge of the garden, which holds nearly a thousand animal skeletons, including dinosaurs – a diplodocus and allosaurus – which are the highlights. The 10-tonne, 6m-tall Dufort mammoth, discovered in 1869, was returned to the gallery in 2023 and is worth popping by to see. Other highlights are the terrestrial and aquatic vertebrates arranged in a large herd, as though in movement.

At the west end of the garden are the **Grande Galerie de l'Évolution**, with displays of more than 7000 preserved animals, and the **Galerie de Minéralogie et de Géologie**, with its vast collection of crystals and gems from all over the world. A festival of lights with colourful animal and plant sculptures is held every winter – it's great fun for the little ones (just wrap up warm!).

SPECH/SHUTTERSTOCK ©

Jardin des Plantes

Maubert
Architectural Feats Past and Present

Located in the heart of the Latin Quarter, Maubert has its own produce market and is close to attractions like the Cluny National Museum of the Middle Ages, a rich, enthralling exploration of the origins of the area, as well as 13th-century Collège des Bernardins, a historical Cistercian university college with a vaulted limestone gallery, now a cultural-events venue. Eastwards, on the river, are the Jean Nouvel–designed Institut du Monde Arabe and recently reopened La Tour d'Argent, an iconic restaurant said to be one of the oldest in the city.

Collège des Bernardins

TOP RIGHT: BEPSY/SHUTTERSTOCK ©. BOTTOM RIGHT: JEROME LABOUYRIE/SHUTTERSTOCK ©

Place Monge

Place Monge
Roman Vestiges and Lunch at a Mosque

In the south of the neighbourhood, place Monge is located between rue Mouffetard and the Jardin des Plantes and is scattered with wonderful greenhouses and must-see museums and galleries.

A short walk away is the Arènes de Lutèce, an amphitheatre built by the Romans, who would come here to watch gladiator fights. Today it is a quiet space where writers showcase their works during the annual literary festival that takes place across the neighbourhood each June. Also make sure you drop by the bathhouse and restaurant at the nearby Grande Mosquée de Paris.

Jussieu
Sorbonne Strolls and a Sculpture Park

Jussieu metro station is the closest station to the **main Sorbonne campus**, which has a mineral collection open to visitors on weekday afternoons (plus Saturdays in winter). Wander along rue Cuvier between the campus and the Jardin des Plantes and you'll reach the **Musée de la Sculpture en Plein Air**. This outdoor sculpture museum in the Tino Rossi garden was named after a well-liked Corsican singer and is scattered with whimsical sculptures by artists such as César and Constantin Brâncuși. Locals also gather here in the evenings to swing and tango to their hearts' content.

Start at **1 place St-Michel** and the magnificent **2 Fontaine St-Michel**, then walk along the River Seine for views across the water to the Cathédrale Notre Dame de Paris, stopping at the **3 bouquinistes** (booksellers) along the way. Take **4 rue de la Huchette**, passing the storied jazz club **5 Caveau de la Huchette,** and stop at the bookshop **6 Shakespeare & Company**, its shelves lined with English-language books. Head westward on **7 rue St-Julien-le-Pauvre**, a charming street with medieval buildings, to the **8 Abbey Bookshop**, before heading in the direction of the Jardin du Luxembourg to browse at the bookshop **9 Red Wheelbarrow**. Walk east to the **10 Université Panthéon-Sorbonne**, a renowned centre of intellectual pursuit, which nurtured the minds of numerous literary luminaries, including Sim-

one de Beauvoir and André Gide. Continue on to see the glorious neoclassical **11 Panthéon**. This monumental mausoleum is a symbol of intellectual achievement, where the remains of some of France's greatest thinkers have been laid to rest, including those of literary figures like Voltaire, Victor Hugo and Émile Zola. Stop for coffee at **12 TRAM** before walking to **13 71 rue du Cardinal Lemoine**, where James Joyce once lived, then on to Ernest Hemingway's former apartment at **14 74 rue du Cardinal Lemoine**. Continue to **15 place de la Contrescarpe**, a square where parties took place at clubs and cafes like the former Café des Amateurs at numbers 2–4. Pass via **16 6 rue du Pot au Fer**, where George Orwell once took up bed and board. Then finish on **17 rue Mouffetard**, an atmospheric medieval street known for its lively market.

Beautiful Bookshops
A Book-Lover's Paradise

Paris' beauty has fuelled countless French authors and expat writers who have lived and worked here over the centuries. The city's literary heritage is palpable at bookshops like the whimsical Shakespeare and Company, the Abbey Bookshop and the more recent TRAM, which also has a cafe, as well as at the famed *bouquinistes*, secondhand booksellers who line the Seine and sell vintage treasures including old books, magazines and posters.

Shakespeare and Company

Literary Events
A Book Festival in a Roman Arena

Rub shoulders with ghosts of the Parisian literary set by delving into the area on a guided tour. You can also meet contemporary writers at events like book signings, talks and readings that take place in the area's various bookshops. Check their websites for up-to-date information on future events. Also, every summer the **Festival Quartier du Livre** takes over the whole area with talks and book sales. It's held in the first week of June at venues across the Latin Quarter, including the Arènes de Lutèce and Collège des Bernardins.

Arènes de Lutèce

Writers' Abodes
From Joyce to Hemingway

Writers have long sought solace and inspiration in Paris, including James Joyce, Ernest Hemingway and George Orwell, who all lived here. James Joyce's flat, at 71 rue du Cardinal Lemoine (through a secret alley that opens onto a leafy courtyard), is where he finished his novel *Ulysses*. Hemingway lived close by, at number 74, for over a year with his first wife Hadley. Conveniently for the party-loving novelist, his apartment was right above one of the hottest dance halls in town, the Bal au Printemps. He was a loyal regular here at English writer and editor Ford Madox Ford's soirees. Nearby at 6 rue du Pot de Fer, George Orwell lived in a boarding house, noted as 'Hotel X' in his memoir *Down and Out in Paris and London*, before he moved to London.

ERICBERY/SHUTTERSTOCK ©

Le Procope

A WORKING CENTURY-OLD BOOKSHOP

Popular even before the days of Instagram, **Shakespeare and Company** has been a hub for expats since 1919. Originally it stood at 12 rue de l'Odéon as a bookshop and library, and regulars included Ernest Hemingway and F Scott Fitzgerald. When WWII broke out it was forced to close. In 1951 new owner George Whitman reopened the English-language bookshop in its current location at 37 rue de la Bûcherie, in a building that served as a monastery. More than 70 years later it's still a must-visit spot for its bewitching atmosphere and selection of works.

Historical Restaurants

MAP P206

Time Travelling with Each Bite

Among the city's historic treasures old and new, three renowned restaurants have stood the test of time in the Latin Quarter: Le Procope, Polidor and La Tour d'Argent. More than places to dine, they are living pieces of Parisian history. Each venue has its own unique ambience and culinary traditions, and offers an unforgettable journey into the heart of French gastronomy. Immerse yourself in their timeless spirit and taste the flavours that have delighted generations of epicureans.

Established in 1686, **Le Procope** is one of Paris' oldest restaurants. Step inside and be immersed in a bygone era thanks to the wood-panelling decor, antique mirrors and heavy flower-patterned carpets. Don't miss Le Procope's specialities, such as coq au vin and snails.

Make time for lunch at **Polidor**, which opened in 1845 and has kept its original *crèmerie* (creamery) façade. An unassuming bistro, it retains its authentic character, featuring rustic wooden tables and vintage decor, and has attracted writers and artists for over a century. It's renowned for its hearty, home-style cooking – try the bœuf bourguignon or blanquette de veau façade.

 ENGLISH-LANGUAGE BOOKSHOPS IN THE LATIN QUARTER

Abbey Bookshop
A store with books stacked up all the way to the ceiling, with regular author readings.

Red Wheelbarrow
Across the road from the northeast entrance to the Jardin du Luxembourg, it stocks plenty of new releases.

San Francisco Book Company
Marvellous store that buys and sells secondhand books, many of which are recent works.

Perched on the banks of the Seine, overlooking Cathédrale Notre Dame, **La Tour d'Argent** is a legendary restaurant that has delighted discerning palates since 1582. Savour specialities like the renowned pressed duck. Make sure to ask for a tour of the wine cellar. Housing over 450,000 bottles, it has remained intact for decades thanks to the owner's grandfather burying it during WWII to hide it from the Nazi invasion. The panoramic views of the city from the dining room add an extra touch of enchantment to the experience.

Arty Odéon

MAP P206

Cinemas and Paris' Oldest Bas-Relief

Named after the neoclassical Roman-inspired Théâtre de l'Odéon (inaugurated in 1782), one of the most famous in the city for its classic and contemporary plays, the Odéon area is at the crossroads of St-Germain-des-Prés and St-Michel. The metro is marked by an Odéon cinema and there is a clutch of arthouse cinemas scattered across the Latin Quarter that are popular with figures in the film industry. The art deco **Le Champo** opened in 1928 and is where director François Truffaut liked to go to see other directors' film retrospectives. Other notable independent cinemas include **Christine21** and **Cinéma St-André des Arts**, on the street of the same name. **Studio Galande** is another cinema to have on your list, especially if you want to see *The Rocky Horror Picture Show*, which they've shown every Friday and Saturday evening for the last four decades.

While you're here, pay attention to the bas-relief above the door of St-Julien-le-Pauvre (St Julian the Poor) in a rowing boat. It's a medieval sculpture from the 14th century, cited as being the oldest in Paris. Nearby, pass by the grand Faculty of Medicine and stop for a pastry at the Pâtisserie Viennoise, which is close to a century old. Then get a glimpse of some of the city's most fashionable art set at **Gallery Mennour**, which represents big-name artists including Daniel Buren and Lee Ufan across its four Paris locations.

St-Michel: Gateway to the Latin Quarter

MAP P206

Roman History and Notre Dame Views

The St-Michel area has a rich history. It is connected to the Île de la Cité, the island on the Seine where the Cathédrale Notre Dame de Paris stands, just across the water. It was once a Roman settlement named Lutetia, and the Romans built

THE BOUQUINISTES, THEN & NOW

Lining the top of the riverbanks at quai de la Tournelle, Pont Marie and quai du Louvre, you'll spot faded boxes that open to reveal secondhand bookstalls (*bouquinistes*) selling out-of-print books, rare magazines, postcards and old posters, all waiting to be rediscovered. In the 16th century, itinerant peddlers sold their wares on Parisian bridges. Sometimes their subversive (eg Protestant) materials would get them into trouble with the authorities. By 1859 the city had wised up: official licences were issued and eventually the permanent boxes were installed.

WHERE TO EAT CLOSE TO ODÉON

Colvert	L'Avant Comptoir de la Terre	Ze Kitchen Gallerie
Brilliant bistro in charming, updated old-world surroundings, Colvert serves heartwarming creative cuisine. €€	A tapas menu of French classics hangs from the ceiling and there's a buzzy ambience. €€	Top-notch contemporary French food from Michelin-star chef William Ledeuil. €€

Rue Mouffetard

BEST LATIN QUARTER STAYS

Hôtel des Grandes Écoles
Hidden in a closed-off alleyway next to the former abode of James Joyce, this charming three-star hotel has a gorgeous courtyard with tables. €€

Le 66
A handful of rooms with wooden beams and original fireplaces, and a conservatory that makes it feel like you're sojourning in the French countryside. €€

Hôtel Dame des Arts
This slick newcomer is infused with urban chic. The rooftop terrace with incredible views of the Eiffel Tower is worth crossing town for. €€

a bridge to connect the island to the left bank of the River Seine, which is near present-day St-Michel.

The area got its name after a 13th-century chapel nearby, inspired by the 11th-century Benedictine St-Michel Abbey in Normandy's picturesque town of Mont St-Michel. In the Middle Ages, as the prestigious Sorbonne University expanded, the area around what is now St-Michel became the educational centre of Paris. Students, scholars and teachers gathered here, creating a vibrant hub for intellectuals. Today, sadly, very little remains of the area as it once was, with many spots being replaced by tourist eateries and bars along its large boulevard, which crosses the Latin Quarter from the iconic Fontaine St-Michel to the Jardin du Luxembourg. The fountain, a local landmark, was built in the 19th century and depicts the archangel Michael defeating a dragon. To the east, the **quai de Montebello** is an offbeat picnic spot with unbeatable views of Notre Dame.

A Medieval Road in the Latin Quarter
Rue Mouffetard's Quirks and Bars

The cobbled rue Mouffetard acquired its name in the 18th century, when the now underground River Bièvre, Paris' second river, became the communal waste disposal for local tanners

🍴 WHERE TO EAT CLOSE TO ODÉON

Treize au Jardin
A pretty cafe with outdoor seating looking over the Jardin du Luxembourg serving homemade organic food. €€

Allard
Part of the Alain Ducasse empire, this characterful bistro specialises in excellent traditional French cuisine. €€€

La Pérouse
Dating to Louis XIV's reign, this legendary spot on the literary scene has private dining rooms. €€€

and wood pulpers. The odours gave rise to the name *Mouffette* ('skunk'), which evolved into Mouffetard. The street is now filled with market stalls (except on Mondays), cheap eating spots and lively bars.

The road begins in the south of the Latin Quarter. Close to the metro Censier Daubenton end is a small produce market. Few authentic establishments have survived to this day, but they include the **Église St-Médard**, which dates back to the 16th century and features intricate stained-glass windows. It is the only church in the area to have survived the French Revolution and Second Empire town planning.

Built in the 1970s, the pocket-sized arthouse cinema **L'Epée de Bois** ('the wooden sword') has two screens and shows recent (non-dubbed) French and other European flicks, and stands on the spot of a centuries-old theatre of the same name. The cinema **Le Grand Action**, 10 minutes away, shows cult international films too.

The street runs all the way to the storied place de la Contrescarpe, where writers like Hemingway, Joyce and de Beauvoir would go to mingle into the early hours. Otherwise, it's lined with studenty bars and pubs such as **Margen's**, and **Le Chouff'Bar**, **Le Bar'ouff** and **Brewberry** on nearby rue du Pot au Fer. Also nearby is the bowling alley **Bowling Mouffetard**, with luminous lighting and themed nights, which makes for a fun outing.

At the markets around rues Mouffetard, Maubert and Monge you can pick up a few nibbles for a picnic in the warmer months or to take home as souvenirs or gifts for friends and family. The sellers in these markets offer local artisanal products such as hams and cheeses as well as organic fruit and vegetables. The markets really come alive in the mornings on weekends, when local shoppers nip down to stock up on groceries and stop for a coffee or a pre-lunch apéritif.

Architecture Worship
Vestiges of the Middle Ages

The Latin Quarter's impressive Roman and medieval roots can be seen throughout the neighbourhood, so if you have time for one thing while here, it has to be strolling around the area to catch glimpses of its incredible architectural heritage. Top picks include the **Arènes de Lutèce**, a 2nd-century Roman amphitheatre that seated 10,000 people for gladiator fights. Found by accident in 1869 when rue Monge was under construction, it's now used by locals for playing football and boules.

AN INSIDER'S LATIN-QUARTER SPOTS

Neil Kreeger, food guide, takes visitors into the heart of the area, past and present.
neil.kreeger@gmail.com

Jinji
I love this store's curation of lesser-known international brands, and that here, trends and seasons don't matter – just quality and style.

Square René Viviani
This beautiful green space, boasting views of Notre Dame, is home to Paris' oldest tree, planted at the turn of the 17th century. It's one of my favourite places to sit and contemplate.

Fromagerie Androuët
Launched in 1909, Androuët is one of the stars of the Parisian cheese scene. It is my go-to *fromagerie* for discovering cheeses from across the country.

Maison d'Isabelle
Winner of a butter-croissant competition in 2018, Isabelle's *viennoiseries* are still the best. That buttery aroma gets me every time!

COFFEE-SHOP PIT STOPS FROM THE PANTHÉON TO NOTRE DAME

TRAM
Coffee lovers will want to stick around for drinks or lunch while perusing the handpicked selection of books. €€

Nuage
Lures digital nomads with its cosy spaces in an old church (where Cyrano de Bergerac apparently studied). €€

Odette
An upstairs tearoom dishing out cream-filled choux (puff pastries) inside a charming 17th-century abode. €€

Don't miss the magnificent **Église St-Étienne du Mont**, built between 1492 and 1655, whose highly ornate façade will make you gasp in amazement. The tomb of Ste Geneviève lies in a chapel in the nave's southeastern corner. The patron saint of Paris, she was born at Nanterre in 422 and is said to have turned away Attila the Hun from Paris in 451. A highly decorated reliquary near her tomb contains all that is left of her earthly remains: a finger bone. Fans of the Woody Allen film *Midnight in Paris* will recognise the stone steps on the northwestern corner as the place where Owen Wilson's character is collected by a vintage car and transported back to the 1920s.

Adjacent to the church is the star attraction, the Panthéon, a regal Roman-inspired resting place for some of the country's greatest minds. You'll also notice the remains of the **Philippe II Augustus wall**, the oldest city wall in Paris. Today, visible parts pass through buildings and car parks, including on rue Clovis, where the rubble and brick core are exposed.

Other architectural marvels include the **Collège des Bernardins**. Dating back to 1248, this former Cistercian college originally served as the living quarters and place of study for novice monks. It's now an art gallery and Christian culture centre, with events ranging from lectures to film screenings and music performances. There's a stunning stone vaulted ceiling in the main hall. Closer to St-Michel is **Église St-Séverin**, a Gothic church containing one of the oldest bells in Paris, cast in 1412. Also of note are the seven stained-glass windows depicting the seven sacraments, designed by Jean René Bazaine in 1970. One of the oldest churches in Paris is **St-Julien-le-Pauvre**, where piano recitals (of Chopin, Liszt and others) are staged at least two evenings a week. You'll need a ticket to attend.

BEST QUICK BITES IN THE LATIN QUARTER

The area has quite a few restaurants, but for something quick and cheap in between sightseeing, try these.

Petits Plats de Marc
Easy plates of quiches and salads, made with seasonal ingredients. There are also vegetarian and vegan options. €

Pot O'Lait
Try the tasty *galettes* (savoury buckwheat crêpes), generously filled with ingredients like goat's cheese and smoked salmon. €

Croq'Fac
S*andwicherie* with varied bread options, ranging from ciabattas to baguettes, filled with virtually any combination of items that take your fancy. €

MORE COFFEE SHOPS IN THE LATIN QUARTER

Dose	Tea Caddy	Compagnon 2
Get your caffeine hit with artisan-roasted craft coffee and follow with a lunch of homemade quiche. €€	Founded by a certain Miss Klinklin in 1928, it's a fine spot for a casual English afternoon tea. €€	Replacing the popular Circus Bakery is the stylish Café Compagnon's second location. €€

If you don't have time to visit many monuments, this tour will give you a glimpse of the Latin Quarter's incredible history and essential stops in half a day.

Start at **1 St-Michel**, braving the crowds for a glimpse of Cathédrale Notre Dame across the River Seine. Peek at the medieval-style street **2 rue Galande** around the corner, and move on to the château-like **3 Cluny Musée National du Moyen Âge**, with its Roman thermal bath remains. As you edge closer to the grandiose Faculty of Medicine, you'll pass the art deco **4 Le Champo**, one of a handful of arthouse cinemas in the area. Stop for a pastry at the unchanged near-century-old **5 Pâtisserie Viennoise** before setting off again. Continue to the **6 Collège des Bernardins**, a former 13th-century Cistercian college, and then to the Jean Nouvel–designed

7 Institut du Monde Arabe, a centre for learning about the Arab world, near the Seine. Take a stroll around the 2nd-century **8 Arènes de Lutèce**, a Roman-era amphitheatre, then head west on rue Clovis to see a section of the **9 wall of Philippe II Augustus**, the oldest city wall in Paris. Continue up the slight hill to see the **10 Église St-Étienne du Mont** and its marvellous façade, adjacent to the **11 Panthéon**, the star of the Latin Quarter, where the great thinkers of France rest. Across the square is the **12 Panthéon-Sorbonne University**; this is one of the most famous buildings of the Sorbonne network. Walk southwards, past place de la Contrescarpe, and continue along **13 rue Mouffetard** to see some of its medieval remnants. Finish close to the Jardin des Plantes at the **14 Grande Mosquée de Paris** for a steam bath and a bite to eat.

DANCING ON THE SEINE

Grab a partner and dance after dark to the tango, foxtrot or some of the best toe-tapping rock and roll while watching the moonlight shimmer on the River Seine. Most evenings in the small amphitheatre at the water's edge, close to the **Jardin Tino Rossi** and outdoor sculpture gardens, locals gather to dance from around 7pm until midnight. It's held come rain or shine, although more people come out in the warmer months.

TANYA USTENKO/SHUTTERSTOCK ©

Cluny Musée National du Moyen Âge

Iconic Museums
Roman Remains and an Arab Institute

As well as monuments and restaurants, the Latin Quarter also has its fair share of museums. Travel back in time to medieval France (814–1450 CE) at the **Cluny Musée National du Moyen Âge**, which showcases sublime treasures, from medieval statuary, stained glass and objets d'art to its celebrated series of tapestries, such as the famed *Lady and the Unicorn* (1500). Don't miss the adjoining 1st-/2nd-century Gallo-Roman Thermes de Cluny (baths), on which the museum is built. In the Roman era, they spanned an area of roughly 6000 sq metres and were among the largest ancient remains in northern Europe, notably thanks to the preservation of a vast vaulted room, the *frigidarium*. Its vaults rise to over 14m high and they are among the best preserved in northern France. Designed by architect Bernard Desmoulin, the contemporary entrance building houses the ticket office, bookshop, souvenir boutique and cloakroom. Following renovations, it now has enhanced explanatory panels and interactive displays. It is also possible to access the 1st-floor late-Gothic chapel, La Chapelle de l'Hôtel de Cluny, with rich carvings of Christ on the cross, 13 angels and floral and foliage ornaments. Make time to visit the beautiful gardens too.

JAZZ CLUBS IN THE LATIN QUARTER

Le Petit Journal St-Michel
Open since 1971, this classic restaurant hosts live jazz bands outside and in the basement.

Caveau de la Huchette
A medieval cellar used as a courtroom and torture chamber during the Revolution, it's hosted many jazz greats.

Papa's Jazz Club
In St-Germain-des-Prés, this moodily lit institution hosts top jazz artists while dinner of French fare is served.

Another museum you should set some time aside for is the **Institut du Monde Arabe (IMA)**, perched on the banks of the River Seine inside a sleek contraption of a building by star architect Jean Nouvel. It features a metallic screen of moving geometric motifs designed to look like a *mashrabiya*, a window of ornate latticework often found in Islamic architecture, where the motifs are actually 240 light-sensitive shutters that automatically open and close to control the amount of light and heat in the building. The IMA was founded by France and 18 Arab countries with the aim of creating a research hub about the Arab world. It was established due to the perceived lack of representation for the Arab world in France, and it seeks to provide a secular location for the promotion of Arab civilisation, art, knowledge and aesthetics. The IMA is comprised of a museum, library, auditorium, meeting rooms and a rooftop restaurant, Dar Mima, which whisks up food with influences from North African countries, such as fish tagine and couscous. The real selling point here is the view across the Paris rooftops.

Artistic Treasures

Cultural Institutes and Contemporary Go-Tos

Despite the area being one of the oldest in Paris, the Latin Quarter brims with arty findings old and new. For travellers looking to put a contemporary spin on their visit to the neighbourhood, drop in at charismatic **Kamel Mennour's gallery spaces**, three of which are in the area, with an off-shoot in the 8th *arrondissement*. Mennour founded his first gallery in 1999, his hard graft propelling him onto the international art circuit. Starting out by selling artworks door-to-door, today he represents 40 of the art world's biggest names, from Anish Kapoor to Alberto Giacometti.

With so many students around, it's only natural that there should be more of a grassroots art scene too. Hybrid arts hub **Césure** has recently opened its doors inside an old Sorbonne campus building, where old dorms and common rooms have been turned into exhibition spaces, artist studios and residencies. Led by several associations and collectives, the takeover will initially last two years, during which time various events will be held, from plays to parties (check the Césure website to see what's on).

Add the **Institut Finlandais** to your list too: it's an independent and multidisciplinary cultural space with a pared-back cafe and various events taking place year-round. The **Centre Culturel Irlandais** is also worth checking out for its well-curated exhibitions of Irish visual artists from all

LATIN QUARTER PUB CULTURE

Being a student hub, the Latin Quarter has always been a hub for late-night antics.

Cave la Bourgogne
On pretty square St-Médard, it's perfect for soaking up the local vibes.

Le Violon Dingue
'The Crazy Violin' has sports showing on big screens upstairs and quizzes downstairs.

Le Piano Vache
A 1970s rock den with live music on the weekends.

Bombardier
An old English pub with the best view of the Panthéon.

Pub St-Hilaire
Usually packed out with students who come for a pool game and the hearty food.

Le Verre à Pied
A classic old-world bar-tobacconist that's pretty much unchanged since the 1800s.

Le Chouff'Bar
A relaxed tavern serving Belgian beers and shots of all kinds.

Brewberry
More modern bar, with over 20 craft beers.

 WHERE TO EAT AROUND THE PANTHÉON

Bar à Iode	Le Coupe-Chou	Baieta
A cosy little spot for reasonably priced oysters – there are prawns and smoked salmon too. €€	A centuries-old institution with an open fireplace, serving duck *magret* and other French classics. €€	Where culinary sensation Julia Sedefdjian whisks up Niçoise creations like her take on bouillabaisse. €€

DON'T-MISS RESTAURANTS

AT
Switch things up from French food with Michelin-starred chef Atsushi Tanaka's contemporary inspired dishes. €€€

Café de la Nouvelle Mairie
Serving traditional bistro food done well, around the corner from the Panthéon on a fountained square. €€

Les Papilles
A pocket-size bistro, wine bar and *épicerie* (specialist grocer) with excellent market-driven fare and natural wine. €€

Galerie de Paléontologie et d'Anatomie Comparée

over the world. There are also artist residencies and a physical and digital library. For cutting-edge design, the Parisian pioneer is **Galerie Kreo**. It's the go-to for clued-up designers and collectors, located on the cusp of the Latin Quarter and St-Germain-des-Prés, where most galleries are clustered.

The Latin Quarter with Kids

Dinosaurs, Rainforest and an Amphitheatre

If you've got kids, summer in Paris is always easier to explore as there are plenty of parks and gardens for them to run around in. You can picnic in the **Jardin du Luxembourg** in the west end of the Latin Quarter, or visit the **Arènes de Lutèce**, a 2nd-century Roman amphitheatre with plenty of space to play football, boules and other sports. There is also a small playground in the adjoining **square Capitan** for a quick go on a slide.

 WHERE TO SHOP IN THE LATIN QUARTER

CityPharma
Beauty products from French and international brands and over-the-counter supplements at discounted prices.

Parfums de Nicolaï
An under-the-radar perfume brand with fresh fragrances, from invigorating verbena to sultry musk.

Album BD
Lose yourself in the world of comic books, with artwork and figurines as well.

The Jardin des Plantes is packed with museums that will fascinate both little and big kids, such as La Ménagerie, a small zoo with various animal species from orangutans to pythons and pink flamingos. There's also a corner with tons of reptiles and amphibians in aquariums. The star attraction is the **Muséum National d'Histoire Naturelle**, with its world-class **Galerie de Paléontologie et d'Anatomie Comparée**, which has fossils and dinosaur skeletons that kids will love. More recently, the impressive, 6m-tall Dufort mammoth has been returned to the site. And don't miss the **Grande Galerie de l'Évolution**, with thousands of preserved animal specimens displayed in a vast metal and glass 19th-century gallery. The **Galerie de Minéralogie et de Géologie** is also worth checking out, especially as a new meteorite has just landed for all to see. Otherwise, there's plenty to see in the gardens too, such as the labyrinths to get lost in and wonderful greenhouses hiding quiet little worlds of rainforest that are scattered with exotic trees and flowers.

GREEN SPACES TO CATCH YOUR BREATH

Jardin du Luxembourg
The Latin Quarter can be quite overwhelming due to the amount of visitors, so seek some respite at this gorgeous garden, with picnic spots and iconic metal green garden chairs by a fountain.

Jardin des Plantes
Scattered with museums, it's also got lawns and flowers as well as beautiful greenhouses in which you can escape from it all.

Cluny Musée National du Moyen Âge
The recently restored gardens here have a particular calm about them and are a good reward after a visit to the excellent museum that shines a light on the area's history.

Muséum National
d'Histoire Naturelle

WHERE TO SHOP IN THE LATIN QUARTER

CrocoDisc
Selling and buying records since the late 1970s, CrocoDisc specialises in all sorts of genres (except classical).

Brûlerie des Gobelins
Coffee roasters since 1957, this is a chic spot stuffed with a variety of coffees to buy.

Shakespeare & Company
If you're not sure what souvenirs to buy, a tote bag and a good read are always fine ideas.

TOP TIP

Be prepared to walk, as the sprawling 6th and 7th *arrondissements* are not well connected to each other by public transport. Comfortable walking shoes are a must to deal with the old cobbledstone streets. Don't worry – even the most chic of Parisians wear sneakers these days!

IMAGINEERING/SHUTTERSTOCK ©

Above: Musée Rodin (p245); Right: Le Bon Marché (p233)

DON'T MISS

MUSÉE D'ORSAY
See Paris' second-most-visited museum, home to one of the finest collections of impressionist and postimpressionist works.
p228

LE BON MARCHÉ
Shop at the world's first department store, a temple of French luxury. **p233**

CAFÉ DE FLORE
Sip a drink in the birthplace of existentialism, the perfect cafe for people-watching. **p235**

St-Germain & Les Invalides

IN THE FOOTSTEPS OF CREATIVE GIANTS

The ever-chic neighbourhoods of St-Germain and Les Invalides, in the Left Bank's 6th and 7th *arrondissements*, have long been the storied stomping grounds of modern history's greatest thinkers.

In the Middle Ages, the Left Bank was considered the countryside of Paris, dominated by open fields, known in French as *près* – hence the name St-Germain-des-Près. But the development of the Abbey de St-Germain in the 6th century (where the Église St-Germain-des-Prés is now located) quickly turned the place into a spiritual and intellectual hot spot.

The area really came into its own at the turn of the 20th century: its lively cafe scene attracted creative people from across the globe with its promises of rich intellectual banter over endless carafes of cheap table wine. Writers such as Ernest Hemingway, George Orwell and James Joyce wrote their chefs-d'oeuvre at the tables of Les Deux Magots, while philosophers like Jean-Paul Sartre and Simone de Beauvoir were busy pondering existentialism across the road at the Café de Flore. Also adding to the creative mix was L'École des Beaux-Arts, where some of the past century's greatest artists, such as Pierre Bonnard and Edgar Degas, came to hone their craft.

Although today the neighbourhoods have largely been gentrified – it's now home to some of the city's most pricey and sought-after real estate – reverberations of its colourful past still echo proudly through its immaculately preserved cobbledstone streets.

As you wander about, be sure to keep an eye out for plaques signposting the former abodes of creative titans. You'll quickly realise that almost every great thinker of the past 200 years had once called this area home.

FRANCK LEGROS/SHUTTERSTOCK ©

MAISON GAINSBOURG
Take a self-guided tour of French musician Serge Gainsbourg's personal abode. **p237**

ÉGLISE ST-SULPICE
Step inside the second-largest church in Paris, home to spectacular works by Delacroix and Jean-Baptiste Pigalle. **p240**

MUSÉE RODIN
Visit the museum and sculpture garden dedicated to sculptor Auguste Rodin, known for works like *The Thinker.* **p245**

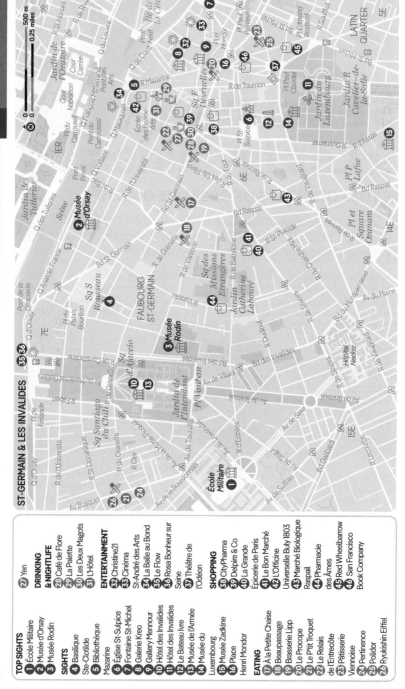

ST-GERMAIN & LES INVALIDES

0   500 m
0   0.25 miles

TOP SIGHTS
1 École Militaire
2 Musée d'Orsay
3 Musée Rodin

SIGHTS
4 Basilique
  Ste-Clotilde
5 Bibliothèque
  Mazarine
6 Église St-Sulpice
7 Fontaine St-Michel
8 Galerie Kreo
9 Gallery Mennour
10 Hôtel des Invalides
11 Le Bateau Ivre
12 Musée de l'Armée
13 Musée des Invalides
14 Musée du
  Luxembourg
15 Musée Zadkine
16 Place
  Henri Mondor

EATING
17 À la Petite Chaise
18 Beaupassage
19 Brasserie Lipp
20 Le Procope
21 Le P'tit Troquet
22 Le Relais
  de l'Entrecôte
23 Pâtisserie
  Viennoise
24 Pertinence
25 Polidor
26 Ryukishin Eiffel

27 Yen

**DRINKING
& NIGHTLIFE**
28 Café de Flore
29 La Palette
30 Les Deux Magots
31 L'Hôtel

ENTERTAINMENT
32 Christine21
33 Cinéma
  St-André des Arts
34 La Balle au Bond
35 Le Flow
36 Rosa Bonheur sur
  Seine
37 Théâtre de
  l'Odéon

SHOPPING
38 CityPharma
39 Delpire & Co
40 La Grande
  Épicerie de Paris
41 Le Bon Marché
42 L'Officine
  Universelle Buly 1803
43 Marché Biologique
  Raspail
44 Pharmacie
  des Âmes
45 Red Wheelbarrow
46 San Francisco
  Book Company

CityPharma

A Pharmaceutical Pilgrimage for Beauty Addicts

In the heart of St-Germain is the city's most famous pharmacy, CityPharma: a place of pilgrimage for both local and international beauty lovers looking to stock up on French beauty products. Sprawled over two floors and across two separate buildings, the pharmacy offers the lowest prices in Paris on all pharmaceutical products. Stock up on the usual cult favourites (Crème Embryolisse moisturiser, Klorane shampoos) and don't hesitate to ask for help navigating the labyrinth of products – the staff are incredibly knowledgeable.

Steak-frites

Le Relais de l'Entrecôte

The Best Steak-Frites in Paris

Le Relais de l'Entrecôte is the most famous place in the capital for *steak-frites* – and its rue St-Benoit restaurant is its oldest location. There's only one thing on the menu here – you guessed it – steak and fries, served with the institution's top-secret special pepper sauce. All you have to do is pick the *cuisson* (how you'd like your steak done) and a wine to wash it down with. As the restaurant doesn't take reservations the queues can be long, so aim to get here for opening at 6.30pm or for a late dinner at around 9pm.

Le Bateau Ivre, Rue Férou

Rimbaud's 'The Drunken Boat'

A Mural of the Poet's Famous Ballad

Wander down quaint rue Férou (where Hemingway once lived) in the 6th *arrondissement* and you'll notice a wordy mural that's unlike any of the other graffiti scrawled across the city's façades. Take a step back from the wall and you can parse together the lengths of French poet Arthur Rimbaud's masterpiece 'Le Bateau Ivre' (The Drunken Boat). Written when he was just a teenager, the symbolist ballad recounts a journey aboard a sinking ship at sea. The rue Férou mural was commissioned in 2012 by the French government, with support from a Dutch poetry society, as an homage to the poet. Local folklore has it that Rimbaud first recited it at a location nearby – hence the mural's peculiar setting.

TOP RIGHT: MS Y BAILEY/SHUTTERSTOCK ©. BOTTOM RIGHT: ERICBERY/SHUTTERSTOCK ©

LEFT: KIEVVICTOR/SHUTTERSTOCK ©, RIGHT: MERIXELL TORNE/SHUTTERSTOCK ©

Scan this QR code to book tickets in advance.

TOP SIGHT

Musée d'Orsay

The second-most-visited museum in France after the Louvre, the Musée d'Orsay is housed in a former railway station and contains one of the most important collections of impressionist and postimpressionist works in the world. With its sublime architecture and masterpieces from Monet and Cézanne, plan on spending at least half a day here.

DON'T MISS

Manet's *Le Déjeuner sur l'herbe*

Van Gogh's *Starry Night Over the Rhône*

Degas' *La Petite Danseuse de Quatorze Ans*

Monet's *Londres, le Parlement*

Renoir's *Bal du Moulin de la Galette*

Cézanne's *Apples and Oranges*

A Living History of Architecture

As you enter the Musée d'Orsay, take a pause to notice the layout of the ground floor, with sculptures in two straight rows, and small galleries annexed along the outer edges of the space. It was organised to mimic the layout of the original railway station within which it is housed. Given the sheer significance of the encasing building, it was decided from the outset that the Musée d'Orsay would elevate the history of architecture to the same revered rung as that of the history of art. Accordingly, galleries dedicated to the museum's impressive collection of architectural drawings by the likes of Gustave Eiffel and Viollet-le-Duc interject those allocated to fine art. At the end of the ground floor is a space dedicated to the history of Paris' urban development. Look below you and you'll notice an intricate scaled model of the city as it stood in 1914.

The Impressionists

Most people visit the Musée d'Orsay for its collection of impressionist works and rightly so: the 5th floor of the museum is largely consecrated to the movement. By tracing the galleries in a clockwise direction you'll get a fairly comprehensive overview of the development of the movement from impressionism to postimpressionism to neoimpressionism. Here is where the movement's masterpieces, such as Monet's *Londres, le Parlement,* Van Gogh's *Starry Night Over the Rhône* and Edgar Degas' sculpture *La Petite Danseuse de Quatorze Ans* are exhibited alongside other fabled modern works like Cézanne's *Nature morte* series.

Cinema as Art

Few people know that from its beginnings the Musée d'Orsay has devoted one of its sections to the history of cinema and cinematography, innovating an approach that considers film as art, and not simply as technique or entertainment. On the 5th floor, tucked away alongside the impressionist collection, is a gallery tracing the medium's history and technical developments, with projections of short clips from pivotal films in the medium's history. To complement this venture, the Musée d'Orsay often holds screenings in its auditorium of some of the most important works of cinema from the early 20th century. Check the official website for a schedule.

History Through a Contemporary Lens

Although the focus of the Musée d'Orsay is modern art from the period between 1848 and 1914, several times a year the museum invites the biggest names in today's contemporary art scene, such as Jean-Philippe Delhomme, Marlene Dumas and Peter Doig, to curate exhibitions featuring their own works interwoven with selections from the permanent collection. By placing contemporary art in direct dialogue with historical masterpieces, it urges us to consider the works with a fresh perspective while emphasising their enduring importance. On one Thursday evening per month, the museum also hosts 'Curious Thursdays', when young artists from other creative worlds (like dance and music) are invited to perform among the art. Check the website for schedule details.

Interior, Musée d'Orsay

THEMED TOURS

It's impossible to view the entire collection in one day – instead it's advisable to pick one or two of the themes mentioned as entry points. Alternatively, take one of the museum's themed guided tours. Held daily in English, French and Italian, the 1½-hour tours are centred around fun themes such as masterpieces, animals and parties.

TOP TIPS

● Book your ticket online in advance so that you can skip the snaking queues to enter.

● The best time to visit is when it opens at 9.30am or on Thursday evenings when the museum is open until 9.45pm.

● Rent an audioguide, which provides commentary from the museum's curators on over 300 works.

● Entry to the museum is free on the first Sunday of every month, but you'll have to reserve a time slot in advance via the museum's website.

● Break up your visit with a pause in the museum's gilded tearoom, which was formerly the railway station's dining room.

L'Officine Universelle Buly 1803

À la Petite Chaise

(Supposedly) The Oldest Restaurant in Paris

À la Petite Chaise claims to be the oldest restaurant in Paris (although it's a title challenged by neighbouring institution La Tour d'Argent). The restaurant was founded in 1680 by wine merchant Georges Rameau, who had the novel idea of serving food to accompany his wines for sale. Today, the menu at this charming institution remains rooted in the classics, such as onion soup and *tartare de boeuf*, yet it is always of exceptional quality. What's more, it's open seven days a week for both lunch and dinner.

L'Officine Universelle Buly 1803

A Contemporary Apothecary

L'Officine Universelle Buly 1803 is a contemporary revival of the fragrance and beauty empire founded by French *parfumier* Jean-Vincent Bully in 1803. The shop front at 6 rue Bonaparte pays perfect homage to the brand's 19th-century roots – everything down to the elegant packaging, the demurely dressed staff and the wood-panelled interiors conjure up images of magical apothecaries from a bygone era. Today Buly is known for its delicately perfumed body lotions and soaps as well as its spectacular array of artisanal combs and brushes. The leather-boxed lip balms, which can be monogrammed, make a great gift for those back home.

Musée du Luxembourg

Musée du Luxembourg

The Former Museum of Living Artists

Nestled within the Jardin du Luxembourg, the Musée du Luxembourg was opened in 1818 as the first French museum dedicated to living artists. After foreign works pillaged by Napoléon I were returned to their rightful owners in 1815, the museum was conceptualised as a space to stimulate local artistic production, proving to the rest of the world that France was capable of refilling the empty walls with talent from within. After artists died, their works were transferred to the Louvre. Although the museum only plays host to two exhibitions a year (often with an emphasis on 20th-century female artists), the high calibre of its shows and its stunning location within the garden's former orangery make it well worth a visit.

Basilique Ste-Clotilde
Neogothic Grandeur

Located on rue Las Cases in the 7th *arrondissement*, the Basilique Ste-Clotilde, constructed between 1846 and 1856, was the first Parisian church built in the neogothic style. While the western façade is arresting in its grandeur – the twin spires each reach a soaring height of 70m – don't forget to visit the apse: its supporting iron structure was designed by Paris' favourite engineer Gustave Eiffel. Less crowded than other Parisian churches, its quiet, light-dappled interiors provide a moment of respite from the surrounding cityscapes.

Basilique Ste-Clotilde

Bibliothèque Mazarine

Yen
A Celebrity-Favourite Japanese Restaurant

For some of the finest Japanese food in Paris, head to Yen on rue St-Benoit. This incredibly elegant eatery specialises in buckwheat noodles, produced in-house from 100% buckwheat flour (making it suitable for gluten-free diets), and sashimi made from market-fresh produce. To accompany its delicate offerings is one of the most extensive saké lists in the city. It's open Tuesday through Saturday for both lunch and dinner; be sure to book in advance. And keep your eyes peeled for celebrities when you're here – it's rumoured to be one of Charlotte Gainsbourg's favourite lunch spots.

Bibliothèque Mazarine
The Oldest Public Library In France

Located within the Institute of France (the national body conceived to protect French culture) is the oldest public library in the country: Bibliothèque Mazarine. Once the private reading room of Cardinal Mazarin, today it is both a public workspace and national archive, containing a stunning collection of rare and ancient manuscripts. The resplendent reading room is open to the public from 10am to 6pm, Monday through Friday, but you must register on-site for an access card (free for five days, €15 for an annual pass).

All visitors are required to wash their hands before entering the room in absolute silence. As you are not allowed to simply thumb through the treasured volumes, the library organises free (and wonderfully informative) daily guided tours in both French and English.

Marché Biologique Raspail

Paris' Largest Organic Food Market

Every Sunday between 7.30am and 2.30pm on the bd Raspail (between rue de Sèvres and rue de Rennes) is Marché Biologique Raspail, Paris' top organic food market. All the 50 or so stalls here must adhere to the national guidelines on organic produce. This, in turn, means that the prices are higher than at your usual neighbourhood market, but it's a great place for otherwise hard-to-find goods such as freshly baked gluten-free bread, vegan curries and superfood powders like spirulina and maca.

Marché Biologique Raspail

Théâtre de l'Odéon

France's Oldest Monumental Theatre

Just a stone's throw from the Jardin du Luxembourg is the Théâtre de l'Odéon. Opened in 1872, it was the first in the country to have benched seating for its ground-floor audience. Many a famed French playwright debuted works here and today the program remains rather classical. But you don't have to sit through a two-hour play in French to get a taste of the theatre's history: from the outside you can admire the building's imposing neoclassical façade, in the style of Ancient Greek theatres, and then peek inside at its gilded foyer.

Église
St-Germain-des-Prés

Église St-Germain-des-Prés

Home to the First Flying Buttresses in Paris

Before the Notre Dame de Paris was completed, the Église St-Germain-des-Prés, located at place St-Germain, was the central church of worship for Parisians. The church in its current form was built in the 11th century, yet it had been the site of a Benedictine abbey since 558. In the 8th century it was renamed in honour of St-Germain, a former bishop of the city. The church has since undergone many transformations, including the addition of the flying buttresses, but the bell tower on the western façade remains practically unchanged since 990. Don't forget to visit the adjoining Chapelle de St-Symphorien, left over from the original abbey, under which St-Germanus is believed to be buried.

TOP LEFT, ALLENG/SHUTTERSTOCK ©; BOTTOM LEFT, CORTYN/SHUTTERSTOCK ©

A One-Stop Shop for French Luxury
The World's First Department Store

At the intersection of the ever-chic rue du Bac and rue de Sevres stands **Le Bon Marché**, an opulent shopping temple whose elegant architecture matches the luxurious mix of both local and international fashion brands housed within. Founded in 1838 by brothers Paul and Justin Videau, it is where shopping was transformed into an *art de vivre*.

In 1852 Le Bon Marché was taken over by marketing maverick Aristide Boucicaut and his wife Marguerite, who drastically improved the customer experience as well as the working conditions of the employees. Over half of the store's workforce were women – unheard of at the time – and unmarried women were provided accommodation in dormitories located on what is now the top floor of the store.

The Boucicauts also introduced a fixed-price system for goods (haggling was still the way of the market at the time) and installed amenities such as a reading room where husbands could wait while their wives shopped.

Although the eye-watering price tags of the goods for sale are no longer exactly 'a good deal' (the store's name translated into English), to wander Le Bon Marché is to experience the world of historic French luxury – without having to spend a euro. Take the central escalators and gaze up at the magnificent steel-wrought glass ceiling; if it calls to mind the capital's most famous metal monolith, the Eiffel Tower, it's because the building was in fact designed by Gustave Eiffel, along with architect Louis-Charles Boileau. Don't forget to stop in at the bathrooms (complete with an old-school powder room) – the Boucicauts were the first to innovate in-store separate sex bathrooms.

If all the browsing has you peckish, pop next door (or across one of the connecting bridges) to **La Grande Épicerie de Paris**, Le Bon Marché's quality food and produce market. The store had long offered fashionable items like cocoa and coffee, but in 1988 the *épicerie* section was given its own building. Today, it offers not only the finest in local produce but also international products for the homesick tourist or expat. Its basement floor has one of the largest (and most expensive) wine selections in Paris, while the upper levels are home to a restaurant and a selection of homewares.

Le Bon Marché was the inspiration for the novel *Au Bonheur des Dames* (The Ladies' Paradise) by French literary giant Émile Zola. Published in 1883, the book closely chronicled the innovations of the department store – mail-order, home delivery, mass advertising – but also the real role it played in

THE SECRET GARDENS OF ST-GERMAIN & LES INVALIDES

Jardin Catherine-Labouré
Located just a stone's throw from Le Bon Marché, this little-known garden is on the grounds of a former 17th-century convent.

Square Roger-Stéphane
A tiny green oasis at the end of the pedestrian street rue Juliette Récamier, off rue de Sevrès.

Maison de l'Amerique Latine
Hidden within the Latin American cultural centre on bd St-Germain is a lush, grassy courtyard where you can kick back and relax with a beverage in hand.

WHERE TO BUY BOUTIQUE HOMEWARES IN ST-GERMAIN & LES INVALIDES –

Cire Trudon
Once the official candlemaker for the royal courts; the rue de Seine shop front was founded in 1643.

Marin Montagut
Beautiful hand-painted porcelain and other decorative objects created by the French illustrator Marin Montagut.

La Soufflerie
Handblown artisanal glassware: 100% of proceeds benefit the glassmakers to help keep the dying art alive.

JULIE MAYFENG/SHUTTERSTOCK ©

Les Deux Magots

THE OLDEST CAFE IN PARIS

Le Procope, founded in 1686, lays claim to the title of the oldest cafe in Paris (although it hasn't been in continuous operation). By the 18th century, it had become the hot spot of the intellectual elite, with the likes of Voltaire, Benjamin Franklin and Thomas Jefferson all dining here. Local legend has it that Denis Diderot and Jean le Rond d'Alembert began writing the French Encyclopaedia (*Encyclopédie*) at Le Procope over endless cups of black coffee. Today the establishment has been reimagined as an 18th-century-style restaurant, complete with artefacts from its previous lives (like Napoléon's hat), serving up traditional French fare such as escargot and *tête de veau* (calf's head).

destroying local boutique commerce, as all goods were now gathered under one roof.

But more pertinently for Zola, Le Bon Marché represented a step towards women's emancipation during the Industrial Revolution. By employing and housing women, the department store provided them with a sense of independence from their male counterparts and gave them the opportunity to work in public-facing 'city' roles outside the home or factories.

Where Gastronomy Meets Contemporary Art

A Secret Urban Passageway

In direct contrast to the historical Le Bon Marché – and located just nearby, with the main entrance on rue de Grenelle – is the **Beaupassage**, a verdant, contemporary passageway designed to provide epicurean relief from the hustle bustle of the surrounding neighbourhood.

The peaceful urban space reunites the superstars of the French gastronomical scene with a slight twist: each culinary expert had to open a venture that was unlike anything they'd ever done before. As a result, the 10,000-sq-metre space includes a cafe from master *patissière* Pierre Hermé, a *cave à vin* from chef Yannick Alléno and an *épicerie* with ready-to-eat meals from three-Michelin-starred chef Anne-Sophie Pic.

 WHERE TO STAY IN ST-GERMAIN & LES INVALIDES

Hôtel des Académies et des Arts
Boutique hotel with an art gallery in the building where Modigliani once lived. €€€

Hôtel La Belle Juliette
Quirky yet charming rooms and an indoor pool, located near Le Bon Marché. €€

La Villa Madame
Classic-style rooms with an idyllic courtyard in the heart of St-Germain. €€

From 7am until midnight, visitors are free to wander the open-air space, which also includes contemporary public art from the likes of Fabrice Hyber and Marc Vellay, but be sure to check the opening times of each individual boutique.

Literary Libations

Raising a Glass to Hemingway

According to the Parisian adage, '*La Rive Gauche, on va pour penser; la Rive Droite, on va pour depenser*', the Left Bank is where one goes to think, while the Right Bank is for spending money. And think (and drink) on the Left Bank they did – St-Germain is home to some of the most famous dining establishments beloved by the 20th century's greatest writers, artists and philosophers.

Les Deux Magots, located on place St-Germain-dès-Près, is considered by many to be the birthplace of surrealism, as during the 1930s the likes of André Breton, Man Ray and Max Ernst gathered here to plan out the movement's defining manifesto. Lost Generation writers James Joyce and Ernest Hemingway were also regular customers – it is believed that the latter penned his great novel *The Sun Also Rises* at one of the back tables.

Across the road, on the corner of bd St-Germain and rue St-Benoit, is rival literary haunt **Café de Flore**. Although creative people were known to flit between each cafe, Flore had one great advantage: a fireplace-heated upper floor where writers came to work during the frosty winter months. It was here that great existentialist philosophers like Simone de Beauvoir, Jean-Paul Sartre and Albert Camus would write their defining oeuvres.

Today, it comes down to personal preference as to whether to dine at Café de Flore or Les Deux Magots: the two offer similar menus and exceptional vantage points for people-watching. Head to either in the early morning to read the newspaper over a tartine and *chocolat chaud* (made from pure melted chocolate) as the locals do, or go in the early evening for an apéritif.

Down the road on rue de Seine is **La Palette**, a lesser-known but equally storied bar that was frequented by artists such as Picasso and Cézanne. Today, its creative vibe lives on as it's the local hangout spot for students from the nearby fine-arts school L'École des Beaux-Arts.

Although literary folklore would make it seem like artists subsisted entirely on coffee and dry sherry à la Ernest Hemingway, even the most starved of them had to eat at some point – which is why they'd head to **Brasserie Lipp**,

BEST SPECIALITY ALCOHOL STORES IN ST-GERMAIN & LES INVALIDES

Dilettantes Cave à Champagne
A female-run wine store specialising in small-producer champagnes.

La Maison du Whisky Odéon
A spectacular collection of both local and international spirits, with a focus on whiskies.

Augustin Marchand d'Vins
Speciality wine store with a large selection of biodynamic and minimal-intervention wines.

 ERNEST HEMINGWAY'S LOCAL DRINKING SPOTS

Café de la Mairie	La Closerie des Lilas	Le Select
An old-school cafe located on place St-Sulpice, where it's rumoured he began plotting *A Moveable Feast*.	Now a traditional restaurant, this is where the writer would regularly stop for a drink on his way home.	The original 1920s interiors make it feel like Hemingway could still be drinking here today.

SMALLER MUSEUMS IN ST-GERMAIN & LES INVALIDES

Musée National Eugène Delacroix
A museum dedicated to painter Eugène Delacroix, tucked away in the idyllic place Furstemberg.

Musée Maillol
This museum houses the monumental sculptures of artist Aristide Maillol.

La Monnaie
The former French Mint, La Monnaie plays host to exhibitions by contemporary artists.

JEANLUCICHARD/SHUTTERSTOCK ©

La Monnaie

conveniently located directly opposite Café de Flore. Lipp was the favourite of French poets Paul Verlaine and Guillaume Apollinaire and, still today, the interiors and service feel as though they are stuck in the 1920s. Be sure to reserve at least a day in advance as the restaurant is regularly full.

Finish off your literary tour with an after-dinner drink at **L'Hotel**, the hotel on rue des Beaux-Arts where Oscar Wilde died in 1900 of meningitis. Wilde had made what was then known as L'Hotel d'Alsace his home and famously declared in his final days 'My wallpaper and I are fighting a duel to the death. One of us has got to go.' Although the building – and its wallpaper – have since been given a luxurious renovation, the bar of the now five-star hotel remains open for guests wishing to pay homage to the illustrious writer.

St-Germain's Green Lung
Family Fun in Regal Gardens

Surrounding the majestic Palais du Luxembourg, the **Jardin du Luxembourg** was the former residence of Catherine Medici, and is beloved by children and adults alike. Construction of the garden began in 1612, with its terrain expanding across the centuries until it reached its current size in 1865.

 WHERE TO EAT AT A BISTRO IN ST-GERMAIN & LES INVALIDES

Le Petit St-Benoit
Orders are scribbled on red-checked tablecloths at this authentic, old-school bistro. €

Wadja
A cosy restaurant serving up contemporary takes on beloved bistro classics. €€

Bistro de Paris
Opposite the Musée d'Orsay, this classic bistro serves up traditional fare in an art deco setting. €€

Today, the palace houses the French Senate, and the gardens are its official property.

The focal point of the garden is the **grand bassin** (central pond) around which iconic Fermob garden chairs are scattered – the perfect place to enjoy a picnic, read a book or simply rest weary legs. In the summer months, the pond springs to life as toy sailing boats are raced across its waters. Although some people bring their own boats, Les Voilieurs, the pond's official toy-boat club, has a selection available for rental.

If toy boating is not your thing – or it's simply not the right day or season for it – the garden has plenty of other activities for visitors of all ages, from *pétanque* courts to chess tables (although you'll have to bring your own balls or chess set). There's also an orchard, a greenhouse and an apiary to explore – with honey from the garden's bees sold at the end of September during the annual Fête du Miel. During spring and summer, the grassy lawns are open for visitors to picnic on, before being closed for rejuvenation during the winter months.

The garden is especially a verdant wonderland for young children, complete with a playground, sand pit and pony rides. It's also home to Paris' oldest **merry-go-round**, designed by Charles Garnier (the architect of the Opéra Garnier), and is topped with an ancient ring-tilting game: children are equipped with a wooden stick and attempt to snatch rings off the operator as they go around the merry-go-round. To play the game is a rite of passage for many a Parisian kid.

As the opening hours of the garden vary depending on the time of year, be sure to check the official website.

An Artistic Oasis

Sculptor Zadkine's Home and Atelier

Tucked away on rue d'Assas is the little-known **Musée Zadkine**, housed in the former home and atelier of Russian-born sculptor Ossip Zadkine. It's intimate in scale and sentiment, and both the beauty of the building and the works housed within it provide a peaceful escape from the business of the surrounding neighbourhood.

The museum contains some 300 works by the artist, from his monolithic sculptures carved in stone, wood and bronze to more delicate lithographs and photographs. Of note is the section dedicated to the creation of his monumental homage to painter Vincent Van Gogh; the photographs testify to the prolific talent of Zadkine. Although you probably won't need more than 45 minutes to visit the entire collection, set aside extra time to rest weary museum legs in the bucolic garden. Entry to the permanent collection and sculpture garden is free.

SERGE GAINSBOURG'S HOUSE

Until recently, the heavily graffitied former abode of French singer Serge Gainsbourg, located at 5bis rue de Verneil, had never been open to the public – despite being a site of pilgrimage for the crooner's massive fan base.

Now, **Maison Gainsbourg** has been opened to the public: visitors are given an intimate glimpse into his private life by following a 30-minute immersive audioguide. Opposite the house is a museum chronicling the stages of his musical career, complete with a restaurant and cocktail bar (named Le Gainsbarre) – an homage to the late-night venues the musician was so fond of. Be sure to book tickets to the museum and house in advance.

 WHERE TO BUY FOOD FOR A PICNIC IN ST-GERMAIN & LES INVALIDES

Boulangerie Poilâne	Fromagèrie Barthèlemy	Marché St-Germain
Perhaps France's most famous *boulangerie* (bakery), it's known for its sourdough, butter cookies and apple tarts.	The Left Bank's most famous cheese shop, with a huge selection of both popular and rare cheeses.	Covered food market open Tuesday to Saturday with vegetable stands, a fishmonger and charcuterie options.

In the garden's eastern wing is the spectacular **Fontaine Médicis**, named after Catherine Medici, who commissioned the grotto in homage to her home country, Italy. Today, it barely resembles its original design yet reads as a pastiche of the different political movements that have governed Paris.

After Napoléon I added a marble statue of Venus, Baron Haussmann attempted to dismantle the fountain altogether in 1858. It was saved by architect Alphonse de Gisors, who moved the fountain 30m from its original location and added sculptures he'd salvaged during the city's replanning. Behind the grotto, he placed the Fountain of Léda, saved from rue de Vaugirard, and replaced Napoléon's Venus with three sculptures by Auguste Ottin.

Péniche Party
Apéritifs to Float Your Boat

Where the 6th and 7th *arrondissements* meet the Seine are several *péniches* – houseboats docked permanently along the riverbanks. Some are still private homes, while others have been converted into restaurants, bars and clubs – they're a great way to experience the city's most famous waterway.

Rosa Bonheur sur Seine is the most popular *péniche*, known for its club nights and live music (with everything from salsa to jazz). Although the boat is entirely enclosed, the spectacular full-length glass windows give the impression of walking on water. But if you can't find your sea legs, drinks and food can be purchased on board and enjoyed on the nearby riverside benches. Be sure to check out its official Facebook page for a complete schedule. Tickets are required for certain events and often sell out in advance.

If you want a more ambient apéritif, then **La Balle au Bond** will be your pick of the *péniches*. With a plant-lined rooftop terrace and cosy couches, it's the perfect place to relax, drink in hand, while watching the sunset over the Seine. It's open daily for apéritifs and dinner, and on Saturdays and Sundays for brunch.

If you're ready to dance the night away, head to **Le Flow**, a *péniche* with views of the glorious Pont Alexandre III. It regularly hosts live DJ sets on its rooftop. Inside, the club stays open until the early hours on Saturdays and Sundays.

BEST COCKTAIL BARS (ON LAND) IN ST-GERMAIN & LES INVALIDES

Prescription Cosmic Theatre
Hidden behind plush velvet curtains, this lavish cocktail bar is mixology heaven.

Le Castor Club
A speakeasy cocktail club with a country-music soundtrack.

Le Bar des Près
A chic cocktail-and-sushi bar from acclaimed chef Cyril Lignac.

WHERE TO GET COFFEE IN ST-GERMAIN & LES INVALIDES

Café du Clown
Offers speciality coffee and patisserie on the terrace of Marché St-Germain. €

Coutume Café
Cafe and roaster with a delicious brunch and lunch menu, near Le Bon Marché. €

Ten Belles
The Left Bank offshoot of the famous cafe and roasters located near Canal St-Martin. €

The pedestrian-only rue Cler is perhaps the most famous market street in Paris. It's conveniently open all day Tuesday through Saturday, as well as Sunday mornings – plan on spending half a day discovering the street's gastronomical goodies. As it's never a good idea to shop on an empty stomach, begin at **1 Petitbon** for sandwiches and the best coffee in the neighbourhood. Before continuing down rue Cler, take a slight detour west along rue du Champ de Mars to stock up on cheese from local legend **2 Fromager Marie-Anne Cantin**. Trace your steps back to rue Cler and continue north along the street. As no French meal can begin without an apéritif, make a stop at **3 Davoli** for nibbles. Yes, it is an Italian *épicerie* but it sells the finest charcuterie on the street. The best fishmonger on rue Cler, **4 La Sablaise** is located just two doors down the street. If oysters are in season, the staff will happily prepare a platter to go. Pop across the road to **5 Le Repaire de Bacchus** and pick up a bottle of Petit Chablis to wash the oysters down with. But if meat is on your mind, turn around and walk back south, past Petibon, to **6 Boucherie du Perche**. They can advise you on how to cook any cut of meat to perfection. Right next door is **7 L'Artisan Au Bon Jardinier**, for all your fruit and veg needs, with their daily deals located out the front. Saving the best until last, finish up at **8 Le Chocolat Alain Ducasse**, the atelier from the giant of French gastronomy, Alain Ducasse, dedicated entirely to cacao delights.

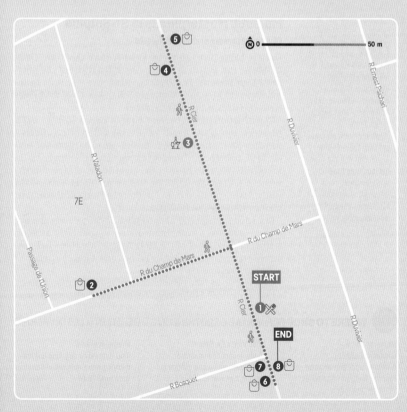

THE GUIDE

ST-GERMAIN & LES INVALIDES PARIS

THE REAL ROSE LINE

A note inside the Église St-Sulpice asserts that, contrary to Dan Brown's claims in *The Da Vinci Code*, the line running through the church 'was never called the Rose Line'.

The real Rose Line is known as the Paris Meridian, which from 1678 to 1884 was the prime meridian on all international maps – until the International Meridian Convention, when it was universally agreed upon that the Royal Observatory in Greenwich, England, would be the reference for zero-degree longitude. France refused, however, to adhere to Greenwich Mean Time, implementing its own system called Paris Time. But during WWI the country found it hard to coordinate internationally on war strategies so in 1911 it officially adopted GMT.

Musée De L'Armée

Majestic Masterpieces in St-Sulpice
Divine Delacroix and Pious Pigalle

Despite being just 1 sq metre smaller than the Notre Dame de Paris, the Église St-Sulpice long lived in its shadow – until Dan Brown's *The Da Vinci Code* drew crowds to the monumental Roman Catholic church in search of the hidden treasures detailed in his epic novel.

Construction of the current church began in 1642 but it passed through the hands of several different architects – which accounts for its unique mishmash of baroque and neo-classical references – until work was halted entirely by the French Revolution. In fact, the right tower on the church's western façade (designed by Italian architect Servandoni, who drew inspiration from London's St Paul's Cathedral) remains unfinished to this day.

But what's so special about Église St-Sulpice are the artworks contained within. Immediately to your right after entering, in the Chapel of the Holy Angels, are three well-preserved wax murals painted by French artist Eugène Delacroix between 1855 and 1861.

Unmissable are the peculiar pair of holy water fonts, located on either side of the nave. Giant clam shells, which were

 WHERE TO SHOP FOR VINTAGE CLOTHING IN ST-GERMAIN & LES INVALIDES

Renaissance – Vintage Fashion
A secret spot among the fashion industry for sourcing vintage treasures.

Tilt Vintage Store
A well-curated selection of affordable vintage clothing and accessories.

Hippy Market
You'll need to dig, but there's many a worthwhile bargain to be found here.

MASSIMO TODARO/SHUTTERSTOCK ©

gifted to King Francis I by the Venetian Republic, sit atop stone bases hand-carved with sea motifs by Jean-Baptiste Pigalle. The white marble statue of Mary, located at the far end of the church, was also sculpted by the prolific artist.

Throughout the year, classical-music recitals are held at the church, with tickets available online from L'Officiel des Spectacles or directly on-site before each performance.

A Cabinet of Military Curiosities
Les Invalides and Musée De l'Armée

At the end of the sprawling Esplanade des Invalides stands the **Hôtel des Invalides**, the hospital commissioned by Louis XIV for wounded soldiers (partially in operation today) and from which some 32,000 weapons were pillaged by revolutionaries before the storming of the Bastille prison on 14 July 1789.

Today, **Les Invalides** also houses the Musée de l'Armée, France's national military museum. With over 500,000 artefacts, it boasts the third-largest collection of weapons and armour in the world. Don't be deterred from visiting if warfare and military paraphernalia are not your thing – the 8000-sq-metre complex is more of a gigantesque cabinet of curiosities with something to pique everyone's interest.

The museum is divided into eight sections: French Classical Cannons, Ancient Armour and Arms (13th–17th centuries), From Louis XIV to Napoléon III (1643–1870), The Two World Wars (1871–1990), Charles de Gaulle Historical Centre, Napoléon I's Tomb, the Cathedral of St-Louis des Invalides and special exhibition rooms (the museum hosts several temporary exhibitions, often centred around contemporary art, several times a year). It's impossible to cover the entire museum in one day – you're better off concentrating on a single section or simply wandering aimlessly, pausing at whatever grabs your attention.

Among the curiosities to be stumbled across within the museum are a taxidermy of Napoléon's last horse, Vizir (check out the Napoléonic branding on the horse's haunches), Jean Auguste Dominique Ingres' monumental painting *Emperor Napoléon on his Throne*, a model of Mont-St-Michel made from playing cards by a monk in the 17th century, and ancient keys to the city of Milan from the late 1700s.

The museum is open seven days a week. Aside from the Cathedral of St-Louis des Invalides, for which entry is always free, a ticket is required.

A TEMPLE OF TAXIDERMY

Founded in 1888 by the eponymous family, the **Deyrolle** taxidermy store located on rue du Bac is more than just stuffed dead animals – to step inside is to travel back in time to the heyday of old-school explorers, adventurers and curiosity cabinets. If the idea of hunting and taxidermy makes you queasy, note that the store has been curated with education in mind – informing visitors about the wonders of our natural world, the scientific systems that make sense of it all, and what we can do now to save it.

WHERE TO SHOP LIKE A LOCAL IN ST-GERMAIN & LES INVALIDES

Kerstin Adolphson	Hervé Chapelier	SuperStitch
Where Parisian artists and chefs come to buy chic but comfortable footwear.	Shopping totes and weekender bags beloved by Parisians.	Bring your old jeans to be spruced up or invest in a timeless pair from these denim connoisseurs.

With dozens of galleries specialising in both contemporary and vintage creations, the Left Bank is window-shopping heaven for both design amateurs and professionals.

Kick off your browsing on rue Las Cases at the showroom of **1 India Mahdavi**, to marvel at the distinctive furniture collection of the French-Iranian designer and architect. A few doors west is the **2 Petits Objets Boutique**, a shop full of Mahdavi's smaller handicrafts that pay homage to ancestorial savoir-faire. Head back the way you came, past the India Mahdavi showroom, and meander your way east to the 6th *arrondissement* along bd St-Germain. Take a small detour left on rue du Bac to peek into **3 Deyrolle** (p241), a life-size cabinet of curiosities. Make your way east along rue Jacob until you arrive at the boutique of **4 Michele Aragon**. Ara-

gon is known for her extensive collection of vintage French textiles – an upholsterer's dream – as well as her handmade tableware. Continue down rue Jacob until you hit rue de Seine; on your left is **5 Isabelle Subra Woolworth**, an antique jewellery dealer offering unique finds for all kinds of price ranges. Further north along rue de Seine is furniture dealer François Laffanour's **6 Galerie Downtown**, a gallery specialising in mid-century designs from the likes of Le Corbusier and Charlotte Perriand. Then finish off your tour by heading back south then east to the two gallery spaces of Kamel Mennour, one located at **7 rue St-André des Arts** and the other at **8 rue du Pont de Lodi**. One of the legends of the Parisian contemporary art scene, Mennour hosts shows from top artists such as Camille Henrot and Daniel Buren.

Under the Golden Dome
Napoléon I's Burial Site

Under the arresting golden **Dôme des Invalides** lie the remains of France's Emperor Napoléon I. Although Napoléon I died in exile on the island of St-Helena in 1821, King Louis Philippe I ordered the repatriation of his remains to Paris in 1840. After all, in his last will, Napoléon wrote 'It is my wish that my ashes may repose on the banks of the Seine, in the midst of the French people, whom I have loved so well'.

The tomb, lavish in materials and intricacies, took over 20 years to complete, during which Napoléon's remains were lain at the nearby Chapelle de St-Jerome. Construction took so long due to the difficulties in importing the speciality stone used: the actual sarcophagus is made from Russian purple quartzite, the green granite base was sourced from Vosges, and the black marble bottom is from Ste-Luce, Martinique.

Surrounding the 6m-deep open crypt, which was designed by Louis Visconti, are 12 statues representing Victory; on the mosaic floor are tiled the names of the battles Napoléon fought in. As you wander the tomb, look down for Napoléon's insignia laid into the marble floors and up at the glorious ceiling frescoes painted by Charles de la Fosse.

Napoléon's Tomb is open every day of the week and entry is included in the ticket to the Musée de l'Armée.

A Bibliophile's Paradise
Nooks and Nooks of Books

Given the famous literary names that once made St-Germain their font of inspiration, it's of little surprise that today the neighbourhood is the publishing heartland of French literature and home to some of the capital's most interesting bookshops.

Paris' most storied English-speaking bookstore, Shakespeare & Company, originally set up shop at 12 rue de l'Odeon, where owner Sylvia Beach famously edited and published James Joyce's chef-d'oeuvre *Ulysses* in 1922. Although the store relocated to the 5th *arrondissement* following its closing during the WWII occupation (Beach refused to sell a copy of Joyce's *Finnegans Wake* to a Nazi officer), several other Anglophone bookshops opened in its wake.

With two locations on the rue de Medicis (which speaks to the sheer volume of books contained inside), the **Red Wheelbarrow** is the largest of the English-speaking stores, hosting regular author talks and signings. Nearby on rue Monsieur le Prince, **San Francisco Book Company** is a labyrinth of secondhand books, complete with ladders so you can sail

BEST SPOTS FOR SWEET TREATS IN ST-GERMAIN & LES INVALIDES

Fruittini
Seasonal fruit filled with ice cream; a delight for both eyes and taste buds. €€

Mori Yoshida
Exquisite pastries with a Japanese twist. Be sure to try the coffee éclair and flan. €

Debauve & Gallais
An 18th-century chocolate shop that was once the official supplier to Napoléon I. €

WHERE TO ENJOY AN APÉRITIF IN ST-GERMAIN & LES INVALIDES

L'Avant Comptoir de la Mer
A tiny counter-service bar with excellent seafood and matching wines.

La Crèmerie
Cosy wine bar with copious charcuterie and cheese platters.

Bar de la Dame des Arts
The best neighbourhood rooftop bar, offering sweeping views of Paris.

L'ÉCOLE DES BEAUX-ARTS

Located on rue Bonaparte is Paris' École des Beaux-Arts, the most competitive fine-arts school in the country. Since its inception in 1648, many of the greatest names in art history have passed through its doors: Degas, Delacroix, Renoir, Moreau and John Singer Sargent, just to name a few.

Although the school is closed to the public (you're not free to simply wander inside), it does host public exhibitions and artists talks from both local and international talent. Check the school's website for a full schedule of events – it's an opportunity to peer inside one of the bastions of French culture.

LEFT: JUNJUN/SHUTTERSTOCK © RIGHT: FROM MY POINT OF VIEW/SHUTTERSTOCK ©

Musée Rodin

the shelves in hunt of beloved titles. For books with 'soul', the recently opened **Pharmacie des Âmes** on rue Vaneau offers a beautifully curated selection of both English- and French-language titles that founder Ramdane Touhami hopes will heal humanity.

For art books, look no further than **Delpire & Co** on rue de l'Abbaye. It has a sublime selection of both new and out-of-print books and magazines, and many an art-industry insider considers it to be the best bookstore in the city.

BEST CONTEMPORARY EATERIES IN ST-GERMAIN & LES INVALIDES

Localino
Laid-back modern Italian restaurant serving up the classics paired with minimal-intervention wines. €€

L'Avant-Comptoir du Marché
Tapas bar from Michelin-starred chef Yves Camdeborde, with a large selection of wines by the glass. €

Bar Etna
A super-friendly cave à manger, with small seafood-focused share plates. €€

A Sculpture Garden for Thinking

A Day at the Musée Rodin

In the heart of the 7th *arrondissement* is one of Paris' most serene museums, the **Musée Rodin**, dedicated to the prolific oeuvre of French sculptor Auguste Rodin. Housed within the Hôtel Biron, a former aristocratic mansion, the museum contains some 6000 sculptures and 8000 drawings by Rodin (though not all are on display!).

Rodin is considered by many an art historian to be the founder of modern sculpture, known for his unparalleled talent to translate the complexities of human emotion into meticulously sculpted clay, bronze and plaster works. Among his most famous sculptures are *The Thinker, The Kiss* and *The Gates of Hell* – all of which are on show at the museum. The museum does a spectacular job of drawing your attention to the humanistic detailing in Rodin's work, with rooms dedicated entirely to body parts like hands, feet and heads.

But what makes this museum so special is its tranquil sculpture garden. Scattered about perfectly manicured hedges and flower beds are several of the sculptor's works, including *The Thinker*. You're free to touch the sculptures and feel for yourself the deft hand of the artist at work.

The Musée Rodin is open Tuesday through Sunday – plan on spending the best part of a day here, allowing ample time to both delve into the depths of the collection and relax in the gardens. An entry ticket provides you with access to both the museum and the garden.

THE HUMBLEST OF FRENCH DISHES

L'oeuf-mayonnaise, which is simply a hard-boiled egg halved and topped with mayonnaise, has long been the emblematic dish of the French bistro – popular dining institutions that were historically the canteen of the working-class population.

For one of the best in town, head to **Le Voltaire**, a former bistro turned upscale eatery on the quai Voltaire (many a French politician is known to lunch here). Miraculously, the price of the *oeuf-mayo* hasn't changed since 1956: it's still only €0.90. Head here early in the evening, before service swings into full action, and the wait staff might let you get away with ordering just an *oeuf-mayo* and a glass of wine.

L'oeuf-mayonnaise

WHERE TO BUY THE BEST CROISSANTS IN ST-GERMAIN & LES INVALIDES —

Boulangerie La Parisienne Madame
Located next to the Jardin du Luxembourg; its speciality is a savoury sea-salt croissant. €

Boulangerie Liberté
Chic, new-wave *boulangerie* with buttery croissants made on-site. €

Maison Bergeron
Consistently voted as having one of the top 10 croissants by the Greater Paris Bakers' Union. €

Montparnasse & Southern Paris

UNDERRATED, ECLECTIC AND FULL OF SURPRISES

If you're in search of a Paris that few visitors take time to explore, southern Paris will appeal to you.

Unpretentious yet seductive, gritty yet full of good vibes, it's a happy mix of typical village-like areas, edgy street art, vast parks and striking architecture. Were it not for a few iconic sites – think Tour Montparnasse and Les Catacombes – the 13th, 14th and 15th *arrondissements* would remain well off the tourist radar. Lacking the prestigious reputation of the more central and northern *arrondissements*, they are often overlooked by foreigners (and even French visitors). Do not make this mistake, and do save time for this sprawling southern sector of Paris.

You can start with fabled Montparnasse, which has brasseries from its mid-20th-century heyday and re-energized backstreets that buzz with local life. Then delve into the huge 15th, one of Paris' most fascinating districts, with plenty of lesser-known corners that beg to be uncovered. This is a very tranquil – but certainly not boring – part of Paris, with lots of greenified areas, wonderful local parks and atmospheric squares. South of Montparnasse, another trove of treasures await in the 14th *arrondissement*. Here, you'll find a few microneighbourhoods with plenty of atmosphere as well as charming facets of the city and great parks that scream 'picnic'.

And then, to the east, there's the ever-regenerating 13th. Is this Paris' bigger surprise? Off place d'Italie, you're going to experience little-known, pocket-sized neighbourhoods that scream village life. The 13th is also home to Paris' largest Chinatown, some striking street art and even more stunning contemporary (and increasingly sustainable) architecture, including the fabulous Duo Towers – a new landmark in the city.

In all, this vast swath of southern Paris is a perfect place to explore if you're looking for a different perspective of the city and a local experience away from the tourist spots.

4KCLIPS/SHUTTERSTOCK ©

DON'T MISS...

CHINATOWN	BUTTE AUX CAILLES	TOUR MONTPARNASSE
Stroll through one of the he most atmospheric Chinatowns in Europe. **p252**	Explore this yet-to-be-discovered neighbourhood with a rural feel off place d'Italie. **p255**	Take in sweeping views of Paris (and the Eiffel Tower), from an iconic building that's hard to beat. **p256**

TOP TIP

The three *arrondissements* – 13e, 14e and 15e – are huge and the distance between Bibliothèque Nationale de France and Parc André Citroën is significant – about 9km. Allow sufficient time by public transport if you want to make the most of the area. Use the metro (line 6) to get from one *arrondissement* to the next.

ULYSSEPIXEL/SHUTTERSTOCK ©

Left: A tree-lined avenue in the 13th *arrondissement*; Above: Parc Georges Brassens (p261)

PARIS RIVE GAUCHE
Share the buzz, energy and zeal for innovation in this fast-evolving district in the 13th. **p257**

MANUFACTURE DES GOBELINS
Visit a venerable cultural institution that has specialised in tapestries since the 18th century. **p260**

PARC GEORGES BRASSENS
Discover one of southern Paris' most attractive green oases: landscaped gardens, a central pond, lawns and fountains. **p263**

MONTPARNASSE & SOUTHERN PARIS

TOP SIGHTS
1 Cimetière du Montparnasse
2 Les Catacombes
3 Rue Daguerre

SIGHTS
4 Ballon de Paris
5 Cité Universitaire
6 Église St-Jean Baptiste de Grenelle
7 Fondation Cartier pour l'Art Contemporain
8 Île aux Cygnes
9 Institut Giacometti
10 Jardin de l'Atlantique
11 Little Brittany
12 Little Tehran
13 Musée Bourdelle
14 Musée de la Libération de Paris – Musée du Général Leclerc – Musée Jean Moulin
15 Parc André Citroën
16 Parc Georges Brassens
17 Parc Montsouris
18 Petite Ceinture du 14e
19 Petite Ceinture du 15e
20 Square St-Lambert
21 Statue of Liberty Replica

ACTIVITIES
62 Aquaboulevard

SLEEPING
63 3 Ducks Hostel
64 Hôtel Max
65 Hôtel Vic Eiffel

EATING
22 Aux Enfants Gâtés
23 Binôme
24 Crêperie de Josselin
25 Crêperie Plougastel

26 Frédéric Comyn
27 Habesha
28 La Closerie des Lilas
29 La Coupole
30 La Rotonde
31 L'Accolade
32 Land&Monkeys
Pernety
33 L'Assiette
34 Le Beurre Noisette
35 Le Casse Noix
36 Le Dôme

37 Le Mauritius
38 Le Sévéro
39 Les Fauves
40 Les Pépites
41 Lokita
42 Maison Binder
43 MoSuke
44 Pernety District
45 Polichinelle
46 Sweet Rawmance

**DRINKING
& NIGHTLIFE**
47 Arthur & Juliette
48 Hexagone Café
49 Poinçon

SHOPPING
50 Atomes
51 Beillevaire
52 Comptoir Corrézien
53 Hazar & Co
54 Il Etait Une
Fois Dix Doigts

55 La Cave des Papilles
56 Le Village Suisse
57 Marché aux Puces
de la Porte de Vanves
58 Marché
Biologique Brancusi
59 Marché de la
Création
60 Marché Edgar
Quinet
61 Marché
Georges Brassens

Les Catacombes

The City's Spine-Prickling Ossuary

It is gruesome, ghoulish and downright spooky, but Les Catacombes remains one of Paris' most visited sights. In 1785 subterranean tunnels of an abandoned quarry were upcycled as storage rooms for the exhumed bones of corpses that could no longer fit in the city's overcrowded cemeteries. By 1810 the skull- and bone-lined catacombs – resting place of millions of anonymous Parisians – had been officially born.

The route through Les Catacombes begins at its spacious 2018-opened entrance on av du Colonel Henri Rol-Tanguy. Walk down 131 spiral steps to reach the ossuary itself, with a mind-boggling number of bones and skulls of millions of Parisians neatly packed along the walls. Visits cover about 1.5km of tunnels in all, at a cool 14°C. The exit is up 112 steps via a minimalist all-white 'transition space' with gift shop at 21bis av René Coty, 14e. Keep in mind that visiting the Catacombes is not for everybody. People with claustrophobia may experience some anxiety in the confined environment. Also note that the Catacombes are not wheelchair accessible.

JRTWYNAM/SHUTTERSTOCK ©

Les Catacombes

Rue Daguerre

Enjoy an Authentic Slice of Parisian Life

Paris' traditional village atmosphere thrives along rue Daguerre, 14e. Tucked just southwest of the Denfert Rochereau metro and RER stations, this narrow street – pedestrianised between av du Général-Leclerc and rue Boulard – is lined with florists, *fromageries* (cheese shops), *boulangeries* (bakeries), patisseries, greengrocers, delis (including Greek, Asian and Italian) and classic cafes where you can watch the local goings on. Shops set up market stalls on the pavement; Sunday mornings are especially lively. It's a great option for lunch before or after visiting Les Catacombes, or packing a picnic to take to one of the area's parks or squares.

Over 30 monumental murals enliven streets and thoroughfares in an area between av de France, rue de Tolbiac and bd Vincent Auriol, with more added every year.

Start from the **1 Chevaleret metro station**. Here you can enjoy the poignant **2 Embrace and Fight** (85 bd Vincent Auriol), by Conor Harrington; *La Madone* (81 bd Vincent Auriol), a masterpiece created by famous artist Inti; and *Les Oiseaux* (The Birds; 91 bd Vincent Auriol), by Pantonio.

Continue west along bd Vincent Auriol and you'll see the monochromatic **3 Le Visage** (The Face; 6 rue Jenner), also by Pantonio, on your right. Then the stunning **4 Rise Above Level** (cnr bd Vincent Auriol and rue Jeanne d'Arc) comes into view, a massive mural by Shepard Fairey. On the opposite side of bd Vincent Auriol, it's impossible to miss the awesome **5 Dancer** (98 bd Vincent Auriol), with a strapline ('*Et J'ai Retenu Mon Souffle*' – And I Hold My Breath), by the collective Faile.

Other great works to look for further west include **6 Le Chat** (cnr bd Vincent Auriol and rue Nationale); monumental *La Marianne* (186 rue Nationale), by Shepard Fairey, which represents the symbol of the French Republic; and the strikingly expressive *Turncoat* (190 rue Nationale), by D*Face (who is from London).

Be awed by the elaborate **7 Sun Daze** (167 bd Vincent Auriol), created by the talented twins How and Nosm, and, on an adjacent building, a splendid portrait of a geisha-like woman (169 bd Vincent Auriol), by British artist Hush.

Follow rue du Château des Rentiers then take a left on rue de Clisson. Marvel at **8 Bach** (57 rue Clisson) before taking rue Jeanne d'Arc on the right and rue Lahire, where you can see another **9 colorful fresco** (13 rue Lahire) by Inti.

THE GUIDE

MONTPARNASSE & SOUTHERN PARIS PARIS

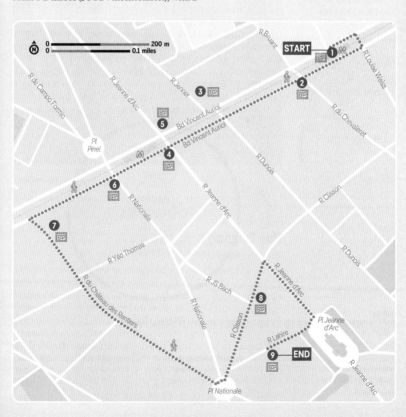

Asian Accents

MAP P.254

Immerse Yourself in Chinatown

Southeast of place d'Italie and near rue de Tolbiac is Paris' largest **Chinatown**. Don't let the massive tower blocks dating from the 1960s deter you from exploring this district, which feels so different from other Parisian neighbourhoods. It's a fascinating piece of Southeast Asia, with plenty of surprises, including culinary delights, colourful festivals and art.

If you're a fan of underground cultures, head to **La Dalle des Olympiades**, off rue de Tolbiac. This vast concrete esplanade with platformed pedestrian zones surrounded by towers has become the focal point for local K-Pop dancers and skateboarders.

On rue Paul Klee, **La Danse de la Fontaine Émergente** ('Dance of the Emerging Fountain') is a large fountain built of stainless steel, plastic and glass, designed by French Chinese sculptor Chen Zhen. Completed in 2008, it looks like a giant stylised dragon winding its way across the square, emerging and submerging from the concrete pavement. High-pressure water flows inside the sculpture.

The most unusual sacred site in Paris must be the **Autel du Culte de Bouddha** (37 rue du Disque) – this small yet colourful Buddhist temple is hidden in an underground car park beneath a tower block.

For any Asian food you can imagine, as well as many decorative and household items, shop at **Tang Frères** (48 av d'Ivry), the biggest Asian store in Paris (and possibly Europe). Nestled beneath the towers on av d'Ivry and av de Choisy you'll find great Vietnamese *pho* noodle bars, family-run restaurants serving homemade dumplings and spicy soups as well as traditional Chinese pastry shops.

CHINESE NEW YEAR

If you happen to be in Chinatown in in late January or February, don't miss Chinese New Year (also known as Spring Festival). With about 2000 participants and more than 200,000 spectators, it's one of the most spectacular events in the city. Celebrations typically last about two weeks and feature colourful parades as well as lion and dragon dances. Expect brightly lit red lanterns, firecrackers and performances by ribbon dancers, drummers, cymbal players and acrobats wearing traditional costumes. It kicks off in front of Tang Frères supermarket on av d'Ivry. For exact dates, check mairie13.paris.fr/culture.

PARIS' CHINATOWNS

Paris has another thriving Chinatown in **Belleville** (p163).

WHERE TO SLEEP AFFORDABLY IN SOUTHERN PARIS

3 Ducks Hostel	Oops	Urban Bivouac Hotel
This hostel, a 10-minute walk from the Eiffel Tower, has a good-time vibe and excellent facilities. €	This colourful design hostel has four- to six-bed dorms and doubles with bathrooms. €	A great base if you want to explore the Paris Rive Gauche area and the Butte aux Cailles neighbourhood. €

Chinese New Year parade, Paris

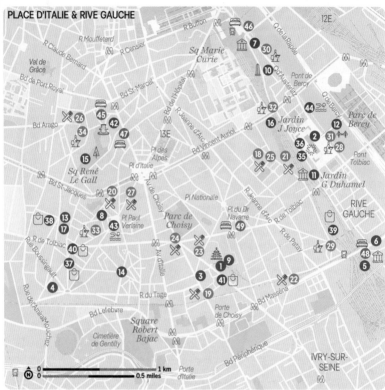

PLACE D'ITALIE & RIVE GAUCHE

SIGHTS
1 Autel du Culte de Bouddha
2 Bibliothèque Nationale de France
3 Chinatown
4 Cité Florale
5 Duo Towers
6 Galerie Itinerrance
7 Institut Français de la Mode
8 La Butte aux Cailles
9 La Dalle des Olympiades
10 La Danse de la Fontaine Émergente
11 La Fab
12 Passerelle Simone de Beauvoir
13 Petite Alsace
14 Square de l'Abbé Georges Hénocque
15 Square René Le Gall
16 Station F
17 Villa Daviel

SPORTS & ACTIVITIES
42 Manufacture des Gobelins
43 Piscine de la Butte aux Cailles
44 Piscine Joséphine Baker

SLEEPING
45 Hôtel Henriette
46 Off Paris Seine
47 Oops
48 TOO
49 Urban Bivouac Hotel

EATING
18 Comme Promis
19 mpérial Choisy
20 La Butte aux Piafs
21 La Felicità
22 Lao Viet
23 Le Bambou
24 Pho Bành Cúon 14
25 Season Square
26 Simone Le Resto
27 Sukhotai

DRINKING & NIGHTLIFE
28 Bateau El Alamein
29 Café Cayo
30 Café Oz Rooftop
31 La Dame de Canton
32 Le Djoon
33 Le Merle Moqueur

34 Simone La Cave see 48 TOO
TacTac Skybar

ENTERTAINMENT
35 EP7
36 MK2 Bibliothèque

SHOPPING
37 Biérocratie
38 Laurent Duchêne
39 Little Jeanne
40 Quatrehomme
41 Tang Frères

Secret Villages

Slices of the Countryside Within Paris

If it's village life and hidden neighbourhoods you're after, the 13th, 14th and 15th *arrondissements* will appeal to you, with a smattering of picturesque, off-the-beaten-track areas. With small houses, flowered gardens, very few cars and no noise, they all have a welcoming bucolic atmosphere.

Much less touristy and congested than other Parisian villages such as Montmartre or Mouffetard, **La Butte aux Cailles** extends on a gently sloping hill immediately west of place d'Italie. Wandering its cobblestoned streets, you'll feel teleported to another era in rural France. Its main thoroughfare is rue de la Butte aux Cailles, lined with numerous laid-back bars, shops and restaurants, but all the adjacent streets are well worth a gander, as is the super relaxing **Parc Brassaï**. A few jewel streets to stroll include passage Boiton, rue des Cinq Diamants, rue Samson, rue Alphand, passage Sigaud, passage Barrault and rue Michal, as well as the adorable rue Daviel with the **Petite Alsace** (Little Alsace) enclave, complete with brick and timbered houses, and **Villa Daviel**, which is lined with superb houses and gardens.

A five-minute walk south of Butte Aux Cailles lies the **Cité Florale**. This micro-neighbourhood is a gem to wander. Built in the 1920s, the Floral City has five streets that were all named after flowers (Iris, Wisteria, Bindweed, Orchid, Volubilis). They are paved and flanked by small houses whose façadess are covered with ivy, vines and flowers, which adds to the serene atmosphere. It's a superb place to explore early in the morning when everything seems to stand still. From here, you can walk east to the leafy **square de l'Abbé Georges Hénocque** and its adjacent streets, including rue des Peupliers and rue Dieulafoy, lined with lovely traditional houses, some of which are made of *pierre meulières* (gritstones).

For some bohemian atmosphere, nothing beats the **Pernety district** (14th), an up-and-coming area nestled on the outskirts of the Montparnasse train station. It has retained its intimate character. With its pedestrian lanes and charming brick buildings, it's entirely different from the purely Haussmannian style. Look for rue des Thermopyles and the adjacent streets. The most convenient metro station is Pernety.

In the 15th, the district around **Église St-Jean Baptiste de Grenelle**, just north of the Félix Faure metro station feels very Parisian, supremely relaxing and is chock-a-block with interesting shops, bars and restaurants.

BEST PANORAMAS IN SOUTHERN PARIS

TOO TacTac Skybar
Take a lift to the 27th floor of this luxury hotel and be wowed by the sensational views of southern Paris.

Tour Montparnasse
Enjoy one of the finest bird's-eye views of Paris from the indoor observatory of this iconic skyscraper (p256).

Café Oz Rooftop
The rooftop bar of the Institut Français de la Mode affords lovely views of the Seine.

Ballon de Paris
This helium-filled balloon (p263) provides unique perspectives of the Tour Eiffel.

 WHERE TO SLEEP IN STYLE IN SOUTHERN PARIS

Hôtel Max	Hôtel Henriette	Off Paris Seine
All 19 rooms at this contemporary boutique hotel have muted colours, modern art and timber floors. €	One of the Left Bank's most stunning boutique addresses, with designer chairs, 1950s lighting and vintage pieces. €€	Paris' first floating hotel is this sleek, 80m-long catamaran-design structure moored off Gare d'Austerlitz. €€

WHY I LOVE SOUTHERN PARIS

Jean-Bernard Carillet, writer, @jb.carillet_ photography

Originally from Metz (Lorraine), I came to Paris as a student to complete a master's degree at La Sorbonne. I was happy to live at the Cité Universitaire de Paris in the 14e and, since then, I've called southern Paris home. I then moved to near place d'Italie in the 13e. I love the serenity, discretion and peacefulness of these districts. They don't boast many iconic attractions but have plenty of little gems that you have to unearth, and that's what makes them so special. The village-y atmosphere that can be enjoyed in a number of areas in all three *arrondissements* (13e, 14e and 15e) is another clincher.

📱 **OTHER VILLAGES**
There's no shortage of hidden villages around the city. Each *arrondissement* has its own gems. Try **Montmatre** (p117), **Batignolles** (p135), **Village St-Paul** (p146) or **Belleville** and **Ménilmontant** (p155).

Parc Montsouris

Take in the Views at Tour Montparnasse
MAP P248

Iconic Building and Mesmerising Views

Spectacular views unfold from this 210m-high, smoked-glass-and-steel office block, built in 1973. A speedy elevator whisks visitors up in 38 seconds to the indoor **observatory** on the 56th floor, with multimedia displays. Finish with a hike up the stairs to the 59th-floor open-air terrace (with a sheltered walkway) and bubbly at the terrace's Champagne bar (closed at the time of writing).

From Tour Montparnasse, it's a short walk to **Cimetière du Montparnasse**. This 19-hectare cemetery opened in 1824 and is Paris' second largest after Père Lachaise. Famous residents include writer Guy de Maupassant, playwright Samuel Beckett, sculptor Constantin Brancusi, photographer Man Ray, legendary singer Serge Gainsbourg, and philosopher-writers Jean-Paul Sartre and Simone de Beauvoir.

 ## WHERE TO SLEEP IN STYLE IN SOUTHERN PARIS

Hôtel Vic Eiffel
A short walk from the Eiffel Tower, this pristine hotel has chic orange and oyster-grey rooms. €€

La Maison Lavaud
This gem feels like a home away from home, in a very quiet street close to Parc Montsouris. €€€

TOO Hotel
Opened in 2022, occupying the top floors of the Duo 2 tower designed by Jean Nouvel. Sensational views. €€€

Wander Parc Montsouris

MAP P248

A Bit of Fresh Air

This sprawling lakeside park planted with horse-chestnut, yew, cedar, weeping-beech and buttonwood trees is a delightful picnic spot and has endearing playground areas. With an RER station at the entrance of the park, it's an easy place to get to.

Tip: after your visit, wander the neighbouring 1920s-built **Cité Universitaire** (student halls of residence), south of the park, which is another soothing spot, as well as rue Georges Braque, impasse Nansouty and rue du Parc de Montsouris, immediately to the west – with their paved roads and stately, ivy-clad houses, they offer a real sense of escape.

Aquatic Wonders

MAP P254

Unique Swimming Pools

Built in 1924, the **Piscine de la Butte aux Cailles** is an art deco swimming complex – a historical monument – which takes advantage of the lovely warm artesian well water nearby. It has a spectacular vaulted indoor pool and, since 2017, Paris' only Nordic pool. In the depths of winter, Parisians head here to swim 25m laps in a five-lane outdoor pool, heated to a toasty 27°C.

Floating on the Seine, the striking **Piscine Joséphine Baker** is named after the 1920s American singer. The 25m x 10m, four-lane pool and large sun deck are especially popular in summer when the roof slides back. In July and August, plus weekends from late May to September, admission is limited to two hours.

If you want to please the kids, consider the **Aquaboulevard**, just outside *bd Périphérique* (the ring road) in the 15e. It's a huge tropical 'beach' and aquatic park with water slides, waterfalls and wave pools.

Explore Paris Rive Gauche

MAP P254

Paris' Most Innovative District

Paris' largest urban redevelopment since Haussmann's 19th-century reformation continues apace in the 13e *arrondissement*. Centred on a once-nondescript area south of the Latin Quarter spiralling out from the big busy traffic hub of place d'Italie, the renaissance of the area known as Paris Rive Gauche was heralded in the 1990s by the controversial **Bibliothèque Nationale de France** and the arrival of the high-speed Météor metro line (now called line 14). With four glass towers shaped like half-open books, the National

BEST AFRICAN RESTAURANTS IN SOUTHERN PARIS

MoSuke
Young chef Mory Sacko cooks up delicious dishes that combine African and Japanese influences. €€

Lokita
Expect West African dishes with a modern twist at this great venture in the Pernety area. €

Le Mauritius
Enjoy great Mauritian and Malagasy cuisine at this unpretentious eatery near Les Catacombes. €

Habesha
This Ethiopian restaurant not far from Tour Montparnasse has a good reputation. €

 WHERE TO EAT BISTRO FARE

Comme Promis
Seasonal ingredients are used to prepare dishes both classic and contemporary at this gem of a bistro. €€

Aux Enfants Gâtés
There are just 20 seats at this bistro with retro marine-blue walls and Bordeaux banquettes. €€

L'Accolade
Neighbourhood eatery famous for its creative, modern French '*bistronomie*' – bistro-style gastronomy. €€

ANDREI ANTIPOV/SHUTTERSTOCK ©, ARCHITECT: JEAN NOUVEL

Duo Towers

DRINKING & NIGHTLIFE IN SOUTHERN PARIS

The comings and goings of the Gare Montparnasse and its historic brasseries keep things lively. Southwest of place d'Italie, rue de la Butte aux Cailles and the surrounding Butte aux Cailles molehill have a plethora of fabulous options popular with students and locals; places here have a loyal clientele and lack the pretension of more trendsetting neighbourhoods. You can also head to rue du Chevaleret and av de France in Paris Rive Gauche district, a burgeoning area with great options. Especially in summer, you can't beat the floating bars and clubs on the Seine just off Bibliothèque Nationale de France.

Library of France, opened in 1995, was one of President Mitterrand's most ambitious and costliest projects. Some 12 million tomes are stored on 420km of shelves, and the library can accommodate 2000 readers and 2000 researchers. It also hosts excellent temporary exhibitions (entrance Est), mostly in the visual arts.

These initial developments were followed, among other additions, by the **MK2** and **EP7** entertainment complexes on av de France, the Piscine Joséphine Baker (p257) swimming pool and Off Paris Seine hotel – both afloat the Seine – and the **Passerelle Simone de Beauvoir** (2006), providing a cycle and pedestrian link to the Right Bank. And work isn't slated to stop for several more years.

Pivotal to this 130-hectare redevelopment zone is the Paris 7 university campus hosting some 30,000 students. Other institutions to have moved in include the **Institut Français de la Mode** (the French fashion institute) in the stylised former warehouse Les Docks. Framed by a lurid-lime wavelike glass façade, it mounts fashion and design exhibitions and events throughout the year. Other draws include huge riverside terraces, the odd pop-up shop and a popular rooftop bar.

The area's mainline train station, **Gare d'Austerlitz**, is undergoing a massive makeover by celebrated French architect

WHERE TO EAT BISTRO FARE

L'Assiette
Chef David Rathgeber, from Auvergne, focuses on age-old traditional French dishes. Superb decor, too. €€

La Butte aux Piafs
Cherry-red chairs hold down the pavement terrace of this bistro on the edge of La Butte aux Cailles. €€

Le Beurre Noisette
Filled with locals, the chocolate-toned dining room here is wonderfully convivial. €€

Jean Nouvel. The station itself will be overhauled (including €200 million alone on the grand hall's glass roof, beneath which hot-air balloons were manufactured during the 1870 siege of Paris), and new shops, cafes and green spaces will open up in the surrounding streets. The renovation is due to wrap up in 2024.

Another iconic rehabilitation is **Station F**, the world's largest start-up campus, in business since mid-2017, where 3000 entrepreneurs from all over the globe dream up groundbreaking new projects and businesses, supported by 30 different incubators and accelerators. Guided tours take visitors on a 45-minute waltz through the gargantuan hangar – a railway depot built in 1927–29 to house trains from Gare d'Austerlitz. Spaces open to the public include Station F's Anticafé co-working space and enormous Italian restaurant **La Felicità**, with five different kitchens, three bars and a twinset of original, graffiti-covered train wagons.

And then there's the futuristic, iconic **Duo Towers**, which were completed in 2021. Both were designed by Jean Nouvel. Their inclined shape has changed the Parisian skyline, and they have become a landmark in southern Paris. Duo 1 and Duo 2 are 180m and 122m high respectively. Duo 1 is the third-tallest building in Paris, after Tour Eiffel and Tour Montparnasse. Duo 2 features **TOO**, a luxury hotel designed by Philippe Starck. Inaugurated in 2022, it ranges across 10 floors and comes with a gastronomic restaurant and a fantastic skybar.

Track updates on this evolving area at parisrivegauche.com.

Artistic Treasures

MAP P254

Offbeat Galleries

There are plenty of options for art enthusiasts. In the 14e, make a beeline for the **Fondation Cartier pour l'Art Contemporain**. Designed by Jean Nouvel, this stunning glass-and-steel building is a work of art in itself. It hosts temporary exhibits on contemporary art (from the 1980s to today) in a diverse variety of media – from painting and photography to video and fashion, as well as performance art. Artist Lothar Baumgarten created the wonderfully rambling garden.

French fashion designer and art collector agnès b opened **La Fab** gallery in a striking new building by SOA Architects in the 13e in 2020. Her 5000-plus strong collection of contemporary works is presented in themed exhibitions on the ground floor that change every three to four months. On the 1st floor, the 'galerie du jour' is styled like a home where everything, from the art to the furniture, is for sale.

LA SEINE MUSICALE

A landmark addition to Paris' cultural offerings, La Seine Musicale opened on the Seine island of **Île Seguin** in 2017. Constructed of steel and glass, the egg-shaped auditorium has a capacity of 1150, while the larger, modular concrete hall accommodates 6000. Ballets, musicals and concerts from classical to rock are all staged here, alongside exhibitions. Outside are amphitheatres, while up above is a panoramic rooftop garden with landscaped lawns. There's also a restaurant, a brasserie, a cafe and a bar on the premises. It's the first of several arts venues, including a contemporary-art museum, planned as part of the Île Seguin's transformation from a Renault factory to a cultural island.

 WHERE TO EAT BISTRO FARE

Le Cassenoix	Simone Le Resto	Le Sévéro
The Nutcracker is everything a neighbourhood bistro should be. Dishes incorporate top-quality ingredients. €€	Pavement-terrace tables at a vibrant neobistro where inventive menus are created from high-quality products. €€	Steaks served with sensational *frites* (fries) are the mainstay of this upmarket bistro run by an ex-butcher. €€

PARIS' MARKETS

Paris' markets are part of the city's identity. Each one has its own charm and character. Other great markets to consider include **Marché des Enfants Rouges** (p152) and **St-Ouen** flea market (p126).

Petite Ceinture du 15e

BEST ASIAN RESTAURANTS IN THE 13E

Pho Bành Cúon 14
This buzzy restaurant is wildly popular with in-the-know locals for its super-fresh *pho* (soup). €

Lao Viet
This great little eatery serves up some of the 13e's best Vietnamese and Laotian cuisine in a cosy interior. €

Impérial Choisy
Renowned for its Cantonese cuisine and its top-quality Peking duck. €

Sukhotai
A cosy Thai restaurant off place d'Italie. €

Le Bambou
Come here for some of the best Vietnamese specialities in southern Paris. €

Testament to the 13e's ongoing creative renaissance, **Galerie Itinerrance** showcases graffiti and street art and can advise on self-guided and guided street-art tours of the neighbourhood that take in many landmark works by artists represented by the gallery. Exhibitions and events change regularly.

Travel Back in Time at the Manufacture des Gobelins

MAP P254

Meet Highly Skilled Craftspeople

Off place d'Italie in the 13e, don't miss this prestigious yet relatively unknown (even by Parisians) French institution. *Haute lice* (high warp) tapestries have been woven on specialised looms here since the 18th century along with Beauvais-style *basse lice* (low warp) tapestries and Savonnerie rugs. Superb examples of carpets and tapestries woven here are showcased in its gallery. Note that the Manufacture des Gobelins is not a museum but an actual workplace. Guided tours (in French) of the workshops are conducted on Wednesdays. There's no shop selling tapestries as all works are for official use only.

WHERE TO PARTY IN THE 13E

Bateau El Alamein
This deep-purple boat has a Seine-side terrace for sitting amid tulips and enjoying live bands.

La Dame de Canton
Floating *boîte* (club) aboard a Chinese junk hosting pop and indie to electro, hip-hop, reggae and rock.

Le Djoon
Glass-and-steel bar and loft club that's a stylish weekend venue for soul, funk, deep house, garage and disco.

Petite Ceinture du 15e

Paris' Most Unusual Trail

This little marvel of a walking path is not to be missed if you want to see Paris from a different perspective – it really feels like entering another world.

Long before the tramway or even the metro, the 35km Petite Ceinture (Little Belt) steam railway encircled the city of Paris. Constructed during the reign of Napoléon III between 1852 and 1869 as a way to move troops and goods around the city's fortifications, it became a thriving passenger service until the metro arrived in 1900. Most passenger services ceased in 1934 and goods services in 1993, and the line became an overgrown wilderness. Until recently, access was forbidden (although that didn't stop maverick urban explorers scrambling along its tracks and tunnels).

Of the line's original 29 stations, 17 survive (in various states of disrepair). Plans for regenerating the Petite Ceinture railway corridor have seen the opening of several sections with walkways alongside the tracks. Other areas remain off-limits. In the 15e *arrondissement*, the Petite Ceinture du 15e stretches for 1.3km, with biodiverse habitats including forest, grassland and prairies supporting 220 species of flora and fauna. In addition to the endpoints, there are three elevator-enabled access points along its route: 397ter rue de Vaugirard; opposite 82 rue Desnouettes; and place Robert Guillemard. On the eastern side of Parc Georges Brassens, a *promenade plantée* (planted walkway) travels atop a stretch of the Petite Ceinture's tracks by Porte de Vanves.

Not enough for you? From there, get to 96bis rue Didot in the 14e, which is the access point for the 750m-long **Petite Ceinture du 14e**, which goes to Porte d'Orléans – another delightful section.

Find more information at petiteceinture.org.

Atmospheric Markets

MAP P249

Shop Like a Parisian

One of the friendliest in Paris, the **Marché aux Puces de la Porte de Vanves** flea market has over 380 stalls. Av Georges Lafenestre has lots of 'curios' that don't quite qualify as antiques. Av Marc Sangnier is lined with stalls of new clothes, shoes, handbags and household items for sale.

If you happen to be in the 14e on a Saturday morning, consider heading to the **Marché Biologique Brancusi**. This open-air market has a huge selection of *biologique* (organic) and locally sourced produce.

MONTPARNASSE & SOUTHERN PARIS PARIS

WHERE TO PICNIC LIKE A PARISIAN

Parisian jeweller **Marie-Louise Orlach**, who works in the 14e, shares her favourite places for a picnic.
@marielouiseorlach

Cité Universitaire
This campus is also a large, quiet and leafy park open to the public – a great place to break for a picnic.

Île aux Cygnes
This is a first-rate picnic destination on the banks of the Seine, with Eiffel Tower and Statue of Liberty views.

Square St-Lambert
Another picnic heaven in the heart of the 15e. Stock up on goodies on nearby rue du Commerce.

Square René Le Gall
In the 13e, this is a fabulous green escape (and a secret spot) off place d'Italie. Find picnic treats on nearby rue des Gobelins.

🛍️ **WHERE TO SHOP IN THE 13E** ─────────────

Atomes
This concept store sells homewares, apparel, jewellery, bags and other accessories – all made by Parisian designers.

Le Village Suisse
Paintings, ceramics, engravings, furniture, sculptures, lights and more in a 'village' in a courtyard complex.

Hazar & Co
Lovely first concept store in the 14e with apparel, accessories, jewellery and homewares rarely found elsewhere.

ALEXANDRE ROSA/SHUTTERSTOCK ©

GREEN ESCAPES

There are plenty of splendid urban parks around the city, including the **Bois de Vincennes** (p183) and the famous **Jardin du Luxembourg** (p216).

Parc André Citroën

MOST HISTORICAL BRASSERIES IN MONTPARNASSE

La Closerie des Lilas
Brass plaques tell you exactly where Hemingway and other luminaries stood, sat or fell at the 'Lilac Enclosure' (opened 1847). €€

Le Dôme
A 1930s art deco extravaganza, monumental Le Dôme is one of the swishest places around for shellfish platters. €€

La Rotonde
Around since 1911, elegant La Rotonde is renowned for its superior food. €€

La Coupole
Opened in 1927, La Coupole is famous for its mural-covered columns, dark wood panelling and soft lighting. €€

Not your average market, the **Marché de la Création** on bd Edgar Quinet (14e) draws a mixed crowd of locals and travellers in transit from nearby Gare Montparnasse. Expect stalls overflowing with handmade arts and crafts. It takes place on Sundays.

Opposite Tour Montparnasse, **Marché Edgar Quinet** is an open-air street market that teems with neighbourhood shoppers on Wednesdays and Saturdays. There's always a great range of irresistible cheeses, as well as stalls sizzling up snacks to eat on the run, from crêpes to spicy felafels.

If you like the *bouquiniste* along the Seine, you'll adore the enormous **Marché Georges Brassens** on Saturdays and Sundays. This secondhand and antiquarian book market is adjacent to beautiful Parc Georges Brassens in the 15e. More than 60 vendors sell their wares beneath the pavilions of this former abattoir. Most (but not all) books are in French, ranging from €1 paperbacks all the way to pricey, coveted collectors' editions. It's a great place to soak up local life.

WHERE TO SHOP IN THE 13E

Il Etait Une Fois Dix Doigts
This is a lovely creative space, where you can relax, have a drink or a snack, and shop for handmade gifts.

La Cave des Papilles
All of the 1200-plus varieties of wine at this dazzling rue Daguerre wine shop are organic.

Little Jeanne
A great family store, with handmade dolls, toys, clothing, candles, lamps and decorative objects.

Visiting Uncrowded Museums

MAP P248

Off-the-Radar Cultural Gems

You won't find many great cultural institutions in southern Paris, but there are a couple of relatively unknown yet not-to-be-missed museums.

Opened in 2018, **Institut Giacometti** is housed in the former studio of artist Paul Follot, in a gold-tiled art deco private mansion (a listed historical monument). It's dedicated to Swiss artist Alberto Giacometti (1901–66), who lived and worked in the area. The 350-sq-metre space has a reconstruction of Giacometti's studio, along with 350 of his sculptures, 90 of his paintings and over 2000 of his drawings. Admission is by prior online reservation only; you can't just turn up.

In the 15e, **Musée Bourdelle** is well worth a look. Monumental bronzes fill the house and workshop where sculptor Antoine Bourdelle (1861–1929), a pupil of Rodin, lived and worked. The three sculpture gardens are particularly lovely, with a flavour of Belle Époque and post-WWI Montparnasse. The museum usually has a temporary exhibition going on alongside its free permanent collection.

Fans of history will make a beeline for the **Musée de la Libération de Paris – Musée du Général Leclerc – Musée Jean Moulin**. This museum is devoted to the WWII German occupation of Paris, with its focus on the Resistance and its leader, Jean Moulin (1899–1943), Free French general Philippe François Marie Leclerc de Hautecloque, and the Liberation of Paris in August 1944. Chronologically arranged displays include clothing, equipment, personal items and photographs. Opened on 25 August 2019 – the 75th anniversary of the city's liberation – it's housed in the stunning Ledoux pavilions (1787), opposite Les Catacombes.

Back to Nature

MAP P248

Urban Oases

In 1915 automotive entrepreneur André Citroën built a vast car manufacturing plant in the 15e. After it closed in the 1970s, the vacated site was eventually turned into **Parc André Citroën**, a forward-looking 14-hectare urban park. Its central lawn is flanked by greenhouses, dancing fountains and smaller gardens themed around movement and the (six) senses. The sightseeing **Ballon de Paris** is located here. This helium-filled balloon remains tethered to the ground as it lifts you 150m into the air for spectacular panoramas over Paris.

Another enchanting green spot is **Parc Georges Brassens**, with a large pond bordered by lawns and gardens featuring

MOST TEMPTING PATISSERIES IN SOUTHERN PARIS

Laurent Duchêne
Prize-winning croissants are the speciality of this lauded bakery. Plenty of other goodies, too, including macarons and cakes.

Binôme
This enchanting pastry shop sells delectable cakes and exquisite *tartelettes*.

Land&Monkeys Pernety
In the heart of the 14e, this new-generation pastry shop has an awesome array of organic and vegan treats.

Frédéric Comyn
This venture won the 'best baguette in Paris' award in 2022. Also has to-die-for *viennoiseries*, including *pains au chocolat* and éclairs.

 WHERE TO HAVE A DRINK IN THE 13E

Café Cayo	Poinçon	Hexagone Café
Café Cayo is one of those great hybrid addresses – perfect for hanging with locals over coffee, tea or cocktails.	Half trendy bar, half slick bistro, Poinçon is in a restored 1867 railway station that was part of the Petite Ceinture.	Award-winning Breton roaster Caffè Cataldi beans used in addictive espressos, drip-filters and cappuccinos.

Restaurant, 13th *arrondissement*

BEST GOURMET SHOPS IN SOUTHERN PARIS

Beillevaire
For a swath of unusual seasonal French cheeses and other top-quality dairy products, make a pit stop at this outstanding place.

Comptoir Corrézien
Plenty of mouth-watering luxury food products are stocked at this head-spinning deli.

Quatrehomme
This fabulous shop is *fromage* heaven, with tantalising cheeses carefully sourced from all four corners of France.

Biérocratie
Craft beers from France (including Paris-brewed Goutte d'Or and Bonjour and Île-de-France-brewed Parisis) fill this bottle-lined specialist shop.

roses and medicinal and aromatic plants. The sloping hill is home to a wine-producing vineyard and an apiary. Also here is the Monfort theatre (look for the building with a conical roof) and the weekend book market, Marché Georges Brassens (p262).

The small **Jardin de l'Atlantique**, which carpets the roof of the Gare Montparnasse, is a hidden gem. It offers greenery and tranquillity in the heart of the urban tumult.

For a leisurely stroll, nothing beats the artificially created **Île aux Cygnes**, Paris' little-known third island. It was formed in 1827 to protect the river port and measures just 850m x 11m. On the western side of the Pont de Grenelle is a soaring one-quarter-scale **Statue of Liberty** replica, inaugurated in 1889. Walk east along the Allée des Cygnes – the tree-lined walkway that runs the length of the island – for knockout Eiffel Tower views.

Southern Paris for Foodies

MAP P248

From Little Brittany to Little Tehran

Since the 1920s bd du Montparnasse has been one of the city's premier avenues for enjoying Parisian pavement life, with legendary brasseries and cafes.

 WHERE TO HAVE A DRINK IN THE 13E

Le Merle Moqueur
Tiny, retro Mocking Magpie has a certain grungy appeal and serves a huge selection of flavoured rums.

Simone La Cave
Lures a loyal wine-loving set keen to try its latest outstanding natural and biodynamic wine selection.

Arthur & Juliette
Lap up the unpretentious Parisian vibe at this staunchly local neighbourhood bistro.

Near Gare Montparnasse, there's a compact area dubbed '**Little Brittany**'. Due to the Breton population congregating in this area, the station's surrounding streets – especially rue du Montparnasse, 14e, and rue Odessa, 14e, one block west – are lined with dozens of crêperies serving authentic Breton crêpes – hence the name. Traditional favourites include the super-atmospheric **Crêperie de Josselin**, named after a village in eastern Brittany, and **Crêperie Plougastel**, named for the Breton commune near Brest.

The down-to-earth 15e cooks up fabulous bistro fare – along rues de la Convention, de Vaugirard, St-Charles and du Commerce, and south of bd de Grenelle.

In Chinatown, you'll find plenty of great restaurants serving excellent Asian fare. Try av de Choisy, av d'Ivry and rue Baudricourt.

Village-y Butte aux Cailles, 13e, is chock-a-block with interesting addresses: rue de la Butte aux Cailles and rue des Cinq Diamants are the main foodie streets.

The up-and-coming area around Bibliothèque Nationale de France (check rue du Chevaleret and rue de Tolbiac) also has great eating options for all budgets.

Anyone craving authentic Middle Eastern cuisine should make a beeline for rue des Entrepreneurs, 15e. This street is not dubbed '**Little Tehran**' for nothing. It has a number of great Iranian restaurants and food stores that should meet your expectations. *ghormeh sabzi* (herb stew with rice), anyone?

Iranian dish *ghormeh sabzi*

BEST VEGETARIAN RESTAURANTS

Season Square
Homemade soups, burgers and bowls bursting with seasonal veggies are the order of the day here. €

Sweet Rawmance
A pretty lavender and fuchsia-pink façade fronts this welcoming cafe and cake shop, where everything is 100% vegan, gluten-free – and raw. €

Maison Binder
A creative spot dreamed up by two brothers, this easy-going place serves up excellent seasonal, organic fare. €

Polichinelle
Offers a tasty *cuisine légumière* (veggie cuisine). Don't miss the lavish buffet lunch. €€

 WHERE TO BRUNCH IN THE 13E

Les Pépites
Weekend brunch is a deliciously long and languid affair at this vibrant bistro. Most dishes are vegetarian. €

La Verrière
Weekend buffet with fresh breads, salads, fish and meat dishes, scrumptious pastries and vegetarian options. €€

The Fauves
Neobistro for a weekend brunch, with a great selection of pastries, cakes and other treats. €€

Day Trips from Paris

It may be hard to turn away from Paris, but several nearby day trips rival anything within the City of Light.

The top day trip is Versailles: when it comes to over-the-top opulence, the colossal Château de Versailles is in a class of its own, even for France. Elsewhere, Chartres rises above fertile farmland. Its Cathédrale Notre Dame, famed for its beautiful stained glass, dominates this charming, walkable medieval town.

The lavish Château de Fontainebleau graces its elegant namesake town amid lush countryside. The palace is stuffed with original furnishings and details from the time of Napoléon that bring it to life. The alluring riverside village of Giverny is the famous site of the Maison et Jardins de Claude Monet, the former home and flower-filled gardens of the impressionist master. Plus there is artful walking along the Seine.

TOP TIP

Head out right after breakfast on these day trips. You'll beat a lot of the crowds and you'll enjoy an unhurried day.

Chartres

CATARINA BELOVA/SHUTTERSTOCK ©

Find Your Way

TRAIN

Trains link Paris to all four-day trip destinations. Journey times are never more than an hour. Confirm which station your train departs from and buy your ticket using the Navigo Easy card.

BUS

The principal sights at Versailles and Chartres are a short walk from the train station. At Fontainebleau and Giverny, you can make the longer walk or ride a bus one or both ways.

Clermont

Oise

Forêt de Vernon

Magny-en-Vexin

Persan

Beumont

Vernon

Giverny

🏛 *Home & Gardens of Claude Monet*

Cergy ●Pontoise

Écouen

Mantes-la-Jolie

Les Mureaux

St-Denis

St-Germain-en-Laye

Seine

La Défense

✪PARIS

Lagny-sur-Marne

Giverny, p281

Monet created some of the world's most popular art at his famous home and gardens in this charming village.

Versailles

🏛●Versailles

Créteil

Houdan

Maurepas

Massy

Montgeron

Forêt de Rambouillet

Évry

Rambouillet

Corbeil-Essonnes

Versailles, p268

One of France's unmissable sights is a glorious day out. Amidst the grandiosity, you'll understand what the peasants were on about.

Arpajon

Melun

Forêt de Fontainebleau

Chartres

Étampes

Barbizon

🏛 *Cathédrale Notre Dame*

Milly-la-Forêt

Fontainebleau

Château de Fontainebleau 🏛

Chartres, p274

The extraordinary cathedral is an artistic tour-de-force that tells biblical tales using stone and stained glass; save time for the town.

Fontainebleau, p278

Not just a smaller Versailles, Fontainebleau has a longer history and offers a more personal window into its residents' lives.

Pithiviers

Forêt d'Orléans

Montargis

Bellegarde

MISTERVLAD/SHUTTERSTOCK ©

Scan
this QR code
for prices and
opening hours.

TOP SIGHT

Versailles

Sprawling over 900 hectares, the 400-year-old Château de Versailles is France's most famous palace. It's situated in the leafy, bourgeois suburb of Versailles, 22km southwest of Paris. The estate is divided into three main sections: the 580m-long palace; the gardens, canals and pools to the west of the palace; and the Trianon Estate to the northwest.

DON'T MISS

The Palace

Hall of Mirrors

King's & Queen's state apartments

Formal gardens and fountains

Lunch near the Grand Canal

Grand Trianon

Hameau de la Reine

History

The estate began in 1623 as a hunting lodge for Louis XIII. Subsequently, Louis XIV transformed it into a vast, baroque château. Some 30,000 workers and soldiers toiled on the property, the bills for which all but emptied the kingdom's coffers. The Château de Versailles was the kingdom's political capital and the seat of the royal court from 1682 up until the fateful events of 1789 when revolutionaries massacred the palace guard. Louis XVI and Marie Antoinette were ultimately dragged back to Paris, where they were ingloriously guillotined. In the 19th century, Napoléon and Josephine lived on the estate, as did Charles de Gaulle in the 1940s.

The Palace

Work on the palace began in 1661 under the guidance of architect Louis Le Vau (Jules Hardouin-Mansart took over from Le Vau in the mid-1670s); painter and interior designer Charles Le Brun; and landscape artist André Le Nôtre, whose workers flattened hills, drained marshes and relocated forests as they laid out the seemingly endless gardens, ponds and fountains. Le Brun and his hundreds of artisans decorated every moulding, cornice, ceiling and door of the interior with the most luxurious and ostentatious of appointments: frescoes, marble, gilt and woodcarvings, many with themes and symbols drawn from Greek and Roman mythology.

Few alterations have been made to the château since its construction, apart from most of the interior furnishings disappearing during the Revolution and many of the rooms being redecorated by Louis-Philippe (r 1830–48), who opened part of the château to the public in 1837. The château is in the final stages of a lavish €400 million restoration.

Hall of Mirrors

The palace's opulence peaks in its shimmering Galerie des Glaces (Hall of Mirrors). This 75m-long ballroom shines with 17 sparkling mirrored features comprising 357 individual mirrors on one side and an equal number of windows overlooking the gardens and the setting sun on the other.

King's & Queen's State Apartments

Luxurious, ostentatious appointments adorn every moulding, cornice, ceiling and door in the palace's Grands Appartements du Roi et de la Reine (King's and Queen's State Apartments). Rooms are dedicated to Hercules, Venus, Diana, Mars and Mercury.

Other Notable Rooms

The opulent excess is punctuated by various highlights worth seeking out. The **Galerie des Batailles** (Battle Gallery) is longer than the Hall of Mirrors and features 33 huge paintings that recall mostly forgotten French military victories. Take time to savour the thematic decor in the **Salon de la Guerre** (War Room) and the **Salon de la Paix** (Peace Room), which bookend the Hall of Mirrors.

Gardens, Estate & Equestrian Academy

A walk through the sprawling and artful formal gardens, natural areas, huge Grand Canal and the Trianon palaces is a highlight for many visitors. Or take in a horse show at the **National Equestrian Academy of Versailles**.

Getting There & Away

Versailles is best reached by the RER C line, which ends at Versailles Château Rive Gauche (some trains go elsewhere). Other stations with Versailles in their names are a much longer walk from the château and town centre. You can walk everywhere within Versailles, the palace and the estate.

HISTORIC VERSAILLES

Don't miss the historic centre of Versailles town. Build a superb picnic at the market stalls of Les Halles de Versailles on the place du Marché. You'll find fine foods from across France here. And grab a coffee at the surrounding cafes. Pause at the recently restored 17th-century Église Notre-Dame, the town's church with a quiet stone interior.

TOP TIPS

- Prepurchase tickets on the château's website and head straight to Entrance A. Lines for the ticketless stretch seemingly forever.
- Avoid Tuesday, Saturday and Sunday, the busiest days. It's closed Mondays.
- Download the official Château de Versailles app, which is loaded with audio tours and info for the entire estate.
- The four-person rental electric carts are limited to a set route covering a fraction of the estate. Rental bikes and e-bikes allow the most freedom to explore. Tour the Grand Canal with a rowboat. The shuttle train is very slow.

Versailles

A Day in Court

Visiting Versailles – even just the State Apartments – may seem overwhelming at first, but think of it as a house where people ate, drank, worked, slept and conspired and you'll be on the right path.

Some two decades into his long reign, Louis XIV began turning his father's hunting lodge into a palace large enough to house his entire court (to keep closer tabs on the 6000-strong army of courtiers). Sparing no expense, the Sun King employed the greatest artists and crafts-people of the day and by 1682 he'd created the most extravagant dormitory in history.

The royal schedule was as accurate and predictable as a Swiss watch. Although it's impossible to recreate the king's day on a visit, the following itinerary does allow you to pass all of the rooms of interest. You'll start with the **1 Royal Chapel**, where morning Mass was held, followed by the **2 Hercules Drawing Room** and **3 Diana Drawing Room**, both sites of evening entertainment, while the **4 King's Library** was visited after lunch. The **5 Hall of Mirrors** was for the royal procession, and the **6 Council Chamber** for late-morning meetings with ministers. The day would have begun in the **7 King's Bedchamber** and the **8 Queen's Bedchamber**, where the royal couple was roused at about the same time.

VERSAILLES BY NUMBERS

Rooms 700 (11 hectares of roof)

Windows 2153

Staircases 67

Gardens and parks 800 hectares

Trees 200,000

Fountains 50 (with 620 nozzles)

Paintings 6300 (measuring 11km laid end to end)

Statues and sculptures 2100

Objets d'art and furnishings 5000

Visitors 8.1 million per year

VICHIE81 / SHUTTERSTOCK ©

Queen's Bedchamber
Chambre de la Reine
The queen's life was on constant public display and even the births of her children were watched by crowds of spectators in her own bedchamber. **Detour »** The Guardroom, with a dozen armed men at the ready.

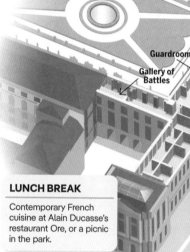

Guardroom

Gallery of Battles

LUNCH BREAK

Contemporary French cuisine at Alain Ducasse's restaurant Ore, or a picnic in the park.

Hercules Drawing Room
Salon d'Hercule
This salon, with its stunning ceiling fresco of the strong man, gave way to the State Apartments, which were open to courtiers three nights a week. **Detour »** Apollo Drawing Room, used for formal audiences and as a throne room.

TWVANURK / SHUTTERSTOCK ©

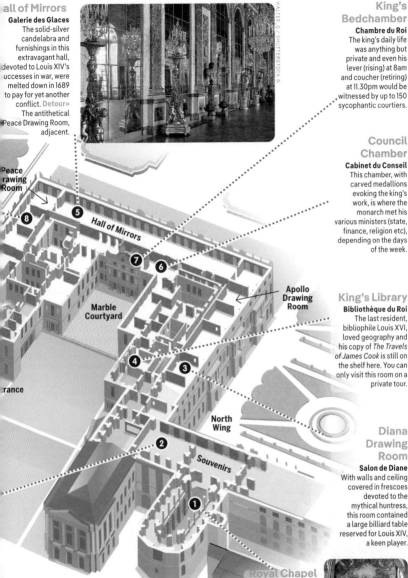

all of Mirrors

Galerie des Glaces
The solid-silver candelabra and furnishings in this extravagant hall, devoted to Louis XIV's successes in war, were melted down in 1689 to pay for yet another conflict. Detour» The antithetical Peace Drawing Room, adjacent.

Peace Drawing Room

Hall of Mirrors

Marble Courtyard

trance

North Wing

Souvenirs

Apollo Drawing Room

King's Bedchamber

Chambre du Roi
The king's daily life was anything but private and even his lever (rising) at 8am and coucher (retiring) at 11.30pm would be witnessed by up to 150 sycophantic courtiers.

Council Chamber

Cabinet du Conseil
This chamber, with carved medallions evoking the king's work, is where the monarch met his various ministers (state, finance, religion etc), depending on the days of the week.

King's Library

Bibliothèque du Roi
The last resident, bibliophile Louis XVI, loved geography and his copy of *The Travels of James Cook* is still on the shelf here. You can only visit this room on a private tour.

Diana Drawing Room

Salon de Diane
With walls and ceiling covered in frescoes devoted to the mythical huntress, this room contained a large billiard table reserved for Louis XIV, a keen player.

Royal Chapel

Chapelle Royale
This two-storey chapel (with gallery for the royals and important courtiers, and the ground floor for the B-list) was dedicated to St Louis, patron of French monarchs. Detour» The sumptuous Royal Opera.

SAVVY SIGHTSEEING

Avoid Versailles on Monday (closed), Tuesday (Paris' museums close, so visitors flock here) and Sunday, the busiest day. Also, book tickets online so you don't have to queue.

WALTER G / SHUTTERSTOCK ©

FOJATO / BUDGET TRAVEL ©

271

Exploring the Vast Estate

The Versailles estate covers over 900 hectares. The main features include the formal gardens and groves that lead down to the Grand Canal. Then amid the hunting forests are two more palaces within the Estate of Trianon and Marie Antionette's Queen's Hamlet. There are surprises in store, as the estate is filled with sculptures, water features and elegant flower gardens. On a pleasant day, you can easily spend a half-day or more exploring.

1 Gardens, Groves & Fountains

The formal gardens were laid out between 1661 and 1700, and feature geometrically aligned terraces, flower beds, tree-lined paths, ponds and fountains. The 400-odd statues of marble, bronze and lead were made by the most talented sculptors of the era.

Amidst soaring walls of trees and hedges are not-to-be-missed highlights such as the Bassin de Bacchus (Bacchus Fountain), the Bassin de Saturne (Saturn Fountain) and the Bosquet de l'Encelade (Enceladus Grove). Surprises abound. The seasonal 'Musical Gardens' program pairs boom-ing classical music with timed sprays of water features.

The Walk: Take your time meandering through the gardens towards the Grand Canal. Pause for the views at the expansive Bassin d'Apollon.

2 Grand Canal

Forming a cross that's 1km by 1.7km and orientated to catch the sunset, the placid waters of the Grand Canal are the dominant feature of the estate. At the east end is a group of good spots to eat as well as a place to rent bikes and e-bikes in case you want to save time reaching the outer reaches of the estate. You can also rent a rowboat and take to the waters.

STONIKO/SHUTTERSTOCK ©

Hameau de la Reine

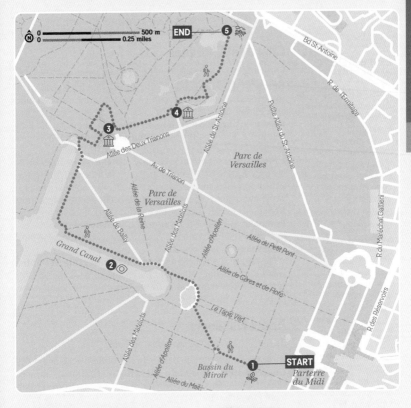

The Walk: No matter how crowded the palace, you can soon feel like you have Versailles to yourself as you walk west along the north side of the water. At the crossing point, turn north.

3 Grand Trianon

In the middle of the park within the Domaine de Trianon are Versailles' two smaller palaces. The pink-colonnaded Grand Trianon was built in 1687 for Louis XIV and his family as a place of escape from the rigid etiquette of the court. Napoléon had it redone in the Empire style and a visit offers a peek at period furniture and decor. The formal gardens behind the palace are dotted with sculptures and offer a serene and shady escape.

The Walk: Take the short walk through elegant flower gardens to the Petit Trianon.

4 Petit Trianon

The ochre-coloured Petit Trianon, built in the 1760s, was redecorated in 1867 by Empress Eugénie, the consort of Napoléon III, who added Louis XVI–style furnishings. You can skip the interior as the allure here is all outside.

The Walk: The English-style Jardins du Petit Trianon have meandering, sheltered paths and include features such as the irresistible Temple de l'Amour (Temple of Love). Stroll the paths a short distance north.

5 Hameau de la Reine

Surprisingly idiosyncratic, the Hameau de la Reine (Queen's Hamlet) is like a film set of a mock village of thatched cottages, a pond, a photogenic mill and lots of barnyard animals. It was constructed from 1775 to 1784 for the amusement of Marie-Antoinette.

Chartres' Churches

Intriguing Sacred Places Around Town

Église St-Aignan is interesting for its wooden barrel-vault roof (1625), arcaded nave and painted interior of faded blue and gold floral motifs (c 1870). The stained glass and the Renaissance Chapelle de St-Michel date from the 16th and 17th centuries. This was the parish church used by Chartres residents as opposed to the pilgrims in the cathedral.

Flying buttresses barely hold up the 12th- and 13th-century **Église St-Pierre**. Once part of a Benedictine monastery founded in the 7th century, it was outside the city walls and thus vulnerable to attack. The fortress-like, pre-Romanesque bell tower attached to it was used as a refuge by monks, and dates from around 1000. The fine, brightly coloured clerestory windows in the nave, choir and apse date from the early 14th century.

The empty shell of the 12th-century **Collégiale St-André** was a Romanesque collegiate church decommissioned in 1791. It was severely damaged in the early 19th century and again in 1944, and now it's an exhibition centre.

Artful Museums

Stained Glass and Medieval Masterpieces

After viewing the stained glass in the cathedral, pause at the **Centre International du Vitrail** (International Stained-Glass Centre), in a half-timbered former granary, to see delicate examples close up.

Chartres' **Musée des Beaux-Arts** (fine-arts museum), accessed via the gate next to the cathedral's north portal, is in the former Palais Épiscopal (Bishop's Palace), built in the 17th and 18th centuries. Peruse 16th-century enamels of the Apostles made for François I, a collection of paintings by Chaïm Soutine and polychromatic wooden sculptures from the Middle Ages.

BEST HOTELS IN CHARTRES

Most of the tourist crowds leave Chartres by 5pm. Being able to wander the streets and ponder the centuries of history in near-solitude is an excellent reason to consider spending the night rather than returning to Paris.

Hôtel Le Bœuf Couronné
The red-curtained entrance lends a theatrical air to this two-star guesthouse in the centre of everything. Some of its modern rooms have cathedral views.

Hotel Le Grand Monarque
With its 1779 façade, a stained-glass ceiling and period furnishings, this epicentral hotel is a historical gem. A host of hydrotherapy treatments are available at its spa.

Campanile Chartres Centre Gare Cathédrale
In a bull's-eye location footsteps from the cathedral and train station, this hotel has spacious rooms.

WHERE TO EAT IN CHARTRES

Boulangerie Duban
Locally grown and milled grains, traditional baked goods, sourdough bread and picnic-ready sandwiches. €

La Chocolaterie
Overlooking the flower market, this corner cafe-tearoom has delectable cakes and fine people-watching. €

Le Geôrges
Michelin-starred multicourse *menus* starring creative mains and desserts at Chartres' most ambitious restaurant. €€€

Walking Chartres will take you up and down the steep streets and stairs between the cathedral's lofty perch and the River Eure. Begin by walking the short distance to rue de la Poissonnerie, where the useful tourist office is housed in the lavishly restored 16th-century **1 Maison du Saumon**. Loop around to **2 place Billard**, where there is usually a market. Follow rue du Soleil d'Or to the **3 Flower Market** and the heart of the shopping district. Choose from several good and non-touristy cafes with terrace seating. Angle around to the rue des Grenets, which features many half-timbered buildings. Pause at the **4 Église St-Aignan**), then continue downhill down to the vast and shambolic **5 Église St-Pierre**. Walk one street over and cross the river. Note the many picturesque footbridges over the water, which was once a noxious sewer with outflow of tanneries and slaughterhouses. Walk north and cross back west over the stone **6 Pont Bouju;** the view north is sublime. Begin the trek uphill along rue du Bourg to the **7 Confluence of rue Saint-Eman and rue des Écuyers,** which has a trove of historic buildings. Look for the superb examples at numbers 17 and 19 on the latter street. Turn left, and after a few steps you'll reach the junction with rue aux Cois with **8 two medieval buildings** one building is shaped like the prow of a ship, while across the way, there's a beautiful turret-shaped, half-timbered staircase. Walk north on rue de la Corroierie to **9 Collégiale St-André**. Follow the sinuous footpath uphill to the **10 Musée des Beaux-Arts**. The former Palais Épiscopal still has flower-filled gardens and places to stop and enjoy the view before you return to the cathedral.

JORISVO/SHUTTERSTOCK ©

Scan this QR code for prices and opening hours.

TOP SIGHT

Chartres' Cathédrale Notre Dame

Step off the train in Chartres and the two very different steeples – one Gothic, the other Romanesque – of its glorious 13th-century Cathédrale Notre Dame loom above. Follow them to check out the cathedral's dazzling blue stained-glass windows, the collection of relics, and the dazzling array of carved stone statuary and decor inside and out.

DON'T MISS

Cathedral entrances

Stained-glass windows

Choir screen carvings

Sainte Voile

Half-timbered houses

Église St-Aignan

History

One of Western civilisation's crowning architectural achievements, the 130m-long Cathédrale Notre Dame de Chartres is renowned for its brilliant-blue stained-glass windows and sacred holy veil. It was built in the Gothic style during the first quarter of the 13th century (to replace a Romanesque cathedral that had been devastated by fire – along with much of the town – in 1194). Effective fundraising and donated labour meant construction took only 30 years, resulting in a high degree of architectural unity.

Today, it is France's best-preserved medieval cathedral, having been spared post-medieval modifications, the ravages of war and the Reign of Terror.

Entrancing Entrances

The cathedral's west, north and south entrances have superbly ornamented triple portals, but the west entrance, known as the **Portail Royal**, is the only one that predates the fire. Carved from 1145 to 1155, its splendid statues, whose features are elongated in the Romanesque style, represent the glory of Christ in the centre, and the Nativity and the Ascension to the right and left, respectively. The structure's other main Romanesque feature is the 105m-high **Clocher Vieux**, also called the **Tour Sud** (South Tower). Construction began in the 1140s; it remains the tallest Romanesque steeple still standing.

Climbing the North Tower

A visit to the 112m-high **Clocher Neuf**, also known as the **Tour Nord** (North Tower), is worth the ticket price and the climb up the long spiral stairway (350 steps). A 70m-high platform on the lacy, Flamboyant Gothic spire, built from 1507 to 1513 by Jehan de Beauce after an earlier wooden spire burned down, affords top-flight views of the three-tiered flying buttresses and the 19th-century copper roof.

Stained-Glass Windows

The cathedral's 176 extraordinary stained-glass windows, almost all of which date back to the 13th century, form one of the most important ensembles of medieval stained glass in the world. The three most exquisite windows, dating from the mid-12th century, are in the wall above the west entrance and below the rose window. Survivors of the fire of 1194, the windows are revered for the depth and intensity of their tones, famously known as 'Chartres blue'.

Choir Screen Drama

Turn your back on the windows (!) and behold the carved-stone statuary of the choir screen that presents the life of Mary in 41 scenes. They capture poignant moments such as number 28, which shows her holding the lifeless body of her son Jesus.

Mary's Holy Veil

In Chartres since 876, the venerated **Sainte Voile** (Holy Veil) – a yellowish bolt of silk draped over a frame, which is believed to have been worn by the Virgin Mary when she gave birth to Jesus – is displayed at the end of the cathedral's north aisle behind the choir.

The relic originally formed part of the imperial treasury of Constantinople but was offered to Charlemagne by Empress Irene when the Holy Roman Emperor proposed marriage to her in 802. Charles the Bald presented it to the town in 876; the cathedral was built because the veil survived the 1194 fire.

Deep in the Crypt

The cathedral's 110m crypt, a tombless Romanesque structure built in 1024 around a 9th-century predecessor, is the largest in France. **Tours** start at the cathedral-run shop, inside near the west entrance.

ON A PILGRIMAGE

You'll likely see hearty souls with backpacks congregating at the cathedral. Chartres is on the pilgrimage route to Santiago de Compostela in Spain. Look for the marker in the pavement that points towards their goal, some 1600km distant. The route has existed for over a thousand years; in the past the cathedral was also a pilgrim campsite.

TOP TIPS

- English guided tours, with expert resident Anne-Marie Woods, depart from the cathedral shop at noon, Tuesday to Saturday from Easter to mid-October.
- The cathedral shop sells hard-to-find guides and books. Look for titles by Malcolm Miller, who dedicated his life to studying the cathedral.
- Bring binoculars to appreciate the detail of the stained glass and carvings (some Chartres shops rent them).
- Get a prime seat in one of the touristy cafes surrounding the cathedral, sit back with a beverage and gaze at the doorways. The more you look, the more you'll see.

LEFT: JACKY D/SHUTTERSTOCK ©; RIGHT: VLASYUK INNA/SHUTTERSTOCK ©

Scan this QR code for prices and opening hours.

TOP SIGHT

Château de Fontainebleau

The town of Fontainebleau grew up around its magnificent château, one of the most beautifully decorated and furnished in France. Although vast, its size pales in comparison to the scope of Versailles – and that's for the good. Many find Fontainebleau to be a much more immersive experience as there is time to savour the château, gardens and grounds.

DON'T MISS

Chapelle de la Trinité

Galerie François Ier

Salle de Bal

Boudoir de la Reine

Chambre de Napoléon

Double-horseshoe staircase

Cour Ovale

History

The resplendent, 1900-room Château de Fontainebleau's list of former tenants and guests reads like a who's who of French royalty and aristocracy. Every square centimetre of wall and ceiling space is richly adorned with wood panelling, gilded carvings, frescoes, tapestries and paintings.

The first château on this site was built in the early 12th century and enlarged by Louis IX a century later. Only a single medieval tower survived the energetic Renaissance-style reconstruction undertaken by François I (r 1515–47). The *Mona Lisa* once hung here amid other fine works of art in the royal collection. During the latter half of the 16th century, the château was further enlarged by Henri II (r 1547–59), Catherine de Médicis and Henri IV (r 1589–1610). Even Louis XIV got in on the act: it was he who hired landscape artist André Le Nôtre, celebrated for his work at Versailles, to redesign the gardens (p268). Fontainebleau was beloved by Napoléon Bonaparte, and Napoléon III was another frequent visitor. During WWII the château was turned into a German headquarters. Later, it served as the Allied and then NATO headquarters from 1945 to 1965.

Grands Appartements

The spectacular **Chapelle de la Trinité** (Trinity Chapel), the ornamentation of which dates from the first half of the 17th century, is where Napoléon III was christened in 1810. Note how the murals play with perspective.

Galerie François 1er, a jewel of Renaissance architecture, was decorated from 1533 to 1540 by Il Rosso, a Florentine follower of Michelangelo. In the seeming acres of carved-wood panelling, François I's monogram appears repeatedly along with his emblem, a dragon-like salamander.

A top sight, the **Salle de Bal**, a 30m-long ballroom dating from the mid-16th century, is renowned for its mythological frescoes, marquetry floor and Italian-inspired coffered ceiling. Its large windows afford views of the **Cour Ovale** (Oval Courtyard) and the gardens. The gilded bed in the 17th- and 18th-century **Chambre de l'Impératrice** (Empress' Bedroom) was never used by Marie Antoinette, for whom it was built in 1787. She actually favoured the **Boudoir de la Reine** (Queen's Bedroom), which attests to her under-appreciated design sensibilities. Note the lovely sunrise on the ceiling. The gilding in the **Salle du Trône** (Throne Room), which was the royal bedroom before the Napoleonic period, is decorated in a rich tableau of golds, greens and yellows.

The **Musée Chinois de l'Impératice Eugénie** (Chinese Museum of Empress Eugénie) offers a change from all the carved wood. It was created in 1863 for the Asian art and curios collected by Napoléon III's wife.

Echoes of Napoléon

Napoléon Bonaparte preferred Fontainebleau to Versailles because he found it more 'intimate'. The **Musée Napoléon I** presents the family history of the emperor, right down to his favourite articles of clothing. A suite of rooms recalls his time in the château: the **Chambre de Napoléon** preserves the decidedly non-minimalist decor of his bedroom. (Don't miss the great man's bathroom, complete with a very short tub.) The **Salon de l'Abdication** is where he called it quits in 1814.

**Swan Lake,
Château de Fontainebleau**

NATURAL WONDERLAND

Fontainebleau is arguably the best springboard for outdoorsy pursuits in the Paris area. The surrounding Forêt de Fontainebleau, an expanse of pine forest and oak trees, sandy clearings and curiously shaped boulders, is a haven for walkers, cyclists and climbers, and begins only 500m from the château. Get info at Fontainebleau's tourist office.

TOP TIPS

● Refreshment and lunch choices within the complex are very limited. Outside the gates in town, you'll find good choices for picnics and meals around rue des Sablons.

● Preserve your flexibility by not buying château tickets in advance as it draws a fraction of the crowds of Versailles.

● There are dozens of daily trains between Paris' Gare de Lyon and the Fontainebleau Avon station.

● You can easily ride the bus from the station to Fontainebleau's town centre and the château's entrance and walk all the way back as part of a tour of the gardens and grounds.

Begin your walk on the northern side of the Château de Fontainebleau in the formal **1 Jardin de Diane**, created by none other than the infamous Catherine de Médicis. Good spots for a picnic abound in this popular public park. Now move into the château complex. As successive monarchs added their own wings to the palace, five irregularly shaped courtyards were created. Start at the largest courtyard, the austere **2 Cour du Cheval Blanc** (Courtyard of the White Horse), which has the château's entrance for visitors. Napoléon, about to be exiled to Elba in 1814, bade farewell to his guards from the magnificent – and iconic – 17th-century double-horseshoe staircase here. For that reason the courtyard is also called the Cour des Adieux (Farewell Courtyard). Cross through the passage to the **3 Cour de la Fontaine** (Fountain Courtyard) and the **4 Étang des Carpes** (Carp Pond). Water from the namesake fountain was once considered so pure that only royalty was allowed to drink it. Immediately west, the informal **5 Jardin Anglais** (English Garden) was created in 1812 and aims to recreate an idealised version of the English countryside. Head east to the oldest and most interesting courtyard, the **6 Cour Ovale** (Oval Courtyard). Although no longer oval but U-shaped due to Henri IV's construction work, it incorporates the keep, the sole remnant of the medieval château. Just south is the geometrically pure expanse of Le Nôtre's formal, 17th-century **7 Jardin Français** (French Garden), also known as the Grand Parterre. Walk east, crossing the Av des Cascades to the sound of just that, cascades, and follow the north bank of the **8 Grand Canal**, which is 1.2km long. It was excavated in 1609 and predates the Versailles canal by more than 50 years. The dense shade trees are a treat on hot days.

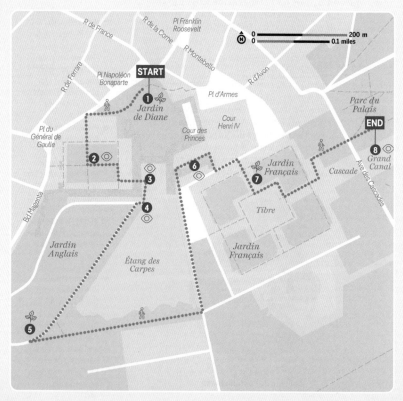

Home of Claude Monet

GIVERNY

Home & Gardens of Claude Monet

Famed Home of Flowers and Beauty

Monet's home for the last 43 years of his life (he died at age 86 in 1926) is open for visits and it's easy to see why he was both so content and so inspired here. His pastel-pink **house** and large, light-filled **studio** (now a gift shop!) stand on the periphery of the **Clos Normand**, his symmetrically laid-out gardens bursting with flowers.

Monet bought the nearby – and even more famous – **Jardin d'Eau** (Water Garden) in 1895 and set about creating his trademark lily pond, as well as the famous **Japanese bridge** (since rebuilt). The charmingly preserved house and iconic gardens are the entire reason for visiting Giverny. Don't expect to see much in the way of original works; rather, you're here to discern the legacy of one of the greatest – and most popular – painters of all time.

In 1883 Monet moved to Giverny with his wife Alice and eight children from two marriages. He planted his new property with a variety of flowers around an artificial pond, the

MONET BEFORE GIVERNY

The undisputed leader of the impressionists, Claude Monet was born in Paris in 1840 and grew up in Le Havre, where he discovered an early affinity with the outdoors. As a teenager, he amused himself by drawing caricatures of teachers and others. In 1860 military service took Monet to Algiers, where the intense light and colours fuelled his visual imagination. The young painter became fascinated with capturing a specific moment in time, the immediate impression of the scene before him, rather than its precise detail.

From 1867 Monet's distinctive style began to emerge, focusing on the effects of light and colour and using the quick, undisguised broken brushstrokes that would characterise the impressionist period. His contemporaries were Pissarro, Renoir, Sisley, Cézanne and Degas.

WHERE TO EAT IN GIVERNY & VERNON

Le Jardin des Plumes
Top-end Michelin-starred restaurant, serving inventive cuisine in a relaxed country-chic setting; has guestrooms. €€€

La Musardière
This sunny terrace is Giverny's most atmospheric table. Casual and creative bistro fare. Sumptuous guestrooms. €€

Gourmandises de Giverny
Upscale deli and sandwich shop with plenty of gift-shop action too. Beautiful pastries. €

WALKING BETWEEN GIVERNY & VERNON

Instead of an overcrowded bus, walk back to the train station in Vernon. It's only a little over 5km along a peaceful riverfront route through the countryside.

From Monet's home, head northwest through the strung-out village along, yes, rue Claude Monet. Go past his gravesite and pause at the many historical plaques about Giverny and the region.

When you reach the busy D5, cross and continue along the cycling and pedestrian footpath through fields of grain along the Seine. Despite the hype of Monet's gardens, you'll soon see that ponds filled with water lilies are a common feature of the Normandy countryside.

In Vernon, stop at the **Collégiale Notre-Dame**, the 12th-century church in the centre of town.

L'Église Ste-Radegonde

Jardin d'Eau, to paint the subtle effects of sunlight on natural forms. It was here that he painted the *Nymphéas* (Water Lilies) series. The huge dimensions of some of these works, together with the fact that the pond's surface takes up the entire canvas, meant the abandonment of composition in the traditional sense and the virtual disintegration of form.

From the late 1870s, Monet also concentrated on painting in series, seeking to recreate a landscape by showing its transformation under different conditions of light and atmosphere. *Haystacks* (1890–91) and the nearby *Rouen Cathedral* (1891–95) are some of the best-known series of his Giverny period.

Try to find a quiet bench in the Water Garden and soak up the surroundings. Purple wisteria is draped artfully over trellises while the Japanese bridge blends into the asymmetrical foreground and background. The tableau creates the intimate atmosphere for which the 'painter of light' was renowned. And yes, there are water lilies, lots of water lilies.

Behind the house, Clos Normand is an ever-changing spectacle as seasons have an enormous effect here. From early to late spring, daffodils, tulips, rhododendrons, wisteria and irises appear, followed by poppies and lilies. By June, nasturtiums, roses and sweet peas are in flower. Around September, there are dahlias, sunflowers and hollyhocks.

 ## WHERE TO STAY IN GIVERNY & VERNON

Restaurant Baudy
Trad old bistro seemingly unchanged since impressionists sat around arguing about the light. €€

Le Parisien
Elegant, modern cafe in Vernon's centre; a good place to stop after the walk from Giverny. €

Boulangerie Festival des Pains
Traditional breads, sandwiches and gorgeous treats made with local berries, in Vernon. €

Monet's bourgeois home – as befits an artist who enjoyed great success in his lifetime – can get too crowded to comfortably enter. But by peering in through some of the doors overlooking the garden, you can see his wonderfully inviting main salon. It's decorated with reproductions of his many works that once graced the walls. Nearby, the same copper pots used to cook his meals still hang from hooks in the kitchen. Just outside, descendants of Monet's egg-layers cluck away happily.

Academic Impressionism

Going Beyond the Facile

Studying the painters and paintings of impressionism, plus the formative influences and legacies of the movement, is the mission of the well-funded **Giverny Musée des Impressionnismes** (Giverny Museum of Impressionisms). It was set up in partnership with the Musée d'Orsay, among other institutions, and the pluralised name reinforces its coverage of all aspects of impressionism. You don't come here to see great original works of art; rather this is the place to learn about many aspects of impressionism through exhibitions that use high-quality reproductions. Topics have included the role of children in impressionism, the portrayal of flowers and how the countryside influenced Renoir.

Monet's Church & Gravesite

Unassuming Final Resting Place

Dedicated to a saint noted for her self-denial, self-mutilation and asceticism , the **L'Église Ste-Radegonde** (Church of St Radegonde) was originally built in the 11th and 12th centuries, expanded in the 15th century and then greatly restored between 2008 and 2010. The church is on the western edge of the village and is most noteworthy for being the site of the Monet family tomb. It's outside around the back and close to a memorial to an RAF crew who died when their bomber crashed nearby in WWII.

TOP TIPS FOR VISITING MONET'S HOME

Check hours in advance from November to Easter, as much of Giverny is closed during the winter months and there's no reason to make the trip as even the gardens are hidden behind walls.

Buy tickets in advance at the Maison et Jardins de Claude Monet website. This also entitles you to use the hassle-free group tours entrance on arrival, which has easy access to the Water Garden. That scrum you see in the distance is people trying to buy tickets on-site.

Giverny has useful eating options, but they are understandably geared towards the masses. Consider assembling a top-notch picnic in Paris and enjoying it in a Giverny garden or along the Seine.

 WHERE TO STAY IN GIVERNY & VERNON

La Parenthèse
Close to Monet's gardens; plush farmhouse rooms and a bright bistro draped with wisteria. €€

La Pluie de Roses
Luxe, welcoming B&B set in gardens in an even quieter part of quiet Giverny. €€

Le Clos Fleuri
Prim B&B down a little lane away from the Monet clamour. Large rooms and beds. €€

TOOLKIT

The chapters in this section cover the most important topics you'll need to know about in Paris. They're full of nuts-and-bolts information and valuable insights to help you understand and navigate Paris and get the most out of your trip.

Arriving
p286

Getting Around
p287

Money
p288

Nuts & Bolts
p289

Accommodation
p290

Family Travel
p292

Health & Safe Travel
p293

Food, Drink & Nightlife
p294

Responsible Travel
p296

LGBTIQ+ Travellers
p298

Accessible Travel
p299

Eiffel Tower (p60)

✈ Arriving

Paris is the main point of entry for most visitors to France. Most international airlines fly to Aéroport de Charles de Gaulle, 28km northeast of central Paris, or Aéroport d'Orly, 19km south of central Paris. Paris also has five major train stations with international services. Whether by plane or train, you'll find easy public-transport options into the city.

Visas

EU citizens have no entry restrictions. From 2024, citizens of countries that can visit the Schengen area visa-free (eg Australia, Canada, UK, USA) will need prior authorisation under the online ETIAS scheme.

Airports

Aéroport de Charles de Gaulle is the busiest airport and is linked to central Paris by the RER B train line. **Aéroport d'Orly is** connected to the RER B line by the Orlyval shuttle train.

Train Stations

International trains use these stations: the UK, Belgium and the Netherlands – **Gare du Nord**; Luxembourg and Germany – **Gare de l'Est**; east Spain, Switzerland and Italy – **Gare de Lyon**; north Spain – **Gare Montparnasse**.

Money

ATMs dispensing euros are easily found in airports, train stations and across central Paris. Currency-exchange (bureaux de change) services to get euros are available in airports and train stations.

Public Transport from Airport to City Centre

Paris

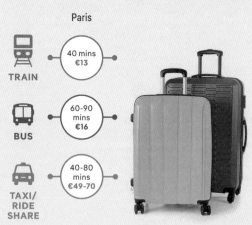

🚆 **TRAIN** — 40 mins €13

🚌 **BUS** — 60-90 mins €16

🚕 **TAXI/ RIDE SHARE** — 40-80 mins €49-70

TRAINS TO/ FROM THE PLANES

Trains are the best way to get to and from Paris' airports. The RER B line from Charles de Gaulle crosses under the middle of Paris, with stops including Gare du Nord, Châtelet–Les Halles, St-Michel–Notre Dame and Luxembourg. Some trains run express through the suburbs, saving about 10 minutes. An even faster express route is slated for 2027. From d'Orly, you can connect to the RER B; beginning in 2024, the airport will also be served by Line 14 of the metro. Aéroport de Beauvais, used by some budget airlines, is a long and slow 75km by bus from Paris.

Getting Around

The convenient Paris metro covers the city, while the comprehensive bus system allows you to sightsee while travelling. For many, however, walking the beautiful streets is the way to go.

TRAVEL COSTS

Metro & bus ride
From €2.10

Children under
10/four
Half-price/free

Mobilis day pass
From €8.45

Paris Visite
five-day pass
€43.30

NAVIGO EASY CARD

The cheapest, easiest way to use Paris' public transport is via the Navigo Easy card. Sold for €2 at metro and RER ticket windows and RATP-affiliated outlets (eg tobacconists and markets), this credit-card-sized fare card is used for all your ticketing needs; or charge up a virtual one on the RATP app.

Navigo, like London's Oyster card or Hong Kong's Octopus card, is a system that provides a full range of fare options. As Paris phases out paper tickets, Navigo Easy cards are the future.

You load the card with value, which is then deducted for each ride. To save money, buy *carnets*, which are credits for 10 rides sold at a discount (this is the cheapest way to ride the metro and buses). One disadvantage of passes is that they're tied to the calendar; eg a seven-day pass always begins on Monday, a monthly pass always begins on the first day of the month.

You can also load train tickets onto your Navigo Easy card. This is good for day trips to places such as Versailles or Giverny, and for journeys to/from the airports. To load tickets of any kind onto your card, use one of the multilingual machines found at metro and train stations. You can also use RATP and SNCF apps on your phone to load tickets and fares.

METRO & RER

The fastest way to get around, the metro runs from about 5.30am to around 1.15am (about 2.15am on Friday and Saturday evenings). RER express trains save time crossing the city and serve the suburbs. It's usually quicker to walk than to take the metro for only one or two stops. Use the IDF Mobilités, RATP and SNCF apps for journey planning, maps and wait times for the next train or bus.

Bus

With no stairs, buses are widely accessible and are good for parents with prams/strollers and people with limited mobility. Bus lines complement the metro: for some journeys a bus is the more direct – and scenic – way to go. Stops shows schedules, routes and often the waiting time until the next bus.

Boat

Combining scenery and convenience, the Batobus is a handy hop-on, hop-off service stopping at nine key destinations along the Seine. In warmer months the service runs regularly through the day and offers the chance for a river cruise at a fraction of the price of a tour boat.

Taxi, Rideshare & Carshare

Find taxis at official stands or via private companies and apps. There are queues of cabs at major train stations. Taxis are expensive but are a blessing if you can't face the metro. Rideshare apps like Uber are active. Find carsharing (*autopartage*) at free2move.com.

Bicycle & Scooter

The **Vélib'** bike-share scheme has over 20,000 bikes, both classic (green) and electric (blue). Buy a subscription online (EU cards only) or at docking stations. There are single-trip, day and multiday options. App-based electric *trottinettes* (scooters) were discontinued in September 2023.

Money

CURRENCY: EURO (€)

Tipping

Taxis Round up to the nearest €1.
Restaurants Bills include a service charge; leave a few extra euros for good service.
Bars/cafes For table service, tip as you would in a restaurant.
Hotels Tip bellhops €1 to €2 per bag. Not expected for concierges, cleaners or front-desk staff.

Digital Payments

Payments via your phone or smartwatch are common in Paris. Tap and pay is becoming ubiquitous, from shops and cafes to the metro.

Credit Cards

Visa is the most widely accepted credit card in Paris, followed by MasterCard. Amex cards are only accepted at more upmarket establishments. Memorise the PIN code for your card in case of the rare instances a payment point requires it – most commonly at automated machines like petrol pumps (or use a debit card).

ATMs

ATMs (*distributeur automatique de billets*) are widespread and can be cheaper than exchanging money. Check if/how much your bank charges for international withdrawals before you travel.

HOW MUCH FOR...

Baguette
Around €1.20

Glass of wine
from €2.50

Two-course bistro menu
from €17

Louvre ticket
€17

HOW TO... Claim VAT Refunds

Non-EU residents over 16 who are visiting France for less than six months can often claim a TVA (*taxe sur la valeur ajoutée*) refund, provided the purchase amount is over €100 and made over a maximum of three days at a retailer that offers tax-free shopping (present your passport for eligibility). The retailer will provide a slip with a barcode that can be scanned at PABLO electronic terminals prior to check-in at the airport.

LOCAL TIP

If paying by card, the electronic device may offer you the option to pay in your home currency. Refuse and select the euro option as this is cheaper.

SAVING MONEY ON MUSEUMS & SIGHTS

Most museums and monuments have discounted tickets (*tarif réduit*) for students and seniors. Children often get in free; the cut-off is anywhere between six and 18 years. Watch for free days.

Paris Museum Pass
Gets you into 50-plus venues; a huge advantage is that pass holders usually enter larger sights at an entrance with shorter queues.

Paris Passlib'
Sold by the Paris Convention & Visitors Bureau, this city pass covers unlimited public transport, admission to dozens of museums, a Seine boat cruise, a bus tour and more.

Nuts & Bolts

OPENING HOURS

The following list covers approximate opening hours. Many businesses close in August for holidays.

Banks 9am–1pm and 2–5pm Monday to Friday; some open on Saturday morning

Bars and cafes 7am–11pm/2am

Museums 10am–6pm; closed Monday or Tuesday

Restaurants noon–2pm and 7.30–10.30pm

Shops 10am–7pm Monday to Saturday; they occasionally close in the early afternoon for lunch and sometimes all day Monday; hours are longer in tourist zones

Internet Access
Free wi-fi is common in many public squares, cultural institutions and cafes.

Weights & Measures
France uses the metric system. Decimal places are indicated by commas.

Smoking
Smoking is illegal in all indoor public spaces, including restaurants, cafes and bars.

GOOD TO KNOW

Time Zone
Central European Time (GMT/ UTC +1)

Country Code
33

Emergency Number
112

Population
2.16 million

Electricity

Type E
220V/50Hz

PUBLIC HOLIDAYS

The following holidays are observed in Paris:

New Year's Day (Jour de l'An) 1 January

Easter Sunday & Monday (Pâques & Lundi de Pâques) Late March/April

May Day (Fête du Travail) 1 May

Victory in Europe Day (Victoire 1945) 8 May

Ascension Thursday (L'Ascension) May (celebrated on the 40th day after Easter)

Whit Monday (Lundi de Pentecôte) Mid-May to mid-June (seventh Monday after Easter)

Bastille Day/ National Day (Fête Nationale) 14 July

Assumption Day (L'Assomption) 15 August

All Saints' Day (La Toussaint) 1 November

Armistice Day/ Remembrance Day (Le Onze Novembre) 11 November

Christmas (Noël) 25 December

Accommodation

Hostels

Paris is home to some state-of-the-art, modern hostels such as Generator, near Canal St-Martin, and, nearby, two by St Christopher's Inns. Expect a range of dorms and private rooms, some with private bathrooms. There are usually cafes, lively common areas and activities. Only Hostelling International (HI) *auberges de jeunesse* (youth hostels) require membership cards.

Apartments

As well as home-share sites like Airbnb and Vrbo, Paris also has a number of *résidences de tourisme* (serviced apartments, aka 'aparthotels'). You'll find oodles of listings for apartments across the city. Some lack lifts (elevators), which can result in a seven-floor walk-up. Others are extremely tiny, though for a price, you can get a grand flat with a balcony and a view.

HOW MUCH FOR A NIGHT IN A...

Midrange hotel
From €150

Hostel dorm
From €25

Studio apartment
From €125

Hotels & Pensions

In Paris, hotel rooms are typically small by international standards, and cheaper properties may not have lifts or air-conditioning. Upper midrange and top-end hotels often have restaurants and bars on-site (but breakfast is rarely included in the price). Prices are high, in line with London and New York City. Hotels, whether humble or grand, are found across the city.

Book Ahead

Paris has no real low season, although room rates may be somewhat less in winter (outside of the holidays) and early spring. Whether you want a hostel bed, a cosy hotel room, a luxurious suite at a grand property or a short-term apartment of any kind, the earlier you book the better. Places to stay in favoured neighbourhoods are always in demand.

Stay in the City

While accommodation outside of central Paris might be marginally cheaper, it is invariably a false economy when travel time and costs are considered. Stay in one of Paris' *arrondissements* (inner-city suburbs) to immerse yourself in Parisian life. There is little joy in ending up in a large generic chain hotel that comes with a long slog on public transport and little interesting street life.

LIMITING SHORT-TERM RENTALS

Given that Paris hotels below five-star status are often more serviceable than superlative, you might want to – literally – think outside the box. Short-term apartment rentals are very popular and often offer excellent value. However, as in other places worldwide that are popular with tourists and that have surging demand for short-term rentals, the local authorities are constantly trying to rein in the market. Getting a licence for a year-round short-term rental is hard for most landlords; rather, they must show that the apartment is their primary residence and may only be rented for four months a year.

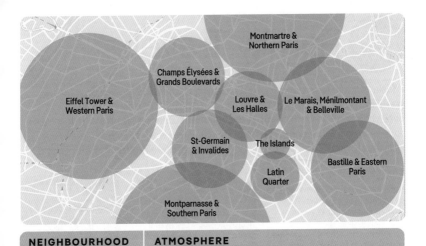

NEIGHBOURHOOD	ATMOSPHERE
Eiffel Tower & Western Paris	Close to Paris' iconic tower and museums. Upmarket area with quiet residential streets. Short on budget and midrange accommodation. Limited nightlife.
Champs-Élysées & Grands Boulevards	Luxury hotels, famous boutiques and department stores, gastronomic restaurants, great nightlife. Some areas extremely pricey. Nightlife hot spots can be noisy.
Louvre & Les Halles	Epicentral location, excellent transport links, famous museums, shopping galore. Not many bargains. Noise can be an issue in some areas.
Montmartre & Northern Paris	Village atmosphere and some lively multicultural areas. Many places have views across Paris. Hilly streets; further out than some areas; some parts very touristy. The red-light district around Pigalle won't appeal to everyone.
Le Marais, Ménilmontant & Belleville	Buzzing nightlife, hip shopping, fantastic eating options in all price ranges. Excellent museums. Lively gay and lesbian scene. Busier on Sundays than many areas. Very central. Can be noisy in areas where bars and clubs are concentrated.
Bastille & Eastern Paris	Fewer tourists, immersing you in a more workaday Paris. Excellent markets, loads of nightlife of all kinds, especially international restaurants. Some areas in the east are isolated.
The Islands	As geographically central as it gets. Accommodation centred on the peaceful, romantic Île St-Louis. No metro station on the Île St-Louis. Limited self-catering shops, minimal nightlife.
Latin Quarter	Energetic boho area with a mix of students and tourists. Myriad eating and drinking options of varying quality, late-opening bookshops. Easy walk to nearby appealing areas.
St-Germain & Les Invalides	Stylish, central location, superb shopping, sophisticated dining, famous cafes, proximity to the Seine and museums. Budget accommodation is in seriously short supply.
Montparnasse & Southern Paris	Good value, less touristy. Has excellent shopping streets, moderately priced restaurants and comfortable vibe. Great outdoor bars. Southern areas not well served by metro.

Family Travel

Parisians adore *les enfants* (children) and the city's residential density means you'll find playground equipment throughout the city. Families have an overwhelming choice of creative, educational, culinary and just plain fun things to see, do and experience. The Paris Tourist Office website lists museums and activities for kids. Discounts at sights and attractions aimed at families abound.

Accommodation

Note that Paris hotel rooms can be smaller than you're used to, so keep that in mind as you think about sharing the room. Some establishments offer rooms aimed specifically at families. Rental apartments will give you – possibly – more space and let you self-cater for younger tastes and habits. Consider lift (elevator) options if you'll be dealing with prams and the like.

Theme Parks

Disneyland Resort Paris is a natural magnet for families. The park is 32km east of the city and incorporates both Disneyland itself and the cinema-themed Walt Disney Studios Park. It's easily reached for day trips on the RER A. **Parc Astérix**, a summer-opening theme park 35km north of the city, features six 'worlds' of adrenaline-pumping attractions and shows for all ages.

Welcoming Children

Most restaurants welcome children; many offer a *menu enfant* (children's menu). Under 18s (or younger) receive discounted or free entry to sights. Rent strollers, car seats and other gear from companies such as Kidelio (kidelio.com). Hotels can often organise babysitters.

Getting Around

Children under four travel free on the metro, RER and bus network. Kids under 10 travel at half-price. Buses have low-floor entrances that are good for prams. The metro system is chaotic at rush hour; some stations have many stairs.

KID-FRIENDLY PICKS

See also Our Picks (p8) and Paris with Kids (p44).

Centre Pompidou (p99)

This modern art hub has kids programs, with workshops and events.

Cité de l'Architecture et du Patrimoine (p65)

Workshops let kids construct miniature art deco buildings.

Cité des Sciences (p135)

The children's museum section allows kids to delve into science in an immersive way.

Promotrain (p125)

A fantastic way to explore Montmartre by avoiding the many steps.

Seine Cruise (p70)

Beloved by all ages.

FABULOUS PARKS FOR KIDS

Major parks have features aimed at kids.

The legendary **Jardin du Luxembourg** (p216) has playgrounds and an old-fashioned carousel. The vintage toy sailing boats are real heart-stealers.

The elegant **Jardin des Tuileries** (p98) also has kid's activities, a summertime amusement park and its own fleet of vintage toy boats

you can sail in the shadow of the Louvre.

The **Parc Floral de Paris** (p185) is easily the best playground for kids eight years and older with outdoor concerts, puppet shows, giant climbing webs, 30m-high slides and a zip line.

On **Canal St-Martin** (p121) you can watch the boats navigate the locks from the nearby parks.

Health & Safe Travel

INSURANCE

Citizens of the EU, Switzerland, Iceland, Norway and Liechtenstein receive free or reduced-cost, state-provided health-care cover with the European Health Insurance Card (EHIC). Each family member will need a separate card. Citizens of non-EU countries should check if there is a reciprocal arrangement for free medical care between their country and France.

Pharmacies & Hospitals

For minor health concerns and to fill prescriptions, see a local *pharmacie* (pharmacy/chemist). For more serious problems, go to *urgences* (emergencies) wards at Paris' *hôpitaux* (hospitals). Pharmacies are marked by a large illuminated green cross outside. At least one in each neighbourhood is open for extended hours; find a complete listing on the Paris Convention & Visitors Bureau website.

Luggage & Bags

Never leave baggage unattended, especially at airports or train stations. This is important not only to deter theft but because unattended bags are viewed as security threats and can cause a major law-enforcement event. Elsewhere, at museums and monuments, bags are routinely checked on entry. Avoid hassles by travelling as light as possible when you're out and about.

PICKPOCKETS

Stay alert for pickpockets, especially on the metro/RER and crowded, touristy areas. *Bornes d'alarme* (alarm boxes) are located on station platforms and some corridors.

Don't Worry

Overall, Paris (and France) is a healthy place: your main risks are likely to be sunburn, foot blisters and mild stomach problems from eating and drinking with too much gusto. Central Paris is well lit and generally safe – single travellers can play it safe by sticking to main streets at night. The important consideration is to use common sense: if an area or situation looks sketchy, leave.

Food, Drink & Nightlife

When to Eat

Restaurants generally open from noon to 2pm for lunch and from 7.30pm to 10.30pm for dinner. Peak Parisian dining times are 1pm and 9pm. Most restaurants shut for at least one full day (often Sunday, Monday and/or Tuesday). August is the peak holiday month and many places are consequently closed during this time.

Etiquette

Table reservations
Booking a table in advance by telephone, email or online is vital.

Bread A basket of fresh bread will be brought to the table. Butter is rarely an accompaniment.

Water Asking for *une carafe d'eau* (jug of tap water) is acceptable.

Coffee Never end a meal with a cappuccino, *café au lait* or cup of tea, which, incidentally, never comes with milk. Order *un café* (an espresso).

Dress Smart casual is best. No baseball caps.

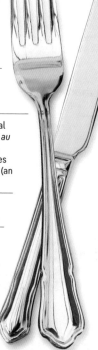

MENU DECODER

Avec/sans With/without

Chaud Hot

Froid Cold

Petit déjeuner Breakfast

Déjeuner Lunch

Dîner Dinner

Entrée Appetiser

Couteau Knife

Cuillère Spoon

Fourchette Fork

Assiette Plate

Verre Glass

Bouteille Bottle

Carte des vins Wine list

Vin blanc White wine

Vin rouge Red wine

Bière Beer

Café Coffee

Eau (minérale) (Mineral) water

Jus (d'orange) (Orange) juice

Lait Milk

Thé Tea

Beurre Butter

Confiture Jam

Fromage Cheese

Huile Oil

Miel Honey

Œuf Egg

Pain Bread

Poivre Pepper

Riz Rice

Sel Salt

Sucre Sugar

Vinaigre Vinegar

Agneau Lamb

Bœuf Beef

Escargot Snail

Huître Oyster

Jambon Ham

Porc Pork

Poulet Chicken

Veau Veal

Asperge Asparagus

Céleri Celery

Champignon Mushroom

Citron Lemon

Fraise Strawberry

Haricots Beans

Légume Vegetable

Pêche Peach

Petit pois Peas

Poireau Leek

Pomme Apple

Pomme de terre Potato

Tomate Tomato

Épicerie Grocery store

Marché Market

When to Eat & Drink

Petit déjeuner (breakfast) Kick-start the day with a *tartine* (slice of baguette smeared with unsalted butter and jam) and *un café* (an espresso), a milky *café au lait* or – especially for kids – a hot chocolate. Croissants (never with butter or jam) are a weekend treat along with *brioches* (sweet breads) and *pains au chocolat* (chocolate-filled croissants).

Déjeuner (lunch) The traditional main meal of the day, lunch translates as a starter and main course with wine, followed by an espresso. Sunday lunch is a long, languid affair taking several hours.

Apéritif The *apéro* (predinner drink) is sacred. Cafes and bars get packed from 5pm onwards.

Dîner (dinner) Traditionally lighter than lunch, but a meal that is increasingly treated as the main meal of the day. Restaurant times are 7pm to 10.30pm.

Baguettes

Buy a baguette from a *boulangerie* (bakery), stuff it with a chunk of Camembert, pâté and *cornichons* (miniature gherkins), and, voilà, picnic perfection! A *baguette tradition/ traditionnelle* will have a little more character and flavour.

Where to Eat & Drink

Bistro (also spelled *bistrot*) Anything from a pub or bar with snacks and light meals to a small, fully fledged restaurant. They often have great-value menus.

Neobistro Trendy in Paris, where this contemporary take on the traditional bistro ranges from checked-tablecloth tradition to contemporary minimalism.

Brasserie Much like a cafe except it serves full meals, drinks and coffee from morning until 11pm or later.

Restaurant Born in Paris in the 18th century, restaurants today serve lunch and dinner five or six days a week.

Buffet (or *buvette*) Kiosk, usually at train stations and airports, selling drinks, filled baguettes and snacks.

Cafe Basic light snacks as well as drinks. You'll find one on seemingly every corner in Paris. They range from humble to grand, in atmosphere and pricing.

Crêperie (also *galetterie*) Casual eatery or food stand specialising in sweet crêpes and savoury *galettes* (buckwheat crêpes).

Salon de thé Trendy tearoom often serving light lunches (quiche, salads, cakes, tarts, pies and pastries) and green, black and herbal teas.

Table d'hôte (literally 'host's table') A meal of set courses with little choice.

THE INGREDIENTS OF A FRENCH MEAL

Knowing these terms will help you navigate through a Parisian meal.

Carte Menu, as in the written list of what's on offer.

Menu Not at all what it means in English, *le menu* in French is a two- or three-course meal at a fixed price.

À la carte Order whatever you fancy from the menu (as opposed to choosing a fixed menu).

Formule Not to be confused with a *menu*, *une formule* is a cheaper lunchtime option.

Plat du jour Dish of the day, invariably good value.

Menu enfant Two- or three-course kids' meal at a fixed price.

Menu dégustation Fixed-price tasting menu served in many top-end restaurants.

Amuse-bouche A complimentary savoury morsel intended to excite and ignite taste buds.

Entrée Starter, appetiser.

Plat Main course.

Fromage Cheese, accompanied with fresh bread; served after the main course and before dessert.

Dessert Served after cheese.

Responsible Travel

Climate Change & Travel

It's impossible to ignore the impact we have when travelling, and the importance of making changes where we can. Lonely Planet urges all travellers to engage with their travel carbon footprint. There are many carbon calculators online that allow travellers to estimate the carbon emissions generated by their journey; try resurgence.org/resources/carbon-calculator.html. Many airlines and booking sites offer travellers the option of offsetting the impact of greenhouse gas emissions by contributing to climate-friendly initiatives around the world. We continue to offset the carbon footprint of all Lonely Planet staff travel, while recognising this is a mitigation more than a solution.

Ride a Bike

Cycle through the city with Paris' bike-share scheme **Vélib'**, which has thousands of classic and electric bikes at citywide docking stations for low-impact travel.

Walk

Walking in Paris is a joy and is easily the most responsible thing you can do while visiting the city. Once out on the ever-fascinating streets, you'll discover that distances are short and steep hills are few.

Hop on a Train/Metro

Public transport in Paris is comprehensive. You'll rarely need to use a cab or a rideshare. The network extends beyond the city, so you can easily reach day-trip destinations by train.

Make over your wardrobe at **Sézane** (sezane.com), a cult-status affordable label that donates many of the proceeds from its sustainably sourced pieces to its own children's charity, Demain.

Look out over Paris from 150m up in the air aboard the helium-filled **Ballon de Paris** (ballondeparis.com). Tethered in the Parc André Citroën, this sightseeing balloon monitors Paris' air quality.

SUSTAINABLE FASHION

Take part in events and more through the **Paris Good Fashion** (parisgoodfashion.fr) initiative, which is focused on improving sourcing, traceability, eco-friendly processes and circular economies as part of Paris' aim to become the world's most sustainable fashion capital.

LEARN RECYCLING

Take an upcycling workshop at eco-conscious cultural centre **La Recyclerie** (larecyclerie.com), in a repurposed vintage train station, whose cafe utilises produce from its own urban farm on the tracks.

Sustainable Dining

Dine farm-to-fork at **Le Perchoir Porte de Versailles** at Europe's largest urban rooftop farm, the 14,000-sq-metre biodiverse Nature Urbaine. The changing menu utilises all the various foods grown in this sustainable setting.

Electric Boats

Chart your own course and explore Paris' waterways by renting an electric-powered boat (no licence required) from **Marin D'Eau Douce** (boating-paris-marindeaudouce.com). You can navigate over 40km of canals and waterways around the city.

Local Markets

Buy fresh produce at Paris' *biologique* (organic) markets, such as Marché Raspail (Sunday), Marché Biologique des Batignolles (Saturday), Marché Biologique Brancusi (Saturday) and Marché Biologique Place du Père Chaillet (Wednesday and Saturday).

Diverse Paris

Discover black Paris on a guided tour with **Entrée to Black Paris** (entreetoblackparis.com), take a walking or kick-scooter tour of Paris' multicultural northeastern neighbourhoods with **Ça Se Visite** (ca-se-visite.fr) and learn about Islamic culture on tours with the **Institut des Cultures d'Islam** (institut-cultures-islam.org).

Snap up bargain-priced unsold items at merchants such as bakeries via the app **Too Good to Go** (toogoodtogo. fr), which helps prevent food waste.

Browse over 1000 exquisite handcrafted items all made in French designers' studios, at **Empreintes** (empreintes-paris. com).

Carbon

In Paris' pursuit of carbon neutrality by 2050, dramatic progress includes a 20% reduction in greenhouse-gas emissions between 2004 and 2018. Help out by refilling your water bottle at fountains all over Paris (see fontaine. eaudeparis.fr).

RESOURCES

Sustainable Paris
Embrace Paris' sustainability initiatives.

Made in Paris
Products sporting the Made in Paris label.

We Love Green
Zero-waste, renewable-energy-powered festival.

LGBTIQ+ Travellers

The city known as 'gay Paree' lives up to its name. Paris is so open that there's less of a defined 'scene' here than in other cities where it's more underground. While Le Marais is the mainstay of gay and lesbian nightlife, you'll find LGBTIQ+ venues throughout the city attracting a mixed crowd.

Annual Events

By far the biggest event on the LGBTIQ+ calendar is Gay Pride Day, in late June, when the annual Marche des Fiertés through Paris via Le Marais provides a colourful spectacle, and plenty of parties over a two-week period. Look for these events at other times.

January The Festival des Cultures LGBT features films, events and more.

March to April The Festival de Films d'Artistes sur le Queer celebrates queer films.

October to November Jerk Off is a huge series of events devoted to queer and alternative culture.

GAY TOURS

For an insider's perspective and recommendations on where to eat, drink, sightsee and party, take a tour with the **Gay Locals** (thegaylocals.com). English-speaking residents lead two tours of 'the Gaybourhood' Le Marais or Montmartre. Its website is a good source of nightlife info.

Nightlife

Le Marais, especially the areas around the intersection of rue Ste-Croix de la Bretonnerie and rue des Archives, and eastwards to rue Vieille du Temple, has long been Paris' main centre of LGBTIQ+ nightlife and is still its epicentre. There are also a handful of bars and clubs close by to its west, particularly around Châtelet. Bars and clubs are generally all gay- and lesbian-friendly.

PARIS' BEST RESOURCE

Centre LGBTQI+ de Paris et Île-de-France (centrelgbtparis.org) is the single best source of information for gay and lesbian travellers in Paris, with a large library, a comprehensive website and periodicals and a sociable bar. It also has details of hotlines, helplines, gay and gay-friendly medical services and politically oriented activist associations.

Gay Paris

In 2001 Paris was the first European capital to elect an openly gay mayor. The city itself is very open – same-sex couples commonly display affection in public. In 2013 France legalised same-sex marriage (and adoption by same-sex couples).

LGBTIQ+ WEBSITES

Spartacus International Gay Guide (spartacus.travel) Travel site with solid recommendations for gay-friendly accommodation in particular.

CitéGay (citegay.com) One of the best all-inclusive gay sites, with a heavily political agenda.

Gay and lesbian cultural venues (parisjetaime.com/eng/article/gay-and-lesbian-cultural-venues-a652) The Paris Tourist Office lists 'the gayest spots in the French capital'.

Accessible Travel

Paris is an ancient city and not particularly well equipped for *visiteurs handicapés* (disabled visitors): kerb ramps are few and older public facilities and the metro are mostly inaccessible for those in a wheelchair (*fauteuil roulant*). Efforts are being made to improve things ahead of the 2024 Olympic and Paralympic Games.

Helpful Paris

In general, although Paris is not always accessible, you will find that most Parisians are more than willing to help and that arrangements can be made at cultural institutions and public places like cafes and restaurants.

Airport

Paris' airports are fully in line with international standards for accessibility. Note, however, that transport to and from the airports may be an issue as many metro stations in the city are not fully accessible.

Accommodation

Hotels and rental apartments are a mixed bag of accessibility. Typically chain hotels in modern buildings meet international standards. But properties in older buildings, especially rental apartments, may lack lifts and other accessibility amenities.

TAXIS

Taxis G7 (g7.fr) has hundreds of low-base cars and over 100 cars equipped with ramps, and drivers trained in helping passengers with disabilities. Guide dogs are accepted in its entire fleet.

Accessible Culture

For information about which cultural venues in Paris are accessible to people with disabilities, visit Accès Culture (accesculture.org). Its information is comprehensive and includes details on all forms of accessibility, from Braille signage to special events.

Public Transport

Much of the vintage metro system in the heart of Paris is not fully accessible; the RATP makes info available through its app and website. Paris buses, however, are all accessible, with low floors and wide doors.

ACCESSIBLE TRAINS

The SNCF has made many of its train carriages more accessible to people with disabilities, including RER trains. For information and advice on planning your journey from station to station, contact the service Accès Plus.

RESOURCES

An excellent first stop is the website of the **Paris Tourist Office** (parisinfo. com/accessibility), for a wealth of useful information organised by theme – getting there and around, attractions, accommodation and cafes/bars/restaurants – as well as practical information such as where to rent medical equipment or locate automatic public toilets. You can download the up-to-date Accessible Paris guide, which is also available in hard copy from tourist information centres in the city.

Accessible Tours

Mobile en Ville makes independent travel within Paris easier for people with mobility challenges. It organises wheelchair *randonnées* (walks) in and around Paris; those in wheelchairs are pushed by 'walkers'; contact the association ahead of your visit to take part.

e Poste
auchat

→

MAISON FONDÉE EN 1761

NÉGUS
DE
NEVERS

FLORENTINS

ORANGETTES

MENDIANTS

À
LA MÈRE
DE FAMILLE
CHOCOLATIER

CONFISEUR

GLACES
CONFITURES
CAKES
ET
SPÉCIALITÉS
MAISON

VINS FINS DESSERTS

À LA MÈRE DE F

THE PARIS

STORYBOOK

Our writers delve deep into different aspects of Paris life

À la Mère de Famille (p83)

A HISTORY OF PARIS IN
15 PLACES

With its cobbled streets, terraced cafes and iconic landmarks, Paris evokes a sense of timelessness, yet the city has changed and evolved dramatically over the centuries. Paris' history is a saga of battles, bloodshed, grand-scale excesses, revolution, reformation, resistance, renaissance and constant reinvention. By Alexis Averbuck

THE EARLY HISTORY of Paris is murky, but the consensus is that a Celtic tribe known as the Parisii established a fishing village in the area in the 3rd century BCE. In the early Middle Ages, most of today's Paris was either a carpet of fields and vineyards or a boggy, waterlogged marsh. From this, Paris the powerful would rise, a city of kings and the seat of power for a country dominating Europe.

The city was not transformed into the modern metropolis it is today until town planner Baron Haussmann (1809–91) completely rebuilt huge swaths of it (demolishing much of medieval Paris in the process). Many chaotic narrow streets were replaced with the handsome, arrow-straight and wide thoroughfares for which the city is now celebrated.

The Latin motto *'fluctuat nec mergitur'* ('tossed but not sunk') was adopted by Paris around 1358. It still appears on the city's coat of arms and became emblematic of the city's spirit following the 2015 terrorist attacks, when Parisians' resilience came to the fore.

These epic rises and falls are not just consigned to museums and archives – reminders of the capital's and the country's history are evident all over the city.

1. Arènes de Lutèce
THE EARLIEST SETTLERS

After beating back the Gauls, the Romans established a town in 52 BCE – Lutetia (Lutèce in French) – with the main public buildings (forum, bathhouse, theatre and amphitheatre) radiating from Île de la Cité onto the Left Bank, near today's Panthéon. Though Lutetia was not the capital of its province, it was a prosperous town, with a population of around 8000. To this day you can visit the Romans' earliest ruins at Crypte Archéologique beneath Notre Dame, and the bathhouse (beneath the Cluny), or even play boules in the amphitheatre at Arènes de Lutèce.

For more on Arènes de Lutèce, see page 211

2. Église St-Germain-des-Prés
RISE OF CHRISTIANITY AND PARIS AS CAPITAL

One of the key figures in early Parisian history was the Frankish king Clovis I (c 466–511). Clovis was the first ruler to unite what would later become France, to convert to Christianity and to declare Paris the capital. Under the Frankish kings, the city once again began to expand, and important edifices such as the abbey at St-Denis and the abbey of

Église St-Germain-des-Prés were erected. Today, the church that stands on the site of the abbey is the oldest in Paris, and it lies smack in the middle of the Left Bank's cool shopping streets.

For more on Église St-Germain-des-Prés, see page 232

3. Notre Dame
MEDIEVAL PARIS

The city's strategic riverside position ensured its importance throughout the Middle Ages. The first guilds were created in the 11th century, and in the mid-12th century the ship merchants' guild bought the principal river port, by today's Hôtel de Ville (City Hall), from the crown. Frenetic building marked the 12th and 13th centuries. The Basilique de St-Denis was commissioned in 1136 and less than three decades later work started on Notre Dame in 1163 and was largely completed by the early 14th century. It is the site of myriad important historical moments, especially royal coronations and weddings.

For more on Notre Dame, see page 190

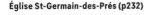

Église St-Germain-des-Prés (p232)

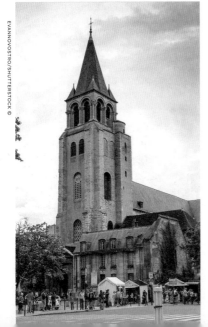

4. Conciergerie & Palais de Justice
REIGN OF THE ROYAL COURT

The history of the Palais de Justice (Law Courts) and the Conciergerie winds through centuries of Parisian life and power. When Hugh Capet was made king in 987 (and Paris became the royal seat) he lived in the renovated palace of the Roman governor, site of the present Palais de Justice. The buildings continued as headquarters of French kings until the 14th century (when they moved to the Louvre). In the 13th century, Sainte-Chapelle was built in six rapid years by Louis IX (St Louis, r 1226–70) at the Palais de Justice, and in 1391 the Conciergerie became a prison, heavily used in the French Revolution as well.

For more on Conciergerie & Palais de Justice, see page 189

5. Château de Fontainebleau
THE FRENCH RENAISSANCE

Under Louis XI (r 1461–83) the city's first printing press was installed at the Sorbonne and churches were built in the Flamboyant Gothic style. But it was during the reign of François I (r 1515–47) that Renaissance ideas of scientific scholarship really assumed new importance, as did the value of secular matters over religious life. Writers such as Rabelais were influential, as were artist and architect disciples of Michelangelo and Raphael, who worked towards a new architectural style designed to reflect the splendour of the monarchy. This is seen at François I's château, blending Italian and French styles to create the First School of Fontainebleau.

For more on Château de Fontainebleau, see page 276

6. Versailles
FROM ROYALTY TO REVOLUTION

Arguably France's best-known king, Louis XIV (r 1643–1715), aka 'Le Roi Soleil' (the Sun King), built an extravagant palace in Versailles and made his courtiers compete for royal favour, quashing ambitious aristocracy and creating the first centralised French state. But by the late 1780s his descendant, indecisive Louis XVI (r 1774–92) and his domineering Vienna-born queen, Marie Antoinette, had alienated virtually every segment of society. When they tried to neutralise the power of more reform-minded delegates at a meeting of the États-Généraux (States-General) in Versailles in 1789, the masses took to the streets. On 14 July a mob stormed the prison at Bastille. Enter the French Revolution.

For more on Versailles, see page 268

7. Arc de Triomphe
NAPOLÉON AND EMPIRE

France's post-Revolutionary government was far from stable when Napoléon Bonaparte returned to Paris in 1799. He found a chaotic republic in which few citizens had any faith. The Arc de Triomphe, built from 1806 to 1836, is a vivid reminder of his ascendancy in December 1804, when he crowned himself 'Emperor of the French' in the presence of Pope Pius VII at Notre Dame. His many reversals of fortune included an odyssey of wars and victories by which France would come to control most of Europe, but also his banishment to Elba and ultimately St Helena in the South Atlantic, where he died in 1821.

For more on Arc de Triomphe, see page 80

8. Grands Magasins
THE BELLE ÉPOQUE

Though a tumultuous political time, the Belle Époque (Beautiful Age) in Paris launched art nouveau architecture, a whole field of artistic 'isms' from impressionism onwards, and advances in science and engineering, including the first metro line (1900) and train station (Gare St Lazare). World Fairs were held in the capital in 1889 (showcasing the Eiffel Tower) and 1901 (in the purpose-built Petit Palais). The Paris of nightclubs and artistic cafes made its appearance around this time, and Montmartre became a magnet for artists and writers. Perhaps the best representatives of this era are the city's *grands magasins*, department stores like Printemps and Galeries Lafayette, replete with art nouveau detailing.

For more on Grands Magasins, see page 87

9. Pigalle's Cabarets
ANNÉES FOLLES (CRAZY YEARS) – PARIS IN THE TWENTIES

In the 1920s, Paris sparkled as the centre of the avant-garde with its newfound liberalism, cutting-edge nightlife and painters pushing into new fields of art like cubism and surrealism. African American musicians brought jazz to France beginning around WWI, and Paris' creative denizens included Josephine Baker, Coco Chanel, Ernest Hemingway, Gertrude Stein, Pablo Picasso, Joan Miró and Salvador Dalí, to name just a few. Montparnasse and the Left Bank became hot spots, as did Pigalle and Montmartre with their speakeasies and cabarets like Moulin Rouge and Le Chat Noir. Soak up the vibe of this area on a walking tour.

For more on Pigalle's Cabarets, see page 127

10. Musée de la Libération de Paris
WWII AND THE OCCUPATION OF PARIS

During WWII, Paris was occupied by Germany, and almost half the population fled the city. The Germans divided France into two: a zone under direct German rule (including Paris); and a puppet state based in the spa town of Vichy. Collaborationists in German-occupied areas (including Paris) helped the Nazis round up 160,000 French Jews and others for deportation to concentration and extermination camps. Learn more at the Memorial de la Shoah (p144). General Charles de Gaulle, France's undersecretary of war, fled to London and established the Forces Françaises Libres (Free French Forces). Colonel Henri Rol-Tanguy led the Free French in Paris during liberation in what is now the Musée de la Libération de Paris.

For more on Musée de la Libération de Paris, see page 263

Galeries Lafayette (p82)

ANDREI ANTIPOV/SHUTTERSTOCK ©

11. Institut du Monde Arabe

COLONIALISM AND
CROSS-CULTURAL INFLUENCE

France's disastrous defeat in Vietnam in 1954 ended its colonial era in Southeast Asia, and the Algerian Revolution (1954–62) ended their longstanding colony there as well. Meanwhile, almost all other French colonies and protectorates in Africa demanded and achieved independence. Some 750,000 pieds noirs (black feet), as Algerian-born French people are known, came to France, and Paris remains a magnet for immigrants of all nations (making up 20% of the population in Paris and 31% in Seine-St-Denis), adding to the region's cultural wealth. A physical metaphor for modern cross-cultural exchange can be seen at the Institute of the Arab World, commissioned in 1981 by 19 Arab states.

For more on Institut du Monde Arabe, see page 211

12. Sorbonne

PIVOTAL YEAR AND FRENCH PROTESTS

The year 1968 was a watershed. In March, a large demonstration against the American war in Vietnam gave impetus to the student movement against capitalism, American imperialism and archaic institutions. In May, police broke up another demonstration, prompting angry students to occupy the venerable Sorbonne University and erect barricades in the Latin Quarter. Workers joined in, with six million people across France joining a strike that virtually paralysed the country. Slogans like 'L'Imagination au Pouvoir' (Put Imagination in Power) took hold. Demonstrating remains a staple of Parisian life – including the Gilets Jaunes Protests sparked in 2018 and 2023's unrest around the police killing of 17-year-old Nahel Merzouk.

For more on Sorbonne, see page 209

13. Pyramide du Louvre

MODERN SOCIETY AND
THE POLITICAL PENDULUM

Paris, despite appearing timeless, is always changing. As the seat of French government it's seen political influence swing many times. De Gaulle resigning in 1969 to be replaced by Gaullist Georges Pompidou. Socialist François Mitterrand leading to Jacques Chirac. Presidential elections in 2007 ushering in dynamic, media-savvy Nicolas Sarkozy. Emmanuel Macron beating back right-wing Marine Le Pen yet again in 2022. Perhaps no one building represents change better than the Louvre. A 13th-century fortress until Charles V (1338–80) moved in, it's seen many renovations, including the IM Pei pyramid completed in 1988 – controversial and iconic at the same time, and always adapting.

For more on Pyramide du Louvre, see page 92

14. Le Bataclan

TURBULENT TIMES

The year 2015 was a harrowing one for the French capital. On 7 January, the offices of *Charlie Hebdo* were attacked after the magazine published satirical images of the Prophet Mohammed; 12 people were killed and 22 injured. On 13 November, coordinated terrorist attacks at a football match, a series of neighbourhood restaurants and a concert at Le Bataclan killed 130 people (89 in Le Bataclan alone), and injured 368. Paris went into lockdown. In the aftermath, Parisians took to cafe terraces and public spaces to symbolise a refusal to live in fear. The long-planned UN Climate Change Conference went ahead, yielding a historic agreement to limit global warming.

For more on Le Bataclan, see page 179

15. Olympic Village

CREATING GREENER CONNECTIONS

In 2014 socialist Anne Hidalgo became Paris' first female mayor (she was reelected in 2020). Hidalgo quickly set about greening the city and minimising car traffic and pollution while ramping up pedestrian and cycling infrastructure. In addition, the gargantuan Grand Paris (Greater Paris) redevelopment project will ultimately connect outer suburbs beyond the bd Périphérique ring road through a massive decentralised metro expansion. As part of these initiatives, the 2024 Olympic Village is being constructed in St-Ouen, St-Denis and Île St-Denis to add to the areas' infrastructure and increase financial vitality beyond the centre – incorporating reusable venues and attempting to lower carbon footprints.

For more on Olympic Village, see page 40

MEET THE PARISIANS

Paris is changing, but without losing what makes it so special and different from the rest of the country. Jean-Bernard Carillet introduces his people.

EVERYONE IN FRANCE agrees that Parisians are different and special. When they travel around the country, it's quite common to hear the following comments: 'pfff, les Parisiens' (oh, these Parisians), uttered with a fatalistic air. As Paris is not synonymous with France, Parisians are, firstly, Parisians, then French. In that order.

Parisians feel like they live on an island amid a sea of rough, unsophisticated provinces. That said, this perception is changing. With the pandemic and remote work, a significant number of Parisians have left Paris for other shores – especially large cites in western France, including Nantes and Bordeaux – and have been totally seduced by the quality of life they have found there. And they have realised that the rest of France is not a *désert culturel* (cultural desert). Other French cities also have vibrancy, complexity and vitality. For Parisians, who have been living in their own bubble, this growing awareness is equivalent to a revolution. The superiority complex is fading away. French regions are taking their revenge on the capital.

Paris has never been so diverse and multicultural. It's a giant melting pot of cultures and lifestyles. Paris mixes influences like no other. Your Parisian neighbour might be from North Africa, Central Africa, Eastern Turkey, the Middle East, China or Eastern Europe. Paris is an inclusive city with a great sense of tolerance and open-mindedness.

One of the major recent changes in Paris has to do with transport. An increasing number of Parisians who had never ridden a bicycle have recently realised that cycling is an efficient way of getting around the city. This move is supported by the mayor of Paris, who has created bike lanes around the city in an effort to greenify the capital. Avenues like the famous rue de Rivoli are now filled with bicycles and *trottinettes* (kick-scooters) on lanes that previously were jammed with cars and taxis. It sometimes feels a bit chaotic – we're in Paris, not Amsterdam – but it's great fun as a visitor to observe Parisians astride their steeds!

A word about protests and strikes. Yes, it is part of our everyday life, and it can be exasperating. We are known to be rebellious and passionate, even if it's against our own interests. One way we demonstrate this is through protests and rallies, which we have developed into an art form. Whether it's to show solidarity with a cause or to voice our dissatisfaction with government policies (remember the 2023 protests against the pension reform), we take to the streets with passion and determination. That's an integral part of the city's identity, and it's not going to change anytime soon.

And when it comes to stereotypes, yes, we still buy our baguette at our favourite *boulangerie de quartier* (neighbourhood bakery).

Who & How Many

There are more than two million inhabitants within Paris, and 12 million inhabitants across the Grand Paris (the whole metropolitan area). That's more than 20,000 people per square kilometre, making it the most populous urban area in the entire European Union.

Pictured clockwise from top left: street cafes; cycling near Eiffel Tower (p60); protesters during a May Day demonstration; a Sunday monring market

I'M A PARISIAN, WITH A TWIST

I'm originally from northern Lorraine, a region that was the industrial powerhouse of France, with ironworks and coal mines dominating the landscape. Then came de-industrialisation and economic decline. I grew up amid an industrial wasteland. I realised that I needed an escape. Paris perfectly ticked all boxes. Like many Parisians, I came to Paris as a student and have stayed ever since, seduced by the energy, creative vibes and sophistication of the city. This was so reinvigorating, and a striking contrast to what I had experienced in my home region. What a change of scene and atmosphere! I was also enthralled by the many intellectual and cultural dimensions that are typical of Paris, and the sense of tolerance and diversity. This city never ages, it simply reinvents itself continuously. Over time, I've learnt to seamlessly intertwine my two identities – I'm both a Parisian and a Lorrain, a perfect 'bobo' (hipster) and a provincial in my own right.

Pont Neuf metro station
JACKY D/SHUTTERSTOCK ©

STORYBOOK

PARIS' MARVELLOUS METRO

PARIS' MARVELLOUS METRO

Parisian life beneath the surface can be just as interesting as above ground and there's no better way to zip around the city than le metro. By Fabienne Fong Yan

FROM THE CRACK of dawn until the late hours, Paris' underground transport system becomes a vibrant network where workers, students, families, singles and even pets cross paths, forging connections as they traverse the city.

Unveiling the Underground

If there's one landmark that visitors cannot overlook while exploring Paris, it's a monumental work that has stood the test of time for over a century. Not the Louvre, nor the majestic Arc de Triomphe, or even the Eiffel Tower. In fact, it is an almost inevitable space where travellers, Parisians and people from diverse backgrounds come together. It's none other than the Parisian metro.

The metro is an intricate network that sprawls throughout the entire city, resembling a nervous system. With nearly 230km of railway, transporting five million passengers every day, operating 365 days a year, it is a ubiquitous presence encapsulating a multitude of stories – architectural, technological and artistic. Throughout the years, it has become part of Paris' identity.

Yet most Parisians possess limited knowledge about it. Beyond its characteristic white tiles, cylindrical tunnels and crowded platforms, the metro is a testament to the modernisation of Paris, when

it propelled the city into the status of an actual metropolis at the dawn of the 20th century.

The Challenging Birth of the Metro

To grasp the metro's role in urban development, we must go back to the late 19th century. The concept of an urban train was accepted, yet its implementation was uncertain. London had adopted an underground steam-powered system, which, despite running for almost four decades, proved highly polluting, drowning passengers in smoke. For years, the French government struggled to find viable technical solutions.

It was the urgency prompted by the 1900 Universal Exposition that pushed the project forward. Paris could not endure trailing behind cities like London and New York. The breakthrough of electric power at the end of the 19th century allowed Fulgence Bienvenüe, the visionary architect who eventually cracked the project, to breathe life into the underground metro. He celebrated his own work with the phrase, 'By the lightning stolen from Jupiter, the lineage of Prometheus is transported into the depths'. The first line of the metro opened in 1900 and marked the beginning of the dense urban network we know today.

Efficiency & Proximity: a Dense Underground Tapestry

After more than 120 years, with 16 lines and 309 stations, the metro now connects all corners of Paris and beyond. The initial philosophy dear to Bienvenüe was to ensure that 'no place in Paris would be further than 400m away from a station and no journey would require more than two connections'. While connectivity has evolved over time, the imperative of proximity has led to the establishment of an efficient urban network, with an average distance of 710m between two stations. This provides Parisians with ample choices when selecting their metro station based on their ultimate destination. In this regard, the Parisian metro stands in contrast to Berlin's or London's urban railways, where several lines run on the same tracks and stations can be quite far apart. Consequently, hopping on and off the metro in the heart of Paris is like boarding and disembarking a bus, offering passengers ease and convenience.

Navigating Paris Like a Local

This density makes the metro the ideal means to explore and discover Paris. Not only can you immerse yourself in the city like a true Parisian, but you can conveniently access all the major tourist attractions. Note that the metro has its own set of traffic rules: keep to the right on escalators and maintain your right-hand position – according to an archaic rule, blocking the flow may result in a fine, although this is rarely enforced.

To experience the city like a local, there are a few tricks. For instance, alight at Trocadéro instead of Bir-Hakeim for a breathtaking view of the Eiffel Tower from the terraces of Palais Chaillot. Choose Abbesses over Anvers for an exit onto a charming square in Montmartre, rather than a bustling avenue. You can identify a seasoned Parisian by their mastery of navigating the metro and linking it to the above-ground map, enabling them to optimise their exit choices and positioning within the carriages.

Metro Stations as Cultural Landmarks

While the metro system results from architectural and technological prowess, it is widely acknowledged that passengers may not always perceive it as such, particularly during peak hours. Although certain sections of the network may appear under constant renovation, efforts are being made to incorporate art into the subterranean world.

Here are a few stations where you can appreciate the underground artwork while discovering city landmarks. Step off at Arts et Métiers to marvel at its steampunk-style station and then dive into centuries of captivating inventions at the Musée des Arts et Métiers.

Get off at Concorde, where the walls are covered with 44,000 ceramic tiles composing the text of the Declaration of Human Rights of 1789, before visiting the Jardin des Tuileries and the Hôtel de la Marine.

At Bastille, the platforms of Line 1 feature a striking mural commemorating the bicentenary of the French Revolution. When heading to the Latin Quarter, don't miss the mosaics of Cluny-La Sorbonne, which recreate the signatures of renowned intellectuals who once graced the area's streets and universities.

Tomorrow's Metro?

The Greater Paris project, launched in 2010, aims to construct an expanded network that will transcend the current star-shaped system, facilitating connections between the surrounding suburban areas. This approach reflects the reality of the city's present density and the shifting commuting patterns, with passengers no longer solely travelling to the city centre but also across the outskirts.

Furthermore, with the 2024 Olympics, the need for a high-performing transport network becomes crucial once again, as it will need to efficiently move and manage the influx of athletes, tourists and locals who will converge upon the city to witness the games.

How will the 21st-century metro meet this challenge?

PARIS ON LOCATION

Since the birth of moving pictures, France has played a major role in influencing cinema worldwide. Are you ready for your close-up? Paris is. By Alexis Averbuck

PARIS IS ONE of the world's most cinematic cities. The world's first paying-public screening took place in the French capital in 1895, and Paris has since produced a bevy of independent and blockbuster film-makers and stars, and is the filming location of countless box-office hits by both home-grown and foreign directors, with some 900 film shoots here per year.

Classic Cinema

Paris is a natural movie star, immortalised in French classics such as *Hôtel du Nord* (1938), set along the Canal St-Martin, and *Les Enfants du Paradis* (1946), set in 1840s Paris, both directed by Parisian film-maker Marcel Carné (1906–96).

The birthplace of the French New Wave (Nouvelle Vague), which emphasised the naturalistic use of on-location shoots, Paris spawned film director Jean-Luc Godard who followed his B&W celebration of Paris in *À Bout de Souffle* (Breathless; 1959) with *Bande à Parte* (Band of Outsiders; 1964), an entertaining gangster film with marvellous scenes in the Louvre. François Truffaut's Paris-set, semi-autobiographical *Les 400 Coups* (400 Blows; 1959), considered one of the best films in French cinematic history, is a moving portrayal of the magic and disillusionment of childhood.

The Modern Era of Parisian Film

Arguably the epicentre of France's film industry, Paris is always producing international hits, moody, meditative studies and stars. Mathieu Kassovitz had a prescient take on social tensions in modern Paris with *La Haine* (Hate; 1995). Also in the 1990s, Parisian Juliette Binoche leapt to fame after diving into the bright-turquoise water of Paris' art deco Piscine de Pontoise, in *Bleu* (Blue; 1993). She wooed cinema-goers with her role as a grieving mother in *Paris, Je T'Aime* (Paris, I Love You; 2006) – 18 short films – each set in a different Parisian *arrondissement*, and continues to do so today.

Honoured with the Palme d'Or at Cannes in 2008, Laurent Cantet's *Entre Les Murs* (The Class; 2008) portrays a year in the school life of pupils and teachers in a Parisian suburb. Based on the autobiographical novel of teacher François Bégaudeau, the documentary-drama is an incisive reflection of contemporary multi-ethnic society.

Also garnering awards is 2019's *Les Misérables*, directed by Ladj Ly, which won the Jury Prize at the Cannes Film Festival. It grapples with racial and social tensions in the northeastern Paris commune of Montfermeil, the setting for parts of Victor Hugo's 1862 novel of the same name.

The terrorist attacks of 2015 are the subject of *Novembre* (2022), taking an investigative perspective, and *Revoir Paris* (2022), taking a personal introspective one.

Parisian actress Isabelle Huppert holds the honour of having the most nominations for France's national César Award. She won one for Paris-based thriller *Elle* (2016), and one of her most recent films, *The Crime Is Mine* (2023), is set in 1930s Paris.

Another Parisian superstar, Léa Seydoux, recently filmed well-regarded romantic-drama *One Fine Morning* (2022) in Paris, directed by Paris-born Mia Hansen-Løve. Other Paris-born directors to look for are Jean Renoir, Claude Chabrol, Claire Denis and Mati Diop.

Television hits set in Paris include *Lupin* (2021–present) starring Omar Sy as a master thief inspired by the fictional Arsène Lupin, a 1900s master of disguise. Thriller fans can stream *Spiral* (2005–20), a police drama. *Dix Pour Cent* (Call My Agent; 2015–present) chronicles the hijinks of a Paris talent agency, and series creator Fanny Herrero also made *Standing Up* (2022), about Parisian stand-up comics.

Foreign Movies Set in Paris

Paris has always been popular with foreign film directors: Bernardo Bertolucci's *Last Tango in Paris* (1972) stars Marlon Brando as a grief-stricken American. Doug Liman's fast-moving flick *The Bourne Identity* (2002) features Matt Damon as an amnesiac government-agent-turned-target against a fabulous Paris backdrop. *Before Sunset* (2004) is the second part of the Richard Linklater, July Delpy and Ethan Hawke *Before* romantic trilogy.

Martin Scorsese's Oscar-winning children's film *Hugo* (2011) pays tribute to cinema and Parisian film pioneer Georges Méliès through the remarkable adventure of an orphan boy in the 1930s who tends the clocks at a Paris train station.

Parts of 2018's *Fantastic Beasts: The Crimes of Grindelwald*, written by JK Rowling and directed by David Yates, were set in Paris. The city also featured in 2018's *Mission: Impossible – Fallout*, which had its world premiere in Paris.

Many a music video has also been filmed in Paris, from Sinead O'Connor's 'Nothing Compares 2 U' to Taylor Swift's 'Begin Again' and The Carters' (Beyoncé and Jay-Z) 'Apesh**t', which was filmed in the Louvre.

Animation

The classic *Ratatouille* (2007) is an American-made comedy about an ambitious rat who aims to be a chef against all odds. *Avril et de Monde Truque* (April and the Extraordinary World; 2015) depicts a fictitious world in 1941 Paris in the steam age, where Avril (and her talking cat) searches for her missing parents. Delightful *Dilili à Paris* (Dilili in Paris; 2018), directed by Michel Ocelot, sees its young heroine Dilili solve a series of kidnappings in Belle Époque Paris. It features famous Parisians from the era, such as artist Toulouse-Lautrec, and astonishingly realistic detail, and won the César Award for Best Feature.

Documentaries

One of the earliest Parisian documentaries is *Rien les Heures* (Nothing But Time; 1926) directed by Alberto Cavalcanti, an experimental silent film showing a day in the life of the city. Writer-director Pierre Bost's *La Libération de Paris* (The Liberation of Paris; 1944) was filmed in secret by units of the French Resistance during the battle for Paris in WWII. *La Seine a Rencontré Paris* (The Seine Meets Paris; 1957), directed by Joris Ivens, is told from the perspective of a boat trip through the city, showing daily life on its banks. Paris' film archive, the Forum des Images, is an excellent place to discover more.

> THE WORLD'S FIRST PAYING-PUBLIC SCREENING TOOK PLACE IN THE FRENCH CAPITAL IN 1895, AND PARIS HAS SINCE PRODUCED A BEVY OF INDEPENDENT AND BLOCKBUSTER FILM-MAKERS AND STARS

Film production near Notre-Dame (p190)

PARIS' ALTERNATIVE ARTS SCENE

Derelict factories and train stations have become Paris' hottest arts venues. By Rooksana Hossenally

A NEW STREAM of hybrid art hubs inside abandoned buildings have become go-tos for locals, jumpstarting change and making the Paris art scene a lot more inclusive.

Outside the (White) Box

France ranks among the top countries in the world for injecting money into the arts, which shows the significance in which culture is held here. Paris has always had an extremely rich and vibrant art scene, as well as a plethora of theatres, cinemas, concert halls, galleries and landmark museums. However, look outside the institutions to smaller venues and grassroots collectives, and you'll find that the scene is even more diverse and multitiered than it first appears.

In the last two decades, smaller venues like La Bellevilloise, Le 104, Mains d'Oeuvres, Ground Control and Le Point Ephémère have been challenging the status

ANDY SOLOMAN/SHUTTERSTOCK ©

quo by putting the spotlight on a broader range of artists from all over the globe, breaking the white-cube mould and opening up the arts to people who aren't necessarily part of the traditional cultural elite.

Art Squats

Before Nicolas Sarkozy became the country's president in 2007 (until 2012), much of the independent scene unfolded in art squats like La Petite Rockette (11e), Grands Voisins (12e), La Miroiterie (20e) and La Suite (13e), among others, where art collectives took over the city's empty buildings and set up their lodgings, studio spaces and hosted events year-round. They operated like fully fledged art venues, elbowing their way onto the established arts circuit. A lot of the work was liberating and experimental. Most squats have since been shut down, save a handful that have been made permanent and given a right to stay. For instance, the 59 Rivoli (1er) is a rare exploit where the artists took over a huge building right on Paris' main shopping street in the heart of the city. It's open to visitors, and stands as a symbol of the power of the local cultural spirit.

Reinvented Railways

In 2016 another chapter began for the local art scene when the SNCF, France's national rail giant, also the city's biggest land owner, decided to sell or lease some of its property in the city and on the outskirts. For instance, La Petite Ceinture (little belt), a disused railway that circles Paris and is scattered with empty stations, is being transformed into a bucolic promenade, its stations having been repurposed into *tiers lieux* (hybrid venues) with bars and restaurants that put on various events from concerts to exhibitions, festivals to markets, like le Hasard Ludique and La Recyclerie (both in the 18e *arrondissement*).

The SNCF even called upon the art community to suggest renewal projects for some of its abandoned buildings such as La Gare (19e), a former train station that's now a jazz club with techno nights in the basement. There's also La Station – Gare des Mines, an experimental music venue built on the remains of an old coal

station in Aubervilliers, and eco-venue La Cité Fertile in Pantin, in an old SNCF goods station that's now a place to eat and drink that hosts year-round events. Other repurposed stations include Poinçon (14e), formerly the Montrouge-Ceinture station, now a restaurant with arty events, and Brasserie d'Auteuil and Andia, two restaurants in the 16e *arrondissement* also inside former train stations.

Post-Pandemic Rejuvenation

Turning old stations into art hubs is nothing new. In the last few years, especially as the world has whirled back into action post-pandemic, Paris has seen the rise of *tiers lieux* and pop-up venues on *friches* (wasteland) as more permanent fixtures, injecting even more diversity into the city's arts offering.

Cultural associations and foundations are increasingly looking to abandoned factories on the city outskirts. In April 2022 artist incubator POUSH took over a 20,000 sq metre derelict perfume factory in the suburb of Aubervilliers, where it now hosts 250 artists from 30 different nationalities for residencies, events and exhibitions, and takes the prize as the city's biggest arts centre. More recently, the Fiminco Foundation has opened a similar art space with residences and a beer garden in Romainville, also on the outskirts of northeastern Paris.

Cultural event organisers like Soukmachines, behind *tiers lieux* like the 6B in an abandoned St-Denis office block, which has been going since 2010, as well as the Halle Papin in Pantin and L'Orfèvrerie nearby, now both closed, are turning their attention to abandoned French film laboratory, l'Eclair in Épinay-sur-Seine, where they've nabbed a six-year lease to keep organising their events and summer family barbecues. The collective has also opened a more permanent spot with the right to stay for 10 years in an old office block in Gennevilliers, a northern Paris suburb. And in Meudon, on the southwest outskirts of the city, an airship factory left empty for four decades opened as a cultural space. It has yet to build an ongoing program to attract a steady flow of returning visitors but the rehabilitation of the very lofty venue is impressive.

STORYBOOK

PARIS' ALTERNATIVE ARTS SCENE

Art in the Heart

While rarer due to lack of space, disused spots in the heart of Paris are also getting the art treatment. Césure, a former Sorbonne University building in the Latin Quarter, has been turned into a creative venue for concerts, plays, exhibitions and events with a restaurant, by the Plateau Urbain cooperative, which rents cut-price space to creatives like artists as well as to students and charities.

Friches of note in Paris (open summer only) include the Jardin21, an urban garden by the canal in the 19e *arrondissement* by the same association that runs longstanding alternative nightlife venue Glazart nearby, and the 88 Ménilmontant in the location of the old Miroiterie, a squat inside an old mirror shop known for its punk-rock concerts.

Many of these old sites testify to the city's past, and dusting them off serves to retell the stories of bygone industries and disappeared railways. It gives them new purpose and puts sleepy suburbs on the map. Restoring these vestiges of the past has also opened up the city's art scene to locals and visitors seeking something more immersive and tangible than what's on offer in Paris' more traditional museums and galleries. The new generation of cultural leaders are showing us there's a different way to interact with the arts, and that you can sip on a pint while doing it.

La Petite Ceinture (p125)

RALPH ROZEMA/SHUTTERSTOCK ©

LES ANNÉES FOLLES &
THE COCKTAIL CRAZE IN PARIS

The crazy years in Paris between the two world wars gave birth to the cocktail, but its history goes further back than that. By Nicola Leigh Stewart

PERHAPS NO DECADE has captured an image of Paris quite like *les Années folles* (the crazy years). The war was over, victory was in the air, and people were ready to celebrate life again. Paris was a carefree and increasingly cosmopolitan city, full of optimism and artistic innovation in every form. It's no wonder, then, that the cocktail became the drink of choice: it was new, creative and fun, and perfectly encapsulated the mood for celebrating life at every opportunity.

It makes sense that a decade called *années folles* would have at least some alcohol involved, but the cocktail's origins in France go even further back, as told by Franck Audoux, owner of Paris cocktail bar CRAVAN, in his book *French Moderne: Cocktails from the Twenties and Thirties*. In fact, it was Napoléon III who first introduced the word 'bar' to the French in the 1840s, during his exile in London, and who was a big fan of the '*coquetel*', a Bordeaux drink that mixed together wine and eau de vie (fruit brandy). Of course, the word seems to be an early version of 'cocktail', although according to Franck, 'there are lots of stories about where the word came from and no one can agree on which one is true'.

It was also Napoléon III who had the idea to host the 1867 Exposition Univer-selle (World Fair), which was a major driver behind bringing the American cocktail to France. Hundreds of international restaurants and bars opened in order to refresh the some 15 million visitors who

Cocktails, Paris

317

would attend the six-month event, including an American bar where 'young women served drinks that were sipped cold through straws', a new way of drinking at the time, says Frank. At the Paris Exposition 1878, cocktails such as sherry cobblers and mint juleps were on the menu at the American bar. By the time the 1889 Exposition came around (bringing 32 million visitors), the first French cocktail book had been published, aimed at helping cafe bar owners and maîtres d'hôtel meet the demands of Paris' new foreign visitors.

It wasn't just international fairs that brought travellers to Paris. Tourism in general was beginning to boom. Thanks to bigger and faster cruise liners, and the founding of Air France in 1933, it was now easier than ever to travel and explore. Curious and creative Americans came to Paris, some of whom wanted to escape the puritanical rules of home: nationwide Prohibition began in the US in 1920 and lasted until 1933, putting a dampener on the Roaring Twenties fun (at least the legal fun). In contrast, on this side of the pond a burst of Anglo-American bars opened in Paris, serving American drinks and British and Irish dishes to appeal to an En-

glish-speaking clientele. Another American influence on the Paris bar scene was horse racing. In the early 1900s most Anglo-friendly bars would be packed out with racing fans and American jockeys, who came and outperformed the previous leaders of the sport, the English. The now world-famous Harry's Bar was one of the bars frequented by famous jockeys when it launched as the New York Bar in 1911, before being bought and renamed by Scotsman Harry MacElhone in 1923. Under Harry it became a meeting point for famed American expatriates of the time including Ernest Hemingway and Scott and Zelda Fitzgerald, and was the birthplace of cocktail classics such as the Bloody Mary, the Blue Lagoon, the White Lady and, it's also claimed, the Sidecar.

But fashionable new drinks weren't limited to these expat-friendly bars. Cocktails could be found everywhere in the city, from bistros to brasseries, although the most famous at the time were huddled together in Montparnasse. Many Americans had flocked to the neighbourhood upon their arrival in Paris and it became a hub for artists, journalists, academics and publishers who ordered Martinis, Alexanders,

Bar shelf, Paris

Sidecars, Manhattans and more in neighbourhood hangouts such as La Closerie de Lilas, La Rotonde, Le Dôme and Le Select – all still open today.

Next door in St-Germain-des-Prés the Hôtel Lutetia, opened in 1910, also became a hot spot for Paris' American and international creative crowd. Hemingway and Picasso were both patrons of the bar, which is now renamed in honour of the hotel's most famous guest, American-born French dancer and singer Josephine Baker. In the 8th *arrondissement*, the Hôtel Plaza Athénée's Jean Lupoiu, one of the key bartenders of the time, made the Relais Plaza bar another fashionable destination after the hotel's restaurant opened in 1936; it was particularly popular with the couturiers who had their *maisons* on the same street. On the menu at cocktail hour were two drinks named after the hotel: the Plaza Athénée and the Relais-Plaza. But perhaps Paris' most famous bartender at the time was Franck Meier who oversaw the Ritz Hotel's Bar Cambon, better known simply as the Ritz Bar, where guests would sip on future classics such as the Bee's Knees.

THE HÔTEL LUTETIA, OPENED IN 1910 BECAME A HOT SPOT FOR PARIS' AMERICAN AND INTERNATIONAL CREATIVE CROWD ... HEMINGWAY AND PICASSO WERE BOTH PATRONS OF THE BAR

Although the cocktail was an American drink, these new creations were often made with French spirits. Before the cocktail craze took off in Paris there was already a culture for l'apéritif and so bartenders reached for the numerous French spirits already behind the bar such as Noilly Prat, Dolin, Suze, Cointreau and Chartreuse to shake and stir their new creations. The enthusiasm for the drinks wasn't lost on the brands either, who sponsored some of the cocktail competitions that sprang up in the late 1920s, another major driving force behind the cocktail's popularity. Some of these events welcomed amateur and even celebrity participants but the 1929 First International Championship of Professional Bartenders was, as the name suggests, for the Paris pros, and saw 40 bartenders from establishments such as Harry's New York Bar take part. The public were able to buy a ticket to enter and judge the cocktail winners, but had to try all 40 drinks to do so.

These days, the cocktail scene in Paris is thriving once again. The city's influential bartenders are leading the way with their creative concoctions, but they occasionally take a look back to the *les années folles* as a source of inspiration. Dirty Lemon, known for its excellent Boulevardier (invented in Paris in 1927), likes to riff on other 1920s classics such as the Negroni and the Martini, while Le Syndicat has put its own spin on a French 75 by swapping out the gin for Armagnac. A recent menu at Copper-Bay took inspiration from Frank Meier's Bee's Knee to create the lemon and honey-based Silky. Back over at CRAVAN, Franck Audoux might have written the book, literally, on 1920s and '30s Parisian cocktail culture but he stresses that his own drinks form 'a contemporary menu dedicated to the palette of today'. He has reworked a couple of recipes from the time in line with this concept, namely the signature Yellow Cocktail and the Tunnel, but if you're looking for a taste of the past then it's CRAVAN's original location that will take you there more than the drinks: a beautiful art nouveau–listed building designed by French architect Hector Guimard.

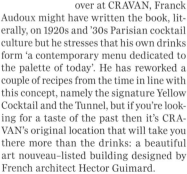

INDEX

Map Pages **000**

Map Pages **000**

Map Pages **000**

"Elegant and iconic, bejewelled by treasures, with its hourly sparkles that illuminate the evening skyline, the Eiffel Tower needs no introduction."
– ALEXIS AVERBUCK

"The Musée du Louvre is undeniably Paris' pièce de résistance, boasting 35,000 works of art on display, including iconic masterpieces, spread across four floors"
– FABIENNE FONG YAN

Mapping data sources:
© Lonely Planet
© OpenStreetMap http://openstreetmap.org/copyright

THIS BOOK

Destination Editor
AnneMarie McCarthy

Production Editor
Graham O'Neill

Book Designer
Norma Brewer

Cartographer
Hunor Csutoros

Assisting Editors
Janet Austin, Nigel Chin, Monique Choy, Fionnuala Twomey

Cover Researcher
Marc Backwell

Thanks Sofie Andersen, Clare Healy, Karen Henderson, Katerina Pavkova, Charlotte Orr

Published by Lonely Planet Global Limited
CRN 554153
14 edition – Mar 2024
ISBN 978 1 83869 198 1
© Lonely Planet 2024 Photographs © as indicated 2024
10 9 8 7 6 5 4 3 2 1
Printed in China

LEFT: KYLE WAGAMAN/SHUTTERSTOCK ©. RIGHT: VERNERIE YANN/SHUTTERSTOCK ©